AN ESSENTIAL COURSE
IN
MODERN SPANISH

BY

H. RAMSDEN M.A. Dr. en Fil. y Let.

EMERITUS PROFESSOR OF THE
UNIVERSITY OF MANCHESTER

Nels

D1078935

Thomas Nelson and Sons Ltd
Nelson House   Mayfield Road
Walton-on-Thames   Surrey
KT12 5PL   UK

51 York Place
Edinburgh
EH1 3JD   UK

Thomas Nelson (Hong Kong) Ltd
Toppan Building 10/F
22A Westlands Road
Quarry Bay   Hong Kong

Distributed in Australia by

Thomas Nelson Australia
480 La Trobe Street
Melbourne   Victoria 3000
and in Sydney, Brisbane, Adelaide and Perth

© H. Ramsden 1959

First published by George G. Harrap and Co. Ltd 1959
(under ISBN 0-245-52860-1)

Reprinted nineteen times
Twenty-first impression published by Thomas Nelson and Sons Ltd 1985

ISBN 0-17-444685-3

NPN 9 8 7 6

Printed and bound in Hong Kong

PREFACE

This book was written in answer to a very definite need: that of university students who offer Spanish as one of their Intermediate subjects. Honours students have long been able to consult their Harmer and Norton or their Ramsey, whilst school children and more leisured learners of the language can always choose from a mass of elementary courses. But Intermediate students, who start with no knowledge of the language and who are expected, within eight months, to reach a level approximately equivalent to scholarship standard at G.C.E. Advanced Level, for these there has been no course available, and teachers have been obliged in their classes either to use an advanced course selectively or to use a more elementary course and supplement it with their own notes. Neither method, I believe, is very satisfactory, either for students or for teachers. Hence the present book.

But it is hoped that Intermediate students will not be the only ones to find the work useful. Every attempt has been made to draw up an *essential* course, essential in vocabulary, in idioms, and in grammar. Thus, the choice of vocabulary has been governed largely by the findings of Victor García Hoz on Spanish word frequency.[1] All the words which he lists in his *vocabulario fundamental* (and which he estimates account for two out of every three words used in a given passage) are included in the present course, and all but ten per cent. of the words included in the course are rated by Dr Garcia Hoz among the top quarter of his *vocabulario usual*. In similar fashion, Hayward Keniston's *Spanish Idiom List* (New York, 1929) has proved an invaluable guide to the choice of idioms and special constructions, and over ninety per cent. of cases listed by Professor Keniston with a range frequency of more than 20–50 have been included here. Finally,

[1] V. García Hoz, *Vocabulario usual, común y fundamental* (*Determinación y análisis de sus factores*), C.S.I.C., Madrid, 1953.

the grammar selection has been the outcome of my own analysis of a considerable number of students' exercises and examination scripts. Rare or insignificant details of grammar have been omitted or dealt with in short notes; particularly important and troublesome aspects have been presented at great length with abundant examples, in the hope that the student may acquire a feeling for a given construction and not have to depend solely on his memory of pure grammar.

The course is divided into twenty-five lessons and eight review and development sections, each with its grammar, vocabulary and exercises. In order to help the home student and to give extra practice to the keen class student a key is provided to the second exercise of each lesson and review section. The Spanish sentences of the last review sections are from modern Spanish writers. Perhaps, for some students, they will serve as a stepping-stone to the original works. The effort would be well rewarded.

I should like to express gratitude to my colleagues at the University of Manchester for their help and encouragement in the preparation of this course. In particular, I am indebted to Dr Joaquín González Muela and Dr G. B. Gybbon-Monypenny for discussing with me points of Spanish usage, and to these, and to Miss W. M. D. Wilson and D. José Vergés for reading, criticizing and improving much of the text. D. Mariano Santiago Luque has kindly undertaken the onerous task of reading through the whole of the proofs. Finally, and very especially, I am indebted to my wife, who has made up examples, criticized, checked, prepared the manuscript and generally been a wonderful help at all stages of the work.

H.R.

CONTENTS

7

8

The Spanish Alphabet, Pronunciation, Word Stress, the Written Accent, Syllabification, Punctuation, Capital Letters

INTRODUCTION

The contents of this introductory chapter are presented together here as a means of reference, and will be referred to as required within the body of the book. It is suggested that the student might omit this chapter for the time being and begin straight away with Lesson I.

1. The Spanish Alphabet. This comprises the following twenty-eight letters:

Symbol	Name	Symbol	Name	Symbol	Name
a	a	j	jota	r, rr	ere, erre
b	be (alta)	k	ka	s	ese
c	ce	l	ele	t	te
ch	che	ll	elle	u	u
d	de	m	eme	v	ve (baja) *or* uve
e	e	n	ene	x	equis
f	efe	ñ	eñe	y	ye *or* i griega
g	ge	o	o	z	zeta *or* zeda
h	hache	p	pe		
i	i	q	cu		

Notes: 1. The letter **w** (**ve doble** or **uve doble**) is not found in native Spanish words and is therefore not considered by the Spanish Academy to be part of the Spanish alphabet.

2. The letters **r** and **rr** are classed together as one by the Academy, though **rr** constitutes, in writing, an indivisible letter.

3. All letters are feminine in gender.

una d mayúscula   a capital 'd'
La rr como la ll debe estar   The 'rr,' like the 'll,' must be
  indivisa en la escritura.   undivided in writing.

2. PRONUNCIATION. Compared with English, the Spanish written language offers a remarkably faithful representation of the sounds of the spoken language.

(a) Vowels

Spanish vowels are generally sharper and more vigorously pronounced than English vowels. They are pure sounds free from any change in the position of the vocal organs during emission (contrast the English tendency to diphthongization: *make*, *vote*), and they retain this pure sound even when in unstressed position (contrast the English relaxed pronunciation of unstressed vowels: *able*, *arable*, *separable*; *Tory*, *factory*). The vowel sounds in Spanish are approximately as follows:

a a very open vowel between standard English *cat* and *father* (cf. Northern English *cat*, *mat*): **fama, patata.**

e like the first *e* in *elephant*: **leche, peseta.**

i like *ee* in *seen*, but shorter and sharper: **mínimo, finísima.**

o like *o* in *for*, but shorter and sharper: **foto, Colón.**

u like *oo* in *root*: **puro, ruptura.**

u is silent in the group **qu** (**quita, aquel**); also in **gu**+**e** or **i** unless a diaeresis (**··**) is written over the **u** (**pague, guisante,** but **averigüe, argüiste**).

y when it is a vowel (in the conjunction **y** and at the end of a word: **rey, ley**) it is pronounced like **i.**

(b) Consonants

b and **v.** These have the same sounds in Spanish:

(i) At the beginning of a word and after a nasal consonant (**n, m**) they are like English *b*: **bata, vara, hambre, enviar.**

(ii) Elsewhere they have a 'buzzed' *b* sound (bilabial fricative: lips as for English *b*; sustained sound as for English *v*): **haba, ave, cabra, calvo, alba.**

c (i) Before **e** or **i** = *th* in *think*: **cero, ceniciento.**

(ii) Elsewhere = *c* in *cat*: **poco, fábrica, pacto.**

NOTE: In words like **acción** and **lección** both sounds are present

ch =English *ch*: **chico, muchacho, leche.**

d (i) At the beginning of a word, after nasal consonants and after **l**, like *d* in *darn* (but with the tongue further forward, against the top front teeth): **doy, anda, molde.**

(ii) Elsewhere = *th* in *though* (rather lighter, especially at the end of a word and in the past participle **-ado** ending where the sound is hardly pronounced at all): **seda, madre, ciudad, olvidado.**

f =English *f*: **fama, frente, sufre.**

g (i) Before **e** or **i** = *ch* in Scottish *loch*: **gemelo, coge, surgir.**

(ii) At the beginning of a word and after a nasal consonant = *g* in *gate*: **grande, ganga.**

(iii) Elsewhere a hard sound as in (ii), but with only the slightest contact of the vocal organs: **agua, paga, agrio.**

h silent: **hombre, hacha.**

j = *ch* in Scottish *loch*: **jota, granja, ajo.**

k = English *k*: **kilo, kilómetro** (found only in a few words of foreign origin).

l = English *l*: **león, palo, habla.**

ll = *lli* in *million*, but with the *l* and *y* sounds more closely associated: **llama, calle.**

m = English *m*: **madre, amo, ambos.**

n = English *n*, but with the tongue further forward, against the upper teeth: **nene, andan.**

NOTE: As in English (cf. *tank, bang*) **n** before hard **c** or **g** (also in Spanish, before **j** and soft **g**) nasalizes the preceding vowel and is itself then less firmly articulated (**banco, ganga, monja, longitud**).

ñ = *ni* in *onion*, but with closer association of the *n* and *y* sounds: **niño, ñoño.** (The sign over the **n** is called a *tilde*.)

p = English *p*, but less aspirate: **Pepe, siempre, papa.**

q found only in the groups **que** and **qui**, the **qu** being pronounced like *c* in *cat*: **saque, banquete, quisquilla.**

r, rr pronounced with different degrees of roll:

(i) every **r** that is not at the beginning of a word = one trill: **para, trueno, siempre, cortar.**

(ii) **r** at the beginning of a word = two trills: **roca, río, rabo.**

(iii) **rr** = three trills: **carro, perro, ferrocarril.**

s like *s* in *simple*: **casa, saco, fiesta.**

t = English *t*, but less aspirate and with tongue against top front teeth: **te, tu, patata.**

v see under **b.**

w = Spanish **b** and **v**; found only in words of foreign origin and frequently changed to **v**; **Wamba, wáter, vals (wals), vagón.**

x (i) Between vowels=English *gs* with very lightly pronounced *g*: **examen, éxito.**

(ii) Before a consonant only the *s* sound remains: **expone, excepto.**

y = *y* in *young*, but much stronger: **yo, yugo, mayo, inyección.** For the occasional use of **y** with an **i** sound, see Section (*a*).

z = *th* in *think*: **manzana, zorra, lápiz.** Except in the name of the letter (**zeta**) and a few words of foreign origin **z** is not used before **e** or **i.**

NOTES: 1. The only double consonants in Spanish are **ll, rr, cc** and **nn.** The first two are really letters in their own right (**llama, perro**), **cc** represents two different sounds (**acción**), and **nn**, found almost only in the negatives of words beginning with **n** (**negable—innegable**, *deniable—undeniable*), indicates two distinct enunciations of the same sound: **in/ne/ga/ble.** For the rest, notice: **posible** (*possible*), **atento** (*attentive*), **café** (*coffee*), **inmediato** (*immediate*), etc.

2. No Spanish word may begin with **s**+*consonant*: **especial** (*special*), **estudio** (*study*), **escena** (*scene*), **escaldar** (*to scald*), etc.

3. American pronunciation and that of certain parts of Spain differs from the above Castilian principally in two respects: soft **c** (*i.e.*, before **e** or **i**) and **z** are pronounced like **s** (**cera, zona**), and **y** and **ll** like *si* in *vision* (**mayo, calle**).

(c) The Word Group

The observations in (*a*) and (*b*) have been aimed at the pronunciation of the individual word. But Spanish is characterized by the running together in pronunciation of words linked closely within a given sentence, unlike educated English where a momentary pause or glottal stop may be introduced to prevent the fusion of words (*an/awful/accident* as opposed to *a-nawfu-laccident*). Thus, in Spanish the pronunciation of **su ave** and of **suave** is identical, as also that of **le hemos** and **leemos** (somewhat longer than the single **e** in **vemos**). Similarly, **las alas** and **la sala** are both pronounced *lasala(s)*, and **lo ha echado** and **no he acabado** sound as if they were written *loaechado* and *noeacabado* respectively. Against these examples may be set such English pairs as *a note—an oat(-cake)*, *Ann dotes—and oats*, *began—big Ann*. In each pair the Spaniard would expect the pronunciation of the earlier case to apply to both.

The tendency for words to run together in Spanish shows itself in the absence of the glottal stop. It shows itself, too, in the change of sound that the consonants **b (v)**, **d** and **g** may undergo when, being initial of a word, they are used after a word ending in a vowel. In **bañarse, ver, da, gasta,** for instance, as in **quieren bañarse, procuran ver, él da, Juan gasta,** the **b, v, d, g** are in initial position and therefore have the plosive sound; in **quiere bañarse, procura ver, me da, no gasta,** on the other hand, the same letters are now preceded as well as followed by a vowel (*i.e.*, they have become intervocalic) and thus take the corresponding fricative sound. (See above, Section (*b*), under the letters **b, d, g**.)

3. WORD STRESS IN SPANISH. (*a*) In a word of more than one syllable the stress falls generally on the next to the last (the penultimate) syllable or on the last one. The penultimate syllable bears the stress if the word ends in a vowel, **n**, or **s** (**casa, verde, compran, vendemos**); otherwise, the last syllable bears the stress (**hospital, tenaz, vivir, ciudad**).

(*b*) Any variation from the above is indicated by means of a written (acute) accent: **difícil, lápiz, azúcar** (contrast **senil, feliz, cantar**); **periódico, fábrica, también** (contrast **abanico, salpica, viven**); **sacó, cansé** (contrast **saco, canse**).

(*c*) Brief indications must be made on words of the type **causa, lengua, edificio, oigo, tarea, caer, buey,** in which two or more vowels come together.

(i) **a, e** and **o** are strong vowels, and when two of them come together they constitute separate syllables. Thus, in accordance with (a) above we stress **tarea, caer, poema, peor, oasis, caoba, cree.**

(ii) **u** and **i** (also **y** in final position) are weak vowels. When they come together they constitute a single syllable (a diphthong) with the syllable stress on the second of the two vowels: **viuda, ruído, muy.**

(iii) A strong vowel together with one or more weak vowels constitutes a single syllable, the stress falling upon the strong vowel of the group: **causa, Juan, oigo, idiota, peine, tienda, buey, miau.**

NOTE: Because a strong vowel and one or more weak ones together constitute a single syllable, we stress **lengua, edificio, familia, ingenuo,** in accordance with (a) above. (Contrast **tarea, oboe, mareo, Bilbao.**)

(iv) Any variation from (i)–(iii) above is indicated in writing by means of an accent over the stressed vowel: **vivíamos, país, río, oído, grúa, baúl.** An accented (i.e., stressed) **i** or **u** becomes a syllable in its own right. Thus **Asia** comprises two syllables; **asía** has three.

4. THE WRITTEN ACCENT. (a) The written accent is used in Spanish to indicate word stress that does not conform to a simple basic pattern [§ 3 (b) and (c) (iv)].

(b) It is also used to distinguish in writing between words that would otherwise be identical in form:

(i) Interrogative and exclamative pronouns and adverbs bear an accent whereas their corresponding relative and conjunctive forms do not: **¿dónde?** *where?*, but **donde,** *where*; **¡qué!** *what a!*, but **que,** *that, which*; **¿quién?** *who?*, but **quien,** *who*; etc.

¿Cuándo vas a ir?   When are you going to go?
Cuando viene, habla mucho.   When he comes, he talks a lot.

(ii) The demonstrative pronoun bears an accent when there exists also a corresponding adjectival form: **éste, ésa, aquéllas,**

etc. **Esto, eso, aquello** have no accent because there is no
neuter adjective.

Voy con aquel muchacho.	I am going with that boy.
Voy con aquél.	I am going with that one.

(iii) The following words also are distinguished by the presence
or absence of the accent:

mí	me	**mi**	my
tú	you	**tu**	your
él	he	**el**	the
sí	yes; himself, herself, etc.	**si**	if
dé	he (may, should) give	**de**	of
sé	I know; be!	**se**	himself, herself, themselves
más	more, most, plus	**mas**	but
sólo	only	**solo**	alone
aún	still, yet	**aun**	even

(*c*) In certain monosyllabic verb parts there is hesitation in the
use of the accent:

fui (fuí)	I was; I went	**dio (dió)**	he gave
fue (fué)	he was; he went	**vi (ví)**	I saw
di (dí)	I gave	**vio (vió)**	he saw

(*d*) Against what has been established in § 3, note the following:

(i) When a weak pronoun object is affixed to a verb part that
ends in a stressed vowel (and which therefore bears a written
accent in accordance with the rule expressed in § 3 (*b*)), the accent
remains even though the verb ending is now in penultimate (*i.e.*,
naturally stressed) position.

sacó—sacóla   **cansé—canséme**

(ii) When an adjective bearing a written accent in accordance
with § 3 (*b*) is made into an adverb by the addition of **-mente** to
the feminine singular, the accent is preserved though the main
stress of the word now falls on the syllable **-men-**.

bárbaro—bárbaramente   **magnífico—magníficamente**

(*e*) The accent is frequently omitted from capital letters.

5. SYLLABIFICATION. (*a*) The division of words into syllables is no mere intellectual exercise. Like the system of sounds and stresses it is a faithful reflection in Spanish of the spoken language and a knowledge of its principles will help one's pronunciation. Moreover, word-splitting (at the end of a line) is much more frequent in Spanish than in English and must follow the rules of syllabification in that no syllable may be divided within itself.

(*b*) A syllable in Spanish must contain at least one vowel and begins generally with one consonant, though **ch, ll** and **rr,** and *consonant* + **l** or **r** (except **rl, sl, tl, lr, nr, sr**) cannot be split:

po/pu/lar	lec/ción	in/ne/ga/ble
di/fí/cil	ma/ra/vi/lla	ham/brien/to
te/me/ro/so	ma/rrón	com/pren/der
prac/ti/can/te	tre/gua	mi/la/gro
cons/ti/tu/ye	so/pla	par/la/men/to

(*c*) A syllable begins with a vowel:

(i) at the beginning of a word: **al/to, e/di/ción, ín/te/gro.**

(ii) when two strong vowels, or one strong vowel and a stressed weak vowel, come together [for each then constitutes a separate syllable, § 3(*c*) (i) and (iv)]: **ta/re/a, pe/or, o/a/sis, vi/ví/as, o/í/do, grú/a.**

NOTES: 1. To appreciate the reality of syllabic division in actual pronunciation, one must hear a Spaniard pronounce a word such as **comprender (com/pren/der),** with the strong articulation of the consonants **m** and **n,** and with almost a pause before the next syllable is enunciated. Remember, too, the pronunciation of the word group [§ 2 (*c*)], with the carrying on of a final consonant to form a syllable with a following initial vowel sound: **estos hombres** (*es/to/som/bres*).

2. Against Note 1, remember that adjoining vowels blend, whether or not they belong to the same syllable: **la he de encontrar** is divided syllabically into *la/he/de/en/con/trar* but pronounced *la͡/he/de͡/en/con/trar*, i.e., *lae-den-con-trar*.

6. PUNCTUATION. (*a*) For the English-speaking student the most striking characteristics of Spanish punctuation are: (1) the use of double question and exclamation marks, inverted at the beginning of the question or exclamation and as in English at the end, and (2) the use of the dash to indicate dialogue.

¡Vámonos!, o ¿no quieres?	Let's go, or don't you want to?
— ¿Quieres venir?	"Do you want to come?"
— ¡Qué va!	"No fear!"
— **Juan, márchate** — dijo ella furiosa —. **No puedo soportarte.**	"John, go away," she said angrily. "I can't stand you."
— **No quiero marcharme.** Juan lloraba.	"I don't want to go away." John was crying.

NOTES: 1. Question marks and exclamation marks do not necessarily coincide with the beginning or the end of a sentence.

2. The dash does not correspond exactly to the English inverted commas, for it does not close speech (unless followed by an indication of *saying*, *adding*, *replying*, etc.).

(*b*) Spanish punctuation indications are given as follows:

.	punto	¿	se abre interrogación
,	coma	?	se cierra interrogación
;	punto y coma	¡	se abre admiración
:	dos puntos	!	se cierra admiración
...	puntos suspensivos	«	se abren comillas
		»	se cierran comillas
-	guión	(	se abre paréntesis
—	raya	)	se cierra paréntesis

Start a new paragraph	aparte
Carry straight on	seguido
Capital letter	mayúscula
Small letter	minúscula
Underline	subrayado

7. CAPITAL LETTERS. Within the sentence capitals are used less frequently in Spanish than in English. Thus, though they are used for place and personal names, they are not used for related adjectives or nouns.

España	español (*Spanish*), **el español** (*Spanish* [language]; *Spaniard*)
Andalucía	andaluz (*Andalusian*), **los andaluces** (*the Andalusians*)
Góngora	estudios gongorinos (*studies on Góngora*), **el gongorismo** (*Gongorism*)

Capitals are not used either, in Spanish, for names of days or months, nor for titles, unless abbreviated.

el segundo martes de febrero, the second Tuesday in February
el príncipe don Juan, Prince Don Juan
(el señor) don José Fernández, Mr José Fernández
Sr. D. José Fernández, Mr José Fernández (*on envelopes*)
El sombrero de tres picos, The Three-Cornered Hat

*Pronunciation, the Noun, the Definite
and Indefinite Articles, the Three Verb
Conjugations (Present Indicative)*

LESSON I

8. PRONUNCIATION. Read § 2 and study the pronunciation of
the vowels and of the consonants **d, b, v, h, j, r, s.** Study also the
introductory indications on Spanish word stress [§ 3 (*a*) and (*b*)].
Read aloud the words listed in the vocabulary at the end of this
lesson.

9. THE NOUN. Nouns in Spanish are either masculine
(**muchacho,** *boy*; **hospital,** *hospital*) or feminine (**tienda,** *shop*;
mujer, *woman*). The plural form is obtained by adding **-s** or **-es**
to the singular: **-s** is added when the singular form ends in a vowel
(**muchachos,** *boys*; **tiendas,** *shops*); **-es** when it ends in a consonant (**hospitales,** *hospitals*; **mujeres,** *women*).

10. THE DEFINITE ARTICLE. This has various forms in Spanish:
it is **el** before a masculine singular noun, **los** before a masculine
plural noun, **la** before a feminine singular noun, and **las** before a
feminine plural noun.

el muchacho, the boy	**los muchachos,** the boys
el hospital, the hospital	**los hospitales,** the hospitals
la tienda, the shop	**las tiendas,** the shops
la mujer, the woman	**las mujeres,** the women

11. THE INDEFINITE ARTICLE. **Un** is used before a masculine
singular noun; **una** before a feminine singular noun.

un muchacho, a boy	**muchachos,** boys
un hospital, a hospital	**hospitales,** hospitals
una tienda, a shop	**tiendas,** shops
una mujer, a woman	**mujeres,** women

NOTE: There is no Spanish equivalent of the French partitive
article: **vino,** *wine* (Fr. *du vin*), **hombres,** *men* (Fr. *des hommes*).

12. VERBS: THE THREE CONJUGATIONS.   There are three classes (or conjugations) of verbs in Spanish: those whose infinitive (English *to* —) ends in **-ar** belong to the first conjugation (**comprar,** *to buy*; **mandar,** *to send*), those ending in **-er** belong to the second conjugation (**vender,** *to sell*; **comer,** *to eat*) and those in **-ir** belong to the third conjugation (**vivir,** *to live*; **escribir,** *to write*).

13. VERBS: THE PRESENT INDICATIVE.   The present indicative tense is formed by adding to the stem (the infinitive minus **-ar, -er** or **-ir**) certain personal endings:

I. **-ar** verbs take **-o, -as, -a, -amos, -áis, -an.**
II. **-er** verbs take **-o, -es, -e, -emos, -éis, -en.**
III. **-ir** verbs take **-o, -es, -e, -imos, -ís, -en.**

I. *infinitive:* **comprar** (to buy)   *stem:* **compr-**

Singular

first person:	**compro**	I buy, do buy, am buying
second person:	**compras** / **usted compra**	you buy, do buy, are buying
third person:	**compra**	he (she, it) buys, does buy, is buying

Plural

first person:	**compramos**	we buy, do buy, are buying
second person:	**compráis** / **ustedes compran**	you buy, do buy, are buying
third person:	**compran**	they buy, do buy, are buying

II. *infinitive:* **vender** (to sell)   *stem:* **vend-**

Singular

first person:	**vendo**	I sell, do sell, am selling
second person:	**vendes** / **usted vende**	you sell, do sell, are selling
third person:	**vende**	he (she, it) sells, does sell, is selling

22

Plural

first person: **vendemos**   we sell, do sell, are selling

second person: $\begin{cases} \textbf{vendéis} \\ \textbf{ustedes venden} \end{cases}$ } you sell, do sell, are selling

third person: **venden**   they sell, do sell, are selling

III. *infinitive:* **vivir** (to live)   *stem:* **viv-**

Singular

first person: **vivo**   I live, do live, am living

second person: $\begin{cases} \textbf{vives} \\ \textbf{usted vive} \end{cases}$ } you live, do live, are living

third person: **vive**   he (she, it) lives, does live, is living

Plural

first person: **vivimos**   we live, do live, are living

second person: $\begin{cases} \textbf{vivís} \\ \textbf{ustedes viven} \end{cases}$ } you live, do live, are living

third person: **viven**   they live, do live, are living

NOTES: 1. The pronoun subject is not usually expressed in Spanish but is indicated in the verb ending.

Compro un periódico.   I buy (do buy, am buying) a paper.
Vendemos el libro.   We sell the book.
Viven en la tienda.   They live in the shop.

It is usual, however, to express the pronoun subjects **usted** (*you*, sing.) and **ustedes** (*you*, pl.).

2. There are two second-person forms in Spanish: the familiar and the polite. The familiar form is the first one of each pair given (**compras, compráis,** etc.) and is used to address members of one's family, friends of one's own age, children, inferiors and animals. The polite (or **usted**) form is the one used in normal polite conversation. The polite form always takes the same verb endings as the third person. **Usted** may be abbreviated in writing to **Vd., Ud.** or **V.,** and **ustedes** to **Vds., Uds.** or **VV.** The pronunciation is not affected.

VOCABULARY

(Each Spanish noun is listed with its definite article, though the English article is omitted. To facilitate the learning of the gender, it is recommended that a noun be memorized always with its article expressed.)

a	to	**Madrid**	Madrid
el amigo	friend	**mandar**	to send
la carta	letter	**mi**	my
la casa	house	**la muchacha**	girl
comer	to eat, to have a meal	**el muchacho**	boy
comprar	to buy	**la mujer**	woman, wife
de	of, from, about	**la pera**	pear
en	in, at	**el periódico**	(news)paper
escribir	to write	**recibir**	to receive
la fábrica	factory	**la tienda**	shop
el hospital	hospital	**trabajar**	to work
leer	to read	**vender**	to sell
el libro	book	**vivir**	to live
		y	and

EXERCISES

I. (a) *Pronounce the following words and explain the presence of the written accent where there is one:* dedo, mandar, Madrid, vino, vive, bebe, heno, hambre, jota, mojado, jamón, pero, perro, árbol, fábrica, seso, escribe, sus.

(b) *Put into the plural:* una carta, la mujer, el periódico, la tienda, un muchacho, el libro, una fábrica.

(c) *Put into the singular:* los amigos, tiendas, las cartas, libros, mujeres, los hospitales, las peras.

(d) *Read aloud and translate into English:* compro, compran, usted compra, mandas, manda, mandáis, vende, venden, ustedes venden, leo, leemos, leéis, vivimos, vivís, vive, escriben, usted escribe, escribo.

(e) *Translate into Spanish:* she sends, they are sending, you (*singular familiar*) do send, he works, you (*plural polite*) work, you (*pl. fam.*) work, we eat, you (*sing. pol.*) do eat, they eat, you (*pl. fam.*) read, they are reading, she reads, you (*pl. pol.*)

receive, he does receive, I receive, you (*pl. fam.*) live, you (*sing. pol.*) are living, we live.

II. (*a*) *Study and translate*[1]: 1. Ustedes compran libros y periódicos. 2. Comemos en la fábrica. 3. Usted vende peras. 4. Recibo una carta de mi amigo. 5. Vivimos en una casa en Madrid. 6. Mi amigo trabaja en el hospital. 7. Usted manda libros a las muchachas. 8. El muchacho vende un periódico a mi mujer. 9. Las mujeres trabajan en una fábrica. 10. Los muchachos comen peras en el hospital.

(*b*) *Translate:* 1. The boys are writing to my friend. 2. You (*sing. pol.*) sell the book to a girl. 3. The girls receive the letters from my friend. 4. The boy sends a book to my wife. 5. We are writing to the hospitals. 6. My friend works in a factory in Madrid. 7. They live in my house. 8. The woman is reading a book. 9. The boys send a letter to the girl. 10. We have a meal in a shop.

III. (*a*) *Study and translate:* 1. Usted lee el libro. 2. Trabajamos en una tienda. 3. La mujer compra un periódico. 4. Ustedes escriben cartas a los muchachos. 5. Recibes una carta de un amigo. 6. Mandáis periódicos a los hospitales. 7. Los muchachos viven en Madrid. 8. Mi mujer escribe una carta a un hospital. 9. Vendo un libro a una muchacha. 10. Las muchachas leen los libros.

(*b*) *Translate:* 1. You (*pl. pol.*) buy the books. 2. A boy reads the newspaper. 3. We receive a letter from my wife. 4. You (*sing. pol.*) eat pears in my house. 5. A boy is selling papers. 6. The woman buys a paper. 7. We are sending the letters to a friend. 8. They work in a shop. 9. She sells the books to the girls. 10. You (*pl. fam.*) live in Madrid.

[1] The key to Exercises 11 (*a*) and (*b*) of every Lesson is to be found near the end of the book (pp. 347–370). Besides acting as a test of progress, the key will at times introduce idiomatic uses or translations arising from the grammar of the lessons. Both parts of the exercise should be written down before checking and kept for subsequent retranslation as each Review Section is reached.

A *and* DE *with the Definite Article,
Negation, Interrogation, Interroga-
tives, Relatives and Conjunctions,*
DAR *and* IR, *Pronunciation*

LESSON II

14. A AND **de** WITH THE DEFINITE ARTICLE. (*a*) The preposition
a (*to*) joins with the masculine singular definite article **el** to give
al. Otherwise there is no contraction.

al hombre, to the man	**a los hombres,** to the men
a la mujer, to the woman	**a las mujeres,** to the women

NOTES: 1. In English the preposition *to* introducing the indirect
object is frequently omitted and the order *direct object—indirect
object* inverted (*i.e.,* instead of saying *He gives a book to the boy* we
say *He gives the boy a book*). This is not possible in Spanish; the
preposition **a** must always appear before a noun used as indirect
object (**Da un libro al muchacho**).

2. There is no contraction with the indefinite article: **a un, a una.**

(*b*) Similarly, **de** (*of, from, about*) joins with the masculine
singular definite article to give **del.**

del periódico, of the news- paper	**de los periódicos,** of the news- papers
de la fábrica, of the factory	**de las fábricas,** of the factories

NOTES: 1. The English *'s* and *s'* are translated into Spanish by
means of the preposition **de** with inversion of the word order:
el periódico de Juan, *John's newspaper* (lit., *the newspaper of
John*); **el amigo de los muchachos,** *the boys' friend* (lit., *the
friend of the boys*).

2. There is no contraction with the indefinite article: **de un,
de una.**

15. NEGATION. The negative in Spanish is formed by placing
the particle **no** immediately before the corresponding verb form.
No compramos la tienda. We do not buy the shop.

Usted no vende plumas. You do not sell pens.
El muchacho no vive en Madrid. The boy does not live in
Madrid.

16. INTERROGATION. A question is expressed in Spanish by
inversion of the order *subject—verb* (where a subject appears). It
is further indicated by double question marks in writing and by a
rising intonation in speech.

¿Habla mi amigo de Madrid? Is my friend talking about
Madrid?
¿Dónde trabaja usted? Where do you work?
¿No vende la casa a mi amigo? Is he not selling the house to
my friend?
¿Por qué bebe vino? Why does he drink wine?

17. INTERROGATIVES, RELATIVES AND CONJUNCTIONS. Interrogative words in Spanish (*cf.* English *who? which? where?* etc.) have
corresponding forms used as relatives or conjunctions. To
distinguish them, an accent is written on the words of the interrogative series [§ 4 (*b*) (i)].

Interrogatives		*Relatives and Conjunctions*	
¿qué?	what? which?	**que**	who, whom, which, that
¿quién(es)?	who? whom?	**quien(es)**	who, whom
¿dónde?	where?	**donde**	where
¿adónde?	where (... to)?	**adonde**	(to) where, to which
¿cuándo?	when?	**cuando**	when
¿cómo?	how?	**como**	as
¿por qué?	why?	**porque**	because

¿Qué compra el padre de Juan? What is John's father
buying?
el libro que compro, the book (which) I buy
¿Qué libros lee usted? Which books do you read?
el amigo que vende peras, the friend who sells pears
¿Quién escribe la carta? Who is writing the letter?

27

el muchacho a quien escribo, the boy to whom I write
¿Dónde trabajas?   Where do you work?
la fábrica donde trabajo, the factory where I work
¿Cuándo come peras?   When does he eat pears?
Come peras cuando no trabaja.   He eats pears when he is not
  working.
¿Por qué no bebe usted?   Why aren't you drinking?
No bebo porque no tengo vino.   I'm not drinking because I
  haven't any wine.

NOTES: 1. It is important to distinguish between the relative pronouns **que** and **quien(es)**. **Que** refers to things:

  la pluma que escribe, the pen that writes
  la pluma que compro, the pen that I buy
  la pluma con que escribo, the pen with which I write

It also denotes persons, except after a preposition when **quien** (plural **quienes**) is used:

  el amigo que trabaja, the friend who works
  el amigo que tengo, the friend that I have
but **el amigo con quien trabajo,** the friend with whom I work

2. In English a relative pronoun or the conjunction *that* may often be omitted. This is not possible in Spanish: *the letter I write* must be translated as **la carta que escribo,** *I believe he is not going* as **Creo que no va.**

3. In English a preposition is frequently separated from the interrogative or relative to which it belongs, and placed after the verb (often with omission of the relative as in Note 2).   In Spanish the preposition must be placed immediately before the word to which it refers.

¿Con quién trabaja usted? Whom do you work with?
¿En qué tienda trabaja?   Which shop does he work in?
el amigo con quien trabajo, the friend I work with
la pluma con que escribo, the pen that I write with

4. The relative **que** and interrogative **qué** are invariable (*i.e.*, the same in singular and plural); **quien** and **¿quién?** have plural forms **quienes** and **¿quiénes?** respectively.

¿Qué plumas vende usted?   What pens do you sell?
las plumas que vende, the pens he sells

¿**Quiénes compran libros?** Who (=which people) buy books?
los amigos con quienes trabajo, the friends I work with

18. Two Irregular Verbs : **dar.** and **ir.**

	dar, *to give*		**ir,** *to go*	
(1)	doy	damos	voy	vamos
(2)	das	dais	vas	vais
	usted da	ustedes dan	usted va	ustedes van
(3)	da	dan	va	van

Notes: 1. In irregular verbs, too, the **usted(es)** forms of the verb are the same as those of the third person. This applies to all verbs in all tenses.

2. Since **dais** and **vais** are words of a single syllable [see § 3 (*c*) (iii)], the accent would be superfluous. Contrast **compráis, mandáis,** etc., accented in accordance with § 3 (*b*).

3. **Ir** is used with the preposition **a** and an infinitive to translate the English *to go to* + verb, *to go and* + verb. Like its English counterpart, **ir** in this construction may indicate future action as well as movement.

Va a comprar un lápiz. He goes and buys a pencil. (*Also:* He is going to buy a pencil.)

Vamos a leer el libro. We are going to read the book.

19. Pronunciation. Study the Spanish pronunciation of the letters **c, z, q, u, ll, y** [§ 2], and read aloud the words listed in the vocabulary below.

Notes: 1. Before **e** and **i** the light English *th* sound (as in *think*) is represented in Spanish by **c**; elsewhere **c** would give a hard sound (like *c* in *cat*) and **z** is used. The letter **z** is not used in Spanish before **e** or **i** [for exceptions see § 2 (*b*)]. Thus, to form the plural of words which in the singular end in **z** (**el lápiz,** *pencil*; **la vez,** *time*), it is not sufficient to add **-es** in accordance with § 9; the **z** must be changed to **c** (**el lápiz, los lápices**; **una vez,** *once*; **dos veces,** *twice*).

2. There is an accent on the **o** of **lección** (*lesson*) to indicate that the stress is on the last syllable [§ 3 (*a*) and (*b*)]. In the plural the stress is on the same syllable but it is no longer the last one. No

accent is therefore written (**lección**, **lecciones**). Compare: **nación**, **naciones**; **afán**, **afanes**; **inglés**, **ingleses**.

3. Though **y** in final position is pronounced like **i**, it counts as a consonant for the formation of the plural (*i.e.*, it takes **-es** not **-s**, § 9): **el rey** (*king*), **los reyes**; **la ley** (*law*), **las leyes**.

VOCABULARY

beber	to drink	**ir**	to go
la calle	road, street	**Juan**	John
la ciudad	town, city	**el lápiz**	pencil
con	with	**la lección**	lesson
dar	to give	**la madre**	mother
estudiar	to study	**la manzana**	apple
hablar	to talk, to speak	**no**	no, not
hay	there is, there are	**el padre**	father
		la pluma	pen
la hermana	sister	**tengo**	I have
el hermano	brother	**el vaso**	tumbler, glass
el hombre	man	**el vino**	wine

See also the words listed in § 17

EXERCISES

I. (*a*) *Pronounce the following words and explain written accents:* acera, cáncer, ciudad, cuidado, periódico, lección, lecciones, lápiz, lápices, rezábamos, porque, ¿qué?, quinqué, cura, quisquilla, cuatro, llegar, mayor, yeso, y, rey, leyes, yo.

(*b*) *Put into the plural:* a un muchacho, al amigo, a la ciudad, a una hermana, a un hospital, al hermano, del periódico, de la lección, de un hombre, de una fábrica, del lápiz.

(*c*) *Put into the singular:* a los hombres, a mujeres, a las ciudades, a los hospitales, a ciudades, de los lápices, de lecciones, de las madres, de los periódicos.

(*d*) *Translate:* No mandan. ¿Trabajas? ¿No manda usted? ¿Dónde vive usted? No recibimos. ¿Recibes? Dan. No voy. ¿Va usted? Vais. ¿No dan ustedes? ¿Adónde va? La hermana de Juan. Del amigo de mi padre. Al padre de los muchachos.

(*e*) *Translate:* I do not eat. Does he drink? He doesn't work. Don't they read? What are they writing with? Where do you (*sing. pol.*) work? They don't send. I am not working. Do you (*pl. fam.*) work? She gives. Does he go? They don't give. I am going. What are you (*pl. fam.*) giving? They are not going. The boy's brother. To John's father. From the girls' mother.

II. (*a*) *Study and translate:* 1. Escribo una carta al padre del muchacho. 2. ¿Adónde vais con el padre de Juan? 3. Como no tengo peras, como manzanas. 4. La madre de los muchachos vive en la ciudad. 5. ¿Qué lee usted cuando no trabaja? 6. ¿A qué periódico escribes la carta? 7. ¿Cuándo van ustedes a comprar la tienda donde trabajo? 8. Hay un hombre que vende lápices. 9. Doy a mi hermano la pluma con que escribo la carta. 10. ¿De qué lecciones habla el muchacho?

(*b*) *Translate:* 1. What do the women sell? 2. Who is he writing the letter to? 3. He gives the boy my pen. 4. Do you (*sing. pol.*) not receive letters from my sister? 5. Where are you (*pl. pol.*) going? 6. My brother doesn't read the books he buys. 7. There's a woman who sells pens to the boys. 8. Why do you (*pl. fam.*) not read the papers? 9. Which pencils do you (*pl. pol.*) write with? 10. How do you (*sing. pol.*) write the letters you send to my brother?

III. (*a*) *Study and translate:* 1. Doy el libro a un amigo de mi hermano. 2. ¿Por qué no escribes una carta a mi padre? 3. Vendo los libros al padre de Juan. 4. ¿Cuándo va usted a mandar los libros al hospital? 5. Mi padre da un vaso de vino a mi hermano. 6. Recibo una carta del padre de mi amigo. 7. ¿Con qué pluma vas a escribir las lecciones? 8. Vamos a ir al hospital con el hermano de un amigo. 9. ¿No trabaja usted en la fábrica de mi padre? 10. La mujer da una manzana al muchacho.

(*b*) *Translate:* 1. Why are you (*sing. pol.*) going to write a letter to John's father? 2. The boy buys a pencil because he is going to study. 3. Where does the man sell the apples? 4. We are going with John to my father's shop. 5. When are you (*sing. fam.*) going to study the lessons? 6. My mother doesn't read the letters she receives. 7. He talks about my brother's house. 8. Who do you (*pl. pol.*) give the newspapers to? 9. They send the boy a book. 10. The woman sells the girl apples and pears.

LESSON III

20. ENDINGS AND AGREEMENT OF ADJECTIVES.   An adjective in Spanish, like the definite article, agrees in number (*i.e.*, singular or plural) and gender (*i.e.*, masculine or feminine) with the noun it qualifies.   From the masculine singular, quoted in dictionaries and vocabularies, we can deduce the remaining forms.

(1) *Adjectives which have a masculine singular ending in* -o (**barato**, *cheap*; **amarillo**, *yellow*).   The feminine singular is formed by changing the **-o** to **-a** (**barata, amarilla**).   The plural is obtained by adding **-s** to the singular (masc. pl. **baratos, amarillos**; fem. pl. **baratas, amarillas**).

un libro barato, libros baratos, a cheap book, cheap books
la pluma barata, las plumas baratas, the cheap pen, the cheap pens

Notice that the adjective is placed after the noun.

(2) *Adjectives of nationality or regional origin ending in a consonant in the masculine singular* (**español**, *Spanish*; **andaluz**, *Andalusian*).   The masculine plural takes **-es** (**españoles, andaluces**).[1]   The feminine takes **-a** in the singular (**española, andaluza**) and **-as** in the plural (**españolas, andaluzas**).

> **un periódico español,** a Spanish paper
> **periódicos españoles,** Spanish papers
> **una casa andaluza,** an Andalusian house
> **casas andaluzas,** Andalusian houses

NOTE: Adjectives of nationality and regional origin are written in Spanish with a small initial letter, as also the corresponding name of the inhabitants and of the language: **el español,** *the Spaniard,*

[1] For the change of **z** to **c** before **e** or **i** see § 19, Note 1.

33

Spanish; **un inglés,** *an Englishman*; **el inglés,** *the Englishman, English*; **una inglesa,** *an English women/girl.*

(3) *Other adjectives* (*i.e.*, those not ending in -o in the masculine singular, nor indicating nationality or regional origin if they end in a consonant: **verde,** *green*; **difícil,** *difficult*). The feminine singular has the same form as the masculine (**verde, difícil**). The plural is formed by adding -s to the singular if this ends in a vowel (masc. and fem. pl. **verdes**), and -es if it ends in a consonant (masc. and fem. pl. **difíciles**).

un vaso verde, vasos verdes, a green tumbler, green tumblers
la pera verde, las peras verdes, the green pear, the green pears
un idioma difícil, a difficult language
idiomas difíciles, difficult languages
la lección difícil, the difficult lesson
las lecciones difíciles, the difficult lessons

21. MORE ABOUT AGREEMENT. If the adjective qualifies more than one noun the following applies:

(1) If the nouns are all masculine the adjective is used in the masculine plural.

un vaso y un plato rotos, a broken glass and plate

(2) If the nouns are all feminine the adjective takes the feminine plural form.

una mujer y una muchacha andaluzas, an Andalusian woman and girl

(3) If the nouns are of different gender the adjective is generally in the masculine plural.

un muchacho y una muchacha españoles, a Spanish boy and girl

NOTE: In English an indefinite article used before one noun may be understood but unexpressed before another. In Spanish the article must usually be repeated. The same applies to the definite article: **los médicos y las enfermeras que trabajan aquí,** *the doctors and nurses who work here.*

22. Position of Adjectives. Adjectives in Spanish are usually placed after the noun. Notice, however, the following:

(1) *Always placed before the noun* are adjectives which limit rather than describe: cardinal numbers used as such (**una lección,** *one lesson*; **dos lecciones,** *two lessons*)[1]; adjectives of quantity such as **mucho** (*much, a lot of*; pl. *many, a lot of*), **poco** (*little, not much*; pl. *few, not many*), **tanto** (*so much*; pl. *so many*), **demasiado** (*too much*; pl. *too many*), **varios** (*several*), **¿cuánto?** (*how much?*; pl. *how many?*); and the invariable interrogative adjective **¿qué?** (*which? what?*).

¿Cuántas cartas va a escribir? How many letters is he going to write?

Tengo muchos hermanos. I have a lot of (many) brothers.

Leen pocos periódicos. They don't read many papers.

¿Qué libros compra usted? Which books are you buying?

(2) *Used more frequently before the noun than after it* are: certain common adjectives such as **bueno** (*good*), **malo** (*bad*), **pequeño** (*small, little*), **hermoso** (*beautiful, lovely*), **nuevo** (*new*), **joven** (*young*) and **viejo** (*old*); ordinal numbers (**primero,** *first*; **segundo,** *second*; etc.), and **último** (*last*).

una pequeña muchacha, una muchacha pequeña, a small girl

un viejo señor, un señor viejo, an old gentleman

la primera vez, la vez primera, the first time

(3) *Used before and after the noun,* but with a different meaning, are:

	before the noun	after the noun
distinto	different (=sundry)	different (=not the same)
grande	great	big
mismo	same	himself, herself, themselves, myself, etc.
pobre	poor (=to be pitied)	poor (=impecunious)

---

[1] Cardinal numbers, in Spanish as in English, may also be used with ordinal sense and are then placed after the noun: **en la página veinte** (*on page twenty*) as opposed to the purely cardinal use in **Este libro tiene veinte páginas** (*This book has twenty pages*).

35

(4) An adjective which is used frequently before the noun nevertheless comes after it when the adjective is itself modified by an adverb.

un libro muy bueno, a very good book
una casa bastante vieja, rather an old house
un profesor demasiado joven, too young a teacher
una muchacha más pequeña, a smaller (*lit.*, more small) girl
el hermano más joven, the youngest (*lit.*, most young) brother

23. AN IRREGULAR VERB: **ser.**

ser, *to be*

(1)	soy	somos
(2)	eres	sois
	usted es	ustedes son
(3)	es	son

¿Es usted inglés?	Are you English?
Mi madre es española.	My mother is Spanish.
Estas tiendas son muy buenas.	These shops are very good.

24. PRONUNCIATION. Study the Spanish pronunciation of the letters **g, j,** and **ñ** (§ 2). Revise § 3 (*a*) and (*b*) and study § 3(*c*).

VOCABULARY

amarillo	yellow	**la flor**	flower
andaluz	Andalusian	**el idioma**	language
azul	blue	**inglés**	English
barato	cheap	**más**	more, most
bastante	rather, fairly, quite	**muy**	very
		para	for
bonito	nice, pretty	**pero**	but
el coche	car	**rojo**	red
la cosa	thing	**el señor**	gentleman
difícil	difficult, hard	**ser**	to be
dos	two	**un(o), -a**	one (*also* a)
español	Spanish, Spaniard	**verde**	green
fácil	easy	**la vez**	time (= occasion)

See also the words listed in § 22

EXERCISES

I. (*a*) *Pronounce the following and explain written accents:* genio, lago, gana, egregio, coge, jaula, ajo, junto, niño, cañones, cañón, vivís, rodea, saeta, Bilbao, compráis, lección, sabio, adiós, herejía, estío, aún.

(*b*) *Put into the plural:* una cosa barata, el lápiz amarillo, la casa más grande, un idioma difícil, el muchacho andaluz, una tienda española, la primera lección, un señor muy viejo, el español y el inglés, una buena muchacha.

(*c*) *Put into the singular:* los coches rojos, las muchachas españolas, vinos andaluces, los idiomas más fáciles, señores ingleses, de los periódicos españoles, flores muy hermosas, en las fábricas más pequeñas, las pobres mujeres.

(*d*) *Translate:* En el segundo libro. Un viejo señor andaluz. Muchas lecciones difíciles. ¿Qué libros? Pocos periódicos españoles. Muchachos muy jóvenes. En una casa más grande. Mi padre mismo. Una calle bastante nueva. Las muchas veces que voy a Madrid.

(*e*) *Translate:* An Andalusian girl. A very nice house. The first lesson. Two great Spaniards. So many factories. A cheap pen and pencil. Many difficult lessons. The first glasses of wine. Which Spanish towns? They give different flowers. It is a different thing.

II. (*a*) *Study and translate:* 1. Hay muchas hermosas tiendas en Madrid. 2. Pocos señores ingleses viven en casas andaluzas. 3. ¿A quién va usted a dar tantas flores? 4. La muchacha española vende muchos periódicos ingleses. 5. ¿Qué libros son los más baratos? 6. Juan estudia la primera lección y mi hermano la tercera. 7. Las flores azules son muy hermosas. 8. Vamos a ir con la madre de Juan al nuevo hospital inglés. 9. ¿Cuántas cartas escribe la muchacha española? 10. La mujer vende las flores rojas a mi hermana y las amarillas a mi madre.

(b) *Translate:* 1. I buy a green pencil and a yellow pen. 2. What are the Spanish girls selling? 3. You (*pl. fam.*) drink a lot of Spanish wine. 4. Who are we going to sell the yellow flowers to? 5. My Spanish friends sell very nice pens and pencils. 6. Where do you (*sing. pol.*) buy so many cheap things? 7. They study two difficult lessons and one easier one. 8. The houses of Madrid are bigger, but the Andalusian ones are nicer. 9. Who are you (*sing. pol.*) studying the third lesson with? 10. We sell so many things that my father is going to buy a new shop.

III. (a) *Study and translate:* 1. ¿De qué habla mi amigo inglés? 2. Habla de un viejo señor que vive en Madrid. 3. La casa de mi hermano es muy grande y muy bonita. 4. ¿No recibes cartas de muchos amigos españoles? 5. Voy a comprar una pluma y un lápiz amarillos. 6. ¿Cuántas lecciones van ustedes a estudiar? 7. Los muchachos andaluces leen pocos libros ingleses. 8. Mi padre habla inglés y mi madre habla español. 9. Mi pobre hermana estudia muchos idiomas difíciles. 10. Tengo un joven amigo español que vende flores muy hermosas.

(b) *Translate:* 1. The flowers are blue and yellow. 2. Who are you (*pl. pol.*) buying the more difficult books for? 3. My father's house is very small. 4. There are many cheap things in the shops of Madrid. 5. John's sister is studying the third lesson. 6. The Andalusians sell cheap pens to English gentlemen. 7. Few Spaniards live in big cities. 8. We sell many English and Spanish newspapers. 9. I am going to buy a red pencil for my brother and a yellow pen for my sister. 10. The Andalusian girls are going to Madrid in my brother's car.

LESSON IV

25. APOCOPATION OF ADJECTIVES. (*a*) **Uno, alguno, ninguno, bueno, malo, primero** and **tercero** lose their final **-o** when they precede a masculine singular noun.

Tengo un vaso. I have one (*or* a) tumbler.

but **Tengo uno; tengo uno verde.** I have one; I have a green one.

¿Hacen Vds. algún cambio? Are you making any change?

but **Hacemos alguno.** We are making the odd one (*lit.*, some one).

No leo ningún periódico. I don't read any paper(s).

but **No leo ninguno.** I don't read any.

Es un buen alumno. He is a good pupil.

but **Es bueno.** He is good.

Es un mal libro. It is a bad book.

but **Es malo.** It is bad.

El primer capítulo. The first chapter.

but **El primero.** The first one.

El tercer periódico. The third newspaper.

but **El tercero.** The third one.

NOTES: 1. Apocopation does not affect the feminine or the plural of these adjectives, formed in accordance with § 20 (1): **la tercera lección** (*the third lesson*), **las primeras casas** (*the first houses*), **algunos señores** (*some gentlemen*).

2. An accent is written on the apocopated forms **ningún** and **algún** in accordance with § 3 (*b*).

3. **Ningún (ninguno, ninguna)** is used only in negations, the corresponding affirmative form being **algún (alguno,** etc.).

¿Tiene usted alguna objeción? Have you any objection?
No tengo ninguna objeción. I haven't any objection.

4. **Ningún (ninguno, -a)** is virtually not used in the plural.

No leo ningún libro. I don't read any books *or* I read no books (*Contrast:* **Leo algunos libros.** I read some books).

5. **Alguno** and **ninguno** are frequently omitted in Spanish where English *some* and *any* appear.

Compra pan. He buys some bread.
¿Tiene usted amigos aquí? Have you any friends here?
No tengo amigos. I haven't any friends.

6. In English the word *one(s)* is usual after an adjective with noun understood (*the first one, a yellow one, the good ones*). In Spanish the article and adjective alone are used: **el primero** or **la primera, uno amarillo** or **una amarilla, los buenos** or **las buenas.**

(*b*) **Grande** is apocopated to **gran** before a singular noun (masculine or feminine); the plural form (**grandes**) remains unchanged. There is no apocopation when **grande** follows the noun [§ 22 (3)].

un gran amigo, una gran señora	a great friend, a great lady
grandes amigos, grandes señoras	great friends, great ladies
una casa grande, un hospital muy grande	a large house, a very big hospital

NOTE: Before a noun beginning with a vowel it is possible not to apocopate: **un grande amigo** (*a great friend*), **una grande época** (*a great age* [= *era*]), **una grande española** (*a great Spanish woman*).

26. DEMONSTRATIVE ADJECTIVES. The English *this* is translated by the Spanish **este** or its related forms. *That* may be translated by **ese** or **aquel: ese** indicates something near to or associated with the person addressed, **aquel** something more remote. Like other adjectives the demonstratives agree in number and gender with the noun they qualify. They precede the noun. The forms are:

	Singular		Plural	
	masculine	*feminine*	*masculine*	*feminine*
this	**este**	**esta**	**estos**	**estas**
that (near you)	**ese**	**esa**	**esos**	**esas**
that (over there)	**aquel**	**aquella**	**aquellos**	**aquellas**

este hombre, estos hombres, esta mujer, estas mujeres
ese periódico, esos periódicos, esa pluma, esas plumas
aquel inglés, aquellos ingleses, aquella ciudad, aquellas
    ciudades

NOTE: Like the definite and indefinite articles [§ 21, Note] a demonstrative cannot generally, as in English, be expressed before one noun and understood (but unexpressed) before another. It must usually be repeated.

    estos hombres y estas mujeres, these men and women

27. DEMONSTRATIVE PRONOUNS. (*a*) The demonstrative pronouns (English *this one, that one*) are similar to the demonstrative adjectives. There are the same three series, and the pronoun agrees in number and gender with the noun that it replaces. The pronoun is distinguished from the adjective by the presence of a written accent [§ 4 (*b*) (ii)]. We have therefore the following forms:

	Singular		Plural	
	masculine	*feminine*	*masculine*	*feminine*
this (one)	**éste**	**ésta**	**éstos**	**éstas**
that (one) [near you]	**ése**	**ésa**	**ésos**	**ésas**
that (one) [over there]	**aquél**	**aquélla**	**aquéllos**	**aquéllas**

¿Qué periódico tienes?   Which paper have you got?
  Tengo éste, ése, aquél.   I have this one, that one, that
                                 one.

¿Qué casas compra mi padre? — Which houses does my father buy?

Compra éstas, ésas, aquéllas. — He buys these, those, those.

NOTES: 1. The English *one* is contained in the Spanish pronoun [*cf.* § 25, Note 6].
2. **Éste** and its related forms may translate English *the latter* and **aquél** translate *the former*.

Tengo una hermana y un hermano. Éste trabaja pero aquélla no. I have a sister and brother. The latter works but the former doesn't.

(*b*) There are forms of the demonstrative pronoun not listed in the above table: the neuter singular forms **esto, eso, aquello.** Since there are no neuter nouns in Spanish these have no equivalent in the adjective series and consequently require no distinguishing written accent. Neuter demonstrative pronouns refer to something indeterminate or collective, unlike the masculine and feminine accented forms which refer to specific nouns.

esto, this   **eso,** that (near you)   **aquello,** that (yonder)

¿Comprendes todo esto? Do you understand all this?

— **¿Vamos a pie?** — **No.** — **¿Y en coche?** — **Eso sí.**
"Shall we walk?" "No." "Go by car?" "Yes (I'd like that)." (*Lit.*, that yes.)

NOTES: 1. There are no neuter plural forms.
2. The dash is used in Spanish to indicate dialogue [§ 6 (a)].

28. TWO IRREGULAR VERBS: **tener** AND **hacer.**

tener, *to have*		**hacer,** *to do, make*	
(1) tengo	tenemos	hago	hacemos
(2) tienes	tenéis	haces	hacéis
usted tiene	ustedes tienen	usted hace	ustedes hacen
(3) tiene	tienen	hace	hacen

Note: **Tener que** with a following infinitive means *to have to*:
Tengo que trabajar mucho.   I have to work hard.
Tienen que ir a comprar algo.   They have to go and buy something.

29. Pronunciation.   Letters p, b, t, d, k, g, m, n [§ 2 (*b*)].
Notice that in the articulation of **n, t** and hard **d**, the tongue is
further forward than in English, pressed against the back of the
upper front teeth.   This results in a sharper, less aspirate sound.
The pronunciation of the remaining letters, too, differs from the
English pronunciation in that it is firmer, sharper and less aspirate.

VOCABULARY

alguno	some, any	**la ley**	law
alto	high, tall	**ninguno**	none, (not) any
el capítulo	chapter	**Pedro**	Peter
como	as, like	**que**	than
el cuarto	room	**el rey**	king
demasiado	too, too much	**la señora**	lady, wife
el día	day	**sobre**	on, about
España	Spain	**sobre todo**	especially
hacer	to do, to make	**tan**	so, such
la idea	idea	**tener**	to have
interesante	interesting	**todo**	all, every

EXERCISES

I. (*a*) *Pronounce the following and explain written accents:*
Pepita, papá, pupila, bimembre, zambomba, baboso, tableta,
tanteo, titán, duende, diente, diputado, kilo, kilómetro,
ganga, garganta, mimar, memoria, tamboril, nene, pande-
monio, ningún.

(*b*) *Put into the plural:* un hospital grande, algún buen señor,
este lápiz amarillo, la primera vez, ¿qué idioma?, esa mujer
tan hermosa, aquel viejo inglés, un gran amigo.

(*c*) *Put into the singular:* estos muchachos andaluces, algunas ciudades inglesas, esos periódicos españoles, buenos amigos, aquellas fábricas tan grandes, los grandes reyes, malas leyes.

(d) *Translate:* este buen señor, una gran señora, algunas cosas muy bonitas, ninguna fábrica española, algunos de estos señores, ninguno de mis amigos, aquella mujer y aquel muchacho, el muchacho más alto.

(e) *Translate:* no book, some friends, no Spanish girls, that pen and pencil, those things, some of these factories, none of these Andalusian boys, a great king.

II. (a) *Study and translate:* 1. Es muy fácil hacer eso. 2. Mi madre es española y mi padre inglés. 3. Este señor no tiene amigos en Madrid. 4. Todos tenemos las mismas ideas sobre esto. 5. — ¿En qué fábrica trabaja usted? — En ésta. 6. Hablamos español cuando vamos a España. 7. Aquellos muchachos andaluces tienen que trabajar mucho. 8. — ¿Qué es eso? — Es un buen libro español que voy a leer algún día. 9. El primer capítulo es muy difícil pero no tan difícil como el tercero. 10. — ¿Cuántos vasos tienen? — Pedro tiene dos, pero Juan no tiene ninguno.

(b) *Translate:* 1. My poor brother works too hard (= too much). 2. Those gentlemen don't speak English. 3. This is a very interesting idea. 4. Why don't you (*pl. fam.*) buy a smaller (= more small) house? 5. Who receives all these letters? 6. This house is very nice and it has many rooms. 7. Peter has many friends but my brother hasn't any. 8. This hospital is too big for such a small town (= a so small town). 9. These flowers are very beautiful, especially the yellow ones. 10. This third lesson is much more difficult than the first, but it is not so difficult as the second.

III. (a) *Study and translate:* 1. Este señor es un gran amigo de mi padre. 2. Esa pluma que tienes no es muy buena. 3. Vamos a ir todos a Madrid. 4. Mi hermana trabaja en la fábrica de aquel señor. 5. — ¿Tiene usted alguna idea sobre esto? — No, no tengo ninguna. 6. Estas muchachas son españolas, pero trabajan mucho. 7. Este libro es más interesante que aquél. 8. —¿Qué capítulos leen? —Juan lee el primero y Pedro el tercero. 9. Mi hermano es muy joven pero escribe cosas bastante buenas. 10. Aquella señora tiene una fábrica muy grande en Madrid.

(b) *Translate:* 1. The king makes these laws. 2. Those Andalusian girls work in this factory. 3. I have to buy several books for my sister. 4. These rooms are bigger (= more big) than those. 5. "Has he any friends in this town?" "No, he hasn't any." 6. That lady is going to write a letter to the king. 7. We are going to read the first chapter of this new book. 8. This shop is very cheap but it is not bad. 9. That boy writes very interesting letters to my father. 10. The letters he writes to my father are the same ones that he sends to Peter.

LESSON V

30. One of the principal difficulties of Spanish is that of distinguishing between the verbs **ser** and **estar,** both of which translate the English *to be.*

31. Ser AND **estar** (PRESENT INDICATIVE).

	ser, *to be*		**estar,** *to be*	
(1)	soy	somos	estoy	estamos
(2)	eres	sois	estás	estáis
	usted es	ustedes son	usted está	ustedes están
(3)	es	son	está	están

32. ENGLISH *to be* + *adjective.* (*a*) **Ser** indicates an inherent or essential characteristic, with no suggestion of change from any other state; **estar,** on the other hand, denotes an accidental quality, the result of change from or liable to change into a different state.

ser:

   Esta lección es difícil.   This lesson is difficult.

   Aquellas casas son grandes.   Those houses are big.

   Mi madre es española.   My mother is Spanish.

   Esto no es posible.   This is not possible.

   Este amigo es muy inteligente.   This friend is very intelligent.

   Esas flores son amarillas.   Those flowers are yellow.

estar:

   Estamos muy contentos.   We are very pleased.

   Hoy estoy un poco triste.   I'm a little sad today.

   Esta pera no está madura.   This pear is not ripe.

   Las puertas están abiertas.   The doors are open.

   La ventana está rota.   The window is broken.

   Mi madre está enferma.   My mother is ill.

(*b*) Most adjectives can be used with both **ser** and **estar**. Not, however, indiscriminately. The distinction established above still applies.

La muchacha es pálida.   The girl is pale (*of naturally pale complexion*).

La muchacha está pálida.   The girl is pale (*because of illness, shock, etc.*).

Este señor es muy alegre.   This gentleman is very cheerful (*of a cheerful disposition*).

Este señor está muy alegre.   This gentleman is very cheerful (*in a cheerful mood*).

El hielo es frío.[1]   Ice is cold (*inherent characteristic*).

Este té está frío.   This tea is cold (*accidental quality: it has gone cold*).

El azúcar es dulce.[1]   Sugar is sweet (*inherent characteristic*).

Este café está dulce.   This coffee is sweet (*accidental quality: sugar has been added*).

(*c*) Some adjectives have a different meaning according to whether they are used with **ser** or **estar**.

ser cansado	to be tiresome
estar cansado	to be tired
ser listo	to be clever
estar listo	to be ready (prepared)
ser malo	to be bad
estar malo	to be ill

Mi hermana está cansada.   My sister is tired.

¡Qué cansado es este hombre!   How tiresome this man is!

Estos alumnos son muy listos.   These pupils are very bright.

Estamos listos para salir.   We are ready (in order) to go out.

Soy muy malo en español.   I'm very bad at Spanish.

---

[1] Notice that the definite article is used in Spanish with nouns employed in a generalizing sense: *i.e.*, all ice (ice as a whole) is cold; all sugar (sugar in general) is sweet.

Estos muchachos son muy malos. These boys are very bad.
Mi madre está mala. My mother is ill.

NOTES: 1. A similar distinction is occasionally made between **ser bueno** (*to be good*) and **estar bueno** (*to be well*), though in the latter case, as in English, the adverb (**bien,** *well*) is more usual than the adjective (**bueno,** *good*): **Estoy bien,** *I am well*; **Mi madre no está bien,** *My mother is not well*.

2. The exclamation mark is used inverted at the beginning of an exclamation [§ 6].

(d) A General Aid

In deciding whether to use **ser** or **estar** in a given case the following will prove useful: if *in a* (+ adj.) *state* can be substituted for the adjective alone without change of meaning, use **estar**; otherwise (*i.e.*, if *a* (+ adj. + noun) would be a more appropriate substitution) use **ser**.

I am pleased (*i.e.*, in a pleased state).
　Estoy contento.
The pear is ripe (*i.e.*, in a ripe state).
　Está madura.
The house is big (*not* in a big state *but* a big house).
　La casa es grande.
My friend is English (*not* in an English state *but* an English person).
　Mi amigo es inglés.
His father is rich (*not* in a rich state *but* a rich man).
　Su padre es rico.

In a case like *He is cheerful* both substitutions are equally possible: *He is in a cheerful state* and *He is a cheerful person*. But which is meant? If it is the first one, **estar** is used; if the second, **ser**.

33. ENGLISH *to be + an element other than an adjective*. **Estar** is used to indicate position, real or figurative; **ser** is used in all other cases.

estar:

   ¿Dónde estás? Estoy aquí.   Where are you?   I'm here.

   Está detrás de la puerta.   He is behind the door.

   Estamos en un lío.   We're in a mess.

ser:

   ¿Qué es eso?   What is that?

   ¿Qué edificio es? Es uno grande. Es el mismo.   Which building is it?   It is a big one.   It is the same one.

   Vivir en Madrid no es conocer España.   To live in Madrid is not to know Spain.

   Dos y tres son cinco.   Two and three are five.

   ¿De quién es este libro? Es de Juan. Es de usted.   Whose book is this?   It is John's.   It is yours.

   ¿De dónde es? Es de Madrid. Es un buen muchacho.   Where's he from?   He's from Madrid.   He's a good lad.

NOTES: 1. Here, as in § 32, **estar** is the word that localizes, that expresses a real state, as opposed to **ser** which scarcely presents more than an equation, or simple existence. Note the corresponding nouns: **el ser** (*being, existence*), **el estado** (*state*).

2. **Estar** is never followed by a noun complement: **Éste es** (never **está**) **mi padre** (*This is my father*).

34· POSSESSIVE ADJECTIVES.

	Singular		Plural	
	masculine	*feminine*	*masculine*	*feminine*
(1) my	**mi**	**mi**	**mis**	**mis**
(2) your (sing.) *fam.*	**tu**	**tu**	**tus**	**tus**
(2) your (sing.) *pol.*	**su**	**su**	**sus**	**sus**
(3) his, her, its	**su**	**su**	**sus**	**sus**
(1) our	**nuestro**	**nuestra**	**nuestros**	**nuestras**
(2) your (pl.) *fam.*	**vuestro**	**vuestra**	**vuestros**	**vuestras**
(2) your (pl.) *pol.*	**su**	**su**	**sus**	**sus**
(3) their	**su**	**su**	**sus**	**sus**

tu coche, tus coches, your car, your cars
tu idea, tus ideas, your idea, your ideas

nuestro libro, nuestros libros, our book, our books

nuestra casa, nuestras casas, our house, our houses

sus hermanos y su amigo, his brothers and his friend

Mis primos trabajan en su cuarto. My cousins are working in their room.

¿Viven sus amigos en vuestra casa? Do his friends live in your house?

NOTE: Like the article and the demonstrative adjective, the possessive adjective is usually best repeated in Spanish where it is merely understood in English.

> **sus primos y sus hermanos,** his cousins and brothers

35. CARDINAL NUMBERS 1–20.

un(o), -a	one	**seis**	six
dos	two	**siete**	seven
tres	three	**ocho**	eight
cuatro	four	**nueve**	nine
cinco	five	**diez**	ten
once	eleven	**diez y seis** *or* **dieciséis**	sixteen
doce	twelve	**diez y siete** *or* **diecisiete**	seventeen
trece	thirteen	**diez y ocho** *or* **dieciocho**	eighteen
catorce	fourteen	**diez y nueve** *or* **diecinueve**	nineteen
quince	fifteen	**veinte**	twenty

NOTE: Apart from **uno** all these numerals are invariable in form.

cuatro hombres y cinco mujeres, four men and five women

For the use of the various forms **un, uno, una,** see § 25.

Mi tío lee un capítulo.

My uncle reads one (*or* a) chapter.

Mi padre lee dos capítulos y mi tío uno.

My father reads two chapters and my uncle one.

Mi hermano tiene una pluma; mi hermana también tiene una.

My brother has one (*or* a) pen; my sister also has one.

36. PRONUNCIATION.   Letters **f, l, w, x** [§ 2 (b)].

VOCABULARY

abierto	open	**listo**	clever; ready
alegre	cheerful, gay	**maduro**	ripe
aquí	here	**malo**	bad; ill
bien	well	**posible**	possible
cansado	tired; tiresome	**la puerta**	door
contento	pleased, happy, content(ed)	**¡qué!**	how! what a!
dulce	sweet	**¿de quién(es)?**	whose?
enfermo	ill	**roto**	broken
hoy	today	**Sevilla**	Seville
inteligente	intelligent	**el té**	tea
el jardín	garden	**triste**	sad

See also the possessive adjectives listed in § 34 and the numbers in § 35.

EXERCISES

I. (a) *Pronounce the following and explain written accents:* filósofo, filosofía, fanfarrón, lebrel, lila, nexo, examinar, taxi, excepción, éxito.

(b) *Translate:* Está cansada. Somos alegres. Son españoles. Estamos en España. La puerta es verde. La puerta está rota. Soy lista. Estoy listo. ¿Dónde están? Su hermano. Mis amigos. Nuestra casa y nuestros jardines. Catorce flores azules y dos amarillas. Nueve lápices nuevos.

(c) *Translate:* Where are you (*sing. pol.*)? She is here. They (*fem.*) are beautiful. He is very clever. The lady is English. This is not possible. The doors are open. We are ill. You (*fem. sing. pol.*) are tired. I am well. This pen is very bad. We (*fem.*) are very bad at Spanish. Five and six are eleven. Three English gentlemen and a Spanish boy. Our mothers and sisters.

II. (a) *Study and translate:* 1. Su madre no va a la ciudad porque está muy cansada. 2. Estos muchachos andaluces son

51

bastante listos. 3. — ¿Dónde estás? — Estoy aquí en el cuarto de mi hermano. 4. Todos mis lápices son amarillos. 5. Esta pluma está rota. 6. — ¿De quiénes son aquellas casas tan bonitas? — Son de un señor de Sevilla. 7. ¿Qué flores tenéis en vuestro jardín? 8. Las puertas están todas abiertas. 9. No es muy difícil hacer esto. 10. Aquella muchacha andaluza es más alta que muchas inglesas.

(b) *Translate:* 1. This town has many beautiful gardens. 2. We are going to read the first chapter of the book. 3. They are sad because they are not going in their father's car. 4. The pencils are cheaper than the pens. 5. "Whose idea is this?" (= Whose is this idea?) "It is Peter's." 6. We drink a lot of sweet wine but we are not ill. 7. Six and seven are thirteen. 8. He is a very intelligent boy. 9. It is not possible to buy cheap wine here. 10. I am very pleased because all the apples are ripe.

III. (a) *Study and translate:* 1. Está triste porque no van a ir a España. 2. Ese vino es demasiado dulce para mi hermano. 3. ¿Cuántas puertas tiene aquella casa? 4. ¡Qué alegre estás hoy! 5. Tienen muchas flores en su jardín. 6. Tengo muchos más lápices que plumas. 7. ¡Qué altas son las hermanas de aquel senor inglés! 8. ¿De quién son esos libros que tienes? 9. Estas peras son muy grandes pero no están maduras. 10. No es posible estudiar una lección tan difícil.

(b) *Translate:* 1. The yellow flowers are more beautiful than the blue ones. 2. They are tired because they study too much. 3. These houses are all very interesting. 4. She is in the shop with her mother. 5. Our house has rather a small garden with not many flowers. 6. "Where are you from?" "I'm from Seville." 7. Is it possible to do this today? 8. His sister is taller than his mother. 9. This tea isn't sweet enough for your father. 10. They are very cheerful today because the gardens are open.

REVIEW AND DEVELOPMENT
SECTION (I)

37. NOUNS AND THEIR GENDER. Nouns in Spanish are either masculine or feminine and each noun should be memorized with its gender. There are, however, certain guides to the gender of a given noun: (1) in the meaning of the word, and (2) in its ending.

(1) Nouns denoting male beings are masculine and those denoting female beings are feminine:

el hombre	man	**la mujer**	woman
el señor	gentleman	**la señora**	lady
el padre	father	**la madre**	mother
el hijo	son	**la hija**	daughter
el tío	uncle	**la tía**	aunt
el abuelo	grandfather	**la abuela**	grandmother
el rey	king	**la reina**	queen
el toro	bull	**la vaca**	cow

NOTE: A masculine plural may often refer to persons of both sexes.

> **mis padres,** my parents
> **los hijos,** the son(s) and daughter(s), children
> **nuestros tíos,** our aunt and uncle
> **los abuelos,** the grandparents
> **los señores de González,** Mr and Mrs González
> **los Reyes Católicos,** the Catholic Monarchs

(2) (i) Nouns ending in **-o** are masculine:

el libro	book	**el edificio**	building
el capítulo	chapter	**el vaso**	tumbler, glass
el periódico	newspaper	**el vino**	wine

EXCEPTIONS: **la mano** (*hand*), **la radio** (*wireless*).

(ii) Nouns ending in **-a** are feminine:

la hora	hour	**la casa**	house
la fecha	date	**la idea**	idea
la fábrica	factory	**la guía**	guide (book)

EXCEPTIONS: 1. Words from the Greek ending in **-ma**: **el idioma** (*language*), **el telegrama** (*telegram*), **el programa** (*programme*), etc.

2. Words denoting male beings: **el guía** (*guide*), **el guardia** (*policeman*), **el cura** (*priest*), **el papa** (*pope*), etc.

3. **El día** (*day*), **el tranvía** (*tram*), **el mapa** (*map*), **el planeta** (*planet*), **el cometa** (*comet*).

(iii) Nouns ending in **-ie, -ión, -dad, -tad, -tud, -umbre** are feminine:

la superficie	surface	**la amistad**	friendship
la especie	sort, kind	**la libertad**	freedom
la estación	station	**la virtud**	virtue
la negación	negation	**la juventud**	youth
la edad	age	**la cumbre**	peak
la bondad	goodness	**la servidumbre**	servitude

EXCEPTIONS: A few words in **-ie** and **-ión** referring to material objects: **el pie** (*foot*), **el avión** (*aeroplane*), **el camión** (*lorry*), **el gorrión** (*sparrow*).

38. AGREEMENT. Articles and adjectives agree in number and gender with the noun they qualify. Their various forms are as follows:

		Singular		Plural	
		masculine	*feminine*	*masculine*	*feminine*
DEFINITE ARTICLE		**el**	**la**	**los**	**las**
INDEFINITE ARTICLE		**un**	**una**	(See Note 1)	
POSSESSIVE ADJECTIVES	my	**mi**	**mi**	**mis**	**mis**
	your	**tu** **su**	**tu** **su**	**tus** **sus**	**tus** **sus**
	his, her, its	**su**	**su**	**sus**	**sus**
	our	**nuestro**	**nuestra**	**nuestros**	**nuestras**
	your	**vuestro** **su**	**vuestra** **su**	**vuestros** **sus**	**vuestras** **sus**
	their	**su**	**su**	**sus**	**sus**
DEMONSTR. ADJECTIVES	this	**este**	**esta**	**estos**	**estas**
	that (near you)	**ese**	**esa**	**esos**	**esas**
	that (yonder)	**aquel**	**aquella**	**aquellos**	**aquellas**
OTHER ADJECTIVES	*Class 1*	**——o** (barato)	**——a** (barata)	**——os** (baratos)	**——as** (baratas)
	Class 2	**——** (español)	**——a** (española)	**——es** (españoles)	**——as** (españolas)
	Class 3	**——** (verde, fácil)	**——** (verde, fácil)	**——(e)s** (verdes, fáciles)	**——(e)s** (verdes, fáciles)

NOTES: 1. The indefinite article has plural forms **unos** and **unas** meaning *some* (**unos libros interesantes,** *some interesting books*), though the English *some* may frequently be left unexpressed in Spanish or be rendered by **algunos** [§ 25, Note 5].

2. The demonstrative pronouns are distinguished from the corresponding adjectives by means of a written accent. Remember,

55

however, the neuters **esto, eso, aquello,** which have no adjectival equivalent and therefore take no accent.

3. Adjectives are usually placed after the noun in Spanish. However, those which indicate or limit rather than describe (demonstratives, possessives, numerals and adjectives of quantity) precede the noun. Also used frequently before the noun are a few common adjectives such as **bueno, malo, pequeño, hermoso,** etc. [§ 22].

4. Certain Class 1 adjectives lose their final **-o** before a masculine singular noun [§ 25]. Such reduction is known as apocopation.

39. VERBS: PRESENT INDICATIVE. There are *three* conjugations:

		Singular	*Plural*
First Conjugation	(1)	compro	compramos
-ar: comprar	(2)	compras	compráis
		usted compra	ustedes compran
	(3)	compra	compran
Second Conjugation	(1)	vendo	vendemos
-er: vender	(2)	vendes	vendéis
		usted vende	ustedes venden
	(3)	vende	venden
Third Conjugation	(1)	vivo	vivimos
-ir: vivir	(2)	vives	vivís
		usted vive	ustedes viven
	(3)	vive	viven

NOTE: The **usted (ustedes)** verb forms are always the same as the corresponding third-person forms, and in future lessons they will not be listed separately. The student will obtain them by placing **usted(es)** before the forms given for the third person.

40. PRONUNCIATION. Read § 1 and revise §§ 2, 3 and 4 (*a*) and (*b*).

NOTE: Since ch and ll are counted as separate letters coming after c and l respectively in the Spanish alphabet, **chico** will be listed after **cumbre** and **llave** after **luego** in dictionaries and vocabularies.

VOCABULARY

Revise the vocabularies of Lessons I–V, study the words listed in § 37 and notice the names of the principal cities of Spain (listed in descending order of population): **Madrid, Barcelona, Valencia, Sevilla, Málaga, Zaragoza** (*Saragossa*), **Bilbao, Murcia, Córdoba, Granada.**

EXERCISES

I. (*a*) *Pronounce the following and explain written accents:* buscó, busqué, calcular, cuidado, ciudad, cualidad, civilizado, vencí, reducción, zapato, guardar, guerra, apacigüé, cuello, quejoso, jota, pájaro, gime, regatea, general, jugo, babero, víveres, vibra, dedo, hallar, Paquita, mimábamos, cambiáis.

(*b*) *In the following words the stressed vowel is italicized but no accents have been written in.* *Read each word aloud and write in the accents where necessary:* llegu*e*, v*a*ya, caj*o*n, r*a*pido, im*a*gen, franc*e*s, polic*i*a, id*e*a, an*u*ncio, llamat*i*vo, ba*u*l, h*a*game, mir*e*is, ra*i*z, neces*a*rio, tambi*e*n, edici*o*n, m*i*o, envi*a*is, l*i*mpias, s*e*an, gr*u*a, rod*e*ar, r*o*a, viv*i*ais.

(*c*) *Translate:* una tienda muy buena, unas ideas bastante interesantes, un gran amigo de mi padre, muchas ciudades inglesas, un hospital mucho más grande, los primeros capítulos, lecciones muy difíciles, algunas veces, ningún padre andaluz, una mujer muy pobre.

(*d*) *Translate:* those small houses, these Andalusian friends, many Spanish papers, an old English gentleman, green apples, some very big hospitals, my first idea, four English ladies, some good boys, no big houses.

II. (*a*) *Study and translate:* 1. Hacemos dos veces la misma cosa. 2. Estos vinos andaluces son muy buenos. 3. Aquellos señores reciben muchas cartas de sus amigos ingleses. 4. ¿Cuántas veces va usted a tener que ir al mismo hospital? 5. España tiene pocas ciudades grandes. 6. ¿De dónde eres y qué haces aquí en mi casa? 7. Ese libro no es malo, pero tengo uno mucho más interesante. 8. — ¿De quién son estos libros? — Son de algún amigo de mi padre. 9. Es la primera vez que estudiamos esta lección. 10. Está contento porque hoy no trabaja y va a ir a Madrid con su mujer.

(b) *Translate:* 1. They are going to your (*sing. fam.*) father's new shop. 2. Why do you (*pl. fam.*) eat so many apples? 3. A gentleman who lives in the city sends my father a letter. 4. Have you (*sing. pol.*) any book of my brother's? 5. What are these two Spanish girls doing? 6. They have a very nice house and garden in Madrid. 7. These ideas of John's are very interesting. 8. Some day I am going to buy a big house in Spain. 9. The men his father works with are all very intelligent. 10. Which boy are you (*sing. fam.*) going to write to?

III. (a) *Study and translate:* 1. ¿Por qué no escribes al padre de los dos muchachos? 2. Los hermanos de Juan no tienen amigos. 3. Tengo dos coches en la fábrica y uno en la ciudad. 4. Ésta es la tercera vez que hago esto. 5. Aquel señor lee muchos libros y periódicos españoles. 6. ¡Qué difíciles son estas primeras lecciones! 7. Mi madre y mi hermano están contentos porque vamos a Sevilla. 8. —¿Dónde estás? —Estoy aquí en el jardín. 9. Esa idea es muy mala. 10. Vamos a tener que vender una de las casas más pequeñas.

(b) *Translate:* 1. You (*sing. fam.*) are ill because you drink too much wine. 2. Why do you (*pl. pol.*) not sell the hospital? 3. This is one of his father's new cars. 4. What's he doing with your (*pl. fam.*) book? 5. A Spanish boy is living with John's mother and sister. 6. This house is too old for those English gentlemen. 7. They are going to buy a newer one in the city. 8. "What are they doing with the old one?" "I have no idea." 9. Our Spanish friend has a very young mother and a rather old father. 10. Which friend do you (*sing. fam.*) receive most letters from?

IV. *Re-translate the keys given for Lessons I–V [pp. 347–349] and compare your versions with the originals.*

LESSON VI

41. THE IMPERFECT INDICATIVE (English *I was buying, used to buy, bought*).

   I. **-ar** verbs: stem plus endings **-aba, -abas, -aba, -ábamos, -abais, -aban.**

  II. **-er** verbs: stem plus endings **-ía, -ías, -ía, -íamos, -íais, -ían.**

 III. **-ir** verbs: stem plus endings **-ía, -ías, -ía, -íamos, -íais, -ían.**

I. **comprar,** *to buy*	II. **vender,** *to sell*	III. **vivir,** *to live*
compraba	vendía	vivía
comprabas	vendías	vivías
compraba	vendía	vivía
comprábamos	vendíamos	vivíamos
comprabais	vendíais	vivíais
compraban	vendían	vivían

Antes vivíamos en Madrid.   Formerly we lived in Madrid.

Su hermano vendía periódicos.   His brother used to sell newspapers.

¿Qué compraba usted?   What were you buying?

Mi madre estaba enferma.   My mother was ill.

Recibían muchas cartas.   They used to get a lot of letters.

42. IRREGULAR IMPERFECTS.   There are only three irregular imperfects:

ser, *to be*	**ir,** *to go*	**ver,** *to see*
era	iba	veía
eras	ibas	veías
era	iba	veía
éramos	íbamos	veíamos
erais	ibais	veíais
eran	iban	veían

NOTE: The imperfect of **ver** is irregular only in that it has the extra **e**. In the same way the first person singular of the present indicative is irregular: **veo, ves, ve, vemos, veis, ven.** (Notice the absence of the written accent on **veis**; *cf.* **dais** and **vais,** § 18, Note 2).

43. SUBJECT PRONOUNS, FORMS AND USES. It has been stated [§ 13, Note 1] that the subject pronoun is not usually expressed in Spanish but is indicated in the verb ending. Nevertheless, subject pronouns *are* used when there is emphasis on the corresponding English pronoun, or when it is necessary to indicate the authors of an action in greater detail than the verb endings allow. They have the following forms:

Singular	*Plural*
(1) **yo,** I	**nosotros, -as,** we
(2) **tú,** you (*fam.*)	**vosotros, -as,** you (*fam.*)
usted, you (*pol.*)	**ustedes,** you (*pol.*)
(3) **él,** he, it (*masc.*)	**ellos,** they (*masc., or masc. and fem.*)
ella, she, it (*fem.*)	**ellas,** they (*fem.*)

Nosotros trabajábamos hasta las seis, pero ellos terminaban a las cinco.

We used to work until six o'clock but *they* would finish at five.

Vosotros ibais por la mañana y ellos (iban) por la tarde.

You used to go in the morning and *they* (went) in the afternoon.

Tú y yo vamos mañana.

You and I are going tomorrow.

NOTES: 1. In a few cases the use of the subject pronoun may serve to avoid confusion, to indicate, for instance, which of the various meanings of **vivía** (*I* [*he, she, it, you*] *used to live*) is intended. Usually, however, the context alone will make it quite clear and no subject pronoun is therefore expressed. The English-speaking student tends to over-use the Spanish subject pronoun.

2. The subject pronoun **usted(es)** is generally expressed even where there is no stress on the English pronoun and no possibility of confusion.

44. USES OF **tener** AND **hacer.**   (*a*) Revise § 28.

(*b*) Notice the following idiomatic uses of **tener**:

tener frío (*m.*)	to be cold (*of living beings*)
tener calor (*m.*)	to be warm, hot (*of living beings*)
tener sed (*f.*)	to be thirsty
tener hambre (*f.*)	to be hungry
tener sueño (*m.*)	to be sleepy
tener suerte (*f.*)	to be lucky
tener prisa (*f.*)	to be in a hurry
tener miedo (*m.*)	to be afraid
tener razón (*f*).	to be right
tener ganas de (*f.*)	to be keen to, to feel like
tener en cuenta	to bear in mind, to take into account, to consider
tener cuidado (*m.*)	to be careful
tener que hacer	to have things to do
tener que ver con	to have to do with
tener — años (*m.*)	to be — years old

¡Qué frío teníamos!   How cold we were!

Tengo muchas ganas de ir a España.   I want very much to go to Spain.

Tenía que hacer en casa.   He had jobs to do at home.

Tengo muchas cosas que estudiar.   I have a lot of things to study.

Esto no tiene nada que ver con él.   This hasn't anything to do with him.

¿Cuántos años tienes? *or* **¿Qué edad tienes?**   How old are you?

Su hermana tiene trece años.   His sister is thirteen (years old).

NOTE: In cases where the Spanish **tener** + noun corresponds to the English *to be* + adjective, an English adverb must be translated by the corresponding Spanish adjective (e.g., *I am very cold* becomes **Tengo mucho frío,** lit., *I have much cold*).

Teníamos mucha sed.   We were very thirsty.

— ¿**Tiene Vd. hambre?** — **Sí, mucha.** "Are you hungry?" "Yes, very."

(c) **Hacer.** Besides translating the English *to do, to make,* **hacer** is used:

(i) to indicate certain states of the weather.

¿**Qué tiempo hace?**	What is the weather like?
Hace calor. Hace mucho frío.	It is warm. It is very cold.
Hacía buen (mal) tiempo.	It was fine (bad) weather.
Hace buen día.	It's a fine day.
Hace un tiempo malísimo.	The weather is shocking.

(ii) in certain expressions of time (English *ago, before*).

hace diez minutos	ten minutes ago
hacía dos horas	two hours before
hacía muchos días	many days before
hace mucho tiempo	a long time ago
hacía años	years before

VOCABULARY

ahora	now	**mientras**	while, whilst
allí	there	**el minuto**	minute
el año	year	**muchas**	often
ayer	yesterday	**veces**	
caliente	warm, hot	**o**	or
el calor	warmth, heat	**el país**	country
el campo	country(side),		(*political*)
	field	**pasar**	to pass; to spend
a casa	(to) home		(time); to
en casa	at home		happen
casi	almost, nearly	**si**	if
descansar	to rest	**siempre**	always
durante	during, for (*of	**la suerte**	luck, fortune
	time*)	**la tarde**	afternoon,
frío	cold (*adj.*)		evening
el frío	cold (*noun*)	**el tiempo**	weather, time
mañana	tomorrow	**a tiempo**	in time
la mañana	morning	**ver**	to see

a casa de mis padres	to my parents' (house)
en casa de mis amigos	at my friends' (house)
todo el día (año)	all day (year), the whole day (year)
toda la mañana (tarde)	all morning (afternoon and evening)
todos los días (años)	every day (year)
todas las mañanas (tardes)	every morning (afternoon, evening)

Study also the idiomatic phrases listed in § 44.

EXERCISES

I. (*a*) *Study and translate:* Nosotros comprábamos. Ellos vivían. Él bebía mucho. Ella comía más. Todos iban. ¿Qué dabais? Vosotros escribíais. Ellas leían demasiado. ¿Dónde trabajabais? Veía. ¿Quiénes eran? Ustedes bebían. ¿Por qué no comes? ¿Dónde estaba? Yo compraba. Él hacía esto. ¿Adónde ibais? ¿Con qué escribías? Yo leía poco. ¿De qué hablabais? Ella tenía mucha prisa. Teníais sueño. ¿Quién tiene miedo? Hacía mucho calor. No hace mal tiempo. Hacía veinte minutos. El té estaba caliente. El vino estaba muy frío.

(*b*) *Translate (using a pronoun subject where possible):* He used to give. They were going. We ate. Did you[1] use to buy? What were they (*fem.*) writing? She would send. They used to drink too much. I hadn't any idea. Were you receiving? I worked. Where did you use to live? We used to go. Where were you going? We used to work. He didn't use to study. Who was he? Where were you? They used to talk a lot. We used to receive a lot of letters. What was he selling? He hasn't any sisters. They were cold and I was hungry. She had to be careful. He was

---

[1] Henceforth, no indication will be given of which second person is intended. A complete sentence will often provide sufficient context to make one form preferable to the other [§ 13, Note 2]. Otherwise, use the singular polite or, better still, give all four possible forms for extra practice.

very warm. It was very warm. Twelve days before. The tea was cold.

II. (a) *Study and translate:* 1. Hacía mucho frío porque todas las puertas estaban abiertas. 2. Durante el buen tiempo íbamos casi todos los días al campo. 3. Muchas veces mandaban libros y periódicos españoles a sus amigos ingleses. 4. ¿Qué hacías tú cuando ibas al hospital? 5. Yo no veía muy bien el edificio adonde teníamos que ir. 6. Ella no tiene en cuenta el frío que hace ahora en Madrid. 7. A veces, cuando hacía mucho calor o cuando teníamos hambre, íbamos a casa de mis abuelos. 8. Hace muchos años vivía en este país un rey muy inteligente. 9. Si no tiene mucho cuidado, va a tener que ir al hospital. 10. Era muy difícil estudiar tantos idiomas.

(b) *Translate:* 1. "Where were you?" "I was at my grandparents'." 2. The doors of the house were all yellow. 3. My mother and sister used to live in Saragossa. 4. He used to speak a lot of Spanish with his Andalusian friends. 5. You used to work much harder (= much more) than he [did].[1] 6. Why were they all so afraid? 7. Who was right: you or I? 8. We have to bear in mind that in Spain it is much warmer than here. 9. She was hungry and they were very thirsty. 10. Many years ago I used to live in a country where the weather was always fine.

III. (a) *Study and translate:* 1. Escribíamos muchas cartas a nuestros amigos de Madrid. 2. Ellos estudiaban mucho, pero nosotros estudiábamos más. 3. ¿Por qué no vamos a casa de tus tíos? 4. Mientras ella trabajaba en el jardín, yo pasaba los días con unos amigos que tenía allí. 5. ¡Qué prisa tenía! ¿Adónde iba? 6. Hacía bastante calor en casa y él no tenía ganas de estudiar lecciones tan difíciles. 7. Cuando vivíamos en el campo, íbamos casi todos los días a casa de los señores de Fernández. 8. Hacía mal tiempo y todos teníamos mucho frío. 9. Pero ¿qué tiene que ver todo eso con la idea

---

[1] Words in brackets [ ] are not to be translated; words in parentheses ( ) are explanations or recommended means of translation.

que tenías ayer? 10. Mañana no voy a ir porque tengo mucho que hacer en casa.

(b) *Translate:* 1. Where did your brother use to work when he lived in Valencia? 2. We used to buy many French and Spanish newspapers. 3. What did you use to do when you went to your grandparents'? 4. Who were the women who were selling the apples and pears? 5. Which country did he live in when he was younger? 6. Twenty minutes ago I was at the station. 7. They would work all afternoon in the garden, but we used to rest in the house. 8. When it is cold we eat much more than when it is warm. 9. He has to be very careful with his new car. 10. What luck to live in this country, where the weather is always fine!

LESSON VII

45. THE GERUND. (*a*) The Spanish gerund is formed by adding **-ando** to the stem of **-ar** verbs and **-iendo** to the stem of **-er** and **-ir** verbs. It usually corresponds to the English present participle *-ing* or to *by -ing*.

comprando   **vendiendo**   **viviendo**

Pasaba una hora haciendo el ejercicio.

I would spend an hour doing the exercise.

Como uno llega a ser rico es comprando y vendiendo cosas.

It is by buying and selling things that one comes to be wealthy.

(*b*) It may translate other English verb parts when they express time *during which* (but not *upon which*) or cause.

Estando en España hablaba español.

When he was in Spain, he used to talk Spanish.

Siendo jóvenes, trabajaban más.

When (*or* As) they were young, they worked more.

(*c*) On the other hand, a gerund does NOT translate the English *-ing* in the following cases:

(i) after a preposition: an infinitive is used.

antes de recibir la carta, before receiving the letter
después de terminar la lección, after finishing the lesson
sin saber por qué, without knowing why
por estar malo, through being ill

Notice also the use of **al** + *infinitive* to express occasion *upon which*: **al llegar a casa,** *on arriving home*; *when I* (*you,* etc.) *arrive(d) home.*

(ii) when *-ing* fulfils the function of a noun: an infinitive is used, often preceded by the masculine singular definite article.

el murmurar de las fuentes, the murmuring of the fountains
el ir y venir de tanta gente, the coming and going of so many
  people
Me gusta leer. I like reading (*lit.*, Reading pleases me.)

(iii) when *-ing* fulfils an adjectival function: an adjective or
adjectival clause is used.

un libro muy interesante, a very interesting book
padres tan comprensivos y amorosos, such understanding
  and loving parents
vuestro hijo que os quiere, your loving son
una maleta que contenía papeles, a suitcase containing
  papers

GENERAL NOTE: The Spanish gerund is essentially verbal and emphasizes the duration of the action it presents. The further the
English present participle (i.e., *-ing*) deviates from this function
the less likely it is to be translated by the Spanish gerund.

46. THE PROGRESSIVE TENSES. These are used less frequently
than the corresponding English forms (*I am buying*, *he was selling*,
we have been living, etc.) for they imply greater duration or
repetition of the verbal action. They are formed by the appropriate tense of **estar** together with the gerund of the verb in
question.

Está cantando a todas horas. She is singing all day long.
Estábamos terminando la lección. We were finishing the
  lesson.

47. THE PERSONAL **a.** (*a*) Besides being used to introduce the
indirect object [§ 14 (*a*)], the preposition **a** must also be used in
Spanish:

(i) before a noun direct object referring to a specific person.

  Veía el libro. I saw the book.
but **Veía al muchacho.** I saw the boy.

Mandaba cartas a España. He used to send letters to Spain.

but **Mandaba a sus hijos a España.** He used to send his children to Spain.

Estaba buscando su libro. He was looking for his book.

but **Estaba buscando a su padre.** He was looking for his father.

El rey recibe un regalo. The king receives a present.

but **El rey recibe al embajador.** The king receives the ambassador.

(ii) before strong pronouns referring to persons, whether or not these are specific persons.

Busco a éste. I am looking for this man.

— ¿A quién ve? — No ve a nadie. "Whom does he see?" "He sees nobody."

¿Conoce usted a alguien? Do you know anyone?

(*b*) The personal **a** is not used:

(i) before a noun direct object referring to an indeterminate person.

Busco (una) criada. I am looking for a maid.

¿Conoces algún señor de Madrid? Do you know any gentleman from Madrid?

(ii) after **tener.**

Tengo una hermana muy guapa. I have a very pretty sister.

48. NEGATION. (*a*) The simplest type of negation is that in which **no** is placed immediately before the appropriate verb [§ 15]. Other negative particles which may be similarly placed are **nunca** (*never*), **jamás** (*never*), **tampoco** (*neither*), **ni** (*neither, nor*), **ni** (**siquiera**) (*not even*), **nadie** (*no one, nobody*), **nada** (*nothing*) and **ninguno -a** (*none, no*).

Nunca tenía dinero. He never had any money.

Tampoco iba mi hermano. My brother wasn't going either.

Ni estudia ni trabaja. He neither studies nor works.

Ni (siquiera) da los buenos días.   He doesn't even say good
    morning.
Nadie acompaña a mi madre.   No one is going with my
    mother.
Nada ocurría tan a menudo.   Nothing would happen so often.
Ninguno vendía plumas.   None (of them) sold pens.
Ningún español pronuncia así.   No Spaniard pronounces like
    that.

(*b*) These same words may also be placed after the verb but **no**
must then precede it.

No vemos nunca al hermano de usted.   We never see your
    brother.
Yo no voy tampoco.   I'm not going either.
No vendía ni libros ni periódicos.   He sold neither books nor
    papers.
No vendía libros ni periódicos.   He didn't sell books or
    papers.
No vendía ni (siquiera) periódicos.   He didn't even sell
    papers.
No iba nadie a España.   No one was going to Spain.
No pasa nada.   Nothing is happening.
No llegaba tarde ninguno.   None (of them) used to arrive
    late.
No iba ninguna muchacha.   No girls used to go.

NOTES: 1. Contrast English usage in which the use of *not* with the
verb makes the following adverb, pronoun or adjective affirmative
(i.e., *I never go* or *I don't ever go*).
    2. Remember that the adjective **ninguno -a** is used almost only
in the singular [§ 25, Note 4].

(*c*) In the examples with **nada, nadie** and **ninguno** listed
above, these elements are the subjects of their respective verbs.
They may also be the objects (direct, indirect or prepositional).

No veo nada.   I don't see anything.
No trabaja en nada.   He isn't working on anything.
No veo a nadie.   I see no one, *or* I don't see anyone.

No doy este libro a nadie. I am not giving this book to anyone.

No discuto con nadie. I am not arguing with anyone.

Juan no acompaña a ninguna. John doesn't accompany any of them (*fem.*)

No escribo cartas a ninguna. I don't write letters to any of them (*fem.*)

No está de acuerdo con ninguno. He doesn't agree with any of them.

No mandaba a ningún hijo suyo. He didn't use to send any son of his own.

No escribo con ninguna facilidad. I don't write with any ease.

NOTES: 1. See § 25, Note 5, and notice the following differences of emphasis:

No compra libros. He doesn't buy [any] books.

No compra ningún libro. He doesn't buy *any* books.

No compra ni un (solo) libro. He doesn't buy a single (*or* even one) book.

2. **Nada, nadie** and **ninguno,** used as objects, may also precede the verb in accordance with Section (*a*), though the result is rather literary or emphatic (*cf.* the corresponding English forms with inversion).

A nadie conocemos tan vanidoso.
No one do we know so vain.

Con ninguno jugaba más que con el muchacho de al lado.
With none of them did he play more than [he did] with the boy next door (*lit.*, the boy of at the side).

(*d*) More than one of these elements of negation may be present in the same sentence. If one of them is placed before the verb as in (*a*), the negative **no** is not used; if they are both (all) placed after the verb, **no** must precede the verb.

El nunca comprende nada. } He never understands any-
Él no comprende nunca nada. } thing.

Yo tampoco comprendo nunca nada. }I never understand
Yo no comprendo nunca nada tampoco. } anything either.

Él nunca hace nada con nadie. }He never does anything
Él no hace nunca nada con nadie. } with anyone.

(e) **Sin** (*without*) and **antes de** (*before*) take the same negative
words as **no,** but **no** is not then expressed before the verb.

sin decir ni una palabra, without saying a (single) word
sin llegar nunca a tiempo, without ever arriving in time
antes de decidir nada, before deciding anything
antes de hablar con nadie, before talking to anyone

49. FOUR IRREGULAR VERBS: **saber, conocer, salir, valer.**
These verbs have **sé, conozco, salgo, valgo** respectively for
the first person singular of the present indicative. For the rest,
they are regular in all parts so far studied. Their meaning and
use, however, should be noted:

saber, *to know* (*of knowledge, understanding*), *to know how to*

¿Sabe usted cómo hace esto? Do you know how he does this?
No sé dónde vivían. I don't know where they lived.
Sabemos muy bien esta lección. We know this lesson very
well.
No sabe nadar. He doesn't know how to (*or* can't) swim.

conocer, *to know* (*be acquainted with*)

¿Conocías a su mujer? Did you know his wife?
No conozco esta ciudad. I do not know this town.

salir, *to go* or *come out, to set off, to depart, to leave ; to rise*
(*of the sun*)

Salen mañana para Valencia. They are leaving for Valencia
tomorrow.
Salgo del cuarto. I go out of the room.
salir de, to leave (*a place*)
Mañana salgo de Madrid. Tomorrow I am leaving Madrid.
¿A qué hora sale el sol? At what time does the sun rise?

valer, *to be worth*

¿Cuánto vale? How much is it worth? What is the price?
Yo no valgo para esas cosas. I'm no use for that sort of thing.
Este muchacho vale mucho. This boy is very good (*i.e.,* has great worth).
Más vale ir a pie. It's better to walk.

VOCABULARY

antes de	before (*prep.*)	**mirar**	to look at
aprender	to learn	**la plaza**	square
buscar	to look for	**por**	through
cerca de	near, close to	**principal**	main, principal
comprender	to understand	**el regalo**	present, gift
conocer	to know	**saber**	to know
después de	after (*prep.*)	**salir**	to go (come)
la impor-	importance		out, to leave
tancia		**sin**	without
importante	important	**terminar**	to finish
llegar	to arrive	**valer**	to be worth
llegar a	to reach, to	**el vecino, -a**	neighbour
	arrive at	**la visita**	visit
llevar	to take, to carry	**visitar**	to visit

ir (salir) de compras, to go (go out) shopping

See also the words of negation listed in § 48 (*a*).

EXERCISES

I. (*a*) *Study and translate:* Recibiendo. Mandando. Estando. Siendo. Teniendo en cuenta. Después de llegar. Al terminar la lección. Estábamos escribiendo. Él veía a su tío. Nosotros no íbamos tampoco. No veo nada. Él no hablaba con nadie. Nunca llegaban a tiempo. No vemos a nadie. No tengo ninguno. Yo no veo nada tampoco. Nadie tenía miedo. Ni él ni yo teníamos mucho frío. Tampoco hace mal tiempo. Visitábamos a nuestros amigos. No visitaba ni a su padre ni a su abuelo. Esto no vale nada. Por no conocer a su hermano. Sin hablar con nadie. Ni siquiera sabía dónde vivíamos. No conozco a ninguna de sus hermanas. Antes de salir de casa. Vale más no escribir nada.

(b) *Translate:* Doing. Buying. Living. Without resting. Before going. On drinking too much. He is having a meal. We were studying. You were drinking. I am finishing. They were writing to their uncle. I see my parents. They are visiting their friends. He never arrives in time. His brother never arrives in time either. I don't see anyone. He has neither sisters nor brothers. He doesn't understand anything. She doesn't know anyone. I don't know anyone either. We were not talking about anything important. I leave tomorrow. What were you looking for? Without receiving any letters. After leaving the station. Before writing anything. Without looking at any of his children. A gentleman living in the same street.

II. (a) *Study and translate:* 1. Pasábamos muchas horas hablando de los países que íbamos a visitar. 2. Iba a escribir la carta antes de visitar a sus amigos. 3. Ni él ni ella tenían razón; ni nosotros tampoco. 4. No conozco a la muchacha con quien estaba mi hermano. 5. No sé dónde vive ni en qué fábrica trabaja. 6. Nunca recibo tantas visitas como cuando estoy enfermo. 7. No sabíamos dónde estaba la estación. 8. Mandaba a todos sus hijos a España a aprender el idioma. 9. Muchos de nuestros vecinos trabajaban en una fábrica que estaba muy cerca de donde vivíamos. 10. Visitábamos a todos los señores más importantes de la ciudad.

(b) *Translate:* 1. I am never as contented as when I am working in my garden. 2. He didn't use to buy anything for his brother, nor for his sister either. 3. We used to take our friends to the station when the weather was bad. 4. It is better to spend the afternoon resting at home than to go out with the heat as it is now. 5. The building he was talking about is very close to the main square. 6. When we read this, we have to bear in mind that in Spain it is much warmer than here. 7. Do you know where my brother is?

8. My sister had a lot of friends, but my brother hadn't any. 9. When they finished, they used to go out to look for more books. 10. We used to spend the afternoons visiting old friends and talking about things of little importance.

III. (a) *Study and translate:* 1. Muchas veces, al terminar sus lecciones, iba a visitar a sus abuelos. 2. Todos los días veíamos a los mismos señores haciendo las mismas cosas. 3. No iba nadie a visitar a mis padres cuando vivían en Bilbao. 4. ¡Qué prisa tienen ustedes! Nosotros nunca tenemos tanta prisa. 5. Después de estudiar la primera lección, tengo que descansar antes de mirar la segunda. 6. Tenía unos amigos que vivían muy cerca de la plaza principal. 7. Cuando trabajo todo el día, siempre tengo sueño al llegar a casa. 8. Estaban buscando a un amigo que llegaba de Sevilla. 9. Pasábamos las tardes estudiando el idioma, escribiendo cartas o recibiendo alguna visita de los nuevos vecinos. 10. Mientras él trabajaba en el jardín, ella salía de compras con una de las vecinas.

(b) *Translate:* 1. When he goes home, he never takes any present for his mother. 2. How old were you when you worked with my brother? 3. I always finish the first chapter before reading the second. 4. We never go to my grand-parents' when the weather is bad. 5. They are visiting some friends they have in this town. 6. He used to take his sister to the station every morning. 7. I don't know John's mother, nor his father. 8. *She* wasn't looking for anyone. 9. They would work all day without eating anything. 10. They were buying presents for one of their friends who was going to Spain.

LESSON VIII

50. CARDINAL NUMBERS. (*a*) Revise § 35.

(*b*)

21	veinte y uno, -a	300	trescientos, -as
22	veinte y dos	400	cuatrocientos, -as
30	treinta	500	quinientos, -as
31	treinta y uno, -a	600	seiscientos, -as
40	cuarenta	700	setecientos, -as
50	cincuenta	800	ochocientos, -as
60	sesenta	900	novecientos, -as
70	setenta	1,000	mil
80	ochenta	1,001	mil uno, -a
90	noventa	1,100	mil cien(to)
100	cien(to)	2,000	dos mil
101	ciento uno, -a	100,000	cien mil
102	ciento dos	200,000	doscientos (-as) mil
120	ciento veinte	1,000,000	un millón (de)
200	doscientos, -as	2,000,000	dos millones (de)
201	doscientos (-as) uno, -a		

NOTES: 1. In practice the twenties are more often than not written as a single word, an accent being added where necessary to preserve the proper stress: **veintiuno, veintidós, veintitrés, veinticuatro,** etc.

2. Except for the plural hundreds and for numbers ending in **uno,** cardinal numbers are invariable.

cuarenta y cinco plumas, forty-five pens
but **setecientas sesenta y una casas,** seven hundred and sixty-one houses

3. **Uno** is apocopated to **un** when it refers to a following noun [§ 35].

quinientos treinta y un buenos señores, five hundred and thirty-one worthy gentlemen

75

4. **Ciento** is apocopated to **cien** before **mil** or a noun (including **millón**).

cien mil habitantes, a hundred thousand inhabitants
cien personas, a hundred people
cien millones de personas, a hundred million people

5. The English *a, one* is not translated before **ciento** or **mil** (except where it is necessary for the meaning: **veintiún mil,** *twenty-one thousand*). It *is* translated before **millón** which, being a noun, takes the preposition **de** before the object numbered.

mil aviones y un millón de soldados, a thousand aircraft and a million men

6. Counting by hundreds does not go beyond the nine hundreds.

mil sesenta y seis, ten sixty-six
los mil novecientos, the nineteen hundreds

7. *Than* before a numeral is translated by **de.**

más de veinte personas, more than twenty people

51. ORDINAL NUMBERS.

primero, -a	first	**sexto, a**	sixth
segundo, -a	second	**séptimo, -a**	seventh
tercero, -a	third	**octavo, -a**	eighth
cuarto, -a	fourth	**noveno, -a**	ninth
quinto, -a	fifth	**décimo, -a**	tenth

NOTE: The ordinals are rarely used in Spanish beyond the tenth, being replaced by cardinals.

Isabel II (Isabel segunda), Isabella II; Elizabeth II
but **Alfonso XIII (Alfonso trece),** Alphonso XIII

el siglo IV (el siglo cuarto), the fourth century
but **el siglo XVI (el siglo diez y seis),** the sixteenth century

Notice that in titles and centuries ordinals and cardinals alike follow the noun. The English *the* that precedes the number in titles is not translated.

52. THE TIME. (*a*) The time of day is indicated by means of **ser** used in the present or imperfect tense. The word **hora** (*hour*), or its plural **horas,** is understood and indicated by the

use of the feminine definite article. With the first hour **ser** is
therefore used in the singular; with the rest it is used in the plural.
The conjunction **y** indicates time *past* the hour, and **menos** time
to the hour. **Minutos** (*minutes*) is added with the finer divisions
of time (*i.e.*, within the five-minute division).

¿Qué hora es? Son las dos. What time is it? It is two
o'clock.
Es la una y cinco. It is five past one.
Era la una y siete minutos. It was seven minutes past one.
Son las cuatro menos veinte. It is twenty to four.
Son las tres menos catorce minutos. It is fourteen minutes
to three.
Eran las cinco y media. It was half past five.
Son las doce menos cuarto. It is a quarter to twelve.

NOTE: Spanish also has forms corresponding to the English *seven
thirty* (**las siete treinta**), *eight forty-three* (**las ocho cuarenta y
tres**), etc. In official time-tables these are associated with the
twenty-four hour clock system: **a las quince veinte** (*at* 3.20 *p.m.*),
a las trece cincuenta y cinco (*at* 1.55 *p.m.*).

(*b*) The English *a.m.* (also *in the morning*) and *p.m.* (also *in the
afternoon, in the evening, at night*) are rendered as follows:

de la madrugada, in the morning (a.m. before sunrise)
de la mañana, in the morning (a.m. after sunrise)
de la tarde, in the afternoon, in the evening (p.m. until after
nightfall)
de la noche, at night (late p.m. and very early a.m.)

NOTE: Where there is no hour mentioned, *in* and *at* with parts of
the day are translated by **por**: **por la madrugada** (*in the* [*early*]
morning), **por la mañana** (*in the morning*), **por la tarde** (*in the
afternoon, in the evening*), **por la noche** (*at night*). Notice also
examples of the type **ayer por la tarde** (*yesterday afternoon*),
mañana por la mañana (*tomorrow morning*).

(*c*) The definite article, used before the hour of the day, is
retained after a preposition:

a la una menos diez, at ten to one

después de las doce, after twelve o'clock
antes de la una y media, before half past one
para las nueve, for (*or* by) nine o'clock
desde las dos hasta las cinco y cuarto, from two until quarter
    past five

It *may* be omitted, however, in the phrases **de — a —** (*from —
to —*) and **entre — y —** (*between — and —*).

de seis a siete y media, from six to half past seven
entre ocho y nueve, between eight and nine

53. THE DATE. There are two ways in Spanish of indicating
the day of the month:

(1) By using **estar a** (usually in the first person plural) followed by the appropriate cardinal number.

¿A cuántos estamos? What is the date? *or* What date is it?
Estamos a diecisiete. It's the seventeenth.
Estábamos a once de mayo. It was the eleventh of May.

(2) By using **ser** followed by the masculine singular definite
article and the appropriate cardinal number. The article may be
omitted if there is no month expressed.

¿Qué fecha es hoy? What is today's date?
Hoy es (el) diez y ocho. Today is the eighteenth.
Era el doce de abril. It was the twelfth of April.

NOTES: 1. The latter alternative is generally better for past and
future time, and with **primero: Estamos a diez** *but* **Era el diez.**
2. Cardinal numbers, not ordinals, are used to indicate the day of
the month, except that **el primero** and **el (día) uno** are both frequent to indicate the first of the month. The word **día** is often
used in dates, especially when the month itself is unexpressed:
Llega el día 7 (*He arrives on the 7th*)
3. The month is introduced, even after figures, by **de**: (**el**) **20 de
enero** (*20th January*). So also the year: (**el**) **28 de octubre de
1954** (28th October, 1954). At the head of letters the article is not
used: **Madrid, 26 de junio de 1965.**
4. The word *on* before a date or day of the week is expressed in
Spanish by means of the definite article.

el lunes, el martes, on Monday, on Tuesday
los miércoles, los jueves, on Wednesdays, on Thursdays
el dos de marzo, on the second of March

5. Names of days and months begin with a small letter in Spanish
6. The days of the week are: **lunes** (*Monday*), **martes** (*Tuesday*),
miércoles (*Wednesday*), **jueves** (*Thursday*), **viernes** (*Friday*),
sábado (*Saturday*), **domingo** (*Sunday*). All but the last two have
the same form in singular and plural: **los lunes** (*on Mondays*), but
los sábados (*on Saturdays*).
7. The names of the months are: **enero, febrero, marzo, abril,
mayo, junio, julio, agosto, se(p)tiembre, octubre, noviembre; diciembre.**

VOCABULARY

a	at (*of time*)	**menos**	less, minus
aún	still, yet	**la noche**	night
el censo	census	**la página**	page
el cuarto	room; quarter, fourth	**para**	by (*of time*), for
		la persona	person, *pl.* people
desde	since, from		
Felipe	Philip	**la peseta**	peseta (*Spanish money; approx.* ½p.)
el habitante	inhabitant		
hacia	towards; (at) about		
		la población	population
hasta	until, as far as, (up) to	**en punto**	just, exactly (*of time*)
Isabel	Elizabeth, Isabella	**según**	according to
		el siglo	century
más	more, most, plus	**sólo**	only
medio -a	half	**el tren**	train

¿Qué hora tiene usted?   What time do you make it?
Tengo la una, las dos, etc.   I make it one o'clock, two o'clock, etc.

Study the names of the months and the days of the week, § 53,
Notes 6 and 7.

EXERCISES

I. (a) *Study and translate:* Cincuenta y seis capítulos. Treinta
y dos páginas. Más de mil aviones. La página cuarenta y
siete. Noventa y un lápices. Cien tiendas buenas. Ciento
sesenta personas. Quinientas veinte y una casas. Dos millones y medio de habitantes. Mil novecientos cincuenta y
ocho. Mil setecientos setenta y siete. La página veintiuna.
Isabel segunda. Felipe quinto. El siglo once. Después de
la una. A las cinco en punto de la tarde. Hasta las cuatro
menos cuarto de la madrugada. Desde antes de las diez.
A las seis veintiséis. Hacia las dos y media. De siete y
media a ocho y cuarto. Eran las nueve de la mañana. A las
diecinueve cuarenta. Era el siete de febrero. Estamos a once
de diciembre. El quince de marzo. El seis de mayo de mil
novecientos cincuenta y seis.

(b) *Translate:* Twenty-six women. Five hundred and fifty-
five houses. A hundred shops. Two thousand seven hundred people. Seventeen ninety-seven. Nineteen eighty-
four. Six hundred and twenty-one buildings. A hundred
thousand inhabitants. More than a million pesetas. The
seventh chapter. (The) page two hundred and one. Peter
the Second. The nineteenth century. By half past five in
the morning. Before eleven p.m. Until after seven in the
evening. From five to six until ten past eight. At about
ten to one at night. At seven forty-five p.m. It was twenty
past seven. It is almost quarter past one. The first of June.
On the sixteenth of October. 18th January.

II. (a) *Study and translate:* 1. Ahora, en el siglo veinte, no es
difícil conocer varios países. 2. Quinientos sesenta y siete
más setecientos cincuenta y cuatro son mil trescientos veinte
y uno. 3. Él trabajaba desde las ocho de la mañana hasta
las cinco de la tarde. 4. — ¿A qué hora llega el tren de
Sevilla? — Hacia las seis y media. 5. Los lunes íbamos a
casa de mis tíos y los miércoles a casa de mis abuelos.
6. — ¿Qué fecha era? — Era el catorce de enero. 7. Yo
no estudio tantos idiomas como tú. 8. Su padre iba a la
fábrica en el tren de las siete treinta y cinco. 9. Todos

teníamos que estudiar hasta las cuatro menos cinco.   10. A las nueve usted no estaba en casa.

(b) *Translate:* 1. Cervantes was still alive in the year sixteen fourteen.   2. Four hundred and fifty-three plus seven hundred and eighty-nine are twelve hundred and forty-two.   3. I'm going to finish this by tomorrow morning.   4. I work every day from nine to five, but he only works six hours.   5. He reaches Valencia on the twentieth of January and has to be in Barcelona before the first of March.   6. Spain has a population of over thirty-one million inhabitants.   7. This train reaches Seville at six nineteen.   8. We had to be at the station before ten past eight.   9. There are a hundred and twenty-one houses in this street.   10. He is going to arrive on the twenty-seventh of December at about six p.m.

III. (a) *Study and translate:* 1. Según el censo de mil novecientos cincuenta Madrid tenía un millón, seiscientos diez y ocho mil, cuatrocientos treinta y cinco habitantes.   2. Según el mismo censo hay en España veinte ciudades de más de cien mil habitantes.   3. No iban en el mismo tren que nosotros.   4. ¿A qué hora vamos a llegar a la estación?   5. Los martes siempre estoy en casa.   6. — ¿A cuántos estamos? — Estamos a dos de setiembre.   7. El tren llega a las siete y cuarto.   8. — ¿Qué hora es? — Son las once y siete minutos.   9. Voy a terminar todas estas lecciones antes del treinta y uno de julio.   10. Sólo teníamos bastante para cien personas.

(b) *Translate:* 1. They used to work every day from six in the evening until four in the morning.   2. I'm always at home from seven to eight.   3. We have to be at the station by half past five.   4. There are a hundred and thirty-two million people who speak Spanish.   5. "What time do you make it?" "Seven o'clock exactly."   6. The lessons were all very difficult.   7. At what time did you use to arrive home?   8. Today is the fifteenth of April, nineteen fifty-seven.   9. Seven hundred and sixty-nine minus five hundred and fifty-five are two hundred and fourteen.   10. The Málaga train arrives here at nine forty-three p.m.

LESSON IX

54. THE PRETERITE TENSE (English *I bought, I did buy; I sold, I did sell;* etc.).

I. **-ar** verbs: stem plus endings **-é, -aste, -ó, -amos, -asteis, -aron.**

II. **-er** verbs: stem plus endings **-í, -iste, -ió, -imos, -isteis, -ieron.**

III. **-ir** verbs: stem plus endings **-í, -iste, -ió, -imos, -isteis, -ieron.**

I. **comprar**	II. **vender**	III. **vivir**
compré	vendí	viví
compraste	vendiste	viviste
compró	vendió	vivió
compramos	vendimos	vivimos
comprasteis	vendisteis	vivisteis
compraron	vendieron	vivieron

NOTES: 1. Verbs of the second and third conjugations take the same endings.

2. In the first person plural **-ar** and **-ir** verbs (but not **-er** verbs) have the same forms as in the present indicative: **compramos, vivimos** (but **vendemos—vendimos**).

55. THE IMPERFECT AND THE PRETERITE. It is often difficult for the English student to distinguish between the use of the imperfect and the use of the preterite in Spanish. The Spanish imperfect translates the English *was —ing* and *used to —* (at times also *would —*) and in these cases there should be no confusion. The difficulty arises in the translation of the English *I —ed* and *I did —*, and a careful distinction must be made. The imperfect considers verbal action in its duration, without indication of beginning or end (a state of mind free of time limits, for instance, or an action repeated an indeterminate number of times); the preterite, on the other hand, presents verbal action in its completeness, ascribed to a particular moment or to a definite period of time.

Imperfect

¿Qué decías?   What were you saying?
Todos éramos muy felices.   We were all very happy.
Vivían en Madrid.   They lived (=used to live) in Madrid.
Cuando salíamos de clase, íbamos al cine.   When we came out of lectures we would go to the pictures.

Preterite

Al día siguiente vi a mi padre.   The next day I saw my father.
Pasó dos horas con el profesor.   He spent two hours with the teacher.
Estuve [§ 56] tres años en España.   I was in Spain for three years.
¿Llegó usted a tiempo?   Did you arrive in time?

56. IRREGULAR PRETERITES.

ir	fui, fuiste, fue, fuimos, fuisteis, fueron
ser	fui, fuiste, fue, fuimos, fuisteis, fueron
estar	estuve, estuviste, estuvo, estuvimos, estuvisteis, estuvieron
tener	tuve, tuviste, tuvo, tuvimos, tuvisteis, tuvieron
saber	supe, supiste, supo, supimos, supisteis, supieron
hacer	hice, hiciste, hizo, hicimos, hicisteis, hicieron
dar	di, diste, dio, dimos, disteis, dieron
ver	vi, viste, vio, vimos, visteis, vieron

NOTES: 1. **Ver** has been included only because of the question of the accent [below, Note 2]. **Conocer, salir** and **valer** are regular in the preterite.

2. The accented forms **fuí, fué, dió** and **vió** are still frequent, but since 1959 they have not been considered correct by the Spanish Academy. The forms **dí** and **ví**, though found, are neither frequent nor correct.

57. USES OF **ser, estar, ir** AND **dar.**

(a) **Ser.** Revise §§ 30–33 (**ser** and **estar**), § 52 (time), § 53 (date), and note the following:

¿Quién es? Soy yo. Who is it? It is I (*lit.*, I am).

¿Eres tú? (**¿Es Vd.? ¿Sois vosotros? ¿Son Vds.?**) Is it you? (*lit.*, Are you?)

Éramos nosotros. It was us [we] (*lit.*, We were).

NOTE: The subject pronoun in this construction is usually placed after the verb, even when the sentence is affirmative.

(b) **Estar.** Revise §§ 30–33 (**ser** and **estar**), § 53 (date), § 46 (progressive tenses), and distinguish between the following uses with preposition and infinitive:

estar por, not yet to have —; to be inclined to, to have a good mind to

estar para, to be about to, to be on the point of, to be likely to

El tren estaba por salir. The train hadn't yet left.

Estoy por dejar a mi marido. I've a good mind to leave my husband.

El tren estaba para salir. The train was about to leave.

(c) **Ir.** Revise § 18, Note 3, and study the following idiomatic uses of **ir**:

(i) to form the progressive tenses (**ir** emphasizes more than **estar** the gradual progress in the verbal action).

Mi hermana estuvo muy enferma, pero ahora va mejorando.

My sister was very ill, but now she is (gradually) improving.

(ii) **ir bien a alguien,** to suit someone (*lit.*, to go well to someone).

Este sombrero va muy bien a mi hermana.

This hat suits my sister very well.

(iii) **¡Vamos!** Let's go! Come! Come on! Come now!

Vamos a + *infinitive*, Let's — (*besides* We are going to —).

Vamos, hombre, que estoy esperando.   Come on, man, (for)
    I'm waiting.

Vamos a comprar unos lápices.   Let's buy a few pencils.

(*d*) **Dar.** Besides translating English *to give*, **dar** has the
following idiomatic uses:

dar los buenos días a	to say good morning to
dar las gracias a	to say thank you to, to thank
dar un paseo	to go for a walk
dar una vuelta	to go for a walk (round) *or* a spin
dar la vuelta a algo	to go round something
dar de comer	to feed, to give to eat
dar de beber	to water (*animals*), to give to drink
dar a	to look (out) on to
dar con	to come across, to meet with
dar la hora	to strike the hour

Dimos la vuelta a la Plaza de España.   We walked round the
    Plaza de España.

Mi ventana da a la plaza principal.   My window overlooks
    the main square.

Dio la una; dieron las cuatro.   It struck one; it struck four.

NOTE: Like **ser** [§ 52] **dar** is used in the singular with the first hour
(**Da la una**, *It is striking one*) and in the plural with the rest (**Estaban dando las seis**, *It was just striking six*).

VOCABULARY

la canción	song	al lado	at the side, next door
la capital	capital		
la catedral	cathedral	al lado de	beside
enseñar	to teach, to show	luego	then, next
entrar (en)	to come (go) in, to enter	el momento	moment
		el monu-	monument
el hotel	hotel	mento	
el lado	side	el moro	Moor

AN ESSENTIAL COURSE IN MODERN SPANISH

preguntar	to ask	**terrible**	terrible
el restorán	restaurant	**el turista**	tourist
saludar	to greet, to pay one's respects to	**la ventana**	window
		la verdad	truth
siguiente	following	**el viaje**	journey, trip, voyage

en aquel momento	at that moment
al día siguiente	on the following day
a la mañana siguiente	on the following morning
ser verdad	to be true
¿no es verdad? ¿verdad? ¿no?	isn't it? didn't he? aren't they? etc. (*cf.* French *n'est-ce pas?*)
buenos días	good morning, good day
buenas tardes	good afternoon, good evening
buenas noches	good night
(muchas) gracias	thank you (very much), (many) thanks

EXERCISES

I. (*a*) *Study and translate:* Comimos. Visteis. Recibió. Estuve. Tuvieron. Viví. Mandó. Terminamos. Bebió. Fue. ¿Adónde fuiste? ¿Qué hizo? No dieron. ¿Con qué escribieron ustedes? No leí nada. Vivía. Daba los buenos días. Estaban dando las cuatro. Estoy para terminar. ¿Quién es? Somos nosotros. Estamos a veinticinco de noviembre. Estaba por visitar a sus tíos. Esta ventana da al jardín. Estaba buscando a sus padres. Miró la catedral. Dio las buenas noches.

(*b*) *Translate:* They received. I wrote. Did you see? They arrived. We drank. You did not finish. What did they write? What did you talk about? She visited my mother. They went home. What did you buy? He didn't study anything. He worked all day. What did he sell? They arrived in time. Is it you? It isn't they. They are finishing. She was selling. He said good morning. It was striking ten. He came across an old friend. I walked

86

round the building. We looked for my brother. Did you look at the shops?

II. (a) *Study and translate:* 1. Salió de Madrid el veinte de abril, pasó unos días en Zaragoza, y llegó a Barcelona el veintiséis por la mañana. 2. Eran las ocho y media en punto cuando salieron para tu casa. 3. Dio de beber a su hijo porque éste tenía mucha sed. 4. En aquel momento entró un turista a preguntar dónde estaba el Hotel España. 5. Llegamos a Murcia el viernes por la noche, y a la mañana siguiente fuimos a ver la catedral. 6. — Buenas tardes. ¿Cómo está usted? — Muy bien, gracias. ¿Y usted? 7. En la casa de al lado vivía un señor que trabajaba en el mismo hotel. 8. Durante tres días hizo un frío terrible y nadie salió a la calle. 9. Después de visitar la catedral, fuimos a comer a un restorán que estaba muy cerca. 10. Los moros llegaron a España en el año setecientos once y estuvieron allí durante nueve siglos, hasta mil seiscientos diez.

(b) *Translate:* 1. I spent the whole day writing letters. 2. They lived two years in Valencia and then went to live in Barcelona. 3. Did you see my brother when he passed through here? 4. This is one of the friends I studied with in Madrid. 5. They were very pleased because their children were arriving at four o'clock that afternoon. 6. She used to live here before going to live in Burgos. 7. In Granada we saw some very beautiful gardens, but it was terribly hot. 8. The third chapter was too difficult for my brother, but he did the first one very well. 9. Beside the cathedral there is a very nice restaurant where we used to go and eat. 10. You learnt a lot of songs during your trip to Spain, didn't you?

III. (a) *Study and translate:* 1. Era el veinte y uno de octubre cuando llegamos a la capital. 2. El guía iba enseñando a los turistas los monumentos más importantes de la ciudad. 3. Primero fui a una fábrica bastante grande y luego a una muy pequeña. 4. Llegó a las cuatro y media en el tren de

Málaga, pero sólo estuvo dos horas. 5. La ventana de mi cuarto daba a la plaza más hermosa de la ciudad. 6. Vamos a dar un paseo antes de ir a comer. 7. Al día siguiente fui a visitar a mis abuelos que vivían cerca de la catedral. 8. Estaban dando las siete cuando salimos a dar una vuelta por la ciudad. 9. Pasamos la mañana mirando los monumentos, y por la tarde fuimos a casa de unos amigos que vivían muy cerca de la plaza principal. 10. Hacía un frío terrible cuando estuvimos en Madrid y casi no vimos nada de la ciudad.

(b) *Translate:* 1. I spent the whole day speaking English with a tourist who was living in the same hotel. 2. I was there for two hours but I didn't see anyone. 3. They spent an hour looking for a friend who lived near the main square. 4. On passing through Madrid they went to pay their respects to my parents. 5. We were about to have lunch when his sister arrived with a present for my wife. 6. We read the whole of the (= all the) first chapter, but it was rather difficult. 7. It was striking three when we reached the restaurant. 8. I was about to leave Madrid when I came across an old friend who was working in the same factory as my brother. 9. What did they write the letters with if they had neither pens nor pencils? 10. The first day (that) we spent in Seville it was terribly hot and we only saw the cathedral.

LESSON X

58. WEAK OBJECT PRONOUNS (English: he sees *me*, he gives *it to me*, etc.). Weak (*or* unstressed *or* conjunctive) object pronouns are those which in Spanish cannot stand apart from the verb. They are generally placed immediately before it.

Me ve. No me ve. He sees me. He does not see me.

¿Por qué no me da Vd. el libro? Why don't you give me the book?

NOTE: The personal **a** and the indirect object **a** are not used with weak object pronouns.

59. DIRECT AND INDIRECT OBJECT PRONOUNS. (*a*) Spanish has two series of weak object pronouns: those indicating a direct object (English *me*, *him*, *her*, etc.) and those indicating an indirect object (English [*to*] *me*, [*to*] *him*, [*to*] *her*, etc.). In certain persons the two forms coincide.

	Subject	*Object*	
		Direct	*Indirect*
(1)	**yo**	**me**	**me**
(2)	**tú**	**te**	**te**
	usted	**le (lo), la**	**le**
(3)	**él**	**le (lo), lo**	**le**
	ella	**la**	**le**
(1)	**nosotros**	**nos**	**nos**
(2)	**vosotros**	**os**	**os**
	ustedes	**los (les), las**	**les**
(3)	**ellos**	**los (les)**	**les**
	ellas	**las**	**les**

89

(b) Distinctions between the different Forms

(i) The first persons (**me, nos**) and the second persons familiar (**te, os**) present no difficulty, since they have the same forms for the direct and indirect object.

Nos ve muy a menudo. He sees us very often.
Nos habla en español. He speaks to us in Spanish.
¿Quién te dio el libro? Who gave you the book?
Te vi ayer. I saw you yesterday.

(ii) In the second persons polite the direct object forms are **le** (*pl.* **los**) if one addresses male persons, and **la** (*pl.* **las**) if one addresses female persons. The indirect object pronouns for both sexes are **le** (*pl.* **les**). In all these cases the strong pronoun **usted(es)** is frequently added to distinguish them from the third-person uses [see below, Sections (iii) and (iv)].

Le vimos (a usted) ayer.
We saw you (*masc. sing.*) yesterday.
La vi (a usted) en el mercado.
I saw you (*fem. sing.*) in the market.
Los presenté (a ustedes) a mi madre.
I introduced you (*masc. pl.*) to my mother.
Mi padre las acompañó (a ustedes), ¿verdad?
My father went with you (*fem. pl.*), didn't he?
¿No le dio (a usted) los buenos días?
Did he not say good morning to you? (*masc. or fem. sing.*)
Les escribí (a ustedes) la semana pasada.
I wrote to you (*masc. or fem. pl.*) last week.

NOTE: In the first four examples above the **a** that precedes **usted(es)** is the personal **a**; in the rest it is the preposition **a** introducing an indirect object.

(iii) In the masculine of the third person one must distinguish in the singular between a direct object pronoun referring to a thing (**lo**) and a direct object referring to a person (**le**). The plural of both is **los**. The indirect object pronoun is **le, les** for things and persons.

¿Dónde está el lápiz? Yo no lo tengo.

Where's the pencil?   *I* haven't got it.

Allí está mi hermano. ¿No le ves?

There's my brother.   Don't you see him?

Esos libros eran buenos, pero yo no los compré.

Those books were good, but *I* didn't buy them.

Mis padres estuvieron ayer. ¿Los vio usted?

My parents were [here] yesterday.   Did you see them?

Le dimos los buenos días.

We said good morning to him.

¿No les mandó la carta?

Didn't he send them the letter?

(iv) In the feminine of the third person no distinction is made between animate beings and inanimate objects: **la** (*pl.* **las**) is used for the direct object and **le** (*pl.* **les**) for the indirect object.

No la veo. I don't see her.

¿Mi pluma? No la tengo. My pen? I haven't got it.

Las visitó ayer. He visited them (*fem.*) yesterday.

Les contó muchas cosas. He told them many things.

NOTES : 1. As with verb forms [§ 39, Note] so also with weak pronoun objects the second-person polite forms are the same as those of the third person :

le veo	I see him; I see you (*masc. sing.*)
los veo	I see them (*masc.*); I see you (*masc. pl.*)
la veo	I see her; I see you (*fem. sing.*)
las veo	I see them (*fem.*); I see you (*fem. pl.*)
le doy	I give to him, to her; I give to you (*sing.*)
les doy	I give to them; I give to you (*pl.*)

The additional use of **a usted(es)** with second-person polite pronouns avoids possible ambiguity.

2. Though the third-person (and second-person polite) forms given above are those generally considered most acceptable, one should be prepared to meet regional and individual variations in the course of one's reading and intercourse with Spaniards. The most frequent and most permissible are those quoted in brackets under (*a*) above: (i) **lo** used instead of **le** to indicate a masculine

singular direct object: **lo veo,** *I see him, I see you;* (ii) **les** used instead of **los** to indicate a masculine plural direct object: **les veo,** *I see them, I see you.*

60. ORDER OF WEAK OBJECT PRONOUNS. If a direct and an indirect object pronoun come together, the indirect object pronoun is placed first.

Nos enseña un libro; nos lo enseña.
> He shows us a book; he shows us it (it to us).

Te di las plumas; te las di.
> I gave you the pens; I gave you them.

Notice, however, that when two pronouns of the third person come together (or a third person and a second person polite), the indirect object **le** (*pl.* **les**) becomes **se** (*sing.* and *pl.*):

Se lo da. He gives it (*i.e.,* the book) to her.
Se las da a usted(es). He gives them (*i.e.,* the pens) to you
Se los da. He gives them (*i.e.,* the books) to them.

61. THE PLEONASTIC USE OF THE WEAK OBJECT PRONOUN. A noun (or strong pronoun) direct or indirect object may, for emphasis, be placed before the verb. It must then be repeated in weak-pronoun form immediately before the verb.

A sus padres los ve muy poco. He sees his parents very little.
Este libro lo compro para mi hermano. I'm buying this book for my brother.
A éste le doy el primer premio. To this one I give the first prize.
A ellos les parecía muy difícil. It seemed very difficult to *them.*

Such repetition is usual also, especially in conversational style, when an indirect-object noun (or strong pronoun) *follows* the verb.

Se lo di al profesor. I gave it to the teacher.
Este libro se lo mando a un amigo. This book I'm sending to a friend.

62. POSITION OF WEAK OBJECT PRONOUNS. (*a*) It has been stated [§ 58] that weak pronoun objects are generally placed immediately before the verb in Spanish. With infinitives and gerunds, however, they are placed after the verb and written as one word with it—with a written accent if necessary to preserve the word stress [§ 3 (*b*)].

terminar; terminarlo
　　to finish; to finish it (*i.e.*, the book)
terminando; terminándola
　　finishing; finishing it (*i.e.*, the lesson)
Era imposible hablarle de eso.
　　It was impossible to talk to him about that.
Cogiéndome por el brazo, me habló.
　　Seizing me by the arm, he spoke to me.

(*b*) Where the infinitive or gerund depends on a preceding finite verb, the weak pronoun object may be attached to the end of the infinitive or gerund (as in (*a*) above) or be placed before the finite verb (and written separately).

No quiere vernos.
No nos quiere ver.　} He doesn't want to see us.

Voy a dárselo.
Se lo voy a dar.　} I'm going to give it to him.

Estoy terminándolo.
Lo estoy terminando.　} I am finishing it.

Estaban enseñándonoslo.
Nos lo estaban enseñando.　} They were showing us it.

VOCABULARY

acompañar	to accompany, to go with	**la diferencia**	difference
		entre	between, among(st)
anoche	last night		
la botella	bottle	**esperar**	to wait for
cantar	to sing	**el este**	east
contestar	to answer, to reply	**explicar**	to explain
		la libra	pound

93

el mercado	market	**la semana**	week
el norte	north	**sí**	yes
el oeste	west	**el sur**	south
para	in order to	**también**	also, as well, too
un poco (de)	a little	**tarde**	late
	(*quantity*)	**temprano**	early
la poesía	poem, poetry		

el año pasado   last year
la semana pasada   last week

EXERCISES

I. (*a*) *Study and translate:* Lo bebió. Me los dieron. No nos hablaban. Nos lo vendió. Se lo vendí a usted. Usted no me vio. ¿Qué le hiciste? Me las mandaron. Le acompañé a usted. ¿Por qué no le escribís una carta? No las estudia. Les voy a explicar la primera lección. Visitándonos. Voy a verle. Lo iba a buscar. Se lo vamos a mandar. Les mandé unos libros. Se los mandé. No le escribió nadie. ¿Quién los vio a ustedes? Se lo dio a mi padre. Esta carta la escribí yo. Nadie las conocía. No sé quién lo hizo.

(*b*) *Translate:* They saw us. She wrote to us. We visited them (*masc.*). You studied it (*fem.*). I sent them a book. I sent it to them. He did not see you (*masc. sing. pol.*). Did they give it to you (*masc. sing. pol.*)? You did not explain it (*fem.*). They explained it to us. Are you going to finish it? Seeing him. Studying them (*masc.*). I was looking at her. She was looking for him. We were going to visit you (*masc. pl. pol.*). He gave them to me. I'm going to send it him tomorrow. They were explaining them to him. I taught him many songs. I knew him very well. He drank a little tea.

II. (*a*) *Study and translate:* 1. Mi hermano estuvo aquí ayer. ¿Le vio usted? 2. — ¿Conocéis esta canción que aprendí en España? — Sí, la conocemos muy bien. 3. Usted estuvo mucho tiempo en el este de España, ¿verdad? 4. Si

ustedes no comprenden esta poesía, se la voy a explicar.
5. Estaba buscando a sus hijas para llevarlas al restorán.
6. ¿Qué te contestaron cuando les hablaste de esa idea?
7. ¿Qué hizo usted con el regalo que le di para su madre?
8. Se lo di a mi hermana y ella lo mandó a Zaragoza. 9. Hay grandes diferencias entre el norte de España y el sur; también las hay entre el este y el oeste. 10. Yo iba a dárselo al día siguiente al ir a saludar a sus padres.

(b) *Translate:* 1. Why didn't you say good morning to them when you saw them in the market? 2. What did you give him last night when he went to your house? 3. Why did he not explain it all to us when he saw us last week? 4. I went to thank him and show him my new book of poems. 5. I am going to explain to you the lesson we looked at yesterday. 6. He bought this bottle of wine and gave it to me before leaving for the south. 7. I went to visit them but it was late and they were not at home. 8. We were two hours without seeing them. 9. We were looking for them as we passed through the gardens. 10. In the sixteenth century Spain had a population of less than eight million inhabitants.

III. (a) *Study and translate:* 1. Nunca le vi tan alegre como anoche. 2. Nos va a cantar algunas de las canciones que aprendió durante su viaje a España. 3. ¿Qué hizo usted con los libros que le mandé desde España? 4. Recibí cuatro libras ayer y se las voy a dar a usted mañana por la tarde. 5. Le vimos en el mercado y le dimos los buenos días. 6. Le está buscando a usted para enseñarle las cosas que compró en España. 7. El año pasado le vi varias veces en casa de su abuelo, pero nunca le hablé. 8. Al ver el libro, supo que no valía nada, pero no iba a decírselo a su hijo. 9. Estudié muy bien la lección antes de explicarla. 10. Le estuve esperando desde las ocho y cuarto hasta las nueve menos veinte.

(b) *Translate:* 1. He sent it to us last week when he was in Murcia. 2. This book is worthless. Where did you buy it? 3. I went to greet his parents and to thank them.

4. This book that I bought in Spain I'm going to send to my grandfather.   5. I don't know her well but I know (that) she is from Barcelona and that her mother is English.   6. We set out early in order to arrive before twelve o'clock.   7. Did he reply to you when you greeted him?   8. What differences do you see between the Spanish and the English?   9. I am teaching him many of the songs I learnt in Spain.   10. Seven hundred and forty-five minus five hundred and sixty-seven are one hundred and seventy-eight.

REVIEW AND DEVELOPMENT
SECTION (II)

63. The student will probably, by now, have found difficulties in distinguishing between the Spanish imperfect and preterite tenses, despite the general distinction suggested in § 55. Often, shades of meaning difficult to express in English are indicated by the use of one tense rather than the other, and in translating from English to Spanish it may be necessary to take into account a wider context than that of the mere sentence before one can decide which tense to use. It is a difficult problem at first but is one that, with practice and the study of examples, should soon disappear. In the pages that follow we shall consider certain rather more difficult cases than those given in § 55, borderline cases where both tenses are possible in Spanish but with differences of meaning. We shall consider examples first from the English side and then from the Spanish.

(a) *English–Spanish*

(i) *He was very happy when he saw his father.*

If we mean that he was already in a happy state of mind when he saw his father, we shall use the imperfect (**Estaba muy contento cuando vio a su padre**); if we imply that he became contented because he saw his father, we are setting a beginning (*i.e.*, a time limit) to his happiness and we shall therefore use the preterite (**Estuvo muy contento cuando vio a su padre**).

(ii) *The car was very cheap.*

If we mean that the price being asked for the car was a low one or that it was a cheap type of car, we are interested in a state and shall therefore use the imperfect (**El coche era muy barato**);

97

if, on the other hand, we are thinking of the moment at which the deal was proposed or accepted (*i.e.*, he offered it to me at a low price, or I bought it at a low price), the emphasis is on the price in its time limitations and we shall use the preterite (**El coche fue muy barato**).

(iii) *It was difficult to explain.*

If we are thinking only of the essential difficulty of explaining the problem irrespective of time limits within the past (*i.e.*, it was a difficult type of problem to explain), we shall use the imperfect tense (**Era difícil de explicar**); if, on the other hand, we are thinking of the difficulty someone experienced in explaining the problem at a given moment in the past, we shall use the preterite (**Fue difícil de explicar**).

(iv) *He was a very bad king.*

If we make this statement in a narrative sense, opening the way to details on his life, perhaps, or as a background to the happenings of his reign, we shall use the imperfect tense (**Era un rey muy malo**); but if we are thinking of his reign in its completeness, as a bygone moment in history, we shall use the preterite (**Fue un rey muy malo**).

(v) *She could not see her brother.*

If we mean that from where she was standing her brother was not in sight, we are indicating a state: **No veía a su hermano** (For the omission of **poder**, *to be able*, see § 88, Note 3). If, on the other hand, we wish to stress that she made an effort to go and see her brother but that she met with a definite obstacle, then we must use the preterite (with **poder** now, to indicate the effort made): **No pudo ver a su hermano.**

(vi) *He had breakfast every morning at seven.*

Here there is repeated action, so that the imperfect tense would appear to be the obvious choice in Spanish: **Desayunaba todas las mañanas a las siete.** But suppose the action, though repeated, is ascribed to a limited period of time (his holidays, perhaps, or when he was in Spain). There are then two possibilities, which bring us to the finest distinction of all between the preterite and the imperfect: if we wish to emphasize the completeness and pastness of the period of time in question, we shall use the preterite (**Desayunó todas las mañanas a las siete**); if we wish to present the same period narratively, as something living and progressing [*cf.* (iv) above], we shall use the imperfect.

(b) Spanish–English

(i) **Juan no encontraba al profesor.**
   Juan no encontró al profesor.

In the first case John was having no luck in finding the teacher but he was still looking; in the second case, the search is over and the teacher remains unfound. The imperfect tense, then, indicates progression of the action; the preterite its completeness. In English these two examples might be rendered as *John could not find the teacher* and *John did not find the teacher* respectively, though the difference is less clear than in Spanish for the first translation might also correspond to a Spanish preterite [*cf. (a)* (v), above].[1]

(ii) **No tenía en cuenta el tiempo que hacía.**
    No tuvo en cuenta el tiempo que hacía.

The imperfect **tenía** indicates his state of mind, unconscious of weather conditions; the preterite **tuvo** emphasizes his lack of consideration for such conditions at a given moment: the moment in which he made his plans. Free English translations might be, respectively, *He was oblivious of the state of the weather* and *He did not take into account the state of the weather*.

(iii) **Le acompañaba el embajador.**
     Le acompañó el embajador.

In the first case the ambassador plays a less dynamic part in the proceedings, his presence being incidental to what was done during the tour (*The ambassador was with him*); in the second case

---

[1] Only by a very free translation of the imperfect (e.g., *John was not managing to find the teacher*) can we bring out the essential difference in English.

the emphasis is on the action of the ambassador in going with him (*The ambassador went with him*). The imperfect, then, presents the ambassador's presence in its vagueness, as little more than an accompanying state; the preterite presents it in its limits and its restriction to a given moment in the past.

(iv) **Hablaba alemán.**
Me habló en alemán.

In the imperfect we are interested in someone's ability to speak German (*He spoke [=was able to speak] German*); in the preterite the ability reveals itself in a definite action in the past (*He spoke to me in German*). In the first case, then, we have, as it were, a reservoir of potential action; in the second, a canalizing of that reservoir to a given end.

(v) **Lo sabía cuando conocí a tu hermano.**
Lo supe cuando conocí a tu hermano.

In the first case (*I [already] knew about it when I made your brother's acquaintance*) the imperfect of **saber** is used because I was already in a state of knowledge when I met the brother and there is no indication of when that state began; in the second case (*I found out about it when I made your brother's acquaintance*) the preterite is used because my knowledge has now been given a time limit: the time at which I came to know the brother. Notice that the preterite **conocí** in both examples has been translated by *I made the acquaintance of*; **conocía** would be translated by *I was acquainted with* or, simply, *I knew*.

(vi) **¿Con quién estabas cuando te llamé?**
¿Con quién estuviste ayer?

One might object here that the time covered by the imperfect **estabas** in the first sentence (*Whom were you with when I 'phoned you?*) is probably smaller than that covered by the preterite **estuviste** in the second. Once again it is a matter of the presence or absence of time limits and a sense of completeness. In the first case the action of being in someone's company is not confined temporarily; it stretches indefinitely on each side of the momentary action **llamé**. In the second example, on the other hand, the state of being is seen as a whole confined within the limits of the bygone **ayer**.   **¿Con quién estabas ayer?** is also possible, but the emphasis would not then be on the state of being in its completeness, but on its duration, as a setting for actions more limited in time [*cf.* (*a*) (iv) above].

NOTE: In examples (*b*) (ii), (iii) and (iv) the imperfect may also, of course, indicate repetition of the individual definite action as well as suggest state as we have assumed.   Thus, **No tenía en cuenta** may mean *He did not use to take into account*, and **Le acompañaba el embajador** may mean *The ambassador used to go* (or *come*) *with him*, and **Hablaba alemán** may mean *He used to speak German*. This use of the imperfect to indicate *repeated action* as opposed to *temporally unlimited state* is straightforward and has been left out of account in the above examples.

64. Read §§ 5-7.

VOCABULARY

Revise the vocabularies of Lessons VI–X and study the following geographical nouns and adjectives:

(*a*) The continents: **África, América, Asia, Europa, Oceanía.**

(*b*) Countries, nationalities and cities:

Country	Nationality	Important City
Alemania (Germany)	**alemán**	**Berlín**
Austria (Austria)	**austriaco**	**Viena**
España (Spain)	**español**	**Madrid**
los Estados Unidos (U.S.A.)	**norteamericano**[1]	**Nueva York**
Francia (France)	**francés**	**París**
Inglaterra (Britain)[2]	**inglés**	**Londres**

[1] The simple adjective **americano** suggests *Latin American* to the Spanish speaker. Similarly, the corresponding nouns: **Norteamérica** (*America*), **América** (*Latin America, South America*).

[2] **La Gran Bretaña** (*Great Britain*) exists but smacks of imperialism. **Inglaterra** refers indifferently, in common usage, to all parts of the British Isles and **inglés** to all its inhabitants, though the words **escocés** (*Scottish*), **galés** (*Welsh*) and **irlandés** (*Irish*) may be used for closer definitions. **Bretaña** alone means *Brittany*.

Italia (Italy)	**italiano**	**Roma**
Portugal (Portugal)	**portugués**	**Lisboa**
Rusia (Russia)	**ruso**	**Moscú**
Suiza (Switzerland)	**suizo**	**Berna**

NOTES: 1. The continents are feminine in gender. So also are names of countries ending in unstressed **a**; the rest are masculine.

2. In general, the name of the language is the same as the adjective of nationality: **Habla alemán, francés, italiano y portugués** (*He speaks German, French, Italian and Portuguese*).

EXERCISES

I. (*a*) *Study and translate:* Estábamos contentos. Tuvimos que venderlo. Luego lo comprendió. Nadie la acompañó. No lo sabía. Lo supe por la tarde. No veía bien. Le vio más tarde. Íbamos con mis padres. Fueron cuatro o cinco veces. Escribía poesías. Escribió un libro de poesías. Estaba enferma. Eran muy malos. ¿Dónde los vieron? ¿Quién eres? Estábamos mirando un libro. Hacía mucho frío. Tenía mucho calor. El té estaba muy frío. ¿Adónde fuiste ayer? ¿Por qué no lo hizo usted? Él no lee nunca nada. No se lo voy a dar. Están dando las nueve. Estuvimos dos días. Hacía tres años. No llegó nadie. No vio a ninguna de las francesas. No hablé con nadie. Muchachas alemanas y portuguesas. ¿Qué hora era? Eran las cuatro y diez. ¿Qué fecha era? Era el veintidós de octubre. Hablaba alemán y ruso. Después de explicárnoslo.

(*b*) *Translate:* We used to sell. They visited me on Tuesdays. We wrote to them on Monday. I knew him very well. I got to know her in Spain. She was going home. They sent it to us. I gave it to him. We were not buying anything. On seeing him. Before explaining it. I'm not going to do it either. At seven fifty-five. It was the twenty-seventh of September. A hundred new books. At a quarter to four in the morning. He doesn't explain his ideas to anyone. He is six or seven years old. Why were you in such a hurry? What time do you make it? I had to do it by four o'clock. We saw you yesterday morning. They were showing it to him. At what time did the train leave for the north? At about half past seven. Who is it? It's us. Where are you? We're here. He is tall. I was cold. The weather was warm. She is German. They are from Seville. I saw no one here. Don't you know any Andalusian songs?

II. (a) *Study and translate:* 1. Él estaba muy alegre porque sus abuelos llegaban aquel día. 2. ¿Quiénes eran los franceses que hablaban con tu padre? 3. Nuestra idea fue mala porque no tuvimos en cuenta el tiempo que hacía en la capital. 4. Llegó por la noche y a la mañana siguiente salió muy temprano para el norte. 5. Le pregunté al guardia dónde estaba la catedral. 6. ¿Es éste el restorán donde tienen ese vino tan bueno? 7. Esta señora es inglesa, pero conoce muchas canciones francesas y españolas. 8. El miércoles pasado estuvimos todo el día sin hacer nada. 9. Estas poesías las leí siendo muy joven. 10. Íbamos a visitar la catedral, pero no lo hicimos.

(b) *Translate:* 1. His grandparents' house was near the market square. 2. This lady and gentleman spent several years in Italy studying the language. 3. He was finishing the third chapter when we arrived. 4. They didn't know the girl but they knew where she lived. 5. I didn't eat either the apples or the pears because they were still not ripe. 6. The last time I was in Spain a pound was worth more or less a hundred and ten pesetas. 7. "How old is the taller boy?" "He is eight or nine years old." 8. I am very keen to read the book my brother bought when he was in Spain. 9. He had to finish the third lesson before five o'clock. 10. She is showing the lady some flowers she bought at the market.

III. (a) *Study and translate:* 1. Estaba triste porque veía que nadie le contestaba. 2. Es demasiado tarde para ir a comer al restorán donde fuimos ayer. 3. Mi madre y mi hermana estuvieron casi todo el día sin salir de casa. 4. Fue muy difícil explicarle esta diferencia a mi padre. 5. — ¿De dónde son esas canciones tan bonitas que usted cantó anoche? — Son todas del norte de España. 6. Sé que salió de Valencia a las diez menos cuarto de la mañana, pero no sé a qué hora llegó a Barcelona. 7. ¿Por qué tienes tanto miedo? Yo nunca tengo miedo. 8. Los domingos salíamos al campo a pasar el día. 9. — Estas flores son muy hermosas, ¿verdad? — Sí, sobre todo las amarillas. 10. A la mañana siguiente salieron a dar un paseo por la ciudad.

(b) *Translate:* 1. They left Barcelona at about eight o'clock in the morning, had a meal in Saragossa, and reached Madrid a little before ten at night. 2. It was very cold when we arrived home and the windows were all open. 3. That is the wife of the Italian you were with yesterday. 4. Is this not the same girl I saw last year in my father's factory? 5. In this country the king has nothing to do with the laws. 6. Tomorrow morning we are going to visit a very important French gentleman. 7. On seeing his brother, he went and asked him when he was leaving for England. 8. Why did you not go home and finish the lesson? 9. I used to live at his parents' when I went to Barcelona. 10. I am looking at a book he bought in Spain.

IV. *Re-translate the keys given for Lessons VI–X [pp. 350–353] and compare your versions with the originals.*

LESSON XI

65. THE PAST PARTICIPLE (English *bought, sold, lived*, etc.).   The
Spanish past participle forms are:

- I. **-ar** verbs: stem plus **-ado (comprado, dado, estado)**.
- II. **-er** verbs: stem plus **-ido (vendido, sido, tenido)**.
- III. **-ir** verbs: stem plus **-ido (vivido, ido, recibido)**.

EXCEPTIONS: **hecho** (hacer), **escrito** (escribir), **visto** (ver), **abierto**
(abrir), **cubierto** (cubrir, *to cover*), **descubierto** (descubrir, *to
discover*), **roto** (romper, *to break*).   For the written accent on
leído (leer), **poseído** (poseer, *to possess*), etc., see § 3 (*c*) (iv).

66. THE COMPOUND PERFECTIVE TENSES (English *I have bought, I
had bought*, etc.).   In Spanish as in English the compound perfective tenses are formed by some part of the verb *to have* together
with the past participle of the appropriate verb.   However, in
this case the verb *to have* is not **tener**, but another verb re-
served almost exclusively for the formation of compound tenses:
haber.   It is irregular in the present indicative and in the preterite; regular in the imperfect, the gerund and the past participle.

pres. ind.: he, has, ha, hemos, habéis, han
imp. ind.: había, habías, había, habíamos, habíais, habían
preterite: hube, hubiste, hubo, hubimos, hubisteis, hubieron
past part.: habido
gerund: habiendo

67. THE PERFECT INFINITIVE (English *to have bought, to have sold*,
etc.).   This is formed by the infinitive **haber** together with
the appropriate past participle.

Tengo que haberlo terminado para las seis.

I have to have finished it by six o'clock.

Es un gran mérito haberlo hecho solo.

It is a great achievement to have done it alone.

68. THE PAST GERUND (English *having bought, having sold*, etc.). The gerund of **haber** with the appropriate past participle.

Habiendo perdido el tren, tomó el autobús.

Having missed the train, he took the bus.

69. THE PERFECT INDICATIVE (English *I have bought, I have sold*, etc.). The present tense of **haber** with the appropriate past participle.

¿No lo habéis terminado? Have you not finished it?

La he visitado ya. I have already visited her.

Le hemos visto dos veces. We have seen him twice.

No han llegado aún. They still haven't arrived.

¿Ha escrito Vd. a su hermano? Have you written to your brother?

70. THE PLUPERFECT INDICATIVE (English *I had bought, I had sold*, etc.). The imperfect of **haber** with the appropriate past participle.

No había salido de clase. He hadn't come out of lectures.

Habíamos llegado a las siete. We had arrived at seven.

¿Qué había hecho usted? What had you done?

71. THE PAST ANTERIOR. This tense may translate the English pluperfect indicative (*I had bought, I had sold*, etc.) in subordinate adverbial clauses of time and after **apenas** (scarcely) when the accompanying clause contains a preterite. The past anterior is formed by the preterite of **haber** with the appropriate past participle.

Cuando la hubimos terminado, nos dejó.

When we had finished it he left us.

Le avisé en cuanto hubieron llegado.

I informed him as soon as they had arrived.

Apenas se lo hube preguntado, (cuando) apareció su hermano.

Scarcely had I asked him when his brother appeared.

NOTE: The past anterior can be avoided (and generally is, especially in conversation) by the use of the simple preterite tense: **Cuando lo terminamos, nos dejó; Le avisé en cuanto llegaron; Apenas se lo pregunté, (cuando) apareció su hermano.**

72. THREE GENERAL NOTES ON THE COMPOUND PERFECTIVE TENSES. (*a*) The auxiliary (part of **haber**) cannot be separated from the past participle, except by a weak pronoun object.

Han llegado ya (*or* **Ya han llegado.**)   They have already arrived.

but **habiéndoles escrito,** having written to them.

(*b*) The past participle is invariable (*i.e.*, does not agree with the subject, nor with any direct object).

(Ellas) han salido.   They (*fem.*) have gone out.
La he visto.   I have seen her.

Contrast the French (*Elles sont sorties.   Je l'ai vue*); contrast also the Spanish use of **estar** with the past participle to indicate state resulting from previous action (**La mesa está rota,** *The table is broken*; **Estas lecciones no están terminadas,** *These lessons are not finished*).

(*c*) **Tener** may be used instead of **haber** if there is emphasis on the state arrived at rather than on the action.   The past participle is then an adjective qualifying the direct object and agrees with it in number and gender (*cf.* **estar** + past participle, above).

¿Tienes pensada tu respuesta?
Have you thought out your reply?
Le teníamos preparada una cena de despedida.
We had a farewell dinner prepared for him.

73. OTHER WAYS OF TRANSLATING THE ENGLISH COMPOUND TENSES. (*a*) An English perfect tense indicating action begun

in the past and continuing in the present is rendered by the Spanish present.

Está aquí desde las cinco.   He has been here since five o'clock.

¿Cuánto tiempo lleva usted aquí? ⎫ How long have you been
¿Desde cuándo está usted aquí? ⎬ here?

Llevo dos horas esperándole. ⎫
Hace dos horas que le estoy es-   ⎪
**   perando.**   ⎬ I have been waiting for
Estoy esperándole desde hace dos   ⎪ him for two hours.
**   horas.** ⎭

In corresponding cases in the more distant past a Spanish imperfect translates an English pluperfect.

Llevaban media hora trabajando. ⎫
Hacía media hora que estaban ⎪
**   trabajando.**   ⎬ They had been working
Estaban trabajando desde hacía ⎪ for half an hour.
**   media hora.** ⎭

(b) The English I (you, etc.) have just with a past participle is translated by the present tense of **acabar de** with an infinitive. Similarly, I (you, etc.) had just -ed is rendered by the imperfect of **acabar de** with the infinitive.

Acabo de verle.   I have just seen him.
Acabábamos de salir.   We had just gone out.

74. OTHER USES OF **haber.** Besides serving as an auxiliary verb to form compound tenses, **haber** is used also in the following cases:

(1) In **hay** (there is, there are), **había** (there was, there were), **hubo** (there was, there were), **ha habido** (there has been, there have been), **había habido** (there had been). These forms correspond to the third person singular of the verb.[1] There is no plural form.

---

[1] pres. ind. **hay** = **ha** + **y** (cf. French il y a)

Había dos cosas que no le gustaban. There were two things
he didn't like.

Hubo mucha confusión aquel día. There was a lot of confusion that day.

Ha habido otros que lo han hecho. There have been others
who have done it.

(2) To indicate more visible states of the weather than those
expressed by means of **hacer** [§ 44 (c)]. The same third person
singular forms are used as in (1).

Ha habido neblina. It has been misty.

Había luna. The moon was shining.

Hay sol (*also* **Hace sol**). The sun is shining (*also* It is sunny).

(3) In the expression **hay** (**había,** etc.) **que** + infinitive (*one
must*).

Hay que hacer más. We (you, he, etc.) must do more.

Había que terminarlo para las dos. It had to be finished
(*lit.*, One had to finish it) by two o'clock.

(4) In **haber de** + infinitive (*to be* [*destined, obliged*] *to*).

He de hacerlo mañana. I am to do it tomorrow.

¿Cómo había de hablarle? How was he to speak to her?

75. CONJUNCTIONS. (*a*) *And.* To prevent its loss in pronunciation, **y** becomes **e** immediately before (**h**)**i-** (but not before **hie-**).

> **francés e italiano,** French and Italian
> **literatura e historia,** literature and history
> **e imita muy bien al cura,** and he imitates the priest very
> well

but **madreselva y hiedra,** honeysuckle and ivy

(*b*) *Or.* For the same reason **o** becomes **u** before (**h**)**o-**.

> **éste u otro,** this or another
> **mujeres u hombres,** women or men
> **si ves u oyes algo,** if you see or hear anything

(c) *But*, introducing a positive statement set up in opposition to a previous negative one, is translated not by **pero** but by **sino** (or **sino que** before a clause).

no por *pero* **sino por** *sino*, not by *pero* but by *sino*
No es alemana sino polaca.   She is not German but Polish.
No trabaja sino que descansa.   He is not working but resting.

NOTE: **Pero** (or **pero sí** for emphasis) is used in cases like the following where the terms in opposition are not by nature mutually exclusive:

No he visto hoy a su hermana, pero la voy a ver esta tarde.
  I haven't seen his sister today but I'm going to see her this evening.
No he visto a su hermana, pero sí (he visto) a su hermano.
  I've not seen his sister but I *have* seen his brother.

76. IDIOMATIC USES (**gustar, parecer, quedar, sobrar, faltar, hacer falta**). The use of these verbs often presupposes a change of sentence construction, the English subject becoming the indirect object of the Spanish verb, and the English object becoming the Spanish subject.

Thus, **gustar** (*to be pleasing*), by such a change of construction, translates the English *to like, to enjoy*.

Esto me gusta.   I like this (*lit.*, This is pleasing to me).
Le han gustado mucho.   She has enjoyed them very much.
Este libro le va a gustar a Vd.   You are going to like this book.
A mis hermanas no les gustó.   My sisters didn't like it.
Similarly:

	Basic Meaning	*Translates*
parecer	to seem, to appear	to think (of)
quedar	to remain	to have (left)
sobrar	to be more than enough	to have more than enough
faltar	to be missing	to be short of, to lack
hacer falta	to be necessary, to be needed	to need

Parece que no le vamos a ver. It looks as though we are not going to see him.

¿Qué le parecen estas fotos? What do you think of these photos?

Quedan dos problemas. There remain two problems.

¿Cuántas pesetas te quedan? How many pesetas have you left?

Sobran señores como él. There are too many gentlemen like him.

Nos sobra dinero. We have more money than we need.

Faltaban aún los dos hermanos. The two brothers were still missing.

No les ha faltado nunca nada. They have never gone short of anything.

Hace falta convencerle. It is necessary to convince him.

Nos hacía falta otra solución. We needed another solution.

NOTE: With these verbs the order *verb-subject* is usual.

VOCABULARY

abrir	to open	**la familia**	family
acabar de	to have just	**la mesa**	table
apenas	scarcely	**la muerte**	death
coger	to seize, to catch	**no . . . más**	only
en cuanto	as soon as	**que**	
dejar	to leave (*not places*)	**la novela**	novel
		otro	other, another
delante de	in front of	**el perro**	dog
descubrir	to discover	**romper**	to break, to tear
después (de) que	after (*conj.*)	**la silla**	chair
		tomar	to take
detrás de	behind	**el verano**	summer
la dificultad	difficulty	**viajar**	to travel
la dirección	address, direction	**ya**	already
		ya no	now . . . not, no longer
la falta	lack		

Study also the words listed in § 76.

EXERCISES

I. (a) *Study and translate:* No la he terminado. Lo habían visto. Usted no los había descubierto. ¿Qué habéis hecho? Le hemos escrito. ¿Has leído esto? Antes de haberlo terminado. No la han recibido. No habíamos visto a nadie. ¿Por qué no los has visitado? ¿Han ido a verla? No nos había escrito nadie. Cuando terminaron. Después que le hubieron visto. Ha habido muchas visitas. Había otro hermano. Hubo una dificultad. Había que visitarla. No he de explicártelo. Acababa de salir. No ha faltado nadie. No me quedan más que dos libras. Le hacen falta cien pesetas.

(b) *Translate:* We have almost finished. They had already arrived. What have they done? When we had rested. She had visited them. Have you seen him? After having done it all. Having written to them. What had she discovered? After I had opened the door. They haven't visited anyone. Have you finished? He has not written anything. We had replied in the morning. Who had he gone out with? They had broken the table. As soon as I had read it. What have you seen? He has just talked to me about that. Ten or eleven. Big and important. Not a man but a woman. They lack nothing. He had two pencils too many. What does he think of our idea?

II. (a) *Study and translate:* 1. Había pasado toda la mañana trabajando en el jardín. 2. Nadie había llegado a tiempo para explicarles todas las dificultades. 3. Le sobran libras, pero le faltan pesetas. 4. En cuanto salió de casa, fue a la estación principal donde tomó el tren de Madrid. 5. Este año no fuimos a Francia sino a Alemania y después a Suiza. 6. No ha llegado aún el telegrama que le mandé desde Barcelona. 7. Hay que tener en cuenta que en enero y febrero hace mucho frío en Madrid. 8. Al llegar a Londres fuimos a casa de unos señores que habíamos conocido en Austria. 9. Me han gustado mucho los libros que usted me compró en España. 10. Con la muerte de Felipe e Isabel ya no le quedaron más que dos hijos.

(b) *Translate:* 1. We had already finished the first chapter when it struck four o'clock. 2. I have seen her and I have explained the idea to her. 3. There were a lot of Andalusians in the market today, weren't there? 4. After he had visited his aunt and uncle, he went to pay his respects to his grandfather. 5. I had scarcely read the first poem when my father seized the book and asked me where I had bought it. 6. They had still not opened the doors when we got there. 7. He has learnt several languages by teaching them to others. 8. They asked me why I hadn't left them my address. 9. For my parents Spain has always been the loveliest and most interesting country in (= of) Europe. 10. I have just replied to the letter I spoke to you about yesterday.

III. (a) *Study and translate:* 1. Le pregunté por qué no me había dado los buenos días al verme esta mañana cerca de la plaza. 2. En cuanto descubrí la verdad, cogí un tren para Zaragoza. 3. Otro día, al vernos delante de su casa, nos acompañó a la estación. 4. Había que enseñarles el libro de poesías que yo había comprado en Madrid. 5. No hablo español, pero sí conozco bastante bien los países donde lo hablan. 6. Nunca me han hecho tanta falta como ahora las visitas de aquellos amigos de mi juventud. 7. Les gusta mucho el tiempo que hace ahora en España. 8. ¿Cuántas libras te quedaron después de comprar tantos libros? 9. ¿Qué he de hacer si esos señores no llegan a tiempo? 10. Ha explicado muy bien estas poesías, pero hay algunos que aún no las comprenden.

(b) *Translate:* 1. Behind the door there was an old chair they had bought in the market. 2. When we had read the book we sent it to my brother. 3. I have opened the door but nobody has come out. 4. She asked me who we were going to leave the dog with. 5. We had just left when he arrived. 6. He was very tired through having been working all day in the factory. 7. I have seen many books more beautiful than this one but none do I know so interesting. 8. When his family went to live in Madrid,[1] he was seven or eight years old.   9. They have spent almost the whole summer travelling round (= through) Switzerland and Italy.   10. I have not read any of his novels, but I *have* read his poetry.

---

[1] *In Madrid* is normally **en Madrid,** but see the footnote on p. 352.

LESSON XII

77. THE FEMININE ARTICLES **el** AND **un**. (*a*) Before a feminine singular noun beginning with stressed **a-** or **ha-**, **la** is replaced by **el**: **el hambre** *f.* (*hunger*), **el ala** *f.* (*wing*), **el aula** *f.* (*lecture room*), **el álgebra** *f.* (*algebra*), etc. **El** in such cases is not a masculine article but an alternative form of the feminine, and qualifying adjectives take the usual feminine endings: **el ala rota** (*the broken wing*), **las alas rotas** (*the broken wings*). The form **la** is used before an *un*stressed (**h**)**a-**: **la aritmética** (*arithmetic*), **la América del Sur** (*South America*).

(*b*) In the same conditions, **una, alguna** and **ninguna** are replaced by **un, algún** and **ningún** respectively: **un aula pequeña** (*a small lecture room*), **algún alma piadosa** (*some pious soul*), **ningún agua tan pura** (*no water so pure*).

78. THE NEUTER ARTICLE **lo**. (*a*) **Lo** joins with the masculine singular form of an adjective to express the general quality of that adjective without referring it to any specific noun: **lo bueno** (*what is good, good things, goodness*), **lo importante** (*that which is important, the important thing*), **lo principal** (*the main thing*), etc.

Siempre buscaba lo imposible. He always looked for the impossible.
Eso es lo más importante. That's the most important thing.
Lo malo es que nunca llega a tiempo. The bad thing is that he never arrives on time.

(*b*) Before an adjective used as such, **lo** indicates a great amount of the quality represented by that adjective: *i.e.*, in **lo** + adjective + **que es** (**son, parece,** etc.) + subject.

115

Hay que ver lo guapas que son sus hermanas. You should see how (very) good-looking his sisters are.

¡Y con lo difíciles que han resultado estos ejercicios! And (what) with these exercises turning out so difficult!

(c) In a similar sense **lo** may be used also before an adverb.

por lo mucho que trabaja, through the (great) amount of work he does

con lo despacio que avanzábamos, with the slowness of our advance

Fui a visitarle lo antes posible (*or* **lo más pronto posible**). I went to visit him as soon as possible.

79. ELLIPSIS OF A NOUN. A definite article used immediately before **que** or **de** usually corresponds to the English *the one(s)* or to a demonstrative pronoun. The neuter article **lo** is used when there is no reference to a specific noun.

Los que trabajan más, ganan más. Those who work most earn most.

Fue ella la que lo hizo todo. She was the one (*or* It was she) who did everything.

¿Qué libro es éste? Es el que me mandó tu hermano. Which book is this? It is the one your brother sent me.

No leo lo que escribe. I do not read what (= that which) he writes.

Me dio todo lo que tenía. He gave me everything (= all that which) he had.

mis enemigos y los de usted, my enemies and yours

los ejercicios de la primera lección y los de la cuarta, the exercises of the first lesson and those of the fourth

esta chica y la de al lado, this girl and the one next door

80. SPECIAL USES OF THE DEFINITE ARTICLE. The definite article is required in Spanish in the following cases where it is not used in English:

(1) With nouns used in a generic sense.

Los españoles beben vino. Spaniards drink wine.

El vino no es caro en España. Wine is not dear in Spain.
La libertad no es la ambición de todos los hombres. Liberty
is not the ambition of all men.
Lo bueno no es siempre lo más importante. What is good
is not always what is most important.

(2) With names of languages (but not after **de** or **en**, nor immediately after **hablar** or its subject).

    Estudiamos el español. We are studying Spanish.
    El francés ayuda mucho. French helps a lot.
    Habla muy bien el inglés. He speaks English very well.
but **No hablo alemán.** I don't speak German.
    ¿Habla usted árabe? Do you speak Arabic?
    Una lección de ruso. A Russian lesson.
    Canta en italiano. She sings in Italian.

(3) With the names of certain countries: **la Argentina**
(*Argentine*), **el Brasil** (*Brazil*), **el Canadá** (*Canada*), **el Ecuador**
(*Ecuador*), **la India** (*India*), **el Japón** (*Japan*), **el Paraguay**
(*Paraguay*), **el Perú** (*Peru*), **el Uruguay** (*Uruguay*).

    En el Brasil hablan portugués. In Brazil they speak
      Portuguese.
    Habla de su viaje al Japón. He talks about his voyage to
      Japan.
but **Conoce toda España.** He knows the whole of Spain.
    Suiza está al norte de Italia. Switzerland is to the north
      of Italy.
    Vamos a Francia y después a Alemania. We are going
      to France and afterwards to Germany.

(4) Before a proper noun qualified adjectivally.

el pobre Juan, poor John
la Europa occidental, western Europe
el África del Norte, North Africa

This applies also to the names of languages and countries where
the article would not normally be used [above, Sections (2) and
(3)].

Habla español pero no el español de Castilla. He speaks
Spanish but not Castilian Spanish (= the Spanish of Castile).
la España del siglo doce, twelfth-century Spain
la América del Sur,[1] South America
la Gran Bretaña, Great Britain

NOTE: Where the qualifying element is a phrase or clause English
and Spanish usage coincide in using the article.
el Madrid de Luis Candelas, the Madrid of Luis Candelas
la Sevilla que conocen los extranjeros, the Seville that foreigners
know

(5) Before titles (but not in direct address, nor when the title
is in apposition, nor when it is a foreign word, nor with **don,
doña, Santo**).

    la reina Isabel, Queen Elizabeth
    el general Primo de Rivera, General Primo de Rivera
    el presidente Lincoln, President Lincoln
    el señor Pérez; la señora de Pérez, Mr Pérez; Mrs Pérez
    (*lit.,* the wife of Pérez).
    el capitán Ferrer, Captain Ferrer
    el doctor Martínez, Doctor Martínez

but **Buenos días, señor profesor.** Good morning, sir (=
    teacher).
    ¿Cómo está Vd., señor López? How are you, Mr López?
    el secretario, doctor Alonso, the secretary, doctor Alonso
    lord Derby y sir Robert Peel, Lord Derby and Sir Robert
    Peel
    Herr Müller va a comprar esta tienda. Herr Müller is
    going to buy this shop.
    Santa Teresa y San Juan de la Cruz, Saint Teresa and
    Saint John of the Cross
    Don José va a vender su fábrica. Mr López (*lit.,* Master
    Joseph) is going to sell his factory.

    Also **Sudamérica,** used without an article because **Sud-** is here
considered to be part of the noun and not a separate adjective.

NOTES: 1. Since a title, like an adjective, is a form of description, the use of the definite article in this section is closely related to its use in Section (4).

2. Titles (except **San[to]**, **Santa**) do not take a capital letter.

3. **Santo** is apocopated to **San** before a masculine singular proper noun not beginning with **To-** or **Do-**.

   San Pablo, San Pedro, San Andrés, Saint Paul, Saint Peter, Saint Andrew

but **Santo Tomás, Santo Domingo,** Saint Thomas, Saint Dominic

4. **Don** + *christian name* is best translated into English by *Mr* + *surname*. In Spain it is a mark of respect and polite affection to address an elderly person or one of some social standing by means of **don** (*fem.* **doña**) together with the christian name. Thus, one might address (or talk about) the head of the factory where one works as **don Joaquín,** one's landlady as **doña Carmen,** one's teacher as **don Antonio,** etc.

(6) With parts of the body and with clothing the Spanish definite article usually translates the English possessive adjective.

Levantaron la cabeza. They raised their heads.

¿Dónde dejaste el sombrero? Where did you leave your hat?

Tenía el pelo negro y los ojos azules. Her hair was black and her eyes blue (*lit.*, She had the hair black and the eyes blue).

In some such cases a weak indirect object pronoun may be necessary to make the ownership clear.

   Me rompí el brazo derecho. I broke my right arm.

   Le quitaron la chaqueta. They took his coat off.

NOTE: *They raised their heads*, but each person has only one; therefore **la cabeza.** Similarly, **Abrieron los ojos** (*They opened their eyes*), but **Todos abrieron la boca** (*They all opened their mouths*).

(7) In certain expressions of time:

(i) with hours of the day and daily institutions.

Lo terminé antes de las dos y media. I finished it before half past two.

Vamos a tomar el té. Let's go and have tea.

Tengo que comprar cosas para la cena. I have to buy things for dinner.

Siempre nos visita a la hora de la siesta. He always visits us at siesta time.

(ii) to translate *on* with days of the week.

El miércoles fuimos a Londres. On Wednesday we went to London.

Los sábados no trabajo. I don't work on Saturdays.

(iii) with seasons (but not after **de** used to form an adjectival phrase, nor is the article necessary after **en**).

> **La primavera no ha llegado aún.** Spring has still not arrived.
>
> **Me gusta más el verano.** I prefer summer.
>
> **Estaban hablando del otoño.** They were talking about autumn.

but **Lleva ropa de invierno.** He is wearing winter clothing.

> **En (el) verano hace calor.** In (the) summer it is hot.

(iv) in qualified expressions of time.

la semana que viene, la semana próxima, next week
el año pasado, el viernes pasado, last year, last Friday

(8) To indicate rate (the Spanish definite article here translates the English indefinite article).

Lo venden a seis pesetas el kilo. They sell it at six pesetas a kilogramme.

Los compré a doce pesetas la docena. I bought them at twelve pesetas a dozen.

Gana cuarenta pesetas al día. He earns forty pesetas a day.

Ganaba nueve mil pesetas al mes (al año). He earned nine thousand pesetas a month (a year).

NOTE: In these examples the English *a* has been translated in two different ways: by the *definite article* alone, and by the preposition **a** + definite article. The first is used more for quantity, the second for time. But the expressions **al día, al mes, al año** can also be translated respectively by the adjectives **diario, mensual, anual**: **40 pesetas diarias, 9000 pesetas mensuales (anuales)**.

There is yet another means of translating the English *a* of rate: by **por** without the article. It is used especially with the periods of time **hora** (*hour*) and **semana** (*week*).

> **siete pesetas por hora,** seven pesetas an hour
> **cincuenta kilómetros por hora,** fifty kilometres an hour
> **seis veces por semana,** six times a week

(9) The definite article is also used in Spanish with certain public institutions such as **la escuela** ([*primary or specialized*] *school*), **el instituto** ([*state grammar*] *school*), **el colegio** ([*private*] *school*), **la universidad** (*university*), **la cárcel** (*prison, jail*), also with **la ciudad** (*town, city*) and in a number of idiomatic expressions (*e.g.*, **dar los buenos días, dar las gracias, dar la vuelta a**).

> **A las ocho sale para la escuela.** At eight he leaves for school.
> **Pasé la mañana en el colegio.** I spent the morning at school.
> **Le llevaron a la cárcel.** They took him to prison.

81. OMISSION OF THE DEFINITE ARTICLE. The definite article is used in English but omitted in Spanish:

(1) Before a number in the title of a ruler.

> **Carlos V (Carlos quinto),** Charles V (the Fifth)
> **Fernando VII (Fernando séptimo),** Ferdinand VII
> **Luis XIV (Luis catorce),** Louis XIV

(2) Usually before a noun in apposition, unless that noun is individualized.

> **Al día siguiente, veinte de julio, salí para Toledo.**
>   On the following day, the twentieth of July, I left for Toledo.
> **Luego viene Lugo, capital de la provincia.**
>   Then comes Lugo, the capital of the province.

but **Estuvo también su padre, el profesor.**
His father, the teacher, was also there.
Cervantes, el gran escritor español del siglo XVI.
Cervantes, the great Spanish writer of the sixteenth century.

82. A SPECIAL USE OF THE INDEFINITE ARTICLE. The indefinite article is used in Spanish before a qualified abstract noun.

Caía con una regularidad monótona. It fell with monotonous regularity.
Demostró una agilidad sobrehumana. He showed superhuman agility.

NOTE: Adjectives that limit and indicate rather than describe [§ 38, Note 3] do not take **un(a)**.

Le concede demasiada importancia. He gives it too much importance.

83. OMISSION OF THE INDEFINITE ARTICLE. The indefinite article is omitted in Spanish in the following cases where it is used in English:

(1) Before an unqualified noun dependent on a negative (unless there is emphasis on the *one*ness of that noun).

No tengo lápiz ni papel. I haven't a pencil or paper.
No había recibido contestación. He hadn't received a reply.
Salió sin decir palabra. She went out without saying a word.
Entraron sin invitación. They got in without an invitation.

but **No tengo un hermano sino dos.** I haven't one brother but two.
No vimos ni un solo monumento. We didn't see a single monument.
Salió sin decir ni una palabra. She went out without saying a (single) word.

(2) Before an unqualified noun indicating nationality (or regional origin), rank or occupation, used after **ser** (*to be*) or **parecer** (*to seem, appear*).

Es andaluz.   He's an Andalusian.
Mi hermano era profesor.   My brother was a teacher.
Aquel señor parece oficial.   That gentleman looks like an officer.

When the noun is qualified the article must normally be used.

Es un andaluz de fama universal.   He is an Andalusian of universal fame.
Es un profesor que vale mucho.   He is a very good teacher.
Parece un oficial muy bueno.   He seems a very good officer.

It is not used, however, in cases like the following:

Era profesor de instituto.   He was a grammar-school teacher.
Parece oficial de infantería.   He looks like an infantry officer.

The article is *not* used, then, when the person referred to is attributed to a class; it *is* used when that person is picked out of his class as an individual.

(3) Before a noun used in apposition, unless that noun is strongly individualized.

> **Ocurrió a fines del siglo XIX, época en que España perdía sus últimas colonias.**
> It happened at the end of the nineteenth century, a period in which Spain was losing her last colonies.
> **Luego hablé con un tal Martínez, profesor de idiomas en el Instituto.**
> Then I talked to a certain Martínez, a language teacher at the Grammar School.

but **Fui con el señor Sánchez, un amigo de la familia.**
> I went with Mr Sánchez, a friend of the family.

(4) With **otro** ((*an*)*other*), **cierto** ((*a*) *certain*), **ciento** ((*a*) *hundred*), **mil** ((*a*) *thousand*), **medio** (*half* (*a*)), **tal** (*such* (*a*)), **semejante** (*such* (*a*)) and **¡qué!**, (*what* (*a*)!)

cierta carta que le había escrito otro amigo,
a certain letter that another friend had written to him
mil aviones y medio millón de soldados,
a thousand planes and half a million men
¡Qué sorpresa recibir tal noticia!
What a surprise to receive such (a piece of) news!

NOTE: **Un tal** exists with the meaning *a certain*: **un tal señor López,** *a certain Mr López.*

VOCABULARY

el agua *f.*	water	**el kilo**	kilogramme
el ala *f.*	wing	**el kilómetro**	kilometre
el álgebra *f.*	algebra	**levantar**	to raise, to lift up
el aula *f.*	lecture room, classroom	**llevar**	to take, to carry; to wear
bajar	to go (come, take, bring) down, to lower	**meridional**	southern
		el mes	month
el caballo	horse	**negro**	black
la cabeza	head	**ocurrir**	to happen
el café	coffee, café	**el oficial**	officer
caro	dear	**el ojo**	eye
la clase	lecture, class, kind	**la patata**	potato
		el pelo	hair
creer	to believe, to think	**el profesor**	teacher, lecturer
		el pueblo	town, village
curioso	strange, curious	**la revolución**	revolution
después	afterwards	**el soldado**	soldier
extraordinario	extraordinary	**la taza**	cup
		útil	useful
		la vida	life
ganar	to earn	**que viene**	next

Principal Meals:

el desayuno; desayunar	breakfast; to have breakfast
la comida; comer	midday meal (lunch, dinner); to have the midday meal

la cena; cenar   evening meal (dinner, supper); to
have the evening meal

Comer and **la comida** are also used in the more general sense of
to eat and *food* respectively.

Study also the words given in § 80 (3) and (9), and in § 83 (4).

EXERCISES

I. (*a*) *Study and translate:* El ala más grande. Las aulas más
curiosas. Un África poco conocida. Lo útil y lo más hermoso. Esta revolución y la del siglo pasado. Estas patatas
y las que comimos ayer. Los españoles no comen lo mismo
que los italianos. No habla ni francés ni alemán. En el
Canadá y en el norte de los Estados Unidos. El señor
Martínez y la señora de Cantón. Una taza de té y otra de
café. Parece profesor. Es un profesor muy conocido.
Entró en cierta casa. Sale muy temprano para la ciudad.
Estuve ayer con don Juan. De una importancia extra-
ordinaria. ¿Qué idiomas hablan en Suiza? A más de cien
kilómetros por hora. Él ganaba doscientas pesetas diarias.
¿Cuánto ganabas al mes?

(*b*) *Translate:* South America. A terrible hunger. The
nicest lecture room. The possible. What is bad. All who
work. He teaches me French and Italian. How is Mr Zubi-
zarreta this morning? He knows the markets of Brazil and
of Spanish America. A thousand men and a hundred boys.
Half a potato. Spain is in the south of Europe. Nine-
teenth-century England. They thanked me. We walked
round the building. He is going to be a teacher. I had
just greeted you. They have just had lunch. Mrs Fernández. Twentieth-century Madrid. With extraordinary
luck. Of great importance for another friend. He sold
them to me at seven pesetas a kilogramme.

II. (*a*) *Study and translate:* 1. Le gustan mucho los vinos
andaluces. 2. No conozco ningún aula tan pequeña como
ésta. 3. Lo importante era terminarlo todo antes de la hora

del té. 4. Había hablado mucho durante la cena de su viaje a la India y al Japón. 5. ¡Qué vida más triste tener que estar siempre enseñando lo mismo! 6. En cierto pueblo de la España meridional vivía, hace ya muchos años, un tal señor Martínez. 7. Como no era soldado, no sabíamos cómo explicarle la diferencia. 8. Levantó los ojos hacia la ventana donde le había visto hacía unos minutos. Ya no estaba. 9. Estas lecciones son mucho más difíciles que las que estudiábamos el año pasado. 10. La semana que viene salimos todos para la América del Sur.

(b) *Translate:* 1. I haven't a lecture until next Wednesday. 2. The important thing is to do it now, before leaving for Spain. 3. His brother is a language teacher at the grammar school. 4. These books are much more difficult than last year's ones. 5. He is a very good soldier and they are going to make him an officer. 6. Spanish is not as difficult as the algebra we used to study at school. 7. What I don't understand is why he didn't write to us explaining what had happened. 8. I don't know if horses are more useful than dogs, but they *are* more intelligent. 9. Spanish people don't know how to make a good cup of tea, nor do English people know how to make coffee. 10. We are going to go first to France and Germany, and afterwards, if we have enough money left, to Switzerland and Italy.

III. (a) *Study and translate:* 1. A mi madre le gusta más el agua que el vino. 2. Mis hermanas no son tan altas como las de Felipe. 3. Y lo más curioso es que estos señores parecen creer todo lo que escriben. 4. Voy a tener que salir un momento a comprar patatas para la cena. 5. Otro día llegó una señora a preguntar si conocíamos a un tal Pablo Ferrer. 6. Era muy pequeña la puerta y todos tuvimos que bajar la cabeza al entrar. 7. Durante cinco años Machado fue profesor de francés en el Instituto de Soria. 8. Los padres hablan muy bien el alemán y parece que ahora se lo están enseñando al hijo. 9. Los españoles beben más vino que los ingleses porque el vino es más barato en España que en

Inglaterra. 10. Primero nos habló de su viaje al Brasil y luego nos cantó, en portugués, unas canciones que había aprendido allí.

(b) *Translate:* 1. Her eyes were black and she wore a flower in her hair. 2. Coffee is much dearer than here in present-day Spain (= Spain of today). 3. At half past nine I have a Spanish class. 4. His father had been a soldier during the revolution. 5. We didn't know what we were going to do after breakfast. 6. For some [people] friendship is the most important of the virtues. 7. But all that has nothing to do with what he wrote to us last week. 8. I have been studying German for a year but it is much harder than French or Spanish. 9. I need a hundred pounds more in order to make the trip I was talking to you about last month. 10. Last year he was in South America and this year it seems they are going to send him to the United States.

LESSON XIII

84. RADICAL-CHANGING VERBS. (*a*) There are many Spanish verbs with stem vowel in **e** or **o** which, though regular in their endings, undergo a change of stem vowel whenever the word stress falls upon it. In such cases **e** becomes **ie** (**i** in some third-conjugation verbs) and **o** becomes **ue**.

(*b*) Thus the change will take place in the three singular persons and the third person plural of the present indicative (in all these parts of the verb the word stress falls upon the stem), but not in the first and second[1] persons plural.

I. **pensar,** *to think, intend*   **contar,** *to count, relate, tell*

pienso	pensamos	cuento	contamos
piensas	pensáis	cuentas	contáis
piensa	piensan	cuenta	cuentan

II. **perder,** *to lose*   **mover,** *to move*

pierdo	perdemos	muevo	movemos
pierdes	perdéis	mueves	movéis
pierde	pierden	mueve	mueven

III. (i) **mentir,** *to* (*tell a*) *lie*   **dormir,** *to sleep*

miento	mentimos	duermo	dormimos
mientes	mentís	duermes	dormís
miente	mienten	duerme	duermen

   (ii) **pedir,** *to ask* (*for*)[2]

pido	pedimos
pides	pedís
pide	piden

[1] The second-person polite forms are of course included under the term *third person* [§ 18, Note 1].

[2] Note the difference in meaning between **pedir** (*to ask* [*for*], *to request*) and **preguntar** (*to ask, to enquire*): **Le pido un favor,** *I ask him a favour*; **Le pregunté dónde estabas,** *I asked him where you were.*

(c) The change will not take place in any part of the imperfect indicative, for the stress is always on the ending (**pensaba, pensabas,** etc.; **perdía, perdías,** etc.).   Nor will it take place in the infinitive or the past participle (**pensar, pensado; perder, perdido;** etc.).

There should be no change either in the preterite tense or in the gerund, for the word stress throughout falls upon the ending. Verbs of the third conjugation, however, present a special case.

85. RADICAL CHANGES IN THE PRETERITE.   There is no change of stem vowel in verbs of the first and second conjugation: **pensé, pensaste,** etc.; **perdí, perdiste,** etc.   In all radical-changing verbs of the third conjugation, however, stem **e** changes to **i** and stem **o** to **u** in the third persons singular and plural.   There is no change in the remaining persons.

	mentir		**dormir**	
(i)	mentí	mentimos	dormí	dormimos
	mentiste	mentisteis	dormiste	dormisteis
	mintió	mintieron	durmió	durmieron

	pedir	
(ii)	pedí	pedimos
	pediste	pedisteis
	pidió	pidieron

86. RADICAL CHANGES IN THE GERUND.   In the gerund, third-conjugation radical-changing verbs undergo the same stem change as in the third persons of the preterite.

mintiendo   **durmiendo**   **pidiendo**

Verbs of the first and second conjugation have no change: **pensando, perdiendo,** etc.

87. COMMON RADICAL-CHANGING VERBS.

I. Verbs like **pensar:**   Verbs like **contar:**

| **calentar** | to warm | **acordar** | to agree |
| **cerrar** | to close, to shut| **acostar** | to put to bed |

despertar	to wake (up)	costar	to cost
empezar	to begin	encontrar	to find, to meet
sentar	to set down	mostrar	to show
temblar	to tremble	recordar	to remind, to recall, to remember
		soñar (con)	to dream (of)

II. Verbs like **perder**:

Verbs like **mover**:

defender	to defend	devolver	to give back, to return
encender	to light, to switch on	llover	to rain
entender	to understand	soler	to be wont to (*translates* usually)
		volver	to return, to go (come) back

NOTE: **volver** and **devolver** have irregular past participles (**vuelto, devuelto**).

III. Verbs like **mentir**:

Verb like **dormir**:

divertir	to amuse	morir	to die
hervir	to boil		
preferir	to prefer		
sentir	to feel, to be sorry (about)		

NOTE: **morir** has an irregular past participle (**muerto**).

Verbs like **pedir**:

despedir	to say good-bye to, to see off
repetir	to repeat
seguir	to follow, to continue
servir	to serve
vestir	to dress

130

88. IRREGULAR VERBS: **querer, poder, venir, decir.** The following irregular verbs have simple radical changes in many of their parts (the truly irregular parts are in heavy type):

(1) querer, *to want, like, love* (*cf.* perder)

pres. ind.: quiero, quieres, quiere, queremos, queréis, quieren
imp. ind.: quería, querías, etc.
preterite: **quise, quisiste, quiso, quisimos, quisisteis, quisieron**
past part.: querido
gerund: queriendo

(2) poder, *to be able* (*can*) (*cf.* mover)

pres. ind.: puedo, puedes, puede, podemos, podéis, pueden
imp. ind.: podía, podías, etc.
preterite: **pude, pudiste, pudo, pudimos, pudisteis, pudieron**
past part.: podido
gerund: **pudiendo**

(3) venir, *to come* (*cf.* mentir)

pres. ind.: **vengo,** vienes, viene, venimos, venís, vienen
imp. ind.: venía, venías, etc.
preterite: **vine, viniste, vino, vinimos, vinisteis,** vinieron
past part.: venido
gerund: viniendo

(4) decir, *to say, tell* (*cf.* pedir)

pres. ind.: **digo,** dices, dice, decimos, decís, dicen
imp. ind.: decía, decías, etc.
preterite: **dije, dijiste, dijo, dijimos, dijisteis, dijeron**
past part.: **dicho**
gerund: diciendo

NOTES: 1. The verbs **poder** and **querer** do not take a preposition when used before an infinitive.

¿Quiere Vd. acompañarme mañana? Do you wish to go with me tomorrow?

Mañana no puedo (acompañarle). I can't (go with you) tomorrow.

2. **Venir,** like **ir** (and other verbs of motion), takes the preposition **a** before a dependent infinitive:

Viene a verme todos los días.   He comes and sees me every day.

3. The English *can* is not normally translated with verbs of the senses.

¿Ves a mi hermano?   Can you see my brother?

Se oían las olas sobre la playa.   The waves could be heard on the shore.

The use of **poder** would emphasize the physical capability.

Es muy viejo y casi no puede ver.   He is very old and almost cannot see.

4. *Can* implying knowledge or technique as opposed to pure physical ability is translated by **saber.**

¿Sabes nadar (bailar, etc.)?   Can you swim (dance, etc.)?

VOCABULARY

aceptar	to accept	**la manera**	manner, means, way
algo	something		
el aspecto	aspect	**la media-**	midnight
bastante	enough	**noche**	
la confianza	confidence	**el mediodía**	midday
extranjero	foreign	**la parte**	part
el extranjero	foreigner	**la política**	politics, policy
el gobierno	government	**el proyecto**	plan, scheme
la historia	history, story	**subir**	to go (come) up,
la leche	milk		to take (bring)
la luz	light		up

Study the verbs given in §§ 84–88.

EXERCISES

I. (*a*) *Study and translate:* Prefirió. Pide. Cuenta. Murió. Defiende. Muevo. Calientan. Acuesto. Soñábamos. Encontré. Estaba durmiendo. Sentimos. Volvió. Entendí. Divertís. Vistió. Durmieron. Siguiendo. Repite. Mientes. Hirvió. La encendió. Se lo pedí. Los perdió. Me la pidieron. Quisieron. Le digo lo mismo. Dijeron.

No vino. Vienen. No quiero verla. No pudo venir. ¿Qué te pidió?

(b) *Translate:* I am sorry. He asked for. They count. He lost. She found. They move. He loses. He is sleeping. I begin. He shows. They set down. They are sorry. He is trembling. You closed. We followed. I understand. It is raining. He comes back. She serves. They follow me. I dress him. They say good-bye to me. You repeat the same thing. He died. They amused us. He defended her. She wanted. I couldn't do it. I told him the truth.

II. (a) *Study and translate:* 1. Le pidió un vaso de agua y se lo dio a su hijo. 2. Cuando llueve, los señores Martínez suelen venir en coche. 3. Esto me recuerda algo que me ocurrió una vez en Málaga. 4. Parece que han ido a la estación a despedir a un amigo de la familia. 5. Encuentro muy difícil comprender la política que defienden los del gobierno. 6. Ahora empiezo con las dificultades del álgebra y no encuentro manera de entenderlas. 7. Le cuestan mucho menos las cosas que compra en el mercado que las que compra cerca de casa. 8. Prefiere seguir viviendo en la misma casa donde vivían hace años sus padres y abuelos. 9. Mañana empieza lo más importante y difícil, y tiemblo al pensarlo. 10. A las once y media de la noche sube a su cuarto, enciende la luz, y empieza su lección del día.

(b) *Translate:* 1. I want to see what he has done. 2. But did he not ask you for it two months ago? 3. Milk costs more than wine in many parts of Europe. 4. He lied when he said his brother was coming on the following day. 5. She wants to warm the milk before putting her children to bed. 6. They asked me what time it was and I told them it was half past seven. 7. It always rains when I want to go into town and visit my brother. 8. They say that Spanish people prefer coffee to tea, but I don't understand why. 9. I remember my brother used to say more or less the same thing when he came back from Brazil. 10. They followed the foreigner as far as the market but there they lost him and they had to return home.

III. (a) *Study and translate:* 1. El café estaba hirviendo y no sabíamos cómo servirlo. 2. ¿Qué puedo hacer para mostrarle cuánto le quiero? 3. En política yo no pienso como mis padres. 4. Entra en el cuarto, cierra la puerta y sienta a su hijo sobre la mesa. 5. Ocurrió lo mismo cuando su hermano vino de América a pasar el verano. 6. Le divirtió mucho saber que nosotros no teníamos bastante dinero para volver a casa. 7. Suele salir de casa hacia las ocho y a veces no vuelve hasta después de medianoche. 8. Sueña con ser profesor de historia en algún instituto del norte de España. 9. Los que no han salido nunca de su pueblo suelen ser los que con más confianza hablan de los países extranjeros. 10. Repito lo que dije ayer: que no quiero defender una política que no sirve para los tiempos en que vivimos.

(b) *Translate:* 1. He says his brothers don't want to return home. 2. I prefer to buy them something for the house. 3. She dresses her children before preparing breakfast. 4. He died last year during a visit to his brother's. 5. They wake me every morning at a quarter past eight. 6. What time is it when he closes the shop and returns home? 7. "Do you understand this lesson?" "Yes, but I find it very difficult." 8. When I had slept an hour my brother brought me up a glass of milk. 9. They asked for a certain book on different aspects of Spanish life. 10. Gentlemen, this plan that you want to accept is the negation of everything we have done up to now.

LESSON XIV

89. WEAK REFLEXIVE OBJECT PRONOUNS (English *myself*, *yourself*, etc.). The forms are the same for the direct and indirect object.

(1)	**(yo)**	**me** (to) myself	**(nosotros) nos** (to) ourselves
(2)	**(tú)**	**te**	**(vosotros) os**	
	(usted)	**se** (to) yourself	**(ustedes) se** (to) yourselves
(3)	**(él)**	**se** (to) himself	**(ellos)** **se**	
	(ella)	**se** (to) herself	**(ellas)** **se** (to) themselves

Like other weak personal object pronouns, these are placed immediately before a finite verb and attached to the end of an infinitive or gerund [§ 62]. Whether used as direct or indirect objects they precede other weak pronouns [§ 60].

Se miró.	He looked at himself.
Se me echó encima.	He threw himself on top of me.

90. VERBS USED REFLEXIVELY (English *I cut myself, he sees himself*, etc.). (*a*) A reflexive verb is one in which the direct or indirect object. refers back to the subject of the verb.

Juan se ha cortado.	John has cut himself.
Se ha cortado el dedo.	He has cut his finger (*lit.*, to himself the finger).
Nos lavamos.	We washed ourselves.
Nos lavamos la cara.	We washed our faces (*lit.*, to ourselves the face).
Se calienta.	He warms himself.
Se calienta las manos.	He warms his hands (*lit.*, to himself the hands).
Me vestí.	I dressed myself, I got dressed.
Me compré un traje.	I bought myself a suit.

135

NOTE: With these examples compare those listed in § 80 (6). **Me** in **Me rompí el brazo derecho** is a reflexive pronoun indicating that I broke my own arm and not someone else's. Contrast: **Le rompí el brazo derecho,** *I broke his right arm.*

(*b*) Certain transitive verbs in Spanish have a corresponding reflexive form where two different verbs are used in English.

sentar	to set down
sentarse	to sit down (*lit.*, to set oneself down)
acostar	to put to bed
acostarse	to go to bed (*lit.*, to put oneself to bed)
despertar	to wake (up)
despertarse	to awake, to wake up (*lit.*, to wake oneself)
levantar	to raise
levantarse	to get up (*lit.*, to raise oneself), to rise
despedir	to dismiss, to see off (at station, etc.), to say good-bye to (someone who is going away)
despedirse de	to take leave of (*lit.*, to dismiss oneself from), to say good-bye to (someone who is remaining behind).

Él se acuesta antes que yo, y yo me despierto después que él.

He goes to bed before I do and I wake up after him.

Quiero despedirme ahora.

I want to say good-bye now.

Está despidiendo a su hermano.

He's seeing his brother off.

NOTE: A reflexive infinitive may take other pronouns than the **se** with which it is listed in vocabularies (*cf.* second example above). Thus, *before sitting down* will be translated by **antes de sentarme, antes de sentarte, antes de sentarse,** etc., according to the person it refers to.

91. REFLEXIVE PRONOUNS USED WITH RECIPROCAL SENSE (English *we see each other*). (*a*) The Spanish reflexive pronoun refers back to the subject of the verb. It may, however, indicate inter-action between different parts of a plural subject. This is the reciprocal sense of the reflexive pronoun.

Nos vimos ayer.	We saw each other yesterday.
Se odian.	They hate one another.
¿No os hablasteis?	Didn't you speak to one another?

(*b*) In the above examples the Spanish is unlikely to give rise to confusions with the purely reflexive use of the pronouns (*We saw ourselves yesterday, They hate themselves, Did you not speak to yourselves?*). On the other hand, a case like **Se felicitan** might equally well be interpreted as *They congratulate themselves* or *They congratulate one another.* The addition of **el uno al otro** (*fem.* **la una a la otra**) or, in the case of several persons, **los unos a los otros (las unas a las otras)** will make it clear that the latter sense is desired. The article may be omitted in each case: **Se felicitan (el) uno a(l) otro ([la] una a [la] otra,** etc.).

NOTES: 1. **Mutuamente** (*mutually*) and **recíprocamente** (*reciprocally*) may be used instead of **el uno al otro, la una a la otra,** etc.

2. Whatever the term of reciprocity added after the verb, the weak reflexive pronoun is still required before it.

3. There is also a means of emphasizing that it is the purely reflexive (and not the reciprocal) sense that is required, but this will be explained later.

92. OTHER USES OF THE SPANISH REFLEXIVE PRONOUN.

(1) With certain verbs the addition of the reflexive pronoun emphasizes a change of state or gives force and finality to the action of the verb.

morir; morirse	to die
marchar; marcharse	to leave, to go away
quedar; quedarse	to remain
caer; caerse	to fall

Se marchó de aquí a las seis. He left here at six o'clock.

This use of the reflexive pronoun may modify the meaning in English.

ir; irse	to go; to go off (leave)
dormir; dormirse	to sleep; to go to sleep
comer; comerse	to eat; to eat up
llevar; llevarse	to carry; to take away

Y ella se lo comió todo.	And she ate (up) the whole lot.
Nos fuimos a Zaragoza.	We went off to Saragossa.
El niño se durmió en seguida y duerme aún.	The child went straight off to sleep and is still asleep.

(2) The reflexive in Spanish frequently gives passive sense to an active verb, thus translating the English passive or the English *one* (*people, you, we,* etc.; *cf.* French *on*) with the corresponding active verb.

El hijo se llama Pedro. The son is called Peter.

¿Dónde se compran esos zapatos? Where are those shoes to be bought?

Estos trajes se venden muy baratos. These suits are being sold very cheap.

Aquí se habla inglés. English is spoken here.

Esto se entiende fácilmente. This can easily be understood.

Se prohibe fumar. Smoking is forbidden.

No se oía nada. There was nothing to be heard.

Se dice que no va a venir. It is said he is not coming.

¿Cómo se hace el té? How does one make tea?

Primero se hierve el agua. First you (*or* we) boil the water.

Luego se calienta la tetera. Then you (*or* we) warm the teapot.

¿Se puede? May I? Do you mind?

No se puede entrar. One (*or* you) can't go in.

Se aprende mucho escuchando. One learns a lot by listening.

Los domingos no se trabaja. There's no working on Sundays.

Se viene aquí a descansar.   People come here to rest.
Pero en este país no se piensa así.   But in this country people
  don't think like that.

93. THREE IRREGULAR VERBS: **traer, caer, oír.**

traer, *to bring, fetch*

pres. ind.:	traigo, traes, trae, traemos, traéis, traen
imp. ind.:	traía, traías, traía, traíamos, traíais, traían
preterite:	traje, trajiste, trajo, trajimos, trajisteis, trajeron
past part.:	traído
gerund:	trayendo

caer, *to fall*

pres. ind.:	caigo, caes, cae, caemos, caéis, caen
imp. ind.:	caía, caías, caía, caíamos, caíais, caían
preterite:	caí, caíste, cayó, caímos, caísteis, cayeron
past part.:	caído
gerund:	cayendo

oír, *to hear*

pres. ind.:	oigo, oyes, oye, oímos, oís, oyen
imp. ind.:	oía, oías, oía, oíamos, oíais, oían
preterite:	oí, oíste, oyó, oímos, oísteis, oyeron
past part.:	oído
gerund:	oyendo

NOTES: 1. For the written accents on **oímos, caísteis,** etc., see
§ 3 (*c*) (iv).

2. An *unstressed* **i** is never found in Spanish between two vowels:
thus **caía, oía,** but **cayó, cayeron, oyó, oyeron.**

3. **Caer:**

caer enfermo	to fall ill
caer bien a	to suit
Este sombrero le cae muy bien.	This hat suits you very well.

4. **Oír:**

oír + *infinitive*	to hear —(ing)
Le oí subir la escalera.[1]	I heard him come (*or* coming) up the stairs.
oír decir que	to hear (it said) that
He oído decir que es profesor.	I've heard he's a teacher.
oír hablar de	to hear (speak) of (*or* about)
Oí hablar mucho del presidente.	I heard a lot about the president.

VOCABULARY

acercarse a	to approach	**entonces**	then (= at that time)
alguien	someone, somebody	**la explicación**	explanation
el árbol	tree		
así	thus, like this (that)	**la fuerza**	force, *pl.* strength
blanco	white	**la gente**	people
cada (*invariable*)	each, every	**guardar**	to keep, to save
		más bien	rather
el científico	scientist	**el ministro**	minister
China	China	**el mundo**	world
deber	to have to, must	**el niño**	child
la derrota	defeat	**la palabra**	word
desilusionado	disappointed	**el papel**	paper
		pensar de	to think of (*opinion*)
despacio	slowly		
el dueño	proprietor, master	**pensar en**	to think of (= meditate on)
encargar	to entrust	**la pierna**	leg
engañar	to deceive	**la policía**	police

[1] *Cf.* other verbs of the senses: **La vi** (**miré**, etc.) **salir.** *I saw (watched etc.) her go out.* Such a verb of the senses followed by **cómo** and a finite verb emphasises the progress of the action rather than its completeness:
La vi cómo hablaba con su madre. I saw her talking to her mother.
Miró cómo se acercaban las nubes. He watched the clouds approaching.

pronto	soon	**la respuesta**	reply
de pronto	suddenly	**la reunión**	meeting
reconocer	to recognize, to acknowledge	**seguro**	sure, certain
		el silencio	silence
el reloj	watch, clock		

Study also the words and idioms in §§ 90 (*b*), 92 (1) and 93.

EXERCISES

I. (*a*) *Study and translate:* Se vistieron. Se miraron. No quiso acostarse. Nos levantamos. Me despierto. Se sienta. Se han perdido. Me marché. Se enseña el alemán. Me trajo un reloj. Se lo comió todo. Se hace así. No se oía nada. Iba acercándose a la ciudad. No se debe contestar así. Se cayó y se rompió una pierna. No le oigo bien. Se rompió el silencio. Esto se come con patatas. Como se vive, se muere. Se compran coches viejos. Se ve muy bien desde aquí. ¿Qué se dice del nuevo proyecto? Se pidió demasiado.

(*b*) *Translate:* She gets dressed. They warm themselves. We saw each other yesterday. I broke my leg. He got up at seven. She went to sleep in the afternoon. He took his leave. He had died in Brazil. She went away. We wrote to one another. He approached the building. They got dressed. He warmed his hands. It is not known why. It has already been explained. They all fell asleep. It is going to be done soon. They didn't recognize one another. You get a good meal here (= One eats well here). Houses for sale (= Houses are sold; *invert order*). One doesn't understand anything of what he says.

II. (*a*) *Study and translate:* 1. Entraron en el cuarto y se sentaron sin decirse nada. 2. Nunca se sabe lo que piensa la gente si no se les pregunta. 3. Se marcharon sin decir nada a la policía ni al dueño del hotel. 4. Trajo su botella de vino y se sentó a comer al lado de mi mujer. 5. Parece que durante este viaje se descubrieron cosas muy interesantes para los científicos. 6. Se cayó al volver del colegio y se le rompió el reloj que le habían comprado sus padres. 7. No se oye más que el agua que se pierde soñando entre los árboles. 8. Dicen que en China la gente se viste de blanco cuando alguien se muere. 9. Esto se lo oí decir un día a una señora que salía de casa de un ministro del último gobierno. 10. Al des-pertarnos por la mañana, nos sentimos más alegres e hicimos proyectos para los días que pensábamos quedarnos allí.

(b) *Translate:* 1. She gets up at seven and goes to bed at ten. 2. They ate it all up without saving anything for their friends. 3. "One can think one thing and say another." "Yes, but one must not." 4. They got dressed and went out to lunch at a friend's. 5. I usually go to bed at twelve and I get up at about half past seven. 6. He slept for an hour and, on wak-ing up, asked for a glass of water. 7. Englishmen who think this about their neighbours are deceiving themselves without knowing it. 8. We have been more than a year without seeing each other but we write to one another every week. 9. At these hours of the evening, when the tourists have all gone, the gardens are left (=remain) in silence. 10. Never have there been seen so many aeroplanes nor so many soldiers as since the visit of King Peter the Fourth.

III. (a) *Study and translate:* 1. Se rompió una pierna al caerse de un árbol. 2. Me desperté a las ocho, pero sólo me levanté media hora más tarde. 3. Me parece que se lo he oído decir a un amigo de mi padre. 4. El otro día, al salir de la reunión, me fui a cenar con un amigo norteamericano. 5. Entonces fue cuando se supo lo que había hecho el ministro al ver segura su derrota. 6. No se dijeron ni una palabra al en-contrarse después de la reunión. 7. Tal respuesta no se puede aceptar, ni puedo creer la explicación que nos da de sus viajes a Suiza. 8. Se sale de aquí a las seis de la mañana y se llega a Barcelona hacia las cuatro y media de la tarde. 9. Al acercarme a la capital, me sentí de pronto sin fuerzas para seguir con el proyecto que se me había encargado. 10. Se ha dicho muchas veces que los ingleses somos los grandes turistas del mundo. Ahora parece que lo son más bien los norteamericanos.

(b) *Translate:* 1. They were looking at one another without saying anything. 2. They say Spaniards drink a lot of wine but that they don't like water. 3. Why have you not brought me the same wine I asked you for yesterday? 4. It was not known how he had been able to finish it so soon. 5. They looked at each other in silence for a few moments without recognizing one another. 6. He usually gets up before six, but he also goes to bed very early at night. 7. He asked for another cup of tea but he went to sleep before drinking it. 8. We amused ourselves by making paper aeroplanes, and I think the children enjoyed themselves too. 9. He got dressed slowly, thinking of the reply he had to give to the prime (= first) minister. 10. It is not known who did it first but it is believed it was some tourist disappointed by the lack of trams.

LESSON XV

94. PREPOSITIONS.

(a) Simple Prepositions

a	to, at (*of time*)	**hacia**	towards, about (*of time*)
ante	before, at	**hasta**	until, as far as, (up) to
bajo	under	**para**	for, by (*of time*), in order to
con	with		
contra	against	**por**	by, through
de	of, from, about	**según**	according to
desde	since, from	**sin**	without
en	in, on, at	**sobre**	on, upon, about
entre	between, among(st)	**tras**	after

(b) Compound Prepositions

además de	besides	**después de**	after
a(l) través de	through, across	**detrás de**	behind
alrededor de	around, about	**encima de**	on top of, over
antes de	before	**enfrente de**	in front of, opposite
cerca de	near, close to		
debajo de	under(neath)	**fuera de**	outside
delante de	in front of, before	**lejos de**	far from
		más allá de	beyond
dentro de	inside, within		

NOTES: 1. For the relationship between the adverb and the preposition in these latter cases, note the following examples:

¿Quién está delante? Who is in front?
Estoy delante de esta señora. I am in front of this lady.
Vivía muy lejos. He lived a very long way away.
Vivía muy lejos de aquí. He lived a very long way from here.

Además, no leo los periódicos. Besides, I don't read the papers.
Además de ser poeta, escribe novelas policiacas. Besides
being a poet he writes detective novels.

2. Many of the same adverbs (and others) may be *preceded* by **de**
and then serve as adjectives.

> **la parte de fuera,** the outside part
> **los de más allá,** those beyond, those further on
> **la España de hoy,** present-day Spain
> **la casa de al lado,** the house next door

3. Certain prepositions join with **que** to form a compound conjunction: **desde que,** *since* (temporal); **hasta que,** *until*; **para que,**
in order that; **sin que,** *without*; **antes (de) que,** *before*; **después
(de) que,** *after*.

No le he visto desde que llegó. I haven't seen him since he
arrived.

(c) Possible Confusions

(1) *Before*: time (**antes de**), place (**delante de, ante**). **Delante de** indicates more physical position than **ante** which introduces an element of the English *in the presence of, when confronted
by*.

Lo terminó antes de llegar. He finished it before getting
there.
Un paje iba delante del rey. A page boy walked before the
king.
Compareció ante el juez. He appeared before the judge.

(2) *At*: time (**a**), place (**a** for movement, **en** for position), meta-
phorical sense (**ante,** *cf*. (1) above).

Lo hicieron todos al mismo tiempo. They all did it at the
same time.
¿A qué hora llegó a la reunión? What time did he arrive at
the meeting?
Estuve en la exposición. I was at the exhibition.
Se quedó muy triste ante esta idea. He was very sad at
this idea.

(3) *About*: time (**hacia** and **alrededor de**), place (**alrededor de**), = *concerning* (**de, sobre**). In the last sense **sobre** indicates a fuller, more authoritative treatment than **de**.

Llegó hacia (alrededor de) las dos. He arrived about two o'clock.

Había una tapia alrededor del jardín. There was a wall about the garden.

Habló de su viaje. He talked about his trip.

Habló sobre su viaje. He talked about (gave a talk on) his trip.

¿Qué dijo de su hermana? What did he say about his sister?

Leí un libro sobre España. I read a book about Spain.

NOTE: *About* (and *around*) meaning *approximately* is usually translated by the plural indefinite article: **unas cien libras** (*about a hundred pounds*).

(4) *After*: time (**después de**), succession (**tras**).

Después de visitarle, fui a casa. After visiting him I went home.

uno tras otro; día tras día, one after another; day after day

(5) *From*: **desde** is rather more emphatic than **de**.

de cinco a ocho, from five to eight [§ 52 (c)]

desde las cinco hasta las ocho, from five until eight

Había trabajado desde la una. He had worked from one o'clock.

De Madrid a Toledo fui en tren. From Madrid to Toledo I went by train.

Fui a pie desde Madrid hasta Toledo. I walked (all the way) from Madrid to Toledo.

(6) *On*: physical position (**en, sobre**), figurative sense (**sobre**). In the former case the difference is small, **sobre** being rather more emphatic than **en**. **Sobre** and **encima de** often serve to avoid the ambiguity that may occur with **en** (meaning *in* as well as *on*).

Está sentado en una silla. He is sitting on a chair.

Está de pie sobre una silla. He is standing on a chair.

Los platos están en (*or* sobre) la mesa. The plates are on the
table.

Está sobre el (encima del) armario. It is on (on top of) the
cupboard.

Escribió algo sobre la Revolución. He wrote something on
the Revolution.

NOTE: With days and dates the English *on* is rendered by means of
the Spanish definite article [§ 53, Note 4].

(7) *Under*: physical position (**debajo de, bajo**), figurative
sense (**bajo**). In the former case **debajo de** is more concrete
than **bajo** (*cf.* English *underneath*).

Le encontré debajo de la mesa. I found him under(neath)
the table.

Estaban jugando bajo los árboles. They were playing under
the trees.

Estaban bajo el mando de Napoleón. They were under
Napoleon's command.

(8) *Through*: =*on account of* (**por**); otherwise (**por, a(l)
través de**). In the latter sense **por** is usual; **a(l) través de**
indicates greater length or penetration.

por lo que le había dicho su padre, through what his father
had told him

Vinimos por el parque. We came through the park.

Se escapó por la ventana. He escaped through the window.

Se veía como a través de una niebla. It could be seen as
through a mist.

A través de todo el libro se advierte lo mismo. Through-
(out) the whole book one notices the same thing.

(*d*) The preposition **por** (*through*) may add a notion of means,
movement or direction when it is used before a compound preposition indicating place (or before the corresponding adverb).

Saltó por encima de la tapia. He jumped over the wall.

Cinco soldados sostenían el escudo por debajo. Five
soldiers held the shield firm (from) underneath.

Luego atacaron por detrás de la compañía C.   Then they attacked behind C Company.

Examiné la casa con mucho cuidado por dentro y por fuera.   I examined the house very carefully inside and out.

(*e*) The prepositions **antes de** and **después de** are replaced by the conjunctions **antes que** and **después que** when used before the subject of an unexpressed verb.

Mi hermano llegó antes que yo.   My brother arrived before me (*or* before I did).

Se marchó antes que su padre.   He left before his father.

Los demás terminaron mucho después que él.   The rest finished long after him (*or* after he did).

NOTE: Compare with this the distinction between **más de** and **más que**.

Yo escribí más de media página.   I wrote more than half a page.

Yo escribí más que tú.   I wrote more than you.

95. STRONG PERSONAL PRONOUNS.   Besides the weak object pronouns or *con*junctive pronouns (that join *with* the verb, §§ 58–62, 89), there are in Spanish two series of strong or *dis*junctive personal pronouns (*i.e.*, pronouns that stand *apart from* the verb): the reflexive series and the non-reflexive series.   In the first persons and the second persons familiar the two series coincide.

		Reflexive	Non-Reflexive
(1)	(yo)	mí	mí
(2)	(tú)	ti	ti
	(usted)	sí	usted
(3)	(él)	sí	él
	(ella)	sí	ella
(1)	(nosotros)	nosotros	nosotros
(2)	(vosotros)	vosotros	vosotros
	(ustedes)	sí	ustedes
(3)	(ellos)	sí	ellos
	(ellas)	sí	ellas

96. Use of the Strong Personal Pronouns. (*a*) The disjunctive pronouns are used after prepositions. The reflexive series is used if the prepositional object refers back to the subject of the verb; the non-reflexive forms if the prepositional object refers to some person other than the subject. The adjective **mismo (-a, -os, -as)** may, for emphasis, be added to a reflexive pronoun and, more rarely, to a non-reflexive pronoun.

Lo hago para mí (mismo). I do it for myself.

Mi hermano lo hace para mí. My brother does it for me.

A ver si vuelves en ti. Let's see you pull yourself together.

Todos estamos pensando en ti. We are all thinking of you.

Usted se olvida de sí (misma). You (*fem. sing.*) are forgetting (about) yourself.

No podemos olvidarnos de usted. We can't forget you.

Tiene bastante para sí (misma). She has enough for herself.

No tengo bastante para ella. I haven't enough for her.

No nos fiamos de nosotros mismos. We don't trust ourselves.

Estaban hablando de nosotros. They were talking about us.

Ustedes siempre están pensando en sí mismos. You are always thinking of yourselves.

Tengo mucha confianza en Vds. I have a lot of confidence in you.

Se pelean entre sí. They fight amongst themselves.

Hay desacuerdo entre ellos. There is disagreement amongst them.

Se lo mandé a usted mismo. I sent it to you yourself (*i.e.*, your very self).

(*b*) The preposition **con** joins with the disjunctive pronouns **mí, ti** and **sí** to give respectively **conmigo, contigo** and **consigo**.

Quería estudiarlo conmigo. He wanted to study it with me.

¿Lo han discutido contigo? Have they discussed it with you?

¿Han soñado ustedes alguna vez consigo mismos? Have you ever dreamed about yourselves?

(c) The disjunctive pronoun is frequently used to lend emphasis to a direct or indirect personal object expressed by means of a conjunctive pronoun, to define that object more exactly or to prevent ambiguity (i.e., the conjunctive pronoun becomes pleonastic, cf. §61). The personal a is used before the disjunctive pronoun.

Yo no le veo a Juan y él no me ve a mí. I don't see John and *he* doesn't see *me*.

¿Quién le acompañó a usted? Who went with you?

No nos convence ni a él ni a mí. It doesn't convince either him or me.

Se enseñan a sí mismos. They teach themselves [cf. §91 (b), especially Note 3].

The emphasis is greater if the disjunctive pronoun is expressed first.

A ti te veo todos los días. I see *you* every day.

A usted le parece que es mentira, ¿verdad? Pues a mí también. *You* think it's a lie, don't you? Well, so do I.

A nosotros nos parece algo dudoso. It seems rather doubtful to *us*.

(d) When a weak *direct* object pronoun is in the first or second person (i.e., **me, te, nos, os**), a weak *indirect* object pronoun is replaced by **a** with a strong pronoun.

Me manda a usted. He sends me to you.

Nos acercamos a ellos. We approached them.

but **Se me acercó un francés.** A Frenchman approached me.

(e) The use of the disjunctive personal pronoun is not of course limited to persons.

El edificio se hundió por sí mismo.
The building collapsed of its own accord.

Veíamos el río y poco a poco íbamos acercándonos a él.
We could see the river and gradually we were drawing near to it.

Las aguas del Tajo y este castillo que se refleja en ellas.
The waters of the Tagus and this castle (that is) reflected in
them.

A neuter form **ello** exists for cases where the prepositional object
does not refer to a specific noun.

No estoy seguro de ello.   I am not sure about it.

Está muy contenta con todo ello.   She's very pleased with it
all.

VOCABULARY

antiguo	old, ancient	la niebla	fog, mist
la ayuda	help	la opinión	opinion
ayudar	to help	pálido	pale
bailar	to dance	la pared	wall (of house)
convencer	to convince	el piso	floor, flat
el enfermo	invalid, sick person	por allí	over there, that way
el error	mistake	la postal	postcard
el favor	favour	preparar	to prepare
el gato	cat	reaccionar	to react
generalmente	generally	la salida	exit, way out, departure
importar	to matter	saltar	to jump
el letrero	sign, notice	el sol	sun
la llave	key	sorprender	to surprise
la muralla	wall (of town)	sucio	dirty
nadar	to swim	tapia	(garden) wall

Study also the prepositions listed in § 94.

EXERCISES

I. (a) *Study and translate:* Al lado de él.   Delante de mí.
Hacia nosotros.   Fuera de la ciudad y dentro de ella.   Cerca
de ti.   Delante de usted.   Llegó después que yo.   Después de
las dos y media.   Más allá de la plaza.   El edificio de en
frente.   Ganaba más que yo.   Ganaba más de mil libras al
año.   Estaba detrás de su hermano.   Lo hizo por sí mismo.

Lo escriben para sí mismos. Lo compré para él. Me lo dio a mí. No debéis pensar tanto en vosotros mismos. A ellos les parecía un gran error. Las murallas que vimos alrededor de la ciudad. Según lo que dicen sus padres. Lo hizo sin ayuda de nadie. A ustedes no les hemos convencido, ¿verdad? Con los enfermos nunca se sabe.

(b) *Translate:* For us. With me. Close to him. About six o'clock. With them. She did it herself. Are you sure of it? They went without him. In front of the station. Beyond the garden. Near here. Not very far from the cathedral. Without thinking of his brother. Before the meeting. She made it for herself. Can I go with you? He hasn't any confidence in her. According to what they have told us. He used to eat more than I did. They arrived after him. Besides sending him a postcard. The next-door neighbours and those opposite. They were saying it amongst themselves. From five to six I usually work. What does it matter to *you*?

II. (a) *Study and translate:* 1. Estaban todos detrás de la casa, divirtiéndose con los muchachos de al lado. 2. Lo hicieron todo bajo la dirección de un señor de Madrid. 3. He leído un libro muy interesante sobre los viajes de un inglés por España. 4. Los otros piensan lo mismo que tú, pero no quieren volver a lo de antes. 5. Estos muchachos no saben nadar, pero sí saben bailar y además lo hacen muy bien. 6. Sigue pensando lo mismo de siempre, y no sé cómo le vamos a convencer de su error. 7. Mis padres viven un poco más allá de la plaza principal, no muy lejos de donde vives tú. 8. Veíamos la catedral desde fuera de la ciudad, mucho antes de llegar a la estación. 9. Después de decir esto, salió conmigo a visitar a unos amigos que habíamos conocido en la reunión. 10. Como buenos turistas tuvimos que mirar toda la catedral por dentro y por fuera.

(b) *Translate:* 1. It doesn't matter to me what they are saying, but it does to him. 2. I went with him to see if I could help him. 3. The cat jumped on to the table with the dog behind. 4. Over the door he could see a notice but he couldn't read it. 5. She has sold all the chairs and tables and now they have to eat out. 6. She was sitting (=seated) in front of the door preparing the potatoes for dinner. 7. Besides, he has spoken against the scheme only because he lives inside the town. 8. He had taken his wife to have lunch in a small restaurant that he knew beside the market. 9. I usually arrive before my brother but he generally goes off long (=much) after I do. 10. He was looking for the exit when someone seized him from behind.

III. (a) *Study and translate:* 1. ¿Quién estaba contigo cuando llegaron mis padres? 2. No sabía cómo reaccionar ante tales opiniones. 3. Le preguntó por qué no hacían lo mismo con las casas de enfrente. 4. No quiso comprender que ya no era posible pedirle los mismos favores de antes. 5. Quedé muy sorprendido ante tal opinión y no pude convencerle de su error. 6. Sus amigos iban llegando unos tras otros, algunos tristes, otros más alegres. 7. Todos están contra el nuevo proyecto porque creen que se va a tener que trabajar más. 8. A usted le escribí desde Barcelona y al señor Cantón le mandé una postal desde Tarragona. 9. Parece que el doctor Martínez, al no recibir respuesta, tuvo que pedir la llave a los vecinos de al lado. 10. Alrededor del jardín había una tapia no muy alta donde el perro se sentaba a veces a mirar cómo trabajaban los de la casa.

(b) *Translate:* 1. One was underneath and another on top. 2. They discovered him under the table sleeping beside the dog. 3. "What is the date?" "It is the twenty-sixth of October." 4. They wanted to leave the city on Wednesday at four. 5. I told him that his friend had spoken to me three days before. 6. Until that day I had never arrived before him. 7. We wanted to see him before the departure of the train. 8. Do you know a good book on life in sixteenth-century Spain? 9. Besides French, which is the language of her country, this lady speaks English, German, Portuguese and Italian. 10. He arrived at the hotel at quarter to seven in the evening and asked for a room on the fourth floor.

REVIEW AND DEVELOPMENT
SECTION (III)

97. ANALYSIS OF EXAMPLES.   **Ser** indicates existence; **estar** (from the Latin *stare, to stand*) seeks to localize existence, to set limits to it.

(1) **Soy, más, estoy.   Respiro.**

In this line by a modern Spanish poet, Jorge Guillén, **ser** and **estar** are both used in their rather rare absolute sense (*i.e.*, without any other form of predicate), and the essential difference between them is therefore emphasized.   Translated freely the line might read *I exist; more than that, I am here, now, breathing.* **Ser** affirms only the poet's existence (in an abstract, metaphysical sense); **estar** places him firmly, jubilantly, in the material world around.

(2) **¿Quién es?   Soy yo.**   *Who is it?   It is I.*
   ¿Dónde estás?   Estoy aquí. *Where are you?   I am here.*

The same difference that exists between *to be* in Hamlet's *To be or not to be* and the same verb in *What are you going to be?* exists also between **soy** as used in Guillén's line and **es** and **soy** as used here in the former example.   From affirming pure existence, **ser** has come to be no more than a linking word, like an equals sign in mathematics:

Who is [that person I hear]?   I am [that person you hear].

This is the most usual function of **ser**: to equate or to identify unreservedly a subject with an attribute.   In the second case (with **estar**) the equation (*i.e.*, the identity of the person) is taken for granted.   What is wanted now is something more: a placing of the equation within the material world of the senses.   The answer, **Estoy aquí**, does just that, places the equation, without any pretence at establishing a permanent relationship, within the world of experience.

(3) **Como uno aprende es estu-**   *It is by studying that one*
     diando.   *learns.*
    Está estudiando la lección.   *He is studying the lesson.*

In the first example learning is linked with the act of studying in the form of a generalization; in the second case we come down from generalizations to experience, to a concrete case of a person placed emphatically within a set time (the present) and within definite action (that of studying).

(4) **¿Cómo es tu hermano?**   *What is your brother like?*
    ¿Cómo está tu hermano?   *How is your brother?*

In the first case someone is asked for characteristics that will serve to identify the brother (characteristics, then, considered essential to his being). In the second case the question is not about the brother's identity but about his state: not *what sort of a person is your brother?* but *what state is your brother in?*

(5) **¡Qué ridículo eres!**   *How ridiculous you are!*
    ¡Qué ridículo estás!   *How ridiculous you look!*

In the first case we are emphasizing something we consider essential: *What a ridiculous person you are!* In the second case we are expressing a direct personal observation: *What a ridiculous state you are in!*

(6) **Juan es muy alto.**   *John is very tall.*
    Juan está muy alto.   *John is very tall.*

In the first case there is a simple, unemotional statement of fact: John is associated unreservedly with the quality *tall*, without any suggestion that the relationship might be otherwise. In the less common latter case, on the other hand, the *John-tall* relationship is limited, qualified, presented as something newly observed: the speaker is conscious of a change since last he saw John. **Juan está muy alto** may also refer, of course, to an external circumstance: *John is very high up* (*e.g.*, on a mountain or in the social scale).

(7) **La nieve es blanca.** *Snow is white.*
   La nieve está negra. *The snow is black.*

In the first example the *snow-white* relationship is established as an essential, permanent phenomenon (*i.e., Snow is a white thing*). In the second case *snow-black* is obviously not essential, but accidental (*i.e., The snow is in a black state*). It would be wrong ever to say **La nieve es negra** for it is not true. **La nieve está blanca,** on the other hand, would be possible if one wished to emphasize the whiteness one has observed at a given moment. **Estar,** then, as in the previous example, presupposes a personal appreciation of a noun-adjective relationship; **ser** the acceptance of that relationship as something absolute.

The above distinctions, which aim to present the essential difference between **ser** and **estar** irrespective of grammatical divisions, should be borne in mind during one's study of the more formal treatment that follows.

98. USES OF **ser** [*cf.* §§ 31–33]. (*a*) **Ser** may be used absolutely with the sense of *to exist*.

> **Ser o no ser.** To be or not to be.

(*b*) **Ser** is used also to introduce a complement that is:

(1) a noun or pronoun (expressed or understood, with or without adjectival qualification).

Era un señor muy extraño.	He was a very queer gentleman.
¿Quién es? Soy yo.	Who is it? It is I.
¿Cuál es éste? Es el mismo.	Which is this? It is the same one.
Es la una. Son las cinco.	It is one o'clock. It is five.

(2) a numeral.

Seis y siete son trece.	Six and seven are thirteen.

(3) a verb.

Ver es creer.	Seeing is believing (*lit.,* To see is to believe).

156

Es hablando como uno llega a conocer a la gente.	It is by talking that one comes to know people.

NOTE: Progressive tenses, where no simple equation is expressed, take **estar** [§ 97 (3)].

(4) an adjectival element indicating an inherent or essential quality.

El hielo es frío.	Ice is cold (*i.e.*, a cold thing).
Es muy agrio (de carácter).	He is very ill-tempered (*i.e.*, an ill-tempered person).
Su hijo es muy alto.	His son is very tall (*i.e.*, a tall boy).
Era de una sensibilidad extraordinaria.	He was of extraordinary sensitivity (*i.e.*, a sensitive type of person).
Estas cucharas son de plata.	These spoons are silver (*i.e.*, objects of silver).
Machado era de Sevilla.	Machado was from Seville (*i.e.*, a native of Seville).

99. USES OF **estar** [*cf.* §§ 31–33]. (*a*) **Estar** may occasionally be used without any further complement [§ 97 (1)]; usually an adverbial element is understood.

¿Está tu padre? No, no está.	Is your father in? No, he is not.
¿Estamos (de acuerdo)?	(Are we) agreed?

(*b*) For the rest, **estar** is used to indicate position, real or figurative.

No está por aquí.	He is not around here (hereabouts).
Estamos en una situación bastante difícil.	We are in rather a difficult situation.
¿A cuántos estamos? (Estamos) a dos.	What is the date? (It is) the second.

This includes position with respect to a verbal action (*i.e.*, the progressive tenses).

Estaba esperando a su madre.	He was waiting for his mother.
Están bebiendo demasiado.	They are drinking too much.

It also includes position with respect to an adjectival quality (*i.e.*, indicates a state or an attitude rather than an essential characteristic viewed in its permanence).

Este té está frío.	This tea is cold (*i.e.*, in a cold state).
Las paredes están sucias.	The walls are dirty (*i.e.*, in a dirty state).
Está de muy mal humor.	He's in a very bad mood (*i.e.*, in an ill-humoured state; *contrast* **Es muy agrio (de carácter,)** § 98 (*b*) (4)).
Su hijo está muy alto.	Her son is very tall (indicating a notable change, § 97 (6) and § 98 (*b*) (4)).

NOTES: 1. The English *to be hot, to be cold* may be translated into Spanish in four different ways according to whether one refers to persons (**Tengo mucho calor,** *I am very hot*), weather (**Hace un frío terrible,** *It is terribly cold*), an inherent characteristic in an object (**El hielo es frío,** *Ice is cold*), or an accidental characteristic in an object (**Esta sopa está muy caliente,** *This soup is very hot*).

2. **Estar** may at times be replaced by **encontrarse, hallarse** or **quedar**: by **encontrarse** and **hallarse** (both meaning literally *to find oneself*) when there is emphasis on the state of being or simply to indicate position; by **quedar** (lit., *to remain, be left*) to show acquisition of a state.

¿Cómo te encuentras hoy?   How are you (*or* do you feel) today?
Allí se hallaban los mismos señores de siempre.   The same men as ever were (to be found) there.
Quedó muy sorprendida al saber esto.   She was very surprised to learn this.

VOCABULARY

Revise the words listed in Lessons XI–XV

EXERCISES

I. (a) *Study and translate:* Este café está muy dulce. La silla estaba rota. La comida estaba muy caliente. La puerta era verde. Su madre es andaluza. Soy yo. ¡Qué pálida está! Las paredes estaban muy sucias. ¿De quién fue esta idea? Fue del señor Maurín. Está muy alegre hoy. ¡Qué triste es esta poesía! Yo estaba muy triste cuando la escribí. Esa política es mala. La niebla es negra. Yo estaba negro por la niebla. Es muy difícil explicar la diferencia entre *ser* y *estar.*

(b) *Translate:* My father is in Paris. Who is it? It is Mr and Mrs González. His wife is American but he is Spanish. He is a great friend. We are sad because they are soon going away. Where are these soldiers from? They are from the south. The windows were open. It has been foggy. Fog is bad for invalids. He had been in France and Italy. Are you cold? It has been very hot this summer. He is looking at the clock. The water is very cold. She is tired because she has been working in the factory. This postcard is very nice but it is torn.

II. (a) *Study and translate:* 1. Lo importante es no decir a nadie lo que piensan hacer. 2. Se está muy bien aquí, ¿verdad?, con el tiempo que hace desde que llegamos. 3. Ha habido mucha niebla y las ventanas están muy sucias. 4. — ¿Dónde está la salida de la estación? — No estoy seguro, pero creo que está por allí. 5. Me escribió hace tres o cuatro días, pero no me dio su nueva dirección. 6. El pobre gorrión tenía un ala rota y nosotros no sabíamos qué hacer. 7. Estuvimos más de media hora hablando con él, pero no quiso creer lo que le decíamos. 8. Tuve que marcharme sin haber hablado con el dueño ni estudiado el nuevo proyecto. 9. Hace ya muchos años que viene repitiendo lo mismo y pidiendo favores a los distintos ministros. 10. Llevábamos ya más de veinte minutos esperando a cierto amigo andaluz, cuando se nos acercó un turista alemán.

(b) *Translate:* 1. On Thursdays he comes back from school at six o'clock. 2. He asked me for the Spanish book that I gave to you. 3. The walls of my room are yellow but they are very dirty now. 4. Haven't you been to see what they are doing with the new hospital? 5. It is very cold today but we are warm because we have drunk several cups of tea. 6. We were all very tired after having worked so hard (=so much) in the factory. 7. "He was very thirsty and wanted a glass of water." "Why didn't he ask for it?" 8. The truth is that at seven o'clock, when his parents arrived, he had still not finished the third lesson. 9. But they all talked to him in German and he couldn't understand what they were saying. 10. At three o'clock every day, he comes in, closes the door, and counts the money they have earned in the shop.

III. (a) *Study and translate:* 1. Están muy alegres desde que volvieron de su viaje al Brasil. 2. Yo no le conozco ni he sabido nunca dónde vive. 3. Llevo más de media hora esperándole. 4. Estás muy pálida. ¿Qué te ha pasado? 5. — ¿Conoce usted a su madre? — Sí, la conozco. Es muy joven y además muy hermosa. 6. Estuvo bastante enfermo después de la muerte de su mujer y ahora está muy viejo. 7. No saben decir cosas bonitas, pero sí saben hacerlas y eso es lo más importante. 8. Lo siento mucho, señores, pero no puedo ni debo decir lo que piensa hacer ahora el ministro. 9. — ¿De dónde es su amigo? — Es del sur de España, pero hace ya muchos años que vive en este país. 10. Hacía mucho frío cuando estuvimos nosotros, porque estaban abiertas todas las ventanas.

(b) *Translate:* 1. The sun rose at six o'clock and at seven we were in Córdoba. 2. It was cold and raining when I first saw Mr Ferrer. 3. It is almost half past seven and our parents still haven't arrived. 4. To whom have you given the books I was going to show John? 5. In England men drink a lot of water, but in South America they prefer wine. 6. "What is your sister like?" "She is tall and has black hair and blue eyes." 7. Philip is from Peru but he has been living in Spain for more than five years.   8. We went to old Madrid with Mr López, but we were cold and tired and we saw little.   9. Last year she would get up at half past seven in the morning and go to bed at quarter past eleven at night. 10. We have bought a house outside the town, but it is very old and many of the windows are broken.

IV. *Re-translate the keys given for Lessons XI–XV [pp. 353–357] and compare your versions with the originals.*

LESSON XVI

100. VERBS WITH AN INFINITIVE. Used with a dependent infinitive some verbs take no preposition (**me mandó hacerlo**, *he ordered me to do it*), whilst others are followed by **a, de, en, por, con** or **para** (**me ayudó a hacerlo**, *he helped me to do it*; **insistieron en hacerlo**, *they insisted on doing it*; **se esforzó por hacerlo**, *he strove to do it*; **soñó con hacerlo**, *he dreamed of doing it*; **sirve para hacerlo**, *it serves to do it*).

(1) *Verb + Pure Infinitive* (*i.e.*, without a preposition)

(i) A few verbs when used impersonally, with the infinitive as the real subject of the sentence.

Me alegra verla.

I am pleased to see her (*lit.*, To see her cheers me).

Le gusta acompañarnos.

She likes to go with us (*lit.*, To accompany us is pleasing to her).

Hace falta estudiar más.

It is necessary to study more (*lit.*, To study more is needed).

Se me olvidó traértelo.

I forgot to bring it you (*lit.*, To bring it you forgot itself to me).

Me parece haberla visto.

I seem to think I have seen her (*lit.*, To have seen her seems to me).

Nos conviene hacerlo.

It is best that we do it, It is a good (*or* wise) thing for us to do it (*lit.*, To do it is fitting to us).

(ii) Verbs of advising, making, ordering, permitting and preventing, of which the most common are:

aconsejar	to advise to	**hacer**	to make
dejar	to let, to allow to	**impedir**	to prevent

mandar	to order to, to command to	**permitir**	to permit to
		prohibir	to forbid to

A su hija no le permite salir. He doesn't allow his daughter to go out.

No le dejaron terminar. They didn't let him finish.

Nos mandaron hacerlo. They ordered us to do it.

Les prohibió a sus hijos salir. He forbad his children to go out.

NOTES: 1. The infinitive is here the direct object, and the person to whom the advice, command, etc., is directed is the indirect object.

2. An infinitive may have passive sense after these verbs: **Lo mandé hacer** or **Mandé hacerlo** (*I ordered it to be done*, i.e., *I ordered [someone] to do it*), **Hizo abrir la ventana** (*He had the window opened*).

(iii) The verbs of the senses **ver** and **oír**.

La vi llegar, pero no la oí subir.

I saw her arrive but I did not hear her come up.

NOTE: As with the verbs under (ii) so also after **ver** and **oír** an infinitive may have passive sense: **Vio matar a su hijo** (*He saw his son killed*), **Oí decir que no venía** (*I heard it said he was not coming*).

(iv) Certain other verbs when the subject is the same as that of the infinitive. The most common are:

anhelar	to long to	**evitar**	to avoid -ing
buscar	to seek to	**intentar**	to try to
confesar	to confess to	**lograr**	to succeed in -ing
conseguir	to manage to	**merecer**	to deserve to
creer	to believe (that)	**necesitar**	to need to
deber	to have to, must	**negar**	to deny -ing
decidir	to decide to	**ofrecer**	to offer to
decir	to say (that)	**parecer**	to appear to, to seem to
desear	to desire to, to wish to	**pedir**	to ask to
determinar	to determine to	**pensar**	to intend to
esperar	to hope to	**poder**	to be able to, can

163

preferir	to prefer to	**saber**	to know how to
procurar	to try to	**sentir**	to regret to, to be
prometer	to promise to		sorry to
querer	to want to	**soler**	to be wont to
resolver	to resolve to	**temer**	to fear to

Decidió no casarse con él.	She decided not to marry him.
Parecen dudar de lo que dice.	They seem to doubt what he says.
Vd. prometió no decírselo a nadie.	You promised not to tell anyone.
Ella no sabe bailar.	She can't dance.
Siento mucho tener que decirle esto.	I regret very much having to tell you this.

NOTES: 1. This construction should be used in Spanish even where the English has two finite verbs, except that in less literary language a *que* clause is usual after verbs of saying and thinking.

Siento no poder acompañarle.	I'm sorry I can't go with you.
Creo $\left\{\begin{array}{l}\textbf{haberle}\\\textbf{que le he}\end{array}\right\}$ **visto en alguna parte.**	I think I've seen him somewhere.

2. **Deber de** translates the *must* of supposition.

Deben de ser las cinco.	It must be five o'clock

(2) *Verb + a + Infinitive*

(i) Verbs implying motion to a given end.

Entró a hablar con mi padre.	He came in to talk to my father.
Me enviaron a entregárselo.	They sent me to hand it over to him.
Nos sentamos a comer.	We sat down to eat.
Subió a ver lo que pasaba.	He went up to see what was happening.
Vuelve a vernos mañana.	He is coming back to see us tomorrow.
Pasé por su casa a recoger un libro.	I called at his house to pick up a book.

NOTE: **Volver a,** besides meaning *to return and,* also means *again*:

Volvió a explicarnos lo mismo.   He explained the same thing
to us again.

(ii) Verbs of forcing, inviting and exhorting, of which the most
common are:

animar a	to encourage to, to urge to	**invitar a**	to invite to
forzar a	to force to	**obligar a**	to oblige to, to compel to
inducir a	to induce to	**persuadir a**	to persuade to

Le animaron a continuar.   They urged him to continue.
¿Qué la induce a pensar así?   What induces her to think like
that?

NOTE: **Hacer** and verbs of ordering take a pure infinitive [above,
(1) (ii)].

(iii) Verbs of beginning, of which the most common are:

comenzar a	to begin to	**empezar a**	to begin to
echar(se) a	to begin to, to set off -ing	**ponerse a**	to set about -ing
		romper a	to start -ing

Empieza a llover.   It is beginning to rain.
Se echó a reír como un loco.   He burst out laughing like a
madman.

(iv) Certain other verbs, of which the most common are:

acertar a	to happen to	**ayudar a**	to help to
acostumbrarse a	to get used to -ing	**comprometerse a**	to undertake to
alcanzar a	to manage to	**contribuir a**	to contribute to -ing
aprender a	to learn to	**decidirse a**	to decide to
aspirar a	to aspire to	**dedicarse a**	to devote oneself to -ing
atreverse a	to dare to		
autorizar a	to authorize to	**detenerse a**	to stop to

disponerse a	to prepare to, to get ready to	**pararse a**	to stop to
enseñar a	to teach to	**quedarse a**	to remain to, to stay to (*or* and)
exponerse a	to expose oneself to -ing	**resignarse a**	to resign oneself to -ing
negarse a	to refuse to	**resolverse a**	to make up one's mind to
oponerse a	to object to -ing		

Se quedó a comer con nosotros.	He stayed to lunch with us.
Se detuvo a hablar con alguien.	He stopped to talk to somebody.
¿Cómo te atreves a hablarle de esa manera?	How do you dare to speak to him in that way?

(3) *Verb* + **de** + *Infinitive*

(i) Verbs that indicate separation from an action (*i.e.*, leaving off, dissuading, etc.).

acabar de	to finish -ing	**excusar de**	to excuse from -ing
cansarse de	to grow tired of -ing	**guardarse de**	to take care not to
cesar de	to cease -ing		
dejar de	to leave off -ing, to stop -ing	**hartarse de**	to grow tired of -ing
no dejar de	not to fail to, to be sure to	**parar de**	to cease -ing
disuadir de	to dissuade from -ing	**terminar de**	to finish -ing

Acabó (*or* **Terminó**) **de leerlo.**	He finished reading it.
Se cansó de no hacer nada.	She grew tired of doing nothing.
La disuadí de ir sola.	I dissuaded her from going alone.
Me excusé de terminarlo.	I excused myself from finishing it.

NOTE: **Acabar de** also means *to have just* [§ 73 (*b*)].

(ii) Certain other verbs of which the most common are:

acordarse de	to remember to	**haber de**	to be to, to have to
acusar de	to accuse of -ing	**jactarse de**	to boast of -ing
alegrarse de	to be glad to	**maravillarse de**	to wonder at -ing, to marvel at -ing
arrepentirse de	to repent of -ing	**olvidarse de**	to forget to
avergonzarse de	to be ashamed of -ing	**no poder menos de**	not to be able to help -ing
desesperar de	to despair of -ing	**tratar de**	to try to
encargar de	to entrust with -ing	**tratarse de**	to be a question of -ing
encargarse de	to undertake to		

No se acordó de haberle visto.	He didn't remember having seen him.
Me alegro mucho de conocerle.	I am very pleased to know you.
Se encargó de hablar con él.	He undertook to have a talk with him.
No puedo menos de aprobar su acción.	I cannot (help) but approve of his action.

(4) *Verb + en + Infinitive*

Important verbs that take **en** are:

complacerse en	to take pleasure in -ing	**dudar en**	to hesitate to
consentir en	to consent to	**empeñarse en**	to insist on -ing
consistir en	to consist in -ing	**entretenerse en**	to amuse oneself -ing
convenir en	to agree to	**esforzarse en**	to strive to
divertirse en	to amuse oneself -ing	**hacer bien en**	to do well (*or* right) to

hacer mal en	to do badly (*or* wrong) to	**persistir en**	to persist in -ing
insistir en	to insist on -ing	**quedar en**	to agree to
ocuparse en	to busy oneself -ing	**tardar en**	to take (a long) time -ing
pensar en	to think of -ing	**vacilar en**	to hesitate to

Él se empeña en hacer lo mismo.	He insists on doing the same.
No dudó en aceptar tal condición.	He did not hesitate to accept such a condition.
Haces mal en no ayudarle.	You do wrong not to help him.
Tardó bastante en contestarme.	He took a considerable time to reply to me.

(5) *Verb* + **por** + *Infinitive*

(i) Verbs of great longing and striving, the most important being:

esforzarse por	to strive to	**rabiar por**	to yearn to, to ache to
luchar por	to fight to	**suspirar por**	to sigh to, to yearn to

Se esfuerza por hacerlo bien.	He strives to do it well.
Estaba rabiando por marcharse.	He was aching to go.

NOTES: 1. **Anhelar, buscar, desear, esperar** and **querer** (*i.e.*, verbs of less violent longing) take a pure infinitive.

2. **Esforzarse** is also used with **en** [above, (4)].

(ii) Verbs of beginning and finishing *by*:

Empezaron por leer los periódicos.	They began by reading the papers.
Terminó por matarse.	He ended up by killing himself.

NOTE: **Empezar por** (*to begin by* -*ing*) is not to be confused with **empezar a** (*to begin to*); nor is **terminar por** (*to finish by* -*ing*) to be confused with **terminar de** (*to finish* -*ing*).

(iii) Before an infinitive that indicates action still to be done.

El tren aún estaba por salir.	The train still hadn't gone.
Está por escribir la historia de este reinado.	The history of this reign is yet to be written.
La segunda parte queda por hacer.	The second part remains to be done.

NOTES: 1. A Spanish active infinitive may, as in the second and third examples, correspond to an English passive infinitive.

2. **Estar por** also translates the English *to be inclined to, have a good mind to* [§ 57 (*b*)]: *e.g.*, **estoy por decir . . .**, *I am inclined to say* . . . (but have not yet said).

(6) *Verb* + **con** + *Infinitive*

Common verbs which take **con** are:

amenazar con	to threaten to	**soñar con**	to dream of -ing
contentarse con	to content oneself with -ing		
Soñaba con vivir en el campo.		I dreamed of living in the country.	
Se contenta con anotar los ejemplos.		He contents himself with noting down the examples.	

(7) *Verb* + **para** + *Infinitive*

servir para	to serve to	**estar para**	to be about to

Este instrumento sirve para medir la fuerza del viento.
This instrument serves to measure the force of the wind.

NOTE: Also in this lesson can be considered the following two verbs which do not take an infinitive but a gerund: **seguir** and **continuar,** both meaning *to continue, carry on.*

Sigue trabajando como siempre.   He continues to work as ever.

101. ADJECTIVES AND NOUNS WITH AN INFINITIVE. (*a*) An adjective or noun is followed by the pure infinitive only when that infinitive can be considered as the real subject of the sentence.

This is frequently the case after verbs such as **ser, resultar** and **parecer.**

Es fácil hacer esto.   It is easy to do this (To do this is easy).

Es imposible verle hoy.   It is impossible to see him today.

Nos resultó difícil hacerlo.   It proved difficult for us to do it.

Parece prudente dejarle solo.   It seems wise to leave him alone.

Es una lástima tener que ir.   It is a pity to have to go.

Era un error pensar así.   It was a mistake to think thus.

No vale la pena hacerlo.   It is not worth while doing it.

Es mi deber decirle la verdad.   It is my duty to tell him the truth.

(*b*) If the infinitive cannot be considered as the subject of the finite verb a preposition must be used. This preposition is usually **de.**

Esto es fácil de hacer.   This is easy to do.

Nos resultó imposible de hacer.   It proved impossible for us to do.

Es mío el deber de decirle la verdad.   The duty of telling him the truth is mine.

Estoy contento de estar aquí.   I am pleased to be here.

No era capaz de hacerlo.   He was not capable of doing it.

Estaba deseoso de conocerla.   He was desirous of knowing her.

Tenía miedo de vernos.   He was afraid of seeing us.

Es la hora de marcharnos.   It is time for us to go.

¿Me haces el favor de leerlo?   Would you please read it?

Tengo la costumbre de visitarla.   I am in the habit (*lit.*, have the habit) of visiting her.

(*c*) Prepositions other than **de** are used in certain limited cases, of which the following are the most important.

(1) **A** is used after the noun **tendencia** (*tendency*), and with certain adjectives most of which indicate tendency (imposed or from within) towards a given action:

acostum-brado a	accustomed to	**aficionado a**	fond of -ing

atento a	attentive to -ing	**dispuesto a**	prepared to, willing to
convidado a	invited to		
decidido a	determined to	**inclinado a**	inclined to
		obligado a	obliged to
		resuelto a	resolved to

NOTE: In general, the corresponding nouns take **de**: **la costumbre de trabajar** (*the habit of working*), **la obligación de ganarse la vida** (*the obligation to earn one's living*).

(2) **En** is used with nouns and adjectives corresponding to § 100 (4), and with **el primero (único, último) en**, *the first (only one, last one) to*; **(el) inconveniente en**, *(the) obstacle to -ing, disadvantage in -ing*, and **(el) gusto en**, *(the) pleasure in -ing*.

> **Tiene empeño en hacer lo mismo.** He insists on doing the same.
> **Estaba ocupada en terminarlo.** She was busy finishing it.
> **No hay inconveniente en pensarlo.** There is nothing against thinking it.
> **Tengo mucho gusto en conocerle.** I am (very) pleased to meet you.

but **Es el inconveniente de pensar así.** It is the disadvantage of thinking thus.
> **No conoce el gusto de no hacer nada.** He doesn't know the pleasure of doing nothing.

(3) **Para** is used:

(i) in expressions of motive and aim.

No tiene motivo para llorar.
He has no cause for tears.
No es más que un pretexto para no ir.
It is only a pretext for not going.
Es el paso más serio que se ha dado para llegar a una solución.
It is the most serious step that has been taken to reach a solution.

(ii) in expressions of suitability and adequacy.

No tuvo fuerzas para hacerlo.

He hadn't the strength to do it.

Tengo lo necesario para vivir.

I have what is necessary to live on.

Es un momento oportuno para hablarle.

It is a suitable moment to talk to him.

Era una cosa demasiado íntima para hablar delante de testigos.

It was too intimate a matter to talk of in front of witnesses.

Tiene el oído poco apto para apreciar estos matices.

His ear is ill-suited to the appreciation of these nuances.

(4) **Por** is used with nouns expressing haste and striving [*cf.* § 100 (5) (i)].

No tengo ninguna prisa por entrar.

I am in no hurry to go in.

No hizo ningún esfuerzo por aclarar su propia actitud.

He made no effort to clarify his own attitude.

Es la eterna lucha por salir de la incertidumbre.

It is the eternal struggle to escape from uncertainty.

102. VERBS, ADJECTIVES AND NOUNS WITH A CLAUSE. A verb, adjective or noun which takes a preposition before an infinitive, takes the same preposition before the **que** that introduces a corresponding noun clause.

Se acordó de que no estabas. He remembered you were not in.

Es una prueba de que me ama. It is a proof that he loves me.

Estoy seguro de que le conoces. I am sure you know him.

NOTE: If the noun clause can be considered as the subject of the main verb no preposition is used [*cf.* §§ 100 (1) (i), 101 (*a*)].

Es seguro que ha vuelto ya. It is certain that he has already come back.

VOCABULARY

capaz	able, capable	**oportuno**	suitable, oppor-
conducir	to lead, to drive		tune
imposible	impossible	**poco a poco**	gradually, little
el miedo	fear, fright		by little
dar miedo	to frighten	**solo**	alone
la necesidad	need, necessity	**el trabajo**	work
la oportuni- dad	opportunity		

costar trabajo a alguien, to be an effort (difficult) for someone

Study also the verbs, adjectives and nouns listed in §§ 100 and 101.

NOTES: 1. The following verbs included in this lesson are radical-changing verbs that were not listed in Lesson XIII:

    I. like **pensar: comenzar, confesar, negar(se)**
       like **contar: avergonzarse, esforzar, forzar**

    II. like **mover: resolver** (*past part.* **resuelto**)

    III. like **mentir: arrepentirse, consentir**
       like **pedir: conseguir, impedir**

Irregular radical-changing verbs are **detenerse** and **entretenerse** (like **tener**) and **convenir** (like **venir**).

2. Verbs ending in *vowel* + **cer** (**parecer, merecer, com- placerse,** etc.) are like **conocer**: *i.e.,* they take **-zc-** in the first person singular of the present indicative.

EXERCISES

I. (a) *Study and translate:* Consigue llegar. Niega haberlo escrito. Se encarga de mandarlo. Trató de verle. Se re- signa a no ir. Le animé a seguir. Se esfuerza por terminarlo. Se avergonzó de haberlo pensado. Me impide hacerlo. Se arrepintió de haberlo dicho. Consintió en no decir nada. Fue imposible verle. Está resuelta a decírselo. Me com- plazco en mirarla. Soy aficionado a comprar cosas viejas. Hice un esfuerzo por terminarlo. Vino a visitarnos.

(b) *Translate:* He advised him to do it. He let me go alone.

He has forgotten to write to us. They saw me talking to her. I grew tired of thinking about it. I am sorry to have to go. He succeeded in seeing him. You feared to come. They forced him to come in. He is beginning to understand. They are striving to finish. He prevents my doing it. They repented of having broken it. He confesses to having seen me. He has just come in. They managed to get out. I begin again. Are you trying to do the same?

II. (a) *Study and translate:* 1. Hay que procurar tenerlo todo hecho para la semana que viene. 2. Me parecía haberle visto varias veces en casa del primer ministro. 3. Siempre hacen falta personas dispuestas a trabajar en los pueblos pequeños. 4. Nunca para de decirnos todo lo que ha hecho con sus hijos. 5. Fue entonces cuando empezó a sentirse enferma y a insistir en volver a casa. 6. Me acordé de que habían decidido no volver hasta la semana siguiente. 7. Creo que se va aceptando poco a poco la necesidad de ganarse la vida trabajando. 8. Se ha dicho que hizo bien en no contestar a la carta que le habían mandado. 9. Estábamos cansados de la visita y de estar todo el tiempo hablando de cosas tan poco importantes. 10. Me cuesta trabajo acostumbrarme a la idea de vivir solo en una ciudad tan grande como ésta.

(b) *Translate:* 1. I am sure he is capable of doing it alone. 2. They promised not to say anything to anyone. 3. I am glad to have had the opportunity of knowing him. 4. They agreed to wait until the following Monday. 5. I had the idea he didn't want to come and have lunch with us. 6. Are you prepared to teach me to drive this new car I have just bought? 7. We must acknowledge the necessity of accepting such a scheme. 8. He forgot to tell you that his brother wanted to come and see you. 9. I had just read the first chapter when my son came up to say good-bye. 10. A year ago I had the idea you were not working enough and now it almost frightens me to see you working so hard.

III. (a) *Study and translate:* 1. ¿Por qué te empeñas en creer que yo quiero engañarle? 2. Siempre me gusta descansar después de un día de mucho trabajo. 3. No me parecía momento oportuno para hablar de cosas tan importantes. 4. No hubo manera de hacerle comprender que no debía ir sola. 5. A todos nos ha gustado la idea de ir a pasar el verano en casa de los abuelos. 6. No pudo encontrarlos y ahora sintió haberles contado lo del telegrama que le había mandado su padre. 7. Cuando supo esto, no le costó trabajo obligar a su hijo a confesar lo que había hecho. 8. No quiero perder la oportunidad de ir a visitarlos al pasar por allí. 9. La idea consiste en ir comprando casas para luego venderlas más caras. 10. Algunos días me despierta a las siete y media y otros me deja dormir hasta alrededor de las nueve.

(b) *Translate:* 1. He strove to understand what we were explaining to him. 2. She speaks French and now she is beginning to learn Spanish. 3. I am pleased to know you do not regret having helped me. 4. We didn't dare think of the difficulty of doing it alone. 5. She came in to say good-bye to us before leaving for the station. 6. He insists on inviting Mr and Mrs Martínez to dinner. 7. He was the only one to arrive in time to hear the prime minister speak. 8. It was a mistake to try to convince him of the necessity of such a policy. 9. It frightens me to think of what may happen if he refuses to help us. 10. I am sure he intends to spend the summer travelling through Switzerland and Italy.

LESSON XVII

103. THE FUTURE TENSE (English *I shall buy, you will buy,* etc.). The future is formed by adding to the *infinitive* the endings **-é, -ás, -á, -emos, -éis, -án.** This applies to verbs of all three conjugations.

I. comprar	II. vender	III. vivir
compraré	venderé	viviré
comprarás	venderás	vivirás
comprará	venderá	vivirá
compraremos	venderemos	viviremos
compraréis	venderéis	viviréis
comprarán	venderán	vivirán

Compraremos una tienda. We shall buy a shop.
Se venderán periódicos. Newspapers will be sold.
Vivirá aún muchos años. He still has many years to live.

104. THE CONDITIONAL (English *I should buy, you would buy,* etc.). The conditional is formed by adding to the infinitive the endings **-ía, -ías, -ía, -íamos, -íais, -ían.** The same endings are used for the three conjugations.

I. comprar	II. vender	III. vivir
compraría	vendería	viviría
comprarías	venderías	vivirías
compraría	vendería	viviría
compraríamos	venderíamos	viviríamos
compraríais	venderíais	viviríais
comprarían	venderían	vivirían

Dijo que lo compraría.	He said he would buy it.
Venderíamos muchos más, pero no tenemos.	We should sell a lot more, but we haven't [any].
¿Dónde viviría usted?	Where would you live?

105. THE FUTURE PERFECT (English *I shall have bought, you will have bought,* etc.). The future perfect is formed by the future tense of **haber** (irregular: **habré, habrás,** etc.) together with the past participle of the verb.

Mañana lo habrá leído todo.	Tomorrow he'll have read it all.
¿Habrá podido usted hacerlo?	Will you have been able to do it?

106. THE CONDITIONAL PERFECT (English *I should have bought, you would have bought,* etc.). The conditional perfect is formed by the conditional of **haber** (**habría, habrías,** etc.) together with the past participle of the verb.

Dijo que la habría comprado.	He said he would have bought it (*fem.*).
Se habría marchado, pero su hermano llegó a las ocho.	He would have left, but his brother arrived at eight o'clock.

107. IRREGULAR FUTURES AND CONDITIONALS. The *endings* of the future and conditional tenses offer no irregularities; the only irregularities are in the body of the verb (*i.e.,* cases in which it is not the infinitive to which the endings are added).

	Future	*Conditional*
caber	cabré, -ás, -á, etc.	cabría, -ías, -ía, etc. [§ 111]
decir	diré, -ás, -á, etc.	diría, -ías, -ía, etc.
haber	habré, -ás, -á, etc.	habría, -ías, -ía, etc.
hacer	haré, -ás, -á, etc.	haría, -ías, -ía, etc.
poder	podré, -ás, -á, etc.	podría, -ías, -ía, etc.
poner	pondré, -ás, -á, etc.	pondría, -ías, -ía, etc. [§ 111]
querer	querré, -ás, -á, etc.	querría, -ías, -ía, etc.
saber	sabré, -ás, -á, etc.	sabría, -ías, -ía, etc.

salir	saldré, -ás, -á, etc.	saldría, -ías, -ía, etc.
tener	tendré, -ás, -á, etc.	tendría, -ías, -ía, etc.
valer	valdré, -ás, -á, etc.	valdría, -ías, -ía, etc.
venir	vendré, -ás, -á, etc.	vendría, -ías, -ía, etc.

NOTES: 1. The following verbs, though irregular in some of their parts, are quite regular in the future and conditional: **ser, estar, ver, dar, ir, conocer, traer, caer, oír.** Oír will of course lose the accent on the **i** because the stress moves to the ending: **oiré, oirás,** etc.; **oiría, oirías,** etc.

2. Because in the future and the conditional the stress falls on the ending, there will be no change of stem vowel in radical-changing verbs: **pensaré, pensarás,** etc.; **moveré, moverás,** etc.; **pediré, pedirás,** etc.

108. A SPECIAL USE. The Spanish future may indicate supposition or probability with present time, the conditional with imperfect past time, the future perfect with perfect past time and the conditional perfect with pluperfect past time. English usage frequently coincides.

Él estará trabajando como siempre y ella (estará) divirtiéndose por ahí con sus amigas.

I suppose he's working the same as ever, and she's probably out gallivanting with her friends.

¿Qué hora sería cuando llegó? Serían las dos.

What time would it be when he arrived? It was about two o'clock.

Habrás visto la película que ponen en el Capitol, ¿verdad?

I suppose you've seen the film that's on at the Capitol, haven't you?

No habría terminado la lección cuando usted le vio. ¿O sí?

He probably hadn't finished the lesson when you saw him. Or had he? (Or perhaps he had?)

109. OTHER WAYS OF TRANSLATING THE ENGLISH *shall, will, should, would.* (*a*) An interrogative *shall* introducing or asking for a suggestion must be translated by the Spanish present tense;

a corresponding affirmative *shall* may be so translated in conversational style.

¿Lo dejamos para mañana?	Shall we leave it until tomorrow?
¿Qué hago si no contesta?	What shall I do if he doesn't reply?
Voy (*or* **Iré**) **esta tarde si quieres.**	I'll go this afternoon if you want.

(*b*) The English *shall, will, should* and *would* emphasizing action
as intended or destined to take place is usually translated by the
present or imperfect of **haber de.**

Le prometo que he de re-husarlo.	I promise you I shall refuse it.
Yo estaba seguro de que había de volver.	I was sure he would return.

(*c*) The English emphatic forms indicating determination (*I
will, you shall, he shall,* etc.) may be translated into Spanish by
placing the affirmative particle **sí,** *yes* (negative **sí que no**) before
the future tense of the verb. The verb may occasionally be
replaced by **eso.**

— Yo nunca haré esto. — Sí lo harás.	"I shall never do this." "You will." (*lit.,* Yes [indeed] you will do it.)
— Él lo hará. — Eso sí que no.	"He will do it." "He will not." (*lit.,* That indeed not.)
Ella sí que no vendrá.	She shall (certainly) not come.

(*d*) *Should* implying duty or obligation is translated by some
part of **deber,** *to have to, must,* with the pure infinitive.

Esto $\left\{ \begin{array}{l} \textbf{debe} \\ \textbf{debería} \end{array} \right\}$ **tomarse en cuenta.**	This should be taken into account.
$\left\{ \begin{array}{l} \textbf{Debías haberle dicho} \\ \textbf{Habrías debido decirle} \end{array} \right\}$ **la verdad.**	You should have told him the truth.

NOTE: In the simple tense (first example) the present indicative
implies that something *is to be* taken into account, the conditional

that it *ought to be* (but may not be). In the compound tense (second example) this distinction disappears and the versions given are interchangeable.

(*e*) English *will* and *would*, especially in questions and negations, may indicate disposition (*to be willing*) rather than future action. In such a case the verb **querer** is used in Spanish (also **estar dispuesto a,** *to be disposed to*, and, in negative sentences, **negarse a,** *to refuse to*).

¿**Quiere usted decirme dónde está?**	Will you tell me where he is?
No quiere ir; no está dispuesto a ir; se niega a ir.	He won't (is unwilling to, refuses to) go.
No quería hacerlo; no estaba dispuesto a hacerlo.	He wouldn't (was unwilling to) do it.
No quiso hacerlo; se negó a hacerlo.	He wouldn't (was unwilling to, refused to) do it.

NOTE: In the last two examples **no quería** and **no estaba dispuesto a** indicate a state of unwillingness; **no quiso** and **se negó a** suggest downright refusal.

(*f*) Closely associated with the last section are examples in which the English *will* or *would* (often accompanied by the word *please*) implies a request. This is translated into Spanish by means of **querer,** or **hacer el favor de,** or by a combination of the two (**querer hacer el favor de**). The expression **tener la bondad de** is similar but rather less frequent (*cf.* English *Would you be so good as to*).

¿**Quieres ponerme un poco de agua?**	Please will you pour me a drop of water?
¿**Quieres hacer el favor de mirar esto?**	Would you please have a look at this?
¿**Haría usted el favor de pasarme el vino?**	Would you mind passing the wine, please?

110. Todo (*all, the whole of, every, everything*). (*a*) As an adjective **todo** precedes the noun it qualifies. If an article or some other adjective is expressed before the noun, it is placed after **todo**.

> **todo el día,** the whole day (*lit.*, all the day)
> **todo hombre sensato,** every sensible man
> **todas sus buenas ideas,** all his good ideas
> **todos los años,** every year
> **todas estas dificultades,** all these difficulties
> **toda España,** the whole of Spain

(*b*) As a translation of the English *everything, all* (*of it, of them*), *the whole* (*of it, of them*), **todo(s)** is used in conjunction with the appropriate third-person weak object pronoun.

Lo tengo todo. I have everything (*lit.*, I have it all).
La he leído toda. I have read the whole of it (*fem.*).
Los he visto a todos. I have seen them all (persons).
Las ha estudiado todas. He has studied all of them (*fem.*).
Todo lo hace mal. He does *everything* badly.

111. Two Irregular Verbs: **caber** and **poner**.

caber, *to fit in*

pres. ind.:	quepo, cabes, cabe, cabemos, cabéis, caben
imp. ind.:	cabía, cabías, cabía, cabíamos, cabíais, cabían
preterite:	cupe, cupiste, cupo, cupimos, cupisteis, cupieron
future:	cabré, cabrás, cabrá, cabremos, cabréis, cabrán
conditional:	cabría, cabrías, cabría, cabríamos, cabríais, cabrían
past part.:	cabido
gerund:	cabiendo

Yo no quepo aquí. There's no room for me here.
Estos libros no caben todos en mi cartera. My brief-case won't hold all these books.
No cabe duda. There is no doubt (*lit.*, Doubt does not fit in).
Cabe pensar en otra explicación. It is possible to think of another explanation.

poner, to put, place

pres. ind.:	pongo, pones, pone, ponemos, ponéis, ponen
imp. ind.:	ponía, ponías, ponía, poníamos, poníais, ponían
preterite:	puse, pusiste, puso, pusimos, pusisteis, pusieron
future:	pondré, pondrás, pondrá, pondremos, pondréis, pondrán
conditional:	pondría, pondrías, pondría, pondríamos, pondríais, pondrían
past part.:	puesto
gerund:	poniendo

Se puso la mano sobre el corazón. He put his hand on his heart.

El sol se pone. The sun sets.

poner la mesa, to lay the table

ponerse (colorado, pálido, etc.), to turn, grow (red, pale, etc.)

Se puso como un tomate. He went as red as a beetroot (*lit.*, went like a tomato).

ponerse a, to begin to, set about -ing

Nos pusimos a trabajar con ellos. We set to work with them.

Like **poner** are its compounds: **suponer** (*to suppose*), **exponerse** (*to expose oneself*), etc.

VOCABULARY

el cuchillo	knife	**el pretexto**	pretext
la cuenta	account, bill	**el recuerdo**	recollection, souvenir, memory
esperar	to hope, to expect, to wait for		
		resolver	to solve, to resolve
examinar	to examine		
junto	together	**el salón**	sitting-room
la maleta	suitcase	**en seguida**	at once, immediately, straight away
Méjico	Mexico		
mejor	better, best		
el modo	way, means	**suponer**	to suppose, to presuppose
el número	number		
el plato	plate		

hacer una maleta	to pack a suitcase
darse cuenta de	to realize
{**de este (tal, otro) modo** **de esta (tal, otra) manera**}	in this (such a, another) way
esperar (decir, creer) que sí	to hope (say, think) so
esperar (decir, creer) que no	to hope (say, think) not

Revise the verbs listed in Lesson XVI.

EXERCISES

I. (a) *Study and translate:* No querrá ir. Tendremos que pensarlo. Lo haré mañana. No podré acompañarle. Te mandará hacerlo. Usted se expondrá a tener que contestarle. Valdría la pena comprar otro. Convendrán en ir juntos. Había que pensarlo primero. ¿Qué habrá pasado? Deberíamos decirle algo. No estoy dispuesto a hablar con él. Será difícil comprenderlo todo. ¿Por qué no quiere usted contestarme? Estaremos todos pensando en ti. Me gustaría hacerlo. Iríamos todos con usted.

(b) *Translate:* He will see. They will know. It will appear. He will strive to finish it. I shall want to know. He will be able to tell us (it). What would you say? It would be better for us to remain here. I shall go tomorrow. He won't reply. They will lay the table. Will they fit in? There is no other explanation possible. He would have done the same. Will you go with me? What time will it be? He must be ten or eleven years old. I should do it today. Shall I come back tomorrow?

II. (a) *Study and translate:* 1. Se tardará bastante en dar de comer a los pequeños. 2. ¿Abro la ventana o la dejo cerrada? 3. — Los otros no habrán oído nada, ¿verdad? — Espero que no. 4. Tomaremos muy temprano el desayuno y a las ocho estaremos ya en la Estación del Norte. 5. Ocurrirá lo mismo con los nuevos vecinos y sólo podremos salir los jueves por la noche. 6. Supongo que tomarán la visita del abuelo como un pretexto para divertirse. 7. ¿Quieres

subir estas maletas al cuarto número ciento cuarenta y siete?
Está en el quinto piso. 8. Esta guía nos será muy útil para
el viaje que pensamos hacer por el sur de España. 9. ¿Te
parece que ella se dará cuenta de lo que pensamos hacer al
dejarla con los señores de Cantón? 10. Estas flores las
guardaré siempre como mi mejor recuerdo de los días tan
hermosos que hemos pasado aquí.

(b) *Translate:* 1. What will you do if your brother refuses to
help you? 2. He undertook to do it himself but he wouldn't
say by when. 3. We shall have to prepare the whole lesson
for next Thursday. 4. You should try to find another way
of solving all these difficulties. 5. "I shall invite him to have
lunch with us tomorrow." "You will *not*." 6. It would be
better to find some pretext for going to visit him in his house.
7. It will be difficult to get (=persuade) him to go away
without her. 8. He won't allow us to go alone if we don't
promise to come back before nine o'clock. 9. I cannot
acknowledge the necessity of such a scheme nor will I help
you to convince others of its importance. 10. You have
probably heard what the new minister intends to do with
those who took part in the revolution.

III. (a) *Study and translate:* 1. Isabel, ¿quieres ayudarme a hacer
estas maletas? 2. ¿Qué cree usted que harán al darse cuenta
de que nos hemos marchado sin ellos? 3. Tendría unos
treinta y cinco años cuando se murió. 4. Se pondrá muy
triste al saber que pensamos marcharnos esta misma noche.
5. Ya no volverán aquellos días tan alegres que pasábamos
juntos viajando por España e Italia. 6. Dijo que al día
siguiente iría a visitar a unos señores que había conocido en
Segovia. 7. ¿Cómo cree usted que vamos a caber todos en un
salón tan pequeño como éste? 8. ¿Le traigo un cuchillo y un
plato o prefiere usted tomar café en seguida? 9. Dice que
nos escribirá a todos: a ti desde la Argentina, a Felipe desde
Méjico y a mí desde el Brasil. 10. No caben tantas cosas en
una maleta tan pequeña. Deberíamos comprarnos una más
grande.

(b) *Translate:* 1. Will you please return these books to him? 2. Shall I write him a letter explaining what we intend to do? 3. Let's pack the suitcases. I don't know if everything will fit in. 4. I have examined all of them and this is the one I like most. 5. "What time would it be when you reached the station?" "It was just one o'clock." 6. I shall have finished reading this book before next week, but I don't like it. 7. We shall have to convince him of the necessity of accepting our ideas on the new hospital. 8. "What would *you* do on receiving such a letter?" "I should try to persuade him to come and visit me." 9. "He says he won't do it because it is late." "He *will* (do) because I shall order him to (=lo)." 10. I have an American friend who intends to spend all next year travelling round (=through) Europe.

LESSON XVIII

112. THE FORMATION OF THE PRESENT SUBJUNCTIVE

(a) Regular Verbs

I. -ar verbs: stem plus endings **-e, -es, -e, -emos, -éis, -en.**
II. -er verbs: stem plus endings **-a, -as, -a, -amos, -áis, -an.**
III. -ir verbs: stem plus endings **-a, -as, -a, -amos, -áis, -an.**

I. **comprar**	II. **vender**	III. **vivir**
compre	venda	viva
compres	vendas	vivas
compre	venda	viva
compremos	vendamos	vivamos
compréis	vendáis	viváis
compren	vendan	vivan

(b) Radical-Changing Verbs

(1) In accordance with § 84 (a) radical-changing verbs undergo a change of stem under stress (*i.e.*, in the first, second and third persons singular and in the third person plural).

que (yo) cierre	that I (may, should) close
que (tú) cuentes	that you (may, should) relate
que usted pierda	that you (may, should) lose
que (él) mueva	that he (may, should) move
que (nosotros) cerremos	that we (may, should) close
que (vosotros) mováis	that you (may, should) move
que ustedes mientan	that you (may, should) lie
que (ellos) pidan	that they (may, should) ask for

(2) Radical-changing verbs of the third conjugation also have a stem vowel change of **e** to **i** and **o** to **u** in the first and second persons plural [*cf.*, §§ 85 and 86].

186

mentir	pedir	dormir
mienta	pida	duerma
mientas	pidas	duermas
mienta	pida	duerma
mintamos	pidamos	durmamos
mintáis	pidáis	durmáis
mientan	pidan	duerman

(c) *Irregular Verbs*

caber	quepa, quepas, quepa, quepamos, quepáis, quepan
caer	caiga, caigas, caiga, caigamos, caigáis, caigan
conocer	conozca, conozcas, conozca, conozcamos, conozcáis, conozcan
dar	dé, des, dé, demos, deis, den
decir	diga, digas, diga, digamos, digáis, digan
estar	esté, estés, esté, estemos, estéis, estén
haber	haya, hayas, haya, hayamos, hayáis, hayan
hacer	haga, hagas, haga, hagamos, hagáis, hagan
ir	vaya, vayas, vaya, vayamos, vayáis, vayan
oír	oiga, oigas, oiga, oigamos, oigáis, oigan
poder	pueda, puedas, pueda, podamos, podáis, puedan
poner	ponga, pongas, ponga, pongamos, pongáis, pongan
querer	quiera, quieras, quiera, queramos, queráis, quieran
saber	sepa, sepas, sepa, sepamos, sepáis, sepan
salir	salga, salgas, salga, salgamos, salgáis, salgan
ser	sea, seas, sea, seamos, seáis, sean
tener	tenga, tengas, tenga, tengamos, tengáis, tengan
traer	traiga, traigas, traiga, traigamos, traigáis, traigan
valer	valga, valgas, valga, valgamos, valgáis, valgan
venir	venga, vengas, venga, vengamos, vengáis, vengan
ver	vea, veas, vea, veamos, veáis, vean

NOTES: 1. In all irregular verbs which have a final **o** in the first person singular of the present indicative (*i.e.*, in all except **dar, estar, haber, ir, saber** and **ser**) the present subjunctive has the same stem as that first person:

e.g., **caber:**   quepo; quepa, quepas, etc.
    caer: caigo; caiga, caigas, etc.

2. Like **conocer** are other verbs ending in *vowel* + **cer**.

e.g., **parecer:**   parezco; parezca, parezcas, etc. [p. 173, Note 2].

3. Like these irregular verbs are their compounds.

e.g., **suponer:**   supongo; suponga, supongas, etc.
  atraer: atraigo; atraiga, atraigas, etc.
  convenir: convengo; convenga, convengas, etc.

113. The Perfect Subjunctive.   This is formed by the present subjunctive of **haber** with the appropriate past participle.

  que haya comprado   that I (may, should) have bought
  que hayas vendido   that you (may, should) have sold

114. The Use of the Subjunctive.   The subjunctive is most frequently used in subordinate clauses in which the action of the verb is not presented as a fact or reality, but rather as a hypothesis or future possibility.   It is thus used:

(1) After verbs, adjectives and nouns that imply influence on other people or things (*i.e.*, expressions of wanting, requesting, permitting, forbidding, causing, necessity, etc.).   The desired or forbidden or necessary action is not at the moment a fact; it must be made one, or prevented from becoming one.

Quiere que me marche de aquí.   He wants me to leave here.
Prefiero que lo hagas tú.   I prefer *you* to do it.
Me ha pedido que lo devuelva.   He has asked me to give it back.
No debemos permitirle que vaya.   We must not let him go.
Le prohibe a su hijo que vuelva.   He forbids his son to come back.
Haremos que el puente se derrumbe.   We shall make the bridge collapse.
Dile a Juan que se marche.   Tell John to go away.
Le he mandado que lo haga hoy.   I have ordered him to do it today.
Quiere persuadirme a que los acompañe.   He wants to persuade me to go with them.
Hace falta que vayan ellos también.   *They* must go too.

188

Es preciso que hablemos con el autor.   It is necessary for us
to speak to the author.

NOTES: 1. In sentences of the type *I prefer to go, He asks to go, He
let himself fall,* where the wanting, requesting, etc., is aimed at one's
own actions, Spanish uses a pure infinitive construction: **Prefiero
ir, Pide ir, Se dejó caer.**

2. The pure infinitive construction may be used also with verbs
of ordering, preventing, permitting and forbidding (but not of
requesting or telling) even where the influence is on *another* person's
actions. This other person is then expressed as the indirect object
of the first verb.

Le mando hacerlo. ⎫
Le mando que lo haga.⎭ I order him to do it.

Nos permite acompañarlos. ⎫   He allows us to go with
Nos permite que los acompañemos.⎭   them.

but only **Me pide (dice) que lo haga.**   He asks (tells) me to do it.

3. Verbs implying stimulus to action [§ 100 (2) (ii)] may take
a+infinitive or **a que**+subjunctive. In each case the person
acted upon is expressed as a direct object. For the **a** in **a que**
see § 102.

Los he invitado⎰**a venir.** ⎱   I have invited them to come.
            ⎱**a que vengan.**⎰

(2) When the statement in the subordinate clause is presented
as probably or certainly contrary to fact.

Dudo que venga.   I doubt whether he will come (*i.e.,* the statement *he will come* is probably false).

Niega que sea así.   He denies it is so (*i.e.,* the statement *it is so*
is presented as false).

Veo dudoso que nos escriba.   I consider it doubtful whether
he will write to us.

Es increíble que él haya dicho eso.   It is incredible that he
should have said that.

No es cierto que esté trabajando.   It is not true that he is
working.

No creo que se resuelva de ese modo.   I don't think it will
be solved in that way.

No parece que tenga razón.   It does not seem that he is right.

No es seguro que haya llegado.   It is not certain he has arrived.

Contrast:

No dudo que vendrá.   I don't doubt that he will come (*i.e.*, the statement *he will come* is considered to be true).

Creo que no irá.   I think he will not go (*i.e.*, the statement *he will not go* is probably true).

No cabe duda de que esto es verdad.   There is no doubt that this is true.

Estoy convencido de que le veremos.   I'm convinced we shall see him.

Es evidente que no podemos ir.   It is obvious that we cannot go.

NOTES: 1. After an open question the indicative is usual (**¿(No) cree usted que es verdad?** *Do(n't) you think it's true?*), though a subjunctive may occasionally be used to indicate particular doubt.

2. After the negative imperative [§ 117 (*a*)] of a verb of *thinking* or *saying*, the indicative is used:

No creas que soy tonto.   Don't think I'm a fool.

(3) After expressions of possibility and probability.

Es posible que no lo haya hecho.   It is possible that he has not done it.

Puede que esto sea verdad.   It may be that this is true.

Es probable que le veamos.   It is probable that we shall see him.

Existe la posibilidad de que no vuelva.   There exists the possibility that he will not come back.

(4) After subordinating conjunctions when they introduce future or otherwise hypothetical action.

> **Te avisaré en cuanto se marche.**
> I shall let you know as soon as he goes.

but **Me despido en cuanto se presenta su padre.**
> I take my leave as soon as his father appears.

No iremos mientras no conteste a nuestra carta.

We shall not go so long as he does not answer our letter.

but **No le vemos mientras su primo está en Madrid.**

We do not see him whilst his cousin is in Madrid.

Usted se quedará aquí hasta que venga.

You will stay here until he comes.

but **Se quedan de pie hasta que el presidente se marcha.**

They remain standing until the president leaves.

Se lo dirán cuando le vean.

They will tell him so when they see him.

but **Le vemos cuando vamos a su casa.**

We see him when we go to his house.

Lo hacen en secreto de modo que él no se entere.

They do it in secret so that he will not find out.

but **Lo hacen en secreto, de modo que él no se entera.**

They are doing it in secret so that (in consequence) he does not find out.

Lo haré aunque él esté aquí.

I shall do it even if he is here.

but **Lo haré, aunque él está aquí.**

I shall do it, even though he is here.

NOTE: Certain conjunctions and related phrases *always* take the subjunctive:

(i) **antes (de) que** (*before*) and **para que** (*in order that*), because with these conjunctions the action of the subordinate clause is never a reality at the time of the action of the main clause.

Siempre llega antes de que yo me marche.

He always arrives before I leave.

Nos escribe a menudo para que sepamos dónde está.

He writes to us frequently so that we may know where he is.

(ii) **sin que** (*without*), **no es que** (*it is not that*), **no porque** (*not because*), for the action of the subordinate clause is rejected as contrary to fact.

Lo hace sin que le ayude nadie.

He does it without help from anybody

No es que le encuentre antipático.

It is not that I find him unlikable.

Se odian mutuamente y no es porque sean rivales.

They hate one another, and it is not because they are rivals.

(iii) **a condición de que** (*on condition that*), **con tal que** (*provided that*), **a no ser que** (*unless [it be that]*), **a menos que** (*unless*), because the subordinate clause presents a mere hypothesis or condition.

Se lo daré a condición de que no se lo diga a nadie.

I shall give it him on condition that he doesn't tell anyone.

Iré con tal que nadie se entere.

I shall go provided no one finds out.

Es seguro que vendrá, a no ser que se muera antes.

It's certain that he'll come, unless he dies beforehand.

(5) After relative pronouns when the antecedent is hypothetical (*i.e.*, not a specific person or thing).

Estoy buscando a alguien que me limpie los zapatos.

I am looking for someone to clean my shoes.

No hay nadie que piense como yo.

There is nobody who thinks as I do.

No encuentro quien me aconseje.

I cannot find anyone to advise me.

No hay obstáculo que no se pueda vencer.

There is no obstacle that cannot be overcome.

¿Conoces algún inglés que me enseñe su lengua?

Do you know any Englishman who will teach me his language?

Haremos cuanto podamos.

We shall do whatever we can.

Nos encontraremos donde [a Vd.] le parezca mejor.

We shall meet where you think best.

No lo creo por mucho que me lo digas.

I don't believe it however much you tell me so.

Las haremos por difíciles que sean.

We shall do them however difficult they may be.

A dondequiera que vaya el inglés, se porta como en su propia casa.

Wherever the Englishman goes, he behaves as in his own home.

De cualquier manera que se estudie el proyecto, siempre se llega a la misma conclusión.

In whatever way one studies the plan, one always arrives at the same conclusion.

NOTES: 1. If the antecedent is accepted as a reality no subjunctive is used, for the relative clause then becomes a statement of fact. Thus, with the above compare **Conozco a alguien que me limpia los zapatos, Éste es un obstáculo que no se puede vencer, ¿Estamos donde querías?**

For the use and omission of the personal **a** before a personal antecedent, see § 47. The **a** is here omitted before **quien** because **quien**, unlike **alguien**, is not part of the main clause: it is the subject of the subordinate clause, its antecedent being unexpressed.

2. **Cualquier**, in the last example, is an apocopated form of the adjective **cualquiera**, *whichever, whatever*. Note the plural **cualesquier(a)**.

(6) Finally, the subjunctive is used in clauses dependent on expressions of emotion or evaluation. Here the action of the subordinate clause is often a reality, but it is a reality subordinated to the emotion or evaluation; hence the subjunctive.

Siento que usted se marche.

I am sorry you are going.

Me alegro de que esté aquí.

I am glad he is here.

Me extraña que se comporte así.

I am surprised that he behaves like that.

Tiene miedo de que le vuelvan a encontrar.

He is afraid lest they find him again.

Será mejor que vayas a casa.

It will be better for you to go home.

Es raro que lo haya hecho así.

It is strange that he should have done it like that.

Será inútil que les pidamos más.

It will be useless for us to ask more of them.

Encuentro muy justo que él haya muerto de la misma manera.

I find it very just that he should have died in the same manner.

NOTE: Distinguish carefully between the expressions of judgment referred to here and those of belief [Section (2)] which take a subjunctive only in certain cases.

115. A NOTE ON THE SUBJUNCTIVE. The subjunctive constitutes one of the most important aspects of Spanish grammar and one of those in which a careful study of examples will prove most rewarding. Unlike the distinction between **ser** and **estar,** which will cause difficulties at every stage of one's study of Spanish, the difference between the indicative and the subjunctive is one that with practice will soon be felt. Study closely the abundant examples given in § 114 and those contained in the exercises at the end of this and succeeding lessons.

VOCABULARY

la alegría	joy, cheerfulness	**indudable**	without doubt, indubitable
el amor (a)	love (of)		
animar(se)	to cheer, to brighten, to liven (oneself) up	**loco**	mad
		mal	badly
		de manera que	so that
atraer	to attract	**de modo que**	
el cielo	sky	**necesario**	necessary
convenir	to be fitting, to be appropriate	**el nombre**	name
		la organiza-ción	organization
lo(s) demás	the rest, *pl.* the others		
		el peligro	danger
el dinero	money	**el perdón**	forgiveness
dudar (que)	to doubt (whether)	**¡Perdón!**	Forgive me! I beg your pardon!
extrañar	to surprise, to seem strange to		
		por ... que	however
		preciso	necessary; precise
el fantasma	phantom		
feliz	happy	**prestar**	to lend
gastar	to spend	**el puesto**	position, post

| **puesto que** | since (= because) | **vencer** | to conquer, to overcome |
| **vano** | vain | **volverse** | to become, to turn, to go |

Study also the conjunctions used in § 114 (4).

EXERCISES

I. (a) *Give the first and third persons plural of the present subjunctive of:* caber, creer, comprar, morir, pedir, merecer, preferir, resolver, dormir, gastar, arrepentirse, marcharse, perder, contar, poder, oír, saber, poner, estar, ir, sentarse, consentir, decir, dar, comer, convenir, detenerse.

(b) *Study and translate:* Se empeña en que lo aceptemos. No creo que tenga razón. Le digo que lo termine. Es posible que se quede a comer. Cuando yo vuelva. Es mejor que se sepa. Preferimos que no venga. Niego que esto sea verdad. Es indudable que vendrá. Quiero que usted lo piense. Antes de que nos muramos. Hasta que te lo pidamos. No hay ni uno que sepa escribir. Por mucho que queráis. Es preciso que consintáis en hacerlo. Hace falta que no nos arrepintamos de lo que hemos hecho. Sin que nadie la haya visto.

(c) *Translate:* Before they go away. Until he comes. As soon as he has finished. He forbids him to consent. Unless it rains. Without his realizing it. There is nobody who can swim. It is sure that he will want to go with us. However cheap these houses are. I am glad he has asked us for it. I am sorry you must leave so soon. He doesn't want to have to do it alone. It is necessary that we repent. Before we get back. In order that he may say so (= **lo**). That they may deserve it. Even though he should offer it to us. So that they may recognize him.

II. (a) *Study and translate:* 1. Por mucho que trabaje, nunca tendrá tanto dinero como su hermano. 2. Te aconsejo que lo pienses bien antes que sea demasiado tarde. 3. ¿También te parece mal que sienta la muerte de un amigo? 4. Es indudable que aquí no caben más personas. 5. No conviene que sepa lo que hicimos con el otro dinero que nos dejó. 6. Me he vuelto loca de alegría, porque ya no me parece imposible que me quiera. 7. ¿Qué importa que no tengamos las mismas ideas sobre la vida si vivimos felices uno con otro? 8. Es mejor que nadie sepa el nombre de nadie. Así no hay peligro de que se descubra demasiado. 9. ¿No es verdad que pocos días antes de salir de aquí gastaste más de dos mil pesetas comprando cosas para tu viaje? 10. No hay nada que atraiga más en amor que lo imposible, «el vano fantasma de niebla y luz» que decía Bécquer.

(b) *Translate:* 1. I prefer to remain here until they come. 2. It is possible that he will do it tomorrow morning. 3. He is looking for a woman who can read this. 4. I am very pleased they have been so lucky. 5. Do you want me to tell you what *I* should do? 6. We must prevent his realizing what we have done. 7. I doubt whether it will rain, although the sky *is* rather black. 8. You must promise me that you won't go out again without my knowing it. 9. I will not rest (= cease) until he loves this girl as much as he loved the one over the way (= opposite). 10. He hasn't yet returned the book I lent him but he says he will give it to my brother when the latter passes through London.

III (a) *Study and translate:* 1. Parece que a su padre no le ha gustado que se vaya. 2. Se ha expuesto a que todos piensen mal de él. 3. No hace falta que usted pida perdón puesto que no ha hecho nada malo. 4. No encuentro a nadie que esté dispuesto a ayudarme en esto. 5. Está demasiado acostumbrada a que todos hagan lo que ella quiere. 6. En cuanto Pedro la vuelva a ver es indudable que volverá a quererla. 7. No hay inconveniente en que usted lo sepa con tal que no se lo diga a nadie. 8. ¿Es posible que usted haya venido aquí sin saber adónde venía? 9. No hay nada que le anime tanto como vencer una dificultad. 10. No te extrañará que te hable de lo que piensa hacer tu hermano, ¿verdad?

(*b*) *Translate:* 1. I am pleased your uncle has not forbidden you to go with us.   2. We shall go even if it rains all night.   3. I don't say he is as intelligent as you [are].   4. They want us to stay and help them with the meeting.   5. I am afraid I shall not be able to come and see you tomorrow.   6. In this organization there is no position that is not important.   7. But is it possible that you have still not understood?   8. I am sure my grandfather is going to be pleased when he knows this.   9. There is no man, however bad he may be, who is not disposed at times to help others.   10. Forgive me. I didn't know you were here.   I promise you it won't happen again.

LESSON XIX

116. THE FORMATION OF THE IMPERATIVE. Spanish imperative forms exist only for the second persons familiar.

(a) Regular Verbs

I. **-ar** verbs: stem plus **-a** (sing.), **-ad** (pl.): **compra, comprad.**
II. **-er** verbs: stem plus **-e** (sing.), **-ed** (pl.): **vende, vended.**
III. **-ir** verbs: stem plus **-e** (sing.), **-id** (pl.): **vive, vivid.**

(b) Radical-Changing Verbs

In accordance with § 84 (a) these undergo a change of stem vowel in the singular.

cerrar	cierra	cerrad	**contar**	cuenta	contad
perder	pierde	perded	**mover**	mueve	moved
mentir	miente	mentid	**dormir**	duerme	dormid
pedir	pide	pedid			

(c) Irregular Verbs

decir	di	decid	**salir**	sal	salid
estar	está	estad	**ser**	sé	sed
hacer	haz	haced	**tener**	ten	tened
ir	ve	id	**valer**	val	valed
oír	oye	oíd	**venir**	ven	venid
poner	pon	poned			

NOTES: 1. Only the singular of these verbs is irregular.

2. The interjection **he** (*this is, see here*) is listed by some grammarians as an irregular singular imperative of **haber**: **Henos aquí** (*Here we are*), **He aquí donde tenemos que empezar** (*This is where we have to begin*).

3. In popular usage the subjunctive form **venga** replaces **ven** and **venid,** when corresponding to the English *Come on.*

Venga, hombre, ¿qué haces? Come on, man, what are you doing?

117. COMMANDS AND EXHORTATIONS (English *Do this, Let's go, Let him try [if he dare],*[1] *May you regret it.*) (*a*) The imperative and the present subjunctive supply between them the Spanish command and exhortative forms. The imperative is used only in affirmative commands with the second persons familiar; elsewhere (including *negative* commands with the second persons familiar) the subjunctive is used. The conjunction **que** generally introduces exhortative forms in the third person.

Compra estos lápices.	Buy these pencils.
No compres estos lápices.	Don't buy these pencils.
Compre usted este lápiz.	Buy this pencil.
No compre usted este lápiz.	Don't buy this pencil.
Que lo compre Juan.	Let John buy it.
Escribamos nosotros.	Let *us* write.
Que vivan muchos años.	May they live many years.
Que vendan ellos los lápices.	Let *them* sell the pencils.
Que los vendan ellos.	Let *them* sell them.
Que abran la puerta ellos.	Let *them* open the door.
Que abra la puerta Juan.	Let *John* open the door.

NOTES: 1. If the subject is expressed it follows the verb and, if heavily stressed, it may follow a short direct object (*cf.* last two examples).

2. **Que** + subjunctive may be used with exhortative sense for the second persons familiar.

Que tengas buen viaje. May you have (*or* Have) a good journey.
Que no dejéis de escribirnos, ¿eh? Now don't fail to write to us.
This is less abrupt than the simple imperative without **que.**

---

[1] Notice that *let* in such cases does indicate exhortation and not permission, for which **dejar** or **permitir** would be used.

(*b*) Weak pronoun objects are placed *after* an affirmative imperative not introduced by **que** and are attached to it; otherwise they precede.

	Shut the door	Shut it	Do not shut it
(**tú**)	Cierra la puerta.	Ciérrala.	No la cierres.
(**usted**)	Cierre Vd. la puerta.	Ciérrela Vd.	No la cierre Vd.
(**vosotros**)	Cerrad la puerta.	Cerradla.	No la cerréis.
(**ustedes**)	Cierren Vds. la puerta.	Ciérrenla Vds.	No la cierren Vds.

Que la cierre Juan. Let John close it.
Mandémosle una felicitación. Let's send him a greeting.

(*c*) In the first person plural of the subjunctive (**compremos, divirtamos**) the final **s** drops out before an attached **nos,** and in the second person plural familiar imperative (**comprad, divertid**) the final **d** drops out before an attached **os.** Both changes, then, concern reflexive verbs.

sentemos; sentémonos	let us set down; let us sit down
levantemos; levantémonos	let us raise; let us get up
acordad; acordaos	remind; remember
divertid; divertíos	amuse; amuse yourselves

NOTE: The **d** in the plural imperative of **irse** is preserved: **Idos,** *Go away*.

(*d*) The first person plural command form tends to be replaced, especially in conversation, by **vamos a**+infinitive.

Vamos a cruzar la calle. Let's cross the road.
Vamos a sentarnos aquí. Let us sit down here.

NOTE: **Ir** is the only verb that has an imperative form for the first person plural: **vamos** (*let us go*) as opposed to the present subjunctive **vayamos**.

118. POSSESSIVE ADJECTIVES AND PRONOUNS. (*a*) Besides the weak series of possessive adjectives [§ 34] there is also the following strong series:

(1) **mío** (-a -os -as) my, of mine   **nuestro** (-a -os -as) our, of ours

(2) **tuyo** (-a -os -as)⎫your,   **vuestro** (-a -os -as)⎫your,
    suyo (-a -os -as)⎭ of yours   **suyo** (-a -os -as)   ⎭ of yours

(3) **suyo** (-a -os -as) {his, of his   **suyo** (-a -os -as) { their,
                         {her, of hers   { of theirs

The possessive pronouns are formed by setting the definite
article before the adjectival forms: **el mío, la mía, los míos, las
mías** (*mine*), etc.   Adjectives and pronouns agree in number and
gender with the thing possessed.

(b) Uses of the Strong Possessive Adjective
This follows the noun it qualifies and is used instead of the
weak possessive adjective

(1) for emphasis.

   ¿Cuál es la hermana vuestra?   Which is *your* sister?

(2) in direct address (especially when the noun is otherwise unqualified).

      Escucha, amigo mío.   Listen, my friend.
      Muy señor mío.   Dear Sir (*in letters*).

(3) to translate the English *of mine, of yours*, etc.

una ambición suya   an ambition of his (hers, yours, theirs)
esas ideas tuyas   those ideas of yours

(4) after the verb **ser.**

Estas casas no son mías.   These houses are not mine.
La fábrica es vuestra, ¿ver- The factory is yours, isn't it?
dad?

NOTE: The pronouns are used when the possessive serves also to
distinguish:

Esta carta es la mía; la otra será la tuya.
   This letter is mine; the other one will be yours.

(c) The Possessive Pronouns (English *mine, yours*, etc.)

Las dos ideas son buenas, pero la mía es mejor que la tuya.
   Both ideas are good, but mine is better than yours.

No conoce felicidad como la nuestra.

He knows no happiness like ours.

(d) Ambiguity

The adjective and pronoun (**el**) **suyo,** (**la**) **suya,** may mean *his, hers, yours* (sing. and pl.) and *theirs*. To avoid confusion **suyo** may be replaced by **de él, de ella, de usted, de ustedes** and **de ellos (de ellas)** respectively.

Estas casas son de él.	These houses are his.
¿Cuáles son las de usted?	Which are yours?
Éste es un hermano de ellos.	This is a brother of theirs.

NOTE: Similarly, the weak possessive adjective **su(s)** [§ 34] may be replaced by **el (la, los, las) . . . de él (ella, usted,** etc.).

El hermano de él fue con la hermana de usted. His brother went with your sister.

VOCABULARY

el abrigo	(over)coat	**el marido**	husband
atender	to attend to	**meter**	to put (into)
callar(se)	to be silent	**preocuparse**	to be worried, to worry
encargarse de	to take charge of, to be responsible for	**propio**	own
		que	for (*conj.*)[1]
el hombro	shoulder	**querido**	dear, beloved
increíble	incredible	**la sinceridad**	sincerity
el invitado	guest	**usar**	to use
lavar	to wash	**verdadero**	real

ir a pie	to go on foot, to walk
estar de pie	to be standing, to stand
meterse en un asunto	to meddle in an affair

[1] Where there is a cause–effect relationship the Spaniard tends to express it more than the speaker of English. Thus, **que** (*for*) is often used in Spanish where a semi-colon might be more appropriate in English.

Venga, hombre, que vamos a llegar tarde.	Come on, man; we're going to be late.

EXERCISES

I. (*a*) *Study and translate:* Comprémonos otro. Búscale en el
salón. Que hagan lo mismo. Vamos a intentarlo. Diver-
tidle. Arrepentíos. Marchémonos. Procure usted hablar
con él. No vuelvas a casa. Vuelva usted mañana. Haz lo
que te parezca. Dígale que no pida más. Que vengan ellos
a decírnoslo. Cuatro hermanas mías. Nuestra casa y la de
ustedes. Estas palabras suyas. ¡Pobre hijo mío ! Esta es
la llave de él. ¿Dónde está la de usted?

(*b*) *Give the four possible renderings of the following:* Go out
(*e.g.*, sal, salga usted, salid, salgan ustedes). Come in. Finish it. Don't look at her. Think of them. Amuse him.
Ask for another. Go to bed. Go to sleep. Don't waken
him. Get dressed. Don't do it. Go home. Be careful.
You do the same. May you be lucky. May you rest.

(*c*) *Translate:* Let us realize its importance. Let him consent
to go with us. Let it rain. Let him come back tomorrow.
May they be happy. Let them repeat it. Let us study the
different aspects. Let him not go and think that we are
afraid. May they finish soon. Let us stay to dinner. These
cities of ours. Those schemes of his. Dear brother. Your
house and mine. This wine and my friend's. My watch
and yours.

II. (*a*) *Study and translate:* 1. —¿Qué me aconsejas que haga?
— Haz lo que quieras. 2. Ve a decirle a tu hermano que
venga a verme en seguida. 3. No vaya usted a creer todo lo
que dicen estos señores. 4. Venga, hombre; ayúdame a
ponerme el abrigo. 5. Pase usted. Es una verdadera
alegría que se haya decidido a venir a vernos. 6. Mientras
tengamos cabeza sobre los hombros, usémosla como debemos. 7. Pero, hijo mío, ¿qué has hecho? ¿Cómo te has
puesto tan sucio? Ve a lavarte en seguida. 8. Salúdela en
mi nombre y dígale que en cuanto termine aquí tendré
mucho gusto en atenderla. 9. Cuando la veas, dile que lo
piense bien, que mire lo que hace, que un marido como él

no se encuentra todos los días. 10. — Pero estamos todos de pie. Sentémonos. — Yo, si ustedes me lo permiten, prefiero estar de pie. — Como usted quiera. Está usted en su casa. Sentémonos nosotros.

(b) *Translate:* 1. Do not go too far, or (=for) you are going to get lost. 2. It is too warm here. Let us go inside. 3. Don't take that letter to your father. Give it to me. 4. Never let them think they have convinced us of their sincerity. 5. Let's see what he says if we accuse him of having lied to us. 6. Tell him to come and see me at once and you come with him. 7. Would you give him these books of mine when you see him? 8. Elizabeth, lay the table, will you; (for) we're going to have dinner straight away. 9. Don't tell him any more. He must accept our explanation however incredible it may appear. 10. Be so good as to write to them all inviting them to come and spend the week with us in the country.

III. (a) *Study and translate:* 1. Déjamelo ver para que sepa cómo es. 2. Venga, anímate, que estás muy triste hoy. 3. Ven a ayudarme a escribir los nombres de los invitados. 4. Sal de aquí y no vuelvas hasta que yo te llame. 5. No se preocupe usted, que yo me encargo de la comida. 6. No deje usted de ir a visitarle cuando esté en Madrid. Es seguro que estará. 7. Piense usted lo que quiera con tal que no se meta en lo que no es cosa suya. 8. Callémonos ya, y vámonos a la catedral a ver si han llegado los amigos de usted. 9. Ve a decirle que ha hecho muy mal en tomar lo que no era suyo. 10. Hay que hablar con él. Que te conozca, que te vea, que te diga lo que piensa hacer al llegar a la capital.

(b) *Translate:* 1. Go and look for the key I gave you a moment ago. 2. Don't read that paper; it is mine. You read your own. 3. Let us sit down here where it is warmer. 4. Do not go before Mr Martínez finishes speaking. 5. Let's go and see what Mrs Fernández is doing. 6. Show me what you have written and I shall tell you if I like it. 7. Tell him to give me back the book as soon as he has read it. 8. Don't

lie. Let me see it and *I*'ll tell you if it's yours or not.
9. Come on (woman), (for) it's incredible you should take so
long to get dressed. 10. Don't tell me that I am the only
one to realize what he is trying to do.

LESSON XX

119. FORMATION OF THE IMPERFECT SUBJUNCTIVE. There are two forms of the imperfect subjunctive, both of which may be obtained from the third person plural of the preterite. The **-ron** ending is taken away and the endings **-ra, -ras, -ra, -́ramos, -rais, -ran** or **-se, -ses, -se, -́semos, -seis, -sen** are added. There are no exceptions: irregularities in the imperfect subjunctive are the same as those in the third person plural of the preterite.

(a) Regular Verbs

I. **comprar:** compraron, compra-

comprara	compráramos	comprase	comprásemos
compraras	comprarais	comprases	compraseis
comprara	compraran	comprase	comprasen

II. **vender:** vendieron, vendie-

vendiera	vendiéramos	vendiese	vendiésemos
vendieras	vendierais	vendieses	vendieseis
vendiera	vendieran	vendiese	vendiesen

III. **vivir:** vivieron, vivie-

viviera	viviéramos	viviese	viviésemos
vivieras	vivierais	vivieses	vivieseis
viviera	vivieran	viviese	viviesen

(b) Radical-Changing Verbs

I.

cerrar cerraron cerrara (cerrase), cerraras (cerrases), etc.
contar contaron contara (contase), contaras (contases), etc.

II.

perder	perdieron	perdiera (perdiese), perdieras (perdieses), etc.
mover	movieron	moviera (moviese), movieras (movieses), etc.

III.

mentir	mintieron	mintiera (mintiese), mintieras (mintieses), etc.
pedir	pidieron	pidiera (pidiese), pidieras (pidieses), etc.
dormir	durmieron	durmiera (durmiese), durmieras (durmieses), etc.

(c) Irregular Verbs

caber	cupieron	cupiera (cupiese), cupieras (cupieses), etc.
caer	cayeron	cayera (cayese), cayeras (cayeses), etc.
dar	dieron	diera (diese), dieras (dieses), etc.
decir	dijeron	dijera (dijese), dijeras (dijeses), etc.
estar	estuvieron	estuviera (estuviese), estuvieras (estuvieses), etc.
haber	hubieron	hubiera (hubiese), hubieras (hubieses), etc.
hacer	hicieron	hiciera (hiciese), hicieras (hicieses), etc.
ir	fueron	fuera (fuese), fueras (fueses), etc.
oír	oyeron	oyera (oyese), oyeras (oyeses), etc.
poder	pudieron	pudiera (pudiese), pudieras (pudieses), etc.
poner	pusieron	pusiera (pusiese), pusieras (pusieses), etc.
querer	quisieron	quisiera (quisiese), quisieras (quisieses), etc.
saber	supieron	supiera (supiese), supieras (supieses), etc.
ser	fueron	fuera (fuese), fueras (fueses), etc.
tener	tuvieron	tuviera (tuviese), tuvieras (tuvieses), etc.
traer	trajeron	trajera (trajese), trajeras (trajeses), etc.
venir	vinieron	viniera (viniese), vinieras (vinieses), etc.

120. THE PLUPERFECT SUBJUNCTIVE. The pluperfect subjunctive is formed by the imperfect subjunctive of **haber** with the past participle of the appropriate verb.

que hubiera (or hubiese) comprado, that I might (should) have bought, that I had bought

121. THE USE OF THE IMPERFECT AND PLUPERFECT SUBJUNCTIVE. (*a*) The imperfect and pluperfect subjunctives are used in the same conditions as the present and perfect subjunctives [§ 114] but generally after different tenses of the main verb. Thus, the present, future, perfect and future perfect are followed by the present or perfect subjunctive, and the imperfect, preterite, conditional, pluperfect and conditional perfect by the imperfect or pluperfect subjunctive.

Present and Perfect Subjunctives

Quiero que le veas. I want you to see him.

Me extraña que no le hayas visto. I am surprised you have not seen him.

Le pedirá a usted que lo haga. He will ask you to do it.

Les he dicho que vuelvan mañana. I have told them to come back tomorrow.

Le habrá dicho que no vaya. He will have told him not to go.

A ver si lo terminamos antes de que nos vean. Let's see if we [can] finish it before they see us.

Imperfect and Pluperfect Subjunctives

Nos pedía que lo hiciéramos. He used to ask us to do it.

No creía que lo hubiera hecho así. I did not think he would have done it like that.

Me mandó que lo terminara. He ordered me to finish it.

Se marchó sin que yo hubiera llegado. He went away without my having arrived.

Sería preciso que usted se lo dijera. It would be necessary for you to tell him so.

Se había empeñado en que no vinieran. He had insisted that they should not come.

Lo habría hecho así para que nadie se enterara. He would have done it like that so that nobody should find out.

(*b*) The above division is not absolute. Thus, where the action of the subordinate clause is definitely past, an imperfect subjunctive may be used where the tense of the main verb would suggest a present subjunctive.

Es posible que no fuera tan malo como se decía.

It is possible he was not as bad as people said.

Le habrá extrañado que no estuvieras.

He must have been surprised that you were not there.

Usted ha hecho que se marchara.

You have made him go away.

Conversely, where the action of the subordinate clause is clearly present or future, a present subjunctive may be used where the main verb would suggest an imperfect.

¿Qué hiciste para que piense así?

What did you do that he should be thinking thus?

Me pidió que te hable.

He asked me to talk to you (*implies:* and I am going to do so now).

In the latter case **Me pidió que te hablara** would be a more usual translation of the English but would merely *relate* what was asked; it would contain no indication of my reaction to the asking. The feeling of which tense to use comes quickly with practice. Study carefully the examples included in subsequent exercises.

NOTE: In the examples given in this paragraph, the **-ra** ending has been used throughout for imperfect and pluperfect subjunctives. In each case the **-se** ending would be equally acceptable.

122. CONDITIONAL SENTENCES. The conjunction **si** (*if*) must be distinguished from those referred to in § 114 (4). Though a **si** clause never presents a fact, the subjunctive is found only in certain cases.

(1) If the condition is open, with no indication whether it is a reality or not, the indicative is used.

Si trabajo, como más.   If I work, I eat more.

Si trabajaba, comía más.   If I worked, I ate more.

Si he trabajado, también he comido.   If I have worked, I have also eaten.

(2) If the condition is felt to be remote, perhaps even contrary to fact, the imperfect or pluperfect subjunctive is used.

Si me muriera, ¿qué harías tú?   If I should die, what would *you* do?

Si trabajara, comería más.   If I worked, I should eat more.

Si hubiera trabajado, comería más ahora.   If I had worked, I should eat more now.

Si hubiera trabajado, habría comido más.   If I had worked, I should have eaten more.

NOTES: 1. The **-se** form of the subjunctive may be used instead of the **-ra** form given above.

2. A conditional perfect in the main clause is usually replaced by the pluperfect subjunctive (**-ra** form). Thus, a more frequent rendering of the last example would be **Si hubiera (or hubiese) trabajado, hubiera comido más.**

3. The future and conditional tenses are found in **si** clauses only when the **si** can be translated by the English *whether*.

> **No sé si trabajará mañana.**   I don't know if he will work tomorrow.
>
> **No sabía si trabajaría.**   I didn't know if he would work.

but **Si trabaja mañana, comerá más.**   If he works tomorrow, he will eat more.

> **Si quisiera (or Si estuviera dispuesto a) trabajar, ganaría más.**   If he would work, he would earn more.

4. The present subjunctive is not used after **si**.

123. THE USE OF THE SUBJUNCTIVE IN MAIN CLAUSES.

(1) The subjunctive is used for all command and exhortative forms except affirmative commands of the second persons familiar [§ 117].

> **Que lo hagan ellos mismos.**   Let them do it themselves.
>
> **Hágalo usted; háganlo ustedes.**   Do it (*pol.*)
>
> **No lo hagas; no lo hagáis; no lo haga Vd.; no lo hagan Vds.**   Don't do it (*fam.* and *pol.*).

but **Hazlo; hacedlo.**   Do it (*fam.*).

(2) Closely associated with this exhortative use is the use of the subjunctive in expressions of the type **diga lo que diga** (*say*

what he will, whatever he says) and **sea quien sea** (*whoever he is, be he who he may*).

No iré, pase lo que pase. I shall not go, whatever happens.
Fuera cual fuese la explicación, no le perdonaría. Whatever the explanation might be, I should not forgive him.

NOTE: The subjunctive occurs twice in each example of this type: in the main clause because there is exhortation, and in the subordinate clause because there is an indefinite antecedent [§ 114 (5)].

(3) Also close to the exhortative is the use of the subjunctive after **ojalá** (*oh that! may! would that!*). If the wish is expressed as an open possibility the present or perfect subjunctive is used; if it is felt to be remote or contrary to fact or likely to prove so, the imperfect or pluperfect is employed.

¡Ojalá no venga mañana! Heaven prevent his coming tomorrow!
¡Ojalá no hayan hablado con él! Let's hope they haven't talked to him!
¡Ojalá lo pudiera terminar! If only I could finish it!
¡Ojalá no lo hubieras hecho! Would that you had not done it!

(4) Both the subjunctive and the indicative are found after **quizá(s)**, **tal vez** and **acaso** (all meaning *perhaps*). The subjunctive indicates a greater degree of doubt than the indicative.

Quizá lo haga mañana. Perhaps I shall do it tomorrow.
Tal vez no sea verdad. Perhaps it is not true.
Quizá se han equivocado. Perhaps they have made a mistake.

(5) The pluperfect subjunctive usually replaces the conditional perfect except when this expresses supposition or probability [§ 108].

Tú hubieras hecho lo mismo. *You* would have done the same.
Hubiéramos debido avisarle. We should have let him know.

(6) The imperfect subjunctive **debiera** often replaces **debería** (*should, ought to*), and **quisiera** usually replaces **querría** (*should like*).

Debieras terminarlo hoy.   You ought to finish it today.
Quisiéramos pasar el verano allí.   We should like to spend the summer there.

VOCABULARY

adorable	adorable	**existir**	to exist
el camino	road, way	**el fin**	end, aim
celoso	jealous	**por fin**	at last
como si	as if	**la lengua**	language,
considerar	to consider		tongue
cumplir	to fulfil, to	**natural**	natural
	accomplish	**el permiso**	permission
la chica	girl	**el problema**	problem
el chico	boy	**el represen-**	representative
(el) Dios	God	**tante**	
disponer	to dispose, to	**el secreto**	secret
	arrange	**sin embargo**	nevertheless,
enamorarse	to fall in love		however
de	with	**el tipo**	type, sort
evidente	obvious, evident	**el valor**	value, worth
exigir	to demand		

¡por Dios!	for heaven's sake! in heaven's name!
¡Dios mío!	good heavens! dear me!
cuanto antes ⎫	as soon as possible
lo antes posible ⎭	
oye (*fam.*), **oiga** (*pol.*)	I say (*to draw attention*; *lit.*, hear)

EXERCISES

I. (*a*) *Give the first person plural* (*both forms*) *of the imperfect subjunctive of:* pensar, volver, consentir, convenir, entretenerse, atraer, saber, comer, visitar, decir, haber, oír, poner, pedir, dormir, caber, querer, contar, resolver, arrepentirse.

(*b*) *Study and translate:* Sin que nadie lo supiera. Antes de que se hiciera. Le dijo que lo hiciese de la misma manera. No hubierais podido prepararlo. Para que no reaccionara así. Yo no quería que nos fuésemos. Sería mejor que no dijera nada. Si hubieseis estado antes. Si usted tuviera bastante tiempo. Ojalá no me pidiera tantos favores. No queríamos que él viniese.

(*c*) *Translate:* Before he asked me for it. So that I might see it. Unless it was his father. Not because he was a friend of mine. If this were true. If he had said this. What would you do? We should write to them straight away. If they were at home. Would that he were sleeping. He advised him to do it. We insisted on his coming. I was used to its being done in another way. It was incredible that they should all be lying. I am sure he had still not seen you.

II. (*a*) *Study and translate:* 1. Ya le oíste anoche exigirte que te quedes hasta el viernes. 2. Si hubieran venido ayer, hubiéramos hablado con ellos. 3. ¡Dios mío! ¡Yo que me alegraba tanto de que fuese soldado! 4. Sin embargo, era natural que él no pensara más que en su propia familia. 5. No sabíamos cómo impedir que llegara a hablar con el ministro. 6. Pero ¡por Dios! ¿qué quieres que haga? Ya sabes que no me ha dejado ni una peseta. 7. Sería adorable si fuese más alegre y no se pusiese tan celosa. 8. Yo no me hubiera dejado engañar así, aunque me hubiera confesado mil veces su amor. 9. Si Dios quisiera que esa chica se enamorase de un hombre como usted, la pobre madre sería la más feliz de las mujeres. 10. Hasta cumplir los dieciocho años, ni había salido de su pueblo, ni sabía que existieran, fuera de los libros, países donde se hablara otra lengua que el español.

(*b*) *Translate:* 1. However, if this were true I should not be here now. 2. It is evident that he has thought about you a lot. 3. If he is right we shall have to accept the new scheme. 4. I want to ask him to reconsider the reply he gave to our representative. 5. They ordered him to repeat what he had said to the officer. 6. If he had approached the house he would have realized what was happening. 7. Although they can no longer defend their former policy, they continue to convince people of their sincerity. 8. As soon as they entered the room John's father opened all the windows. 9. If he had undertaken to do it alone, I should have given him permission to work in the house. 10. We tried hard (=strove) to keep the secret but we couldn't prevent the truth being known at last.

III. (a) *Study and translate:* 1. Si llovía, pasábamos las tardes en casa sin hacer nada. 2. Tuve que ir yo porque no había otro que conociera el camino. 3. Dijo que se lo diría a su padre en cuanto le volviera a ver. 4. Lo difícil fue encontrar gente que la animara a seguir con su proyecto. 5. Fue como si se hubiera descubierto otra manera de resolver ese tipo de problema. 6. Si viene la señora de Martínez, haga el favor de decirle que los martes no recibo a nadie. 7. Aunque fuera verdad lo que dice, yo no estaría dispuesto a prestarle más dinero. 8. Pídale que venga a verme en cuanto se marche el señor Fernández. 9. Eres dueño de disponer de lo tuyo como mejor te parezca, y nosotros hacemos mal en querer descubrir tus secretos. 10. Quiero que me repitas delante de estos señores lo que me dijiste ayer sobre la revolución que se está preparando en el norte.

(b) *Translate:* 1. They did not allow me to do it. 2. If he says that, I think he is right. 3. I should have asked her to do it, but she was ill. 4. If he had not come that day, we should not have seen him. 5. It was as if suddenly the water began to tell its secrets. 6. I am going to ask him to give me back the book I lent him. 7. It would be better that you did it before John came. 8. If it had rained, we should have stayed to have lunch at Mr and Mrs Martínez's. 9. He was afraid that someone might see them as they came back from the meeting. 10. I am sorry you didn't have enough time to go and see the walls of the city.

REVIEW AND DEVELOPMENT

SECTION (IV)

124. PERSONAL PRONOUNS (FORMS). There are three classes of personal pronoun in Spanish: subject pronouns, weak object (*or* conjunctive) pronouns, and strong object (*or* disjunctive) pronouns. The object pronouns may be further classified into reflexive and non-reflexive, and into direct object and indirect object. The forms corresponding to these different classes may thus be tabulated as follows:

Subject	*Weak Object Pronoun*			*Strong Object Pronoun*	
	reflexive	*non-reflexive*		*reflexive*	*non-reflexive*
	i.o./d.o.	*i.o.*	*d.o.*		
1. yo	me	me	me	mí	mí
2. { tú	te	te	te	ti	ti
{ usted	se	le	le, la	sí	usted
3. { él	se	le	le, lo	sí	él
{ ella	se	le	la	sí	ella
1. nosotros -as	nos	nos	nos	nosotros -as	nosotros -as
2. { vosotros -as	os	os	os	vosotros -as	vosotros -as
{ ustedes	se	les	los, las	sí	ustedes
3. { ellos	se	les	los	sí	ellos
{ ellas	se	les	las	sí	ellas

NOTES: 1. Reflexive pronouns are those which refer back to the subject of the verb.

2. **Usted** may in all cases be written **Vd., Ud.** or **V.**, and **ustedes** be written **Vds., Uds.** or **VV.**

125. THE SUBJECT PRONOUN. The subject pronoun in Spanish is generally omitted, except in the second-person polite forms where it is usually present. In the other persons it is used for emphasis and to avoid possible ambiguity.

Ella quería comprar algo, pero él no tenía dinero.

She wanted to buy something but he hadn't any money.

126. THE WEAK OBJECT PRONOUN. (a) The Spanish weak object pronouns correspond to the English direct and indirect object pronouns and are placed immediately before the verb of which they are the object. See, however, § 62 for the position of the pronoun with a gerund or infinitive, and § 117 (b) for its position in commands and exhortations.

Al terminarlo, se lo entregó a su padre.

When he had finished it he handed it over to his father.

Le tengo que hablar.
Tengo que hablarle. } I have to talk to him.

Me lo iba a dar.
Iba a dármelo. } He was going to give it to me.

Lo acababa de hacer.
Acababa de hacerlo. } I had just done it.

Déjamelo ver.
Déjame verlo. } Let me see it.

NOTE: The placing of the pronoun object of an infinitive with the principal verb (as in the first case of each pair above) is frequent with: verbs that take a pure infinitive, common verbs that take **a** or **de,** and with **tener que.**

(b) If there are two weak object pronouns with a same verb, they range themselves in the following order of precedence: **se,** *indirect object, direct object.*

Se me acercaron dos andaluces. Two Andalusians approached me.

Se lo mandé a mi padre. I sent it to my father.

Me lo devolvió ayer. He gave it me back yesterday.

(c) In the first persons singular and plural and in the second persons familiar there is no distinction in form between the reflexive and non-reflexive pronouns, nor between the direct and indirect object pronouns.

Me lavo.   I wash myself (*reflexive d.o.*).
Me lavo las manos.   I wash my hands (*reflexive i.o.*).
Me lava.   He washes me (*non-reflexive d.o.*).
Me lava las manos.   He washes my hands (*non-reflexive i.o.*).

(*d*) In the remaining cases there are differences between the various series.

(1) The *reflexive* pronoun (direct and indirect object) is **se** in all cases.

Usted se lava.   You wash yourself (*d.o.*).
Se lava.   He washes himself (*d.o.*).
Vds. se lavan las manos.   You wash your hands (*i.o.*).
Ellas se lavan las manos.   They (*fem.*) wash their hands (*i.o.*).

(2) The *non-reflexive* pronouns are:

(i) Indirect object: **le** (singular) and **les** (plural).

Le lavo las manos.   I wash his (her, your) hands.
Les lavo las manos.   I wash their (your) hands.

But **le** and **les** (indicated by rectangles in § 124) both become **se** if they are followed by a weak direct-object pronoun of the third person.

Se las lavo.   I wash them for him (her, you, them).

(ii) Direct object: **la, las** (*feminine*) and **le, lo, los** (*masculine.*)

La veo; las veo.	I see her (it *fem.*); I see them (*fem.*).
La veo (a Vd.); las veo (a Vds.)	I see you (*fem. sing.*); I see you (*fem. pl.*).
Le veo; los veo.	I see him; I see them.
Lo veo; los veo.	I see it; I see them.
Le veo (a Vd.); los veo (a Vds.)	I see you (*masc. sing.*); I see you (*masc. pl.*).

NOTE: **Lo** is often found instead of **le**, and **les** instead of **los** [§ 59 (*b*) Note 2].

(e) Two Special Uses

(1) In certain cases where it replaces a noun the weak pronoun object may translate the English *some*, *any* or *one(s)*.

Los hay muy buenos; las hay muy buenas.

There are some very good ones.

¿Mantequilla? Dudo que la encuentre usted por aquí.

Butter? I doubt whether you will find any around here.

(2) A noun or adjective complement is indicated by the invariable **lo** (English *so*, nothing, or repetition of noun or adjective).

Están muy alegres y también lo estaban ayer.

They are very cheerful and they were (so *or* very cheerful) yesterday too.

Una de dos: o es amiga tuya o no lo es.

One of two [things]: either she's a friend of yours or she isn't.

127. Strong Object Pronouns.   *(a)* These forms are used in Spanish after a preposition.

Se colocó delante de mí.	He placed himself in front of me.
Yo estaba detrás de ella.	I was behind her.
Lo guardó para sí.	He kept it for himself.

Mismo may be added to the pronoun for emphasis.

Se lo di a usted mismo.	I gave it to you yourself.
Lo hizo por sí misma.	She did it by herself.

(b) The English preposition *to*, however, followed by a personal pronoun usually corresponds to the Spanish weak indirect object pronoun.

Lo dio a su padre; se lo dio.   He gave it to his father; he gave it to him.

But notice the following uses of **a** + strong pronoun:

(1) For clarity or emphasis, to *repeat* an object already expressed before the verb in weak-pronoun form.

Le digo a él (ella, Vd.).	I tell him (her, you).
Se perjudicó a sí misma.	She did herself harm.

(2) To *replace* a weak indirect object pronoun when the direct object is in the first or second person familiar.

Me mandaron a ti.	They sent me to you.
Os acercasteis a ellos.	You approached them.
Me presentaron a ella.	They introduced me to her.

(3) After a verb of motion to emphasize movement.

Vino a mí.	He came to me.
but **Siempre me viene con la misma excusa.**	He always comes to me with the same excuse.

(*c*) The preposition **con** joins with **mí, ti** and **sí** (indicated in the table by dotted lines) to give respectively **conmigo, contigo** and **consigo.**

Pensábamos ir contigo.   We intended to go with you.

(*d*) Besides the forms tabulated in § 124 there is also a neuter form **ello,** used when the pronoun does not recall a specific noun.

No está seguro de ello.   He is not sure of it.

(*e*) *Two Notes in Conclusion*

(1) Distinguish carefully between the use of the three strong-pronoun series in the following examples:

Subject	*Reflexive*	*Non-reflexive*
Lo hice yo mismo.	**Lo hice para mí.**	**Lo hizo para mí.**
I made it myself.	I made it for myself.	She made it for me.
Lo hizo ella misma.	**Lo hizo para sí.**	**Lo hice para ella.**
She made it herself.	She made it for herself.	I made it for her.

(2) *By oneself, by myself, by himself*, etc., can usually be translated by **por** + strong reflexive pronoun (+ **mismo**), and by the adjective **solo**. When the meaning is *alone, in solitude*, **solo** must be used.

Lo hicieron {**por sí (mismas).** / **(ellas) solas.**}	They (*fem.*) did it by themselves.
but only **Vivía sola.**	She lived by herself.

VOCABULARY

Revise Vocabularies XVI–XX and the verbs listed in Lesson XVI.

EXERCISES

I. (a) *Study and translate:* Las comimos todas. No le he visto.
¿Cuándo la vio usted? ¿Por qué no lo vendes? Los hemos
ayudado mucho. Quiero dárselo a usted. Nos ha mandado
a usted. Ella estaba detrás de él. Él se fue sin ella. Vaya
usted con él. No me las devolvió. Se lo estaba diciendo.
No nos gusta ni a él ni a mí. ¿Qué les parece a ustedes esta
idea? ¿Cuánto dinero os queda? No se lo diga usted
ahora. Lo compré para él. Él lo compró para sí. Antes
vivía conmigo, pero ahora vive solo. Se lo dimos a ustedes.
Hablé primero contigo. Me las estaba enseñando. No
piensa más que en sí misma.

(b) *Translate:* I saw him. I gave it to her. They went with
her. They saw you. You looked at him. She looked for
them. I taught it to him. We went without him. Shall we
wait for her or not? She was behind me. He did it after
me. I have dreamed of you. She was thinking about him.
He sent me to you. She would have made it for us. She
washed his hands. She kept it for herself. They took him
with them but left me here alone. We went to see them.
She was preparing it by herself. There are some very
interesting ones in Spain. Are you his parents? We are.

II. (a) *Study and translate:* 1. A mí me importa tanto como a
él que esta dificultad se resuelva lo antes posible. 2. Oye,
¿quieres prestarme tu coche, que tengo mucha prisa por
llegar a la estación? 3. Y ¿qué he de hacer si no consiente
en recibirnos o si se niega a aceptar este proyecto? 4. No
voy a poder acabarlo todo, a no ser que pase toda la noche
trabajando en ello. 5. Al llegar a Londres, no le quedaban
más que dos libras y unas ciento cincuenta pesetas.
6. Hicimos todo lo posible por convencerle, pero no quería

dejar sola a su madre. 7. Si hubieras estado en casa, no tendrías necesidad de preguntárselo a nadie. 8. Puesto que no le gusta a usted hablar de política, vamos a hablar de poesía. Usted escribe poesías, ¿verdad? 9. Tiene poca confianza en nuestras ideas, aunque yo no creo que las suyas tengan ningún valor extraordinario. 10. Pero ellos no son los únicos en pensar así. Hace ya tiempo que yo vengo diciendo lo mismo.

(b) *Translate:* 1. I talked to him yesterday but I couldn't persuade him to accept the new plan. 2. The difficult thing is to solve the problem without asking anybody for help. 3. Why don't we write him a letter inviting him to take part in the organization of the meeting? 4. "Shall we walk?" "If you don't mind (use **importar**) I'd rather go by (=**en**) car." 5. Don't fail to visit him when you go to Madrid. He will be very pleased to see you. 6. Even if this were true I should not like to commit myself to following such a policy. 7. I shall not go with them until I am sure they want me to (=they desire it). 8. He confesses to having taken the book without saying anything to anyone. 9. There is no doubt that the minister did well not to accept the policy that the rest wanted to follow. 10. I persuaded her to return home and to remain there until she had had a talk with her father.

III. (a) *Study and translate:* 1. ¿Cómo vamos a impedir que se dé cuenta de lo que ha ocurrido? 2. Pidió permiso para volver a visitarlos al día siguiente. 3. Sin embargo, conviene que lo pensemos bien antes de decidir nada. 4. No estoy dispuesto a repetir ahora lo que he dicho ya mil veces. 5. No quería que nadie fuera a despedirla a la estación. 6. Será mejor que no le digas nada de lo que pensamos hacer al salir de la reunión. 7. Si hubiera sabido ganarse la confianza de los demás, quizá se hubiera hecho más amigo de ellos. 8. Lo más importante es que todos sigan pensando en lo que harán cuando se marche el señor Fernández. 9. ¿No le parece que sería más fácil empezar con lo que estudiábamos la semana pasada? 10. Si piensan quedarse mucho tiempo aquí, conviene que dejen de meterse tanto en cosas que no tienen nada que ver con ellos.

(b) *Translate:* 1. Nevertheless, he ordered us to go and see him at once. 2. She thinks a lot about herself and very little about others. 3. But, for heaven's sake, don't go without saying good-bye to your grandparents. 4. I shall have great pleasure in sending you my latest book of poems. 5. He threatened to go to the police if the proprietor didn't apologize (=ask forgiveness) to him. 6. Will you undertake to come back tomorrow if I promise not to say anything to your father? 7. Since you are here you'd better (use **convenir** impersonally) stay to dinner. 8. It was impossible to discover how he had been able to do it without anybody's knowing. 9. We have been waiting for over half an hour. It looks as though (=It seems that) we shall have to go without him. 10. Don't you remember that I was with you when you bought the coffee? It cost about a hundred pesetas a kilogramme.

IV. *Re-translate the keys given for Lessons XVI–XX [pp. 358–361] and compare your versions with the originals.*

LESSON XXI

128. ADVERBS. (*a*) Many adverbs are formed by the addition of
-mente to the feminine singular of the corresponding adjective
(*cf.* English *-ly*).

severo	severe	**severamente**	severely
estúpido	stupid	**estúpidamente**	stupidly
fácil	easy	**fácilmente**	easily

NOTE: A written accent on the adjective is retained in the adverb.

(*b*) If two or more such adverbs come together, **-mente** is
placed only after the last of the series, the others being represented by the feminine singular form of the adjective.

Trabajaba rápida, intensa y metódicamente.
He used to work rapidly, intensely and methodically.

(*c*) An adverb in **-mente** is frequently avoided by the use of
con with the corresponding noun, or by the phrase **de una
manera (de un modo)** with an adjective, or by some other
prepositional phrase.

con frecuencia, frecuentemente	frequently
por fin, finalmente	finally
por completo, completamente	completely
sin duda, indudablemente	doubtless

Vamos a mirarlo { **más detenidamente.** / **con más detenimiento.** / **de una manera más detenida.** } Let us look at it more carefully.

(*d*) An adjective is often used in Spanish where English has an
adverb.

Estos libros se venden muy baratos. These books are sold
very cheaply.

129. THE COMPARATIVE (English *faster, dirtier, more intelligent, more slowly*). (*a*) The comparative of a Spanish adjective or adverb is formed by placing **más** (*more*) before the simple form.

una persona más simpática, a nicer person
un chico mucho más inteligente, a much more intelligent boy
Éste es más alto que aquél.   This one is taller than that one.
Iré más tarde.   I shall go later.
Hazlo más despacio.   Do it more slowly.

(*b*) Notice, however, the following irregular comparatives:

Adjectives		Adverbs	
bueno	**mejor**	**bien**	**mejor**
good	better	well	better
malo	**peor**	**mal**	**peor**
bad	worse	badly	worse
mucho	**más**	**mucho**	**más**
a lot of	more	a lot	more
poco	**menos**	**poco**	**menos**
little, few	less, fewer	little	less

The adjective **grande** has two comparative forms, **más grande** and **mayor,** the former generally indicating size (i.e., *bigger*) and the latter seniority and superiority (i.e., *older, greater*).   Similarly, **pequeño** has **más pequeño** (*smaller*) and **menor** (*younger, lesser*).

Éstos son peores que los otros.   These are worse than the others.
Cantan mejor que sus hijos.   They sing better than their children.
Tengo más posibilidades.   I have more possibilities.
Él tiene menos pesetas que tú.   He has fewer pesetas than you.
Está menos alegre que ayer.   He is less cheerful than yesterday.

NOTES: 1. Used as adjectives, **más** and **menos** are invariable. **Mejor** and **peor** are class 3 adjectives [§ 38] and are therefore the same in the masculine and the feminine (**mejor, peor**; *pl.* **mejores, peores**).   Used as adverbs they are invariable.

2. **Más bien** exists with the meaning *rather*.

Parece inglés más bien que alemán.   He seems English rather than German.

130. TRANSLATING THE ENGLISH *than*. (*a*) *Than* is usually represented in Spanish by **que** [see examples in § 129].

Él es menos rico que tú.   He is less wealthy than you are.
Más vale tarde que nunca.   Better late than never.

(*b*) *More than* and *less than* before an indication of quantity or number are translated by **más de** and **menos de** [§ 94 (*e*), Note].

Estuvo más de una hora.   He was here for more than an hour.
Son más de las nueve.   It is more than nine o'clock.
Tiene menos de quince años.   He is less than fifteen years old.

NOTE: **No . . . más que** means *only*: **No tiene más que doce años** (*He is only twelve years old*), but **No tiene más de doce años** (*He is not more than twelve years old*).

(*c*) *Than* is also translated by **de** in sentences of the type *He spends more money than* (*that which*) *he earns*, the bracketed *that which*, usually omitted in English, being translated into Spanish by the appropriate definite article (masculine singular in this case to refer back to **el dinero**) followed by **que**: **Gasta más dinero del** (*i.e.*, **de + el**) **que gana.** If the suppressed element in English does not refer to a specific noun it is represented by **lo**.

Él ve más dificultades de las que hay.
   He sees more difficulties than there are.
Tiene menos libros de los que necesita.
   He has fewer books than he needs.
Es más difícil de lo que crees.
   It is more difficult than you think.

131. OTHER TERMS OF COMPARISON.

tan . . . como	as . . . as
tan . . . como para + infinitive	so . . . as to, . . . enough to

tanto ... como	as much ... as; *pl.* as many ... as

$$\text{cuanto} \begin{Bmatrix} \text{más} \\ \text{menos} \end{Bmatrix} \dots \text{tanto} \begin{Bmatrix} \text{más} \\ \text{menos} \end{Bmatrix} \quad \text{the} \begin{Bmatrix} \text{more} \\ \text{less} \end{Bmatrix} \dots \text{the} \begin{Bmatrix} \text{more} \\ \text{less} \end{Bmatrix}$$

No era tan fácil como parecía.
It was not as easy as it seemed.

Es tan alta como su hermano.
She is as tall as her brother.

Ha sido tan amable como para invitarnos.
He has been kind enough to invite us.

Usted no trabaja tanto como ella.
You don't work as hard as she does.

Él tiene tantas hermanas como yo.
He has as many sisters as I have.

Bebemos tanta agua como vino.
We drink as much water as wine.

Cuantas más ventajas tenía, (tantas) más exigía.
The more advantages he had, the more he demanded.

Cuanto más difíciles son los ejemplos, (tanto) más despacio los traduzco.
The more difficult are the examples, the more slowly I translate them.

Cuantos más libros vende, (tantos) menos le quedan.
The more books he sells, the fewer he has left.

Cuanto mayor sea la dificultad, (tanta) más satisfacción tendremos al vencerla.
The greater the difficulty, the more satisfaction we shall have in overcoming it.

NOTE: In the construction **cuanto ... tanto**: (i) **cuanto** and **tanto** decline when used as adjectives (*i.e.*, immediately before **más** or **menos**+noun) and are invariable when used as adverbs (before **más** or **menos**+adjective or adverb); (ii) **tanto (-a, -os, -as)** is more often omitted than used; (iii) the **más** may be contained in an irregular comparative (*cf.* last example: **mayor = más grande**).

132. THE SUPERLATIVE (English *fastest, dirtiest, most intelligent, most slowly*). (*a*) The superlative in Spanish is the same as the comparative, except that, as in English, the article is used with it more often than with the comparative.

Éste es el más inteligente.
> This is the most (*or* more) intelligent one.

(*but* **Éste es más inteligente.**
>> This one is more intelligent.)

¿Cuál es el chico más inteligente?
> Which is the most (*or* more) intelligent boy?

Es la mejor de sus poesías.
> It is the best of his poems.

Es lo peor que he visto.
> It is the worst I have seen.

Fueron los días más felices de su vida.
> They were the happiest days of his life.

¿Cuál es su hija más lista?
> Which is his cleverest daughter?

Es el hombre más rico del país.
> He is the richest man in the country.

NOTES: 1. The English *in* after a superlative is best translated by **de**.
2. When *most* means *the majority of* or *the greater part of* it is translated by **la mayor parte de**. If it is the subject of the sentence and refers to several individuals it takes a plural verb.

> **La mayor parte de sus amigos dirán lo mismo que yo.**
>> Most of his friends will say the same as I do.
> **La mayor parte de las mujeres desean casarse.**
>> Most women wish to get married.

but **¿Quién tiene más amigos?**
> Who has most friends?

(*b*) With the superlative of an adverb the article **lo** is used only when there follows some qualifying element (*cf.*, English popular usage).

> **Fue él quien lo hizo más despacio.**
>> It was he who did it most slowly.

but **Lo hizo lo más despacio que pudo.**
He did it as slowly as he could (*lit.,* the slowest he could).

A ver quién termina más pronto.
Let's see who finishes soonest.

but **Terminará lo más pronto que pueda.**
He will finish as soon as he can.

Esas cosas ocurren cuando menos se piensa.
Those things happen when one least expects.

but **Lo que importa es que ocurran lo menos posible.**
The important thing is that they should happen as little as
possible.

(*c*) The absolute superlative (which intensifies rather than
compares) is formed by adding **-ísimo** to the last consonant of
the simple adjective (with loss of stem accent and with change of
spelling where necessary to preserve the consonant sound, § 19,
Note 1).

rápido	**rapidísimo**	**rapidísimamente**
quick	most quick	most quickly

Esta lección es dificilísima.   This lesson is most difficult.
Son una pareja felicísima.   They are a most happy pair.
Es un señor riquísimo.   He is a most wealthy gentleman.

NOTE: **Muchísimo** translates *very much*.

133. *Now* AND *then*.   (*a*) *Now* is most frequently translated by
ahora.   **Ya** emphasizes that an earlier state is over and done with,
and **ahora bien** links up logically with what has gone before.

Ahora mismo no está.   He isn't in just now.
Ahora comprendo *or* **Ya comprendo.**   Now I understand.
Está ya muy viejo.   He's (gone) very old now.
Ahora bien: todo esto es muy difícil de demostrar.   Now
all this is very difficult to prove.

NOTE: **Ya** also translates *already*, *(no) longer*, *yet* (with an interrogative) and *presently*. Often it serves simply to give strength to a verbal action and may not be translated in English.

> **Lo ha terminado ya.** He has already finished it.
> **Ya no es profesor.** He is no longer a teacher.
> **¿Lo has hecho ya?** Have you done it yet?
> (*but* **No lo he hecho todavía** [*or* **aún**]. I've not done it yet.)
> **Ya verá usted.** You'll see (presently).
> **Ya se lo dije, ¿verdad?** I did tell you, didn't I?
> **— Irás, ¿verdad? — Ya lo creo.** "You'll go, won't you?"
> "I should just think so" (*or* I'll say, *or* You bet, *etc.*).

(*b*) *Then* is most frequently translated by **entonces,** which means both *at that time* and *in that case* (*i.e.*, as a logical connecting link). **Luego** translates *then* meaning *next*. **Pues** and **conque** are conjunctions whose use can best be seen in examples.

Trabajaba entonces en una fábrica. He was then working in a factory.

Luego llegó su padre con otro señor. Then his father arrived with another gentleman.

— No me gusta. — Entonces (*or* **Pues**) **no iremos.** "I don't like it." "We'll not go then."

Repito, pues, que para mí no pido nada. I repeat, then, that for myself I ask nothing.

Conque no te gusta. You don't like it then (*or* So you don't like it).

134. AN IRREGULAR VERB: andar. Andar, *to walk*; *to go, to run* (= *to work, to progress*) is irregular only in the preterite and the imperfect subjunctive.

preterite: anduve, anduviste, anduvo, anduvimos, anduvisteis, anduvieron

imperf. subj.: anduviera (anduviese), anduvieras (anduvieses), etc.

Mire al pequeño cómo anda. Look at the little chap walking.
Anduvo todo el camino. He walked the whole way.
Este reloj no anda. This watch doesn't work.
¿Cómo anda el asunto? How is the matter going?

In popular usage **andar** may at times replace **estar.**

Ando muy mal de dinero. I'm very hard up.

Anda muy enamorada de un primo suyo. She's very much in love with a cousin of hers.

VOCABULARY

el acento	accent	**el lujo**	luxury
el capricho	whim	**el médico**	doctor
claro	clear	**la montaña**	mountain
completo	complete, full (*bus*, etc.)	**nervioso**	nervous
conciso	concise	**de nuevo** } **otra vez** }	again
dedicar	to dedicate, to devote	**la ocasión**	occasion, opportunity
durar	to last	**el otoño**	autumn
la elegancia	elegance	**precioso**	delightful, lovely
elegante	elegant, smart		
la época	period, time	**rápido**	quick
esperar	to hope, to wait for, to expect	**el remedio**	remedy
		el río	river
el estudio	study	**satisfacer** (*like* **hacer**)	to satisfy
estúpido	stupid, foolish		
frecuente	frequent	**el Tajo**	Tagus
la hoja	leaf, sheet	**tímido**	timid
inmediato	immediate	**único**	only, sole, unique
largo	long		
la longitud	length	**la vista**	sight, view

cada vez más	more and more
cada vez menos	less and less
de vez en cuando	from time to time
la Península Ibérica	the Iberian Peninsula

EXERCISES

I. (*a*) *Study and translate:* Inmediatamente. Únicamente. Elegantísimamente. De una manera completamente natural. Se sentó muy nerviosa. Anda más rápido que su padre. Es la vista más preciosa que conozco. Esta señora viste siempre con mucha elegancia. Lo hizo mejor de lo que esperábamos.

No tengo más que un hermano. Cuantos más libros se leen, más se sabe. Es la familia más importante de la ciudad. ¿Quién lo hizo mejor? La primera poesía me gustó muchísimo; las demás ya no tanto. Pensábamos acompañarle, pero ya no podemos. Luego me contó lo que había oído. Ahora andan muy satisfechos con el remedio que les han dado.

(b) *Translate:* Frequently. Cheerfully. Quickly and concisely. In a most curious way. She is taller than her brother. He does it better than his friend. They have more than they deserve. There are fewer people now than yesterday. These books are bad but the others were worse. Let's see who does it best. The difference was greater than I expected. The more she visits us the less we like her. They are not so stupid as to believe that. This is the best he has done. Now the king, besides being the richest man in the country, was also the most intelligent. On the following day they walked more than fifty kilometres.

II. (a) *Study and translate:* 1. Habló clara, concisa y elegantísimamente. 2. Indudablemente, ésta no es la mejor época para conocer el sur de España. 3. Ya va llegando el otoño y los árboles empiezan a perder sus hojas. 4. Este señor tiene el acento más curioso que he oído en mi vida. 5. Ya no nos quedaba más remedio que aceptar el proyecto tal como lo habían preparado ellos. 6. Los ríos más importantes de España son el Tajo, el Duero, el Ebro, el Guadiana y el Guadalquivir. 7. Son dificilísimos los primeros capítulos de este libro, pero ya vamos entendiéndolos. 8. Pedro tiene más años que su hermana, pero no tantos como su amigo Felipe. 9. No, no: yo quiero que satisfaga sus menores caprichos. ¿No es ella la mujer más hermosa de todo Madrid? Pues que sea también la que vista con más lujo. 10. De vez en cuando se vuelve a despertar algo dentro de mí, y vuelvo a soñar, y empiezo de nuevo a hacer proyectos y a volverme a engañar otro poco. Pero esto va siendo cada vez menos frecuente, y también cada vez dura menos.

(b) *Translate:* 1. I have fewer pounds now than when I left home. 2. This is the only way to do it quickly without anyone's seeing us. 3. This problem is more difficult to solve than it appears at first sight. 4. I don't know any view as delightful as the one I have from my window. 5. This is the highest mountain in the Iberian Peninsula but it is not the highest in Spain. 6. Immediately after dinner we went out for a walk round the oldest part of the city. 7. Elizabeth's parents have been ill but now they are better and Elizabeth wants to go back to school. 8. Do it immediately in order that I may know whether I shall need a bigger suitcase. 9. This boy is only ten years old, but he walks much more quickly than his brothers who are all older than he [is]. 10. The longest river in Spain is the Tagus which is over a thousand kilometres long (=has a length of more than a thousand kilometres).

III. (a) *Study and translate:* 1. Entró tímida, mirando nerviosa a un lado y otro. 2. Se habrán marchado ya muchos de los que llegaron ayer. 3. Es completamente natural que él prefiera quedarse con sus padres. 4. Le escribí una carta larguísima, de unas siete u ocho hojas. 5. Es la única vez que me he comprometido a hacer algo más rápido de lo que he podido. 6. Ya tendremos ocasión de mirarlo más de cerca cuando estemos otra vez en casa. 7. Cuanto más se dedica uno al estudio de estos problemas, más se da uno cuenta de lo difíciles que son. 8. El Manzanares es un río poco importante que merece recordarse únicamente por ser el río de la capital de España. 9. Luego, cuando parecía dispuesta a salir, se puso a cantar y a dar vueltas por el cuarto. 10. Llevábamos ya un cuarto de hora hablando así cuando me di cuenta de que la madre hablaba con cierto acento extranjero.

(b) *Translate:* 1. He has more pesetas than he needs for his trip. 2. The more languages I study, the more quickly I learn them. 3. So you intended to go off without saying anything to us, did you? 4. Naturally I don't want to

promise more than I can do.   5. On another occasion he
talked to me of a most interesting journey he had made
through the south of Spain.   6. I advise you to talk to the
doctor, who is usually the most intelligent man in the vil
lage.   7. Look at this car I've bought.   It only cost me a
hundred pounds.   Don't you think it was very cheap?
8. He writes many more letters than he receives, but not so
many as to satisfy all his friends.   9. For me the sixteenth
century is the most interesting period in Spanish history
(=the history of Spain).   10. It is the best time of the year
to study the trees and flowers of this part of Spain.

LESSON XXII

135. Revise the pronunciation of **c, z, qu, j, g, gu, gü** [§ 2].

136. Certain sounds in Spanish have more than one written form. Thus, before a front vowel (**e** or **i**) the English hard *c* sound (as in *cot*) is represented by **qu**; elsewhere by **c**. The different dualities of this type can best be expressed by means of a table:

	Before **e** *or* **i**	*Elsewhere*
k sound (English *c*ot)	**qu**	**c**
th sound (English *th*ank)	**c**	**z**
g sound (English *g*one)	**gu**	**g**
gw sound (English *Gw*en)	**gü**	**gu**
ch sound (Scottish lo*ch*)	**g** or **j**	**j**

137. This duality in the representation of a same sound is important in verb conjugations, where the final sound of the stem or radical must remain constant throughout, though the letter immediately following (*i.e.*, the first letter of the verb ending) will be at times **e** or **i**, and at other times **a** or **o**. Thus, to show, in these different cases, that the *sound* is constant, a change must be made in the *spelling*:

> *e.g.*, **buscar** *but* **busqué**
> **delinquir** *but* **delinco**

This is known as an *orthographic change*; verbs in which it takes place are *orthography-changing* (or *orthographically changing*) *verbs*.

138. -ar Verbs. It will be seen from the table in § 136 that an **-ar** verb with stem ending in **c, z, g** or **gu** will have to undergo

234

an orthographic change (the **c, z, g, gu** becoming respectively **qu, c, gu, gü**) in those parts of the verb where the ending begins with **e**.[1] This occurs in the first person singular of the preterite and throughout the present subjunctive:

-car   *e.g.*, **buscar,** *to look for*

preterite: busqué, buscaste, buscó, etc.

pres. subj.: busque, busques, busque, busquemos, busquéis, busquen

-zar   *e.g.*, **cazar,** *to hunt*

preterite: cacé, cazaste, cazó, etc.

pres. subj.: cace, caces, cace, cacemos, cacéis, cacen

-gar   *e.g.*, **llegar,** *to arrive*

preterite: llegué, llegaste, llegó, etc.

pres. subj.: llegue, llegues, llegue, lleguemos, lleguéis, lleguen

-guar   *e.g.*, **apaciguar,** *to appease, pacify*

preterite: ᐧ apacigüé, apaciguaste, apaciguó, etc.

pres. subj.: apacigüe, apacigües, apacigüe, apacigüemos, apacigüéis, apacigüen.

NOTE: There is no orthographic change in **-jar** verbs because both **g** and **j** may represent the **jota** sound (lo*ch*) before **e** [§ 136].

-jar   *e.g.*, **dejar,** *to leave*

preterite: dejé, dejaste, dejó, etc.

pres. subj.: deje, dejes, deje, etc.

139. -er AND -ir VERBS. In **-er** and **-ir** verbs which have stem ending in **qu, c, gu, gü, g**, the opposite change will take place (*i.e.*, **qu, c, gu, gü, g** will become, respectively, **c, z, g, gu, j**) when the first vowel of the verb ending is **o** or **a**: namely, in the first person singular of the present indicative, and in the whole of the present subjunctive:

-quir   *e.g.*, **delinquir,** *to transgress*

pres. ind.: delinco, delinques, delinque, etc.

pres. subj.: delinca, delincas, delinca, delincamos, delincáis, delincan

---

[1] In no part of the verb does the ending begin with **i**.

-cer, -cir   *e.g.,* **vencer,** *to conquer, overcome*
pres. ind.: venzo, vences, vence, etc.
pres. subj.: venza, venzas, venza, venzamos, venzáis, venzan

NOTE: -cer and -cir verbs in which the letter immediately preceding the c is a vowel undergo a different change in the same circumstances: the c, instead of passing to z, becomes zc, with a consequent change of sound.

e.g., **conocer,** *to know*
pres. ind.   conozco, conoces, conoce, etc.
pres. subj.: conozca, conozcas, conozca, conozcamos, conozcáis, conozcan.

-guir   *e.g.,* **distinguir,** *to distinguish*
pres. ind.: distingo, distingues, distingue, etc.
pres. subj.: distinga, distingas, distinga, distingamos, distingáis, distingan

-güir   *e.g.,* **argüir,** *to argue*   [See below, § 143]

-ger, -gir   *e.g.,* **coger,** *to seize, catch*
pres. ind.: cojo, coges, coge, etc.
pres. subj.: coja, cojas, coja, cojamos, cojáis, cojan

NOTE: With verbs in which the final stem consonant is already j there is no problem: the j remains throughout.
e.g., **tejer,** *to weave*
pres. ind.: tejo, tejes, teje, etc.
pres. subj.: teja, tejas, teja, etc.

140. -iar VERBS.   (*a*) In some -iar verbs, when the stress is not on the ending it falls on the i which then takes an accent [§ 3 (b) and (*c*) (iv)].

e.g., **enviar,** *to send*
pres. ind.: envío, envías, envía, enviamos, enviáis, envían
pres. subj.: envíe, envíes, envíe, enviemos, enviéis, envíen
imperative: envía   enviad

(*b*) Verbs that take the stress (and written accent) upon the **i** are:

(i) those which have no other syllable in the stem [§ 3 (*c*) (iv)]: **liar** (*to bind*), **fiar** (*to entrust*), **guiar** (*to guide*), **criar** (*to breed, bring up*), etc.

(ii) compounds of these and of nouns and adjectives of monosyllabic stem:

[**liar**]   **aliar** (*to ally*), **desliar** (*to unbind*)
[**fiar**]   **confiar** (*to confide*), **desconfiar** (*to distrust*)
[**vía** *way*]   **enviar** (*to send, i.e.*, put on its way), **desviar** (*to divert*)
[**frío** *cold*]   **enfriar** (*to cool*), **resfriarse** (*to catch a cold*)

(iii) verbs ending in **-riar**: **variar** (*to vary*), **averiarse** (*to be damaged, break down*), **chirriar** (*to creak*), **expatriar** (*to expatriate*), etc.

(*c*) In other **-iar** verbs (*i.e.*, the majority) the stem stress falls on the syllable preceding the **i,** and the **i** therefore takes no accent.

limpiar (*to clean*): limpio, limpias, etc.
estudiar (*to study*): estudio, estudias, etc.

141. -uar VERBS. (*a*) Where the stress is not on the ending it usually falls on the **u** which then takes an accent.

e.g., **situar,** *to situate*

pres. ind.: sitúo, sitúas, sitúa, situamos, situáis, sitúan
pres. subj.: sitúe, sitúes, sitúe, situemos, situéis, sitúen
imperative: sitúa   situad

(*b*) In verbs ending in **-guar** and **-cuar**, however, the stress falls on the syllable preceding the **u** and the **u** therefore takes no accent.

apaciguar (*to pacify*): apaciguo, apaciguas, etc.
evacuar (*to evacuate*): evacuo, evacuas, etc.

142. VERBS IN **-eer.** Since an unstressed **i** is never found in Spanish between two vowels, the **i** of the endings **-ió** and **-ie-** here changes to **y.**

e.g., **leer**, *to read*

preterite: leí, leíste, leyó, leímos, leísteis, leyeron

imp. subj.: leyera (leyese), leyeras (leyeses), leyera (leyese), leyéramos (leyésemos), leyerais (leyeseis), leyeran (leyesen)

gerund: leyendo

NOTE: The same applies to verbs in **-aer** and **-oer** but these are rare. **Caer** (*to fall*) and **traer** (*to fetch, to bring*) are the most common, but they are not completely regular verbs. In the verb parts that interest us here, **caer** follows the rule given above (**cayó, cayeron; cayera** [**cayese**], etc.; **cayendo**), but **traer** follows it only in the gerund (**trayendo**), being irregular in the preterite and the imperfect subjunctive (**trajo, trajeron; trajera** [**trajese**], etc.). See § 93.

143. VERBS IN -uir. As with **-eer** verbs, the **i** of the ending **-ió** and **-ie-** changes to **y**. Moreover, in all parts of the verb where the ending does not begin with **i**, a **y** is inserted before that ending.

e.g., **huir**, *to flee, run away*

pres. ind.: huyo, huyes, huye, huimos, huís, huyen

imp. ind.: huía, huías, huía, huíamos, huíais, huían

preterite: huí, huiste, huyó, huimos, huisteis, huyeron

pres. subj.: huya, huyas, huya, huyamos, huyáis, huyan

imp. subj.: huyera (huyese), huyeras (huyeses), huyera (huyese), huyéramos (huyésemos), huyerais (huyeseis), huyeran (huyesen)

imperative: huye   huid

gerund: huyendo

past part.: huido

NOTES: 1. Verbs ending in **-quir** and **-guir** are not included here for the **u** is silent. Verbs in **-güir**, on the other hand, do comply: **argüir** (*to argue*): **arguyo, arguyes**, etc. [§ 139].

2. **Oír** and its compounds might also be included here but they are irregular in certain parts [§ 93].

VOCABULARY

el acuerdo	agreement	**exclusivo**	exclusive
de acuerdo	agreed, in agreement	**fijar**	to fix
		el final	end
averiguar	to ascertain, to find out	**a fines de** ⎱ **a finales de** ⎰	at the end of (time)
el cambio	change	**la literatura**	literature
conceder	to grant	**la llegada**	arrival
confundir	to confuse	**la obra**	work (of art, science, etc.)
constituir	to constitute		
construir	to construct, to build	**pagar**	to pay (for)
contrariar	to go against	**a pesar de**	in spite of
el corazón	heart	**político**	political
unos cuantos	a few	**el principio**	beginning, principle
desde que	since (*conj. of time*)	**al principio**	at first
el director	manager	**a principios de**	at the beginning of (time)
efectuar	to bring about	**publicar**	to publish
el empleado	employee, clerk	**recoger**	to collect, to gather
el ensayo	essay		
entregar	to hand (over *or* in)	**la situación**	situation, position
escoger	to choose	**utilizar**	to utilize, to use
establecer	to establish	**la voluntad**	will

Study the verbs listed in §§ 138–143.

EXERCISES

I. (a) *Give the first person singular of the present subjunctive of:*
coger, trabajar, argüir, avergonzarse, distinguir, merecer,
exigir, dedicar, satisfacer, contrariar, efectuar, delinquir,
apaciguar.

(b) *Study and translate:* Llegué ayer. Hasta que me lo
ofrezca. Sin que se publique. Recoja usted sus libros.
Entréguemelo mañana. Se lo expliqué todo. Prefiero que
conduzcas tú. Es preciso que estudien más. La dejé aquí.
Le aconsejé que lo hiciera. Empiece usted mañana. Que

239

lo busquen ellos. Para que reconozca a su propio hijo. Me envía a hablar con usted. Siga leyendo. Me complazco en mirarla. Aunque nos venzan. Diga lo que diga la gente. Huyó con las manos en la cabeza. Léame un capítulo más. Siempre escojo lo mejor.

(c) *Translate:* When he convinces me. I threatened him. Don't deny it. I handed him the book. I want him to ascertain what has happened. Without their contributing anything. If they approach the building. Lower your head. Even if he manages to do it. What are they building? We don't want them to establish themselves here. Unless we oblige them to pay. I doubt whether he will desire it. It is possible he will begin tomorrow. Devote yourself to more important things. I brought him the book and left it on the table. Don't catch cold.

II. (a) *Study and translate:* 1. Siga leyendo, que ya vamos llegando al final. 2. Estamos todos de acuerdo en que el cambio se efectúe de tal manera. 3. Está muy nerviosa desde que le entregué esa carta a fines de la semana pasada. 4. Es importante que usted fije cuanto antes la fecha de su llegada a París. 5. Recojamos estas hojas y vamos a enseñarlas a su padre cuando llegue a casa. 6. No consigo comprender cómo ha podido usted pasarse todo un año sin hacer nada. 7. Conviene que todos sepan cómo este señor contraría la voluntad y el corazón de su hija. 8. Cuanto mejor conozco España, más me gusta y más ganas tengo de ir a establecerme allí. 9. Me acerqué a la ventana donde estaba ella, y rápidamente, sin que nadie me viera, le entregué la carta. 10. Conviene que usted hable con el director, para que él mismo le explique la situación en que se encuentra desde que se marchó el señor López.

(b) *Translate:* 1. At first he didn't want anyone to read his poems. 2. It was cold and raining when I arrived at the hotel. 3. Shall we ask him to look for someone who will teach us to drive? 4. Mrs Sánchez sends me to speak with the proprietor of this house. 5. He told me to carry on reading because we were now getting near the end. 6. If this is true then she herself must do it when she gets home. 7. When you arrived I was reading a most interesting essay on life in fifteenth-century England. 8. In spite of this I continue to think that the greatest difficulty will be (=consist) in convincing them of our good will. 9. Ascertain whether the minister will go with them when they leave for Canada. 10. This will be a good opportunity to persuade him to let us publish his complete works.

III. (a) *Study and translate:* 1. Acerquémonos y pidámosles algo de comer. 2. ¿Qué he hecho yo para que usted me dedique así una de sus mejores poesías? 3. Quiero que usted vaya a casa del señor Ramírez a recoger unos libros que dejé anoche. 4. La primera vez que se oyó llamar así, creyó que le habían confundido con otro. 5. Lo importante es que se establezca cuanto antes un acuerdo entre los médicos y el gobierno. 6. Busque otra vez la llave cuando ella se haya marchado y tráigamela si la encuentra. 7. La idea consiste en ir construyendo buenos hoteles por todo el país para así atraer a los turistas extranjeros. 8. Pero ¿qué podemos hacer los pobres empleados puesto que el director nos contraría en todo lo que queremos hacer? 9. Nos han concedido permiso para trabajar aquí, pero a condición de que no utilicemos más que los libros que autoricen ellos. 10. — Son muy hermosas estas flores. — Pues escoja usted las que quiera, con tal que me deje unas cuantas para mi mujer.

(b) *Translate:* 1. This is the lady to whom I paid the bill. 2. I shall ask him to ascertain if it is true or not. 3. Catch this tram and get off (=get down) at the *Plaza de España*. 4. I arrived at six in the evening, had supper and went to bed immediately afterwards. 5. We want him to publish the essay he has written on the poetry of Antonio Machado. 6. The important thing is that he should acknowledge the necessity of such a plan. 7. Go and look for my brother and hand him this letter which has just arrived. 8. Nevertheless, his poetry constitutes the most important part of his complete works.   9. I advise you to change the explanation you give of the political situation at the end of the nineteenth century.   10. For six months I devoted myself exclusively to the study of the German language; then I began to study certain aspects of the literature.

LESSON XXIII

144. Ser AND estar WITH THE PAST PARTICIPLE. **Ser** and **estar** may both be used with a past participle, **ser** to introduce action being done (*i.e.*, the passive voice) and **estar** to indicate state resulting from such action. In both cases the past participle agrees in number and gender with the subject of the sentence. The agent of a passive voice is introduced by **por.**

Este libro fue escrito por un español. This book was written by a Spaniard.

Está escrito en español. It is written in Spanish.

La lección fue muy bien explicada. The lesson was explained very well.

La lección está bien explicada. The lesson is well explained.

Había sido convencida. She had been convinced.
Fue convencida. She was convinced (*action*).
Estaba convencida. She was convinced (*state*).

Los árboles son cortados en primavera. The trees are cut in Spring.

Los árboles están cortados. The trees are (= have been) cut.

Fue acompañado por el embajador. He was accompanied by the ambassador.
(Implies action on the part of the ambassador: the ambassador *went* with him, showed him round perhaps.)

Estaba acompañado por el embajador. He was accompanied by the ambassador.
(The ambassador takes a less active part in the proceedings: the ambassador *was* with him, formed [part of] the attendance.)

243

NOTE: In certain cases an English present participle may indicate state. In Spanish the past participle must be used. Common examples of this are:

acostado	lying down	**colgado**	hanging
apoyado	leaning	**reclinado**	reclining
arrodillado	kneeling	**sentado**	sitting

Estaban sentados a la mesa.   They were sitting at the table.
La vi apoyada en un bastón.   I saw her leaning on a stick.

145. AVOIDANCE OF THE PASSIVE VOICE. The passive voice (**ser**/*to be*+ past participle) is used far less in Spanish than in English, and the English passive may often be better rendered into Spanish by other means.

(*a*) Where the agent is expressed (*i.e.*, the doer of the action: written by *a Spaniard*, accompanied by *the ambassador*) the true passive is more frequent than in other cases. Nevertheless, it is often avoided by transposing the verb into the active voice and making the agent into the subject. In such cases inversion of the order *subject–verb* is frequent to indicate exceptional, passive-type emphasis.

Este libro lo escribió un español.
This book was written by a Spaniard.
Le acompañó el embajador.
He was accompanied by the ambassador.

(*b*) Where there is no particular agent expressed or implied, the passive is generally avoided by one of the following means:

(i) by the use of a Spanish reflexive (the most common solution).

Esta lección se explicó muy bien. This lesson was explained very well.
Se convenció. She was convinced.
Los árboles se cortan en primavera. The trees are cut in Spring.

NOTE: In this construction, when the action of the verb is done to inanimate objects these become the real subject of the verb (*e.g.*, **Los árboles se cortan**). When the action is done to persons, on the other hand, there may be confusion with the true reflexive or the reciprocal reflexive (*i.e.*, **Los ministros se matan** would be interpreted as *The ministers kill themselves* or *The ministers kill one another*), and the passive sense is then usually indicated by a variant form of the same construction: the verb is expressed impersonally in the singular, and the persons acted upon are expressed as the direct or indirect object.

Se mata a los ministros.	The ministers are killed.
Se los mata.	They are killed.
Se vio a la madre por la calle.	The mother was seen in the street.
Se la vio por la calle.	She was seen in the street.
No se le autoriza a nadie acento ninguno.	No one is authorized [to have] any accent.
Se le encarga demasiado trabajo.	He is given too much work to do.
Se les ha enseñado el primer capítulo.	They have been shown the first chapter.
Se me citó para las cinco.	It was arranged I should go at (*lit.*, I was dated for) five o'clock.
Se os anunciará mañana.	It will be made known to you tomorrow.

Where the emphasis is on the state arrived at rather than the action (and provided that no confusion is possible with the reflexive proper) the earlier construction may be used even with persons.

> **Se convenció a la chica;**
> **se la convenció.**
> *but also* **La chica se convenció;**
> **se convenció.**

The girl was convinced; she was convinced.

In the former pair there is greater interest in the action of convincing the girl; in the latter it is sufficient that we know she became convinced.

(ii) by using the verb actively in the third person plural, thereby giving the sentence an indeterminate subject (*they, people*).

Explicaron muy bien la lección.   The lesson was explained very well.

La convencieron.   She was convinced.

Cortan los árboles en primavera. The trees are cut in Spring.

(iii) by introducing **uno** (*one*) or **la gente** (*people*) as an indeterminate subject (less common than solutions (i) and (ii); used principally when the verb is reflexive and the use of a further reflexive pronoun as in solution (i) therefore impossible).

Uno
La gente } **no se da cuenta de su importancia.**

Its importance is not realized.

(*i.e.*, **no se da cuenta** means *he does not realize*, and **no se se da cuenta** is not possible.)

(iv) by the use of **hay que** + infinitive (to indicate admonition or obligation).

Hay que cortar los árboles en primavera.

The trees are to be cut in Spring.

146. Por AND **para.** (*a*) Despite the clear distinction between **por** and **para** suggested by the English renderings in § 94 (*a*), these two words are often confused by the non-native speaker of Spanish, especially since both may translate the English preposition *for*. It is important to understand from the beginning their essential difference: **por** most frequently indicates the source or means of an action (English *by, through, out of, for, because of*, etc.); **para,** on the other hand, denotes principally its direction, destination, purpose or suitability (English *for, to, in order to*, etc.).

¿Por qué cogiste mi lápiz? Why (= through what cause) did you take my pencil?
Lo cogí por mi hermano. I took it because of my brother.
. . . por necesidad. . . . out of necessity.
. . . por no tener aquí el mío. . . . because I didn't have mine here (*lit.*, through not having mine here).
. . . porque no estabas. . . . because you were not here.
Lo dejaré por ti. I'll leave it for you (= on your account, *e.g.*, so that I can be with you).
Salí de Madrid por Barajas. I left Madrid via Barajas.

¿Para qué cogiste mi lápiz?   Why (= for what purpose) did you take my pencil?

Lo cogí para mi hermano.   I took it for my brother.

. . . para una clase de español.   . . . for a Spanish class.

. . . para escribir una carta.   . . . (in order) to write a letter.

. . . para que lo viera Juan.   . . . so that John might see it.

Lo dejaré para ti.   I'll leave it for you (*i.e.*, so that you can have it).

Salí de Madrid para Barajas.   I left Madrid for Barajas.

Por:

> **Ha sido atropellada por un coche.**
> She has been knocked down by a car.
>
> **Cuatro por cinco son veinte.**
> Five fours are twenty.
>
> **Le escogieron por su experiencia.**
> They chose him for his experience.
>
> **Lo hago por el amor que te tengo.**
> I do it out of the love I bear you.
>
> **Me felicitó por el nacimiento de mi hijo.**
> He congratulated me on the birth of my son.
>
> **Ganamos por estar bien entrenados.**
> We won because we were well-trained.
>
> **Lo supimos por carta.**
> We learnt about it by letter.
>
> **Me sujetaron por los brazos.**
> They held me fast by my arms.
>
> **Le ataqué por detrás.**
> I attacked him from behind.
>
> **Se casarán por la Iglesia.**
> They will have a church wedding.
>
> **Empecé por el primer capítulo.**
> I began with the first chapter.

Para:

> **Me voy para Madrid (para casa).**
> I'm off to Madrid (off home).

Se estaba vistiendo para el baile.
She was dressing for the dance.
Se están preparando para salir.
They are getting ready to go out.
Está estudiando para un examen.
He is studying for an examination.
Pero éstos no son para ti.
But these are not for you.
Aproveché la ocasión para conocerle personalmente.
I took advantage of the occasion to get to know him personally.
¿Para qué les hace falta tanto dinero?
What do they need so much money for?
No tenía bastante para comprarse otro.
He hadn't enough to buy himself another.
Es muy apropiado para ese fin.
It is well-suited to that end.

(b) *Translating the English 'for'*

The English *for* is translated by **para,** except in the following cases where **por** is used:

(i) when *for* indicates a causal relationship (*i.e.*, =*because of, on account of*).

Le admiro por su confianza.
I admire him for his confidence.
Me desprecia por mis creencias.
He scorns me for my beliefs.
Nos tiene simpatía por la ayuda que le hemos dado.
He is fond of us for the help we have given him.
Lo hago todo por ella.
I do it all for her (*i.e.*, on her account).
contrast **Lo hago para ella.**
I do (*or* make) it for her (*i.e.*, destined to her).
Lo traigo para usted.
I bring it for you.

(ii) when *for* indicates exchange or substitution.

Pagué cien pesetas por esta camisa.
I paid a hundred pesetas for this shirt.

Lo hago por mi hermano.

I am doing it for (= on behalf of) my brother.

contrast **La compré para mi abuelo.**

I bought it for my grandfather.

Lo hago para mi hermano.

I am doing it for (= destined to) my brother.

(iii) when *for* indicates *on* what occasion.

Me lo regaló por mi cumpleaños.

He gave it me for my birthday.

Esto se come mucho por Navidad.

This is eaten a lot for (*or* at) Christmas.

contrast **Lo haremos para mañana.**

We shall do it for tomorrow.

(iv) when *for* indicates for how long something is (or was) intended.

Iré a España por quince días.

I shall go to Spain for a fortnight.

contrast **Está ahorrando para cuando se jubile.**

He is saving up for when he retires.

NOTE: In general the English *for* indicating space of time is best translated by **por** only when the action of the verb marks the mere entering into the space of time. Otherwise (*i.e.*, when the action of the verb covers the whole space of time) **durante** is used, or no preposition.

Me invitó a su casa por un mes.	He invited me to his house for a month.
Voy a Madrid por ocho días.	I am going to Madrid for a week.
but **Trabajaré durante quince días.**	I shall work for a fortnight.
Estuve dos meses en Madrid. **Estuve en Madrid durante dos meses.**	I was in Madrid for two months.

The only important exceptions to this are **por un momento** (*for a moment*) and **por un instante** (*for an instant*): **Por un momento**

(un instante) creí que no venía. *For a moment (an instant) I thought he wasn't coming.*

(v) when *for* introduces an object for which one has gone or been sent.

Envió a su hijo a la farmacia por un frasco de medicina.
She sent her son to the chemist's for a bottle of medicine.

NOTE: If the object of one's movement is a person the above construction is best avoided.

$$\left\{ \begin{array}{l} \textbf{Llamaron} \\ \textbf{Mandaron llamar} \end{array} \right\} \textbf{al médico.} \quad \text{They sent for the doctor.}$$

(vi) when *for* introduces the object of an emotion.

Muestran un gran afecto por mi padre.
They show great affection for my father.

(vii) when *for* indicates support [*i.e.*, on behalf of, *cf.*, § 100 (5) (i)].

Habló por la monarquía.	He spoke for the monarchy.
Peleaban por el dinero.	They were fighting for the money.
Murieron por la patria.	They died for their country.
Optó por salir en seguida.	He elected to leave at once.
Se esfuerza por acabarlo.	He strives to finish it.

NOTE: Here **por** comes very near to the purpose function of **para**. With a following infinitive the functions of the two words may occasionally overlap: thus **Fuimos para** (also **por**) **ver las fiestas** (*We went to see the celebrations.*) With **para** there is greater emphasis on the aim, and with the less frequent **por** a greater emphasis on the inner desire (*i.e.*, **por querer ver las fiestas**), but the difference is small. **Para** is generally the safer alternative for the English student.

(c) Idioms with **por**

¡por Dios!	for heaven's sake!
¡vaya por Dios!	well, I never!
por entonces	about that time
por ahora	for the time being

250

por el momento	for (*or* at) the moment
por mi parte	for my part, on my side
por otra parte	on the other hand
por si acaso	(just) in case
por lo visto	apparently
por ejemplo	for example, e.g.
por supuesto	of course
por lo tanto } **por consiguiente** }	consequently
por fin } **por último** }	finally, at last
por todas partes	all over the place, everywhere
dos veces por semana	twice a week [§ 80 (8) Note]
cien kilómetros por hora	a hundred kilometres an hour
por culpa mía (tuya, etc.)	through my (your, etc.) fault
por la mañana (tarde, etc.)	in the morning (afternoon, etc.)
por primera (segunda, etc.) vez	for the first (second, etc.) time
hacer algo por segunda vez	to do something a second time
llamar (por teléfono)	to ring up, 'phone (up)
por aquí	hereabouts, around here
por allí; por allá; por ahí	thereabouts, around there
por eso	that's why, on that account, for that reason
por ... que	however [§ 114 (5)]

NOTE: **Por allí** indicates a more definite locality than **por allá** and **por ahí**. **Por ahí** is the most vague of the three and, against the rules of accentuation, is usually pronounced with the stress on the **a** (like **hay**).

147. VERBS IN -ducir. In accordance with § 139, the stem **c** of verbs in **-ducir** changes to **zc** before **o** and **a**.

e.g., **conducir**, *to lead, drive* (*a car*)

pres. ind.: conduzco, conduces, conduce, conducimos, conducís, conducen

pres. subj.: conduzca, conduzcas, conduzca, conduzcamos, conduzcáis, conduzcan

Furthermore, verbs of this type are irregular in the preterite and the imperfect subjunctive:

preterite: conduje, condujiste, condujo, condujimos, condujisteis, condujeron

imp. subj.: condujera (condujese), condujeras (condujeses), etc.

VOCABULARY

la admiración	admiration	el instante	instant
el afecto	affection	insustituible	irreplaceable
la amenaza	menace	justificar	to justify
anunciar	to announce, to advertise	la lágrima	tear
		llamar	to call
el bastón	stick	maestro	master (*adj.* and *noun*)
la cama	bed		
castigar	to punish	de prisa	quickly
la conclusión	conclusion	profundo	profound, deep, sound
la conducta	conduct	de pronto	
conseguir	to obtain, to achieve	de repente	} suddenly
		rezar	to pray
declarar	to declare	rico	rich
desde luego	certainly	situar	to situate
el engaño	deception	sustituir	to substitute
el (la) estudiante	student	la traducción	translation
		traducir	to translate
extremo	extreme (*adj.* and *noun*)	la Virgen	the (Blessed) Virgin
falso	false	la voz	voice
la guerra	war		

Study the idioms with **por** listed in § 146 (*c*).

EXERCISES

I. (*a*) *Study and translate:* Esta poesía fue escrita por Machado. Me lo dijo el profesor. No se sabía quién era. No se permite hablar. No se veía nada. Uno se atreve a todo. Está

colgada detrás de la puerta. Se los vio la semana pasada.
Se me acusa sin razón. Se les encarga la mayor parte del
trabajo. Se invitará a sus padres. Se venden pisos. Aquí
se come muy bien. Trabaja por ser pobre. Trabaja para
ser rico. Por entonces murió su madre. Lo dejamos
para entonces. Lo guardé para el día siguiente. El
tren está por salir. El tren está para salir. Estoy por
decirle que no. Estudia para profesor. Hace falta más
confianza por parte de usted. Por mucho que se lo digan.
Lo traduje al inglés. Hace calor para mayo. Me dio las
gracias por lo que les había dicho. No puedo hacer nada
por usted.

(b) *Translate:* It was translated by him. What has been
done? They have been defeated by the Moors. Has it
been published yet? The plan hasn't yet been accepted.
He was seen last night. Nothing has been decided. She
was heard closing the door. And then *she* is accused.
That's not done. It has not been understood. Before it
was explained to me. As soon as it was realized what had
happened. A hundred and fifty kilometres an hour. However impossible it may appear. He was led to a very small
room. Who is this book for? For a moment she thought
he was dying. If we had been told before. How much did
you pay for this book? He brought it for his brother. They
left for Madrid. He came in through the window. I study
in order to understand. I am tired through having studied
so much.

II. (a) *Study and translate:* 1. Todo lo que puede hacerse por
esta pobre señora está hecho ya. 2. A fines de mes nos
marchamos a España por unas semanas. 3. La Península
Ibérica se halla situada en el extremo sudoeste de Europa.
4. Sabían que ni con amenazas ni con lágrimas podía con-
seguirse nada. 5. La obra fue dedicada por él con todo afecto
a su maestro don Ramón Menéndez Pidal. 6. ¿Cómo
quiere usted que convenzamos a los demás si no estamos
convencidos nosotros mismos? 7. Pero la catedral está muy

lejos, de manera que tardarán bastante en volver, por de prisa que vayan. 8. La palabra inglesa *now* se traduce generalmente por **ahora**, aunque también a veces por **ya** y otras por **ahora bien**. 9. Por otra parte, a mí me gusta mucho la traducción que publicó hace años el señor Ramírez. 10. Procuraré estudiar la lección mañana por la mañana, aunque Felipe dice que piensa tenerla terminada para esta noche.

(*b*) *Translate:* 1. Will you please do it for my brother? 2. She is loved by all who know her. 3. Look at this translation. It's very well done, isn't it? 4. I think I've heard something about Segovia from my brother. 5. I punished him for having sold all his books for a few pesetas. 6. On the following morning we got up early and immediately after breakfast we left for Toledo. 7. I am going to try translating this chapter into Spanish, though I am told it will be rather difficult. 8. The doctor was called straight away but it was too late for him to do anything (=something). 9. Certainly I think that he has been deceived, but don't you think that the deception was justified by his own conduct? 10. Without doubt these problems are difficult but they are not so difficult that they cannot be solved by a good student.

III. (*a*) *Study and translate:* 1. Salieron para la India hacia fines de mayo. 2. Ya sé que a Vd. no le gusta el vino, pero lléveselo por si acaso. 3. La admiro por la mucha confianza que tiene en sí misma. 4. Están muy extrañados de que no se les deje entrar a ver lo que ocurre. 5. Y todas las noches rezaba por ti, arrodillada delante de la Virgen que tengo al lado de mi cama. 6. Se han publicado ya muchos libros y ensayos sobre lo que se suele llamar «el problema de España». 7. Yo, desde luego, estoy convencido de que ésta es su obra maestra, pero ha sido muy mal comprendida por la gente. 8. — Pero es muy viejo este libro. ¿Por qué no lo sustituye usted por otro? — Es un libro insustituible para mí. 9. Sin verte, te conozco ya tanto que leo dentro de ti, y puedo pensar por ti y sentir por ti en cualquier instante que quiera recordarte.

10. En el otro extremo de la mesa estaba sentado un tal señor Fernández, muy conocido, según me dijeron, por un libro que había escrito sobre la situación política de España a principios del siglo xx.

(b) *Translate:* 1. But I don't ask you to do it for her; now it is for me. 2. It was about the end of the year when war was declared. 3. The door was opened by a very old gentleman leaning on a stick. 4. He was seen near here this morning but it is not known where he is now. 5. Suddenly the husband was heard approaching, and apparently he was not alone. 6. You have not been told the whole truth; consequently, your conclusions are completely false. 7. It appears that he has been punished for not having told them what he had seen. 8. They slept soundly all night and were wakened on the following morning by their aunt's voice. 9. This is too difficult for me; certainly I'm not going to be able to finish it for next Monday. 10. It has been announced that the government, for its part, will do everything possible to reach an agreement.

LESSON XXIV

148. VERBS THAT TAKE A DIRECT OBJECT IN ENGLISH OR SPANISH.
(*a*) In general, verbs that take a direct object in English also
take a direct object in Spanish and vice versa.

¿Conoces Madrid (a éste; a mi hermano)?
Do you know Madrid (this man; my brother)?

NOTE: In Spanish the preposition **a** is placed before noun or
strong-pronoun direct objects referring to specific persons (see §47
for details—and exceptions).

(*b*) Certain verbs, however, that have a direct object in English
take a prepositional object in Spanish. Common verbs of this
type are:

abusar de	to abuse, to misuse	**dar con**	to meet, to come across
acercarse a	to approach	**desconfiar de**	to distrust
acordarse de	to remember		
apoderarse de	to seize	**disfrutar de**	to enjoy
aproximarse a	to approach	**dudar de**	to doubt, to question
asistir a	to attend (= be present at)	**encontrarse con**	to meet, to find (out)
burlarse de	to mock, to ridicule	**enterarse de**	to discover, to find out
cambiar de	to change	**entrar en**	to enter
carecer de	to lack	**faltar a**	not to fulfil, to break (word, promise)
casarse con	to marry (= take in marriage)		
dar a	to overlook (= look on to)	**fiarse de**	to trust
		fijarse en	to notice
		gozar de	to enjoy

256

ingresar en	to enter	**prescindir**	to omit, to
jugar a	to play (a game)	**de**	ignore, to leave aside
llegar a	to reach (a place)	**renunciar a**	to renounce, to give up
mudar de	to change	**reparar en**	to notice
olvidarse de	to forget	**resistir a**	to resist
oponerse a	to oppose	**salir de**	to leave (a place)
parecerse a	to resemble, to look like	**servirse de**	to use
pasar de	to exceed	**sobrevivir a**	to survive, to outlive
penetrar en	to penetrate, to enter	**tirar de**	to pull

Carece de todo.	He lacks everything.
Hemos cambiado de casa (de ropa).	We have changed houses (our clothes).
Resistió a la tentación de ir.	He resisted the temptation to go.
No hay placer de que no disfruten.	There is no pleasure they do not enjoy.
Se opone a que entren en la casa.	He opposes their entering the house.

NOTE: Some of the above verbs may be used with a direct object but then have a different meaning: **casar**, to marry (=join or give in marriage); **tirar**, to throw, throw away; **cambiar**, to exchange and to change (=make changes in) as opposed to **cambiar de**, to change (=make a change of). **Dudar** alone is used with the weak pronoun object **lo** (=it but not him) and immediately before **que**; **dudar de** is used in all other cases.

Lo he cambiado por otro.	I've changed (=exchanged) it for another.
He cambiado mis planes.	I've changed my (=made changes in my) plans.
He cambiado de planes.	I've changed my (=made a change of) plans.
Han cambiado de opinión.	They have changed their opinion.
Dudaba que viniera.	I doubted whether he would come.

Lo dudo. (*But* **Dudo de esto.**) I doubt it. (I doubt this.)
Dudaba de su sinceridad. She doubted his sincerity.
Duda de lo que digo. He doubts what I say.

(*c*) Conversely, certain verbs that have a direct object in Spanish take a prepositional object in English. Common verbs of this type are:

agradecer	to be grateful for	**lamentar**	to be sorry about
aguantar	to put up with (=endure)	**meditar**	to think over
		mirar	to look at
aprobar	to approve of	**pagar**	to pay for
aprovechar	to take advantage of, to make use of, to profit from	**recordar**	to remind of
		regalar	to present with, to make a present of
buscar	to look for	**reprochar**	to reproach with
considerar	to look upon (=consider)	**rumiar**	to meditate on, to ponder over
cuidar	to look after		
despedir	to say good-bye to	**sentir**	to be sorry about
escuchar	to listen to	**soportar**	to put up with (=endure)
esperar	to wait for		

¿Con qué lo pagaste? What did you pay for it with?

Llevo media hora esperán- I have been waiting for him for
dole. half an hour.

Cuida muy bien a sus hijos. She looks after her children very well.

Les reprochó su pereza. He reproached them for their idleness.

NOTE: An English direct object with one of these verbs becomes the indirect object in Spanish: i.e., *I paid him for it* becomes **Se lo pagué** (lit., *I paid it to him*). See also the last example above.

149. VERBS THAT TAKE AN INDIRECT OBJECT IN ENGLISH OR SPANISH. (*a*) An indirect object in English is translated by an indirect object in Spanish, and vice versa.

A mi madre le he regalado una pulsera y a mi padre una botella de coñac.

I have given a bracelet to my mother and a bottle of brandy to my father.

REMEMBER: 1. In English the preposition *to* introducing the indirect object is frequently omitted. This is not possible in Spanish, nor is it possible for preposition and indirect object to be separated as occurs frequently with English interrogatives and relatives.

Entregó su ejercicio al profesor.	He handed the teacher his exercise.
A todos les infundía confianza.	He would give everyone confidence.
¿A quién diste el recado?	Who(m) did you give the message to?
Es el mismo a quien debo el dinero.	It's the same man I owe the money to.

2. The preposition **a** is not expressed with a weak pronoun object.

Le mandamos un regalo.	We sent him a present.
Nos causó una desilusión.	It caused us a disappointment.
Les proporcionaba grandes ventajas.	It afforded them great advantages.

(*b*) The indirect object forms are used in Spanish also in the following special cases:

(1) To indicate a person directly interested in or related with the action of the verb. The English equivalent is usually: (i) as in Spanish, the ethic dative or dative of interest (*Make them a cup of tea. She bought herself another hat*); (ii) the preposition *for* followed by the person interested (*We are house-hunting for him. Would you do this for me?*); or, (iii) the Spanish dative may be unexpressed in the corresponding English (*I don't know [me, to myself] the lesson. Look [me] at that*). In this last case frequent use of the dative of interest is a characteristic of popular Spanish conversational style.

No me perdona mis faltas.	He doesn't forgive me my mistakes.

¿Le quieres hacer un poco de té?	Would you make him a drop of tea?
Se compró otro sombrero.	She bought herself another hat.
A sus padres les ha causado muchas desdichas.	He has caused his parents much unhappiness.
Oye, a ver si me haces esto.	I say, how about doing this for me?
Le estamos buscando casa.	We're house-hunting for him.
Me lo consiguió un amigo.	A friend got it for me.
Se le ha muerto su padre.	Her father has died (on her).
Se lo bebió todo.	He drank it all (up).
Mira, se lo ha zampado todo.	Look. He's wolfed the lot.
Me lo tengo que meditar.	I have to think it over.
Te lo mereces.	You deserve it.
No me sé la lección.	I don't know the lesson.
Yo tampoco me la sé muy bien.	I don't know it very well either.
Mírame eso.	Just look at that.

(2) (Closely related with (1).) To indicate the owner of parts of the body, clothing, and certain personal belongings and mental faculties to which action is being done. The English possessive adjective is then translated by the Spanish definite article.

Les lavó la cara a sus hijos.	She washed her children's faces.
Me partí un dedo.	I broke (me) a finger.
Se rompió la pierna.	He broke his leg.
Se llevó las manos a la cabeza.	She put her hands to her head.
Se le llenaron los ojos de lágrimas.	Her eyes filled with tears.
Nos pintaron los brazos.	They painted our arms.
Se quitaron la chaqueta.	They took their coats (= jackets) off.
Nos pusimos el sombrero.	We put our hats on.

¿Quieres atarme los cor- dones?	Will you fasten my (shoe-) laces?
Me subió la maleta.	He took my suitcase up.
Le salvaron la vida.	They saved his life.
Le llamó la atención a mi padre.	He attracted my father's atten- tion.

NOTE: The part of the body or clothing is named in the singular if the action is concerned with only one per person:

	Nos lavamos la cara.	We washed our faces.
but	Nos lavamos las manos.	We washed our hands
	Se quitaron el sombrero.	They took their hats off.
but	Se quitaron los guantes.	They took their gloves off.
	Les até la mano derecha.	I tied their right hands.
but	Les até las dos manos.	I tied their two hands.

(3) To indicate the person *from* (or *of*) whom something is con- cealed, requested or acquired.

¿A quién compró Vd. este coche?	Who(m) did you buy this car from?
Le robaron todas sus ri- quezas.	They robbed him of all his wealth.
Esta guerra le arrebató a Es- paña sus últimas colonias.	This war snatched from Spain her last colonies.
Les exigía demasiado a sus ministros.	He demanded too much of his ministers.
Le ocultó la verdad a su padre.	He concealed the truth from his father.

150. VERBS THAT TAKE A PREPOSITIONAL OBJECT IN ENGLISH AND SPANISH. (*a*) Where an English verb and its Spanish equiva- lent take a preposition, the preposition generally corresponds in the two languages or can be explained by reference to certain broad tendencies (*e.g.*, **de** translates English *with* after verbs that imply filling, loading, covering, etc.)

Habla de la posibilidad de ir a la India.	He talks of the possibility of going to India.
Está jugando con su hijo.	He is playing with his son.
El emperador le colmó de honores.	The emperor loaded him with honours.

(b) With certain verbs, however, the prepositions do not correspond and broad generalizations offer no help:

acabar con	to put an end to	**encontrarse con**	to come across (=meet)
alimentarse de (or **con**)	to feed on	**felicitar por**	to congratulate on
arrimarse a	to lean against	**fijarse en**	to take note of
asomarse a	to lean out of, to appear at	**hablar con**	to speak to
compadecerse de	to be sorry for, to take pity on	**interesarse por**	to be interested in, to take interest in
consentir en	to consent to, to acquiesce to	**lindar con**	to border on
		maravillarse de	to wonder at
consistir en	to consist of	**ocuparse de** (or **en**)	to attend to, to look after
contar con	to rely on, to count on	**oler a**	to smell of
convenir en	to agree to	**pensar en**	to think of
dar a	to look on to	**portarse con**	to behave towards
dar con	to come across (=meet)	**prescindir de**	to do without
depender de	to depend on	**reírse con**	to laugh at (=be amused by)
despedirse de	to say good-bye to	**reírse de**	to laugh at (=make fun of)
destacarse sobre (or **en**)	to stand out against	**reparar en**	to take note of
		responder de	to answer for
divertirse con	to be amused by	**saber a**	to taste of, to smack of
enamorarse de	to fall in love with	**soñar con**	to dream of
		tirar de	to pull at, to tug at

tratarse de	to be about, to deal with	**vengarse de**	to take revenge for (*or* on)
triunfar de	to triumph over	**vivir con** (*or* **de**)	to live on
tropezar con	to run into (= come across)		

Se divirtió mucho con esta historia.	He was very amused by this story.
Le felicité por su gran éxito.	I congratulated him on his great success.
Consiente en que lo hagamos así.	He consents to our doing it thus.

NOTES: 1. **Hablar a** suggests that the subject did the talking; **hablar con** that there was discussion (*i.e.*, almost *to have a talk with*).

2. **Pensar de** means *to think of* (= to have an opinion on).

¿Qué piensa usted de él?	What do you think of him?
but **¿En qué piensa usted?**	What are you thinking of?

VOCABULARY

agradable	pleasant	**familiar**	familiar
anterior	previous	**la ilusión**	illusion
el asunto	matter, subject	**el motivo**	motive, reason
el caballero	gentleman	**notar**	to note
el color	colour	**peligroso**	dangerous
cualquiera	any(one), whichever	**la posibilidad**	possibility
la cuestión	question (= problem)	**la pregunta**	question
		probable	probable
definitivo	final, definitive	**reñir**	to scold, to quarrel
la despedida	farewell		
el ejemplar	copy (of book)	**robar**	to steal, to rob
elegir	to elect, to choose	**el sentimiento**	feeling
el enemigo	enemy	**serio**	serious
escapar(se)	to escape	**todavía**	still, yet
es que	the fact is (that)		

hacer una pregunta   to ask a question

Study also the verbs listed in §§ 148 and 150

263

EXERCISES

I. (a) *Study and translate:* Ha faltado a su palabra. Los que sobrevivieron a la guerra. Se opuso al nuevo proyecto. Prescindiendo de tal posibilidad. Le regalé un reloj. No aguanto más. Exige demasiado a los estudiantes. Se arrimó a la pared. No respondo de mí. ¿De qué se trata? Las montañas se destacaban negras sobre el cielo. Me encontré con que se habían marchado ya. Allí tropecé con un turista norteamericano. A ver si me lo haces para mañana. Tengo que hablarle en seguida. Considérense como amigos. La pobre se me iba muriendo día tras día. Se te nota en los ojos. Fíjese bien en lo que digo.

(b) *Translate:* He won't remember me. I drew near to the door. It depends on what my father says. They put on their overcoats. His uncle got it for him. He is interested in algebra. I want *you* to do it for me. He said good-bye to his parents. His hands were trembling. Have you noticed this wall? They had been waiting for him for more than twenty minutes. Then I found out the truth.' He's very like his elder brother. Those who have come don't exceed twenty. Listen to what he says. Will you get my suitcase down? The room smelt of cats.

II. (a) *Study and translate:* 1. No espero a nadie ni estoy para nadie. 2. Tu tío, sobre todo, no cesaba un momento de pensar en ti. 3. No se atreve a confesar lo que ha pensado de mí en estos últimos días. 4. ¿Puedo hacerle una pregunta? No hace falta que me la conteste si no quiere. 5. Fíjese bien en el color de este árbol. Y mire las hojas qué bonitas son. 6. Quería acordarme de su nombre, pero se me había escapado completamente de la memoria. 7. Fue una tarde muy agradable, sobre todo para los que nos interesábamos por las cuestiones políticas. 8. Ya sé que no ha dejado ni un solo día de pedirte perdón por lo mal que se ha portado contigo. 9. Desde luego este asunto me es familiarísimo, pero prefiero callarme a hacerle dudar de sus propias

264

opiniones. 10. Les agradecería mucho, caballeros, que tuvieran la bondad de decir unas cuantas palabras a mi hijo antes de marcharse.

(*b*) *Translate:* 1. I'd rather do it myself than let her do it for me. 2. I want to take advantage of this visit to know his own feelings. 3. On the other hand, we must not count too much on the possibility of such a revolution. 4. It has been said that the young spend their (=the) time dreaming of the impossible. 5. She washes her own hair on Fridays, and she washes her children's on Saturdays. 6. I am waiting for him now but he always arrives late. It must be five o'clock. 7. She asked him for twenty-five pesetas, saying that she would give them back to him on the following morning. 8. The other day I came across an old friend who was about to get married to an Andalusian girl. 9. During the previous week he had triumphed over his enemies by being elected a minister in the new government. 10. I'm sorry I haven't the book here. I lent it to Mr Fernández last week and he hasn't yet given it me back.

III. (*a*) *Study and translate:* 1. No encontrábamos ningún motivo para dudar de su sinceridad. 2. ¿Cómo he de reñirle por una cosa que no puedo menos de aprobar? 3. No se fíe usted de doña Carmen, que es capaz de engañar a cualquiera. 4. Ya es tiempo de cambiar de conducta y de enterarse un poco de lo que es el trabajo. 5. Tú, ve a buscar a tus padres, y yo me quedo aquí a esperar a los míos. No creo que tarden en venir. 6. — Ya no nos gusta el perro que nos compraron el mes pasado. — Pues entonces que lo cambien por otro. 7. ¿Por qué te marchaste sin despedirte de nosotros? Es que te teníamos preparada una cena de despedida. 8. Estas ideas, por buenas que parezcan, pueden ser peligrosas para gente no acostumbrada a pensar en cosas un poco profundas. 9. Se lo pidió a su padre, pero éste no quería que su hija se casara con un estudiante que no vivía más que de sus ilusiones. 10. Voy siendo cada vez más maduro, más serio, más viejo. Todavía no he pensado en

casarme, que será entonces cuando renuncie ya definitivamente a las ilusiones de la juventud.

(b) *Translate:* 1. They are resolved not to let him enter the
house again. 2. Would you be so good as to look for the
address for me? 3. I had my car stolen yesterday and it still
hasn't been found. 4. He no longer remembered those (so)
happy days he had spent with his parents. 5. Will you come
with me and speak to them, or do you prefer to stay here?
6. Don't count on me. It is probable I shall be out of
Madrid when your brother arrives. 7. We shall leave
England on the second of January and spend three weeks in
the south of France. 8. In studying this matter it is very
important that we should leave aside our own feelings.
9. Would you please ask Peter to look for a copy of *Gulliver's
Travels* for me when he is in town, and to send it on to me
as soon as possible? 10. He was very amused by this story
and told it to his brother so that he (= the latter) too could
laugh at it.

LESSON XXV

151. RELATIVE PRONOUNS. (*a*) These are the following:

que	who, whom, which, that
quien(es)	who, whom
el (lo, la) cual, los (las) cuales	who, whom, which, that
èl (lo, la, los, las) que	who, whom, which, that

(*b*) *Preliminary Distinctions*

(1) A relative pronoun may refer to persons or things, and, within its own clause, it may be the subject, the direct object, or the prepositional object of the verb. There are thus six principal functions to be taken into account when deciding which relative pronoun to use in a given case in Spanish:

SUBJECT	(It is the boy) *who* came yesterday. (I have a car) *that* goes very fast.
DIRECT OBJECT	(It is the boy) *whom* we saw yesterday (I have a car) *that* I want to sell.
PREPOSITIONAL OBJECT	(It is the boy) to *whom* we talked yesterday. (I have a car) in *which* I travel a lot.

REMEMBER: These different functions may at times be confused in English by the omission of the relative pronoun (e.g., *It is the boy we saw yesterday*) or by the placing of the preposition after the subordinate verb (e.g., *I have a car that I travel a lot in*) or by both these things together (e.g., *It is the boy we talked to yesterday*). None of this is possible in Spanish.

(2) A relative clause may be restrictive or non-restrictive.

Restrictive	*Non-Restrictive*
The boys who speak Spanish are going to Spain.	The boys, who speak Spanish, are going to Spain.
There is a lady coming whom you already know.	His wife is coming, whom you already know.

In its restrictive use *who speak Spanish* serves to limit the antecedent *boys*, telling us *which* boys are going to Spain; in the non-restrictive use the antecedent is already limited in the speaker's mind (*these boys, those boys*), and *who speak Spanish* serves merely to give an additional fact about them. Similarly, in the other case, the restrictive *whom you already know* helps to indicate *which* lady is coming, whereas the non-restrictive use simply adds a new fact about a lady who is already sufficiently defined. The omission of a restrictive clause takes away something essential from the principal idea it is desired to express; the omission of a non-restrictive clause merely suppresses a subordinate—and independent—idea.

(c) The Subject Relative Pronoun

(1) This is usually **que** for both persons and things.

Es el chico que vino ayer.

It is the boy who came yesterday.

Tengo un coche que va muy rápido.

I have a car that goes very fast.

(2) In a non-restrictive clause, however, **el cual, la cual,** etc., indicating number and gender, may also be used, especially in literary style with persons when **que** might lead to confusion.

Estuvo también su hermano, $\left\{ \begin{array}{c} \textbf{que} \\ \textbf{el cual} \end{array} \right\}$ **trabajaba en la misma ciudad.**

There was his brother there too, who was working in the same town.

Fuimos a despedir a la madre de Juan, $\left\{ \begin{array}{l} \textbf{que} \\ \textbf{la cual} \end{array} \right\}$ volvía a casa.

We went to see John's mother off, who was returning home.

NOTE: **Quien(es)** may be used instead of **el cual,** etc., to refer to persons, and **el que, la que,** etc., to refer to persons and things. **Quien(es)** is not frequent; **el que,** etc., is rare.

(3) The neuter **lo cual** (or **lo que**) must be used when the antecedent is not a specific noun.

Se marchó, lo cual nos gustó a todos.

He went away, which pleased us all.

No está aquí, lo cual me extraña.

He is not here, which surprises me.

(4) In clauses introduced by words such as *it is I who, it was they who, it has been these books which*, the relative pronoun is **quien** or **el que** for persons and **el que** for things.

Somos nosotros $\left\{ \begin{array}{l} \textbf{los que} \\ \textbf{quienes} \end{array} \right\}$ **tenemos que ir.**

It is we who have to go.   We are the ones who have to go.

Eres tú $\left\{ \begin{array}{l} \textbf{el que} \\ \textbf{quien} \end{array} \right\}$ **tiene que hacerlo.**

It is you who have to do it.

Fue España la que quedó aislada.

It was Spain that was left isolated.

NOTE: If the antecedent is a pronoun of the first or second person, the verb in the relative clause may agree with that antecedent in person as well as number (*cf*. the first example: **nosotros — tenemos**), or, more frequently, be expressed in the third person thus agreeing only in number (*cf*. second example: **tú — tiene**).

(d) *The Direct Object Relative Pronoun*

(1) This is usually **que** for both persons and things.

Es el chico que vimos ayer.

It is the boy we saw yesterday.

Tengo un coche que quiero vender.

I have a car I want to sell.

(2) For persons, however, some form of **quien, el que** or **el cual** preceded by the personal **a** may also be used, especially in non-restrictive clauses.

Es el chico $\begin{cases} \textbf{a quien} \\ \textbf{al que} \\ \textbf{al cual} \end{cases}$ **vimos ayer.**

It is the boy we saw yesterday.

Se asustó mucho con la vuelta de Pedro, al que creía muerto.

She was very frightened by the return of Peter whom she believed dead.

Viene su señora, a quien usted conoce ya.

His wife is coming, whom you already know.

(3) and (4). The relative pronouns used here are the same as those employed in the corresponding cases where the relative is the subject of the clause [above (c) (3) and (4)].

Se ofreció como guía, lo cual le agradecimos mucho.

He offered himself as a guide, for which we were very grateful to him.

Sois vosotros $\begin{cases} \textbf{a los que} \\ \textbf{a quienes} \end{cases}$ **vimos ayer.**

It is you we saw yesterday.

(e) The Prepositional-Object Relative Pronoun

The form of the relative pronoun is influenced by the preposition that precedes it. Thus **a, de, en** and **con** most frequently take **que** or **el que** with things and **quien** or **el que** with persons. The remaining prepositions (including compound prepositions ending in **de** or **a**) usually take some form of the pronoun **el cual.**

Es el chico con $\begin{cases} \textbf{quien} \\ \textbf{el que} \end{cases}$ **hablamos ayer.**

It is the boy we talked to yesterday.

Tengo un coche en (el) que viajo mucho.

I have a car in which I travel a lot.

Hable usted con la señora junto a la cual me pondré.

Talk to the lady beside whom I shall place myself.

Había una ventana desde la cual se veía toda la ciudad.
There was a window from which could be seen the whole town.
Escribí una carta, después de lo cual salí a dar un paseo.
I wrote a letter, after which I went out for a walk.

152. OTHER USES OF **quien**.   Besides serving as a relative pronoun to refer to persons after a preposition, **quien** may be used in certain cases without an antecedent:

(i) in place of **alguien que** (*someone who*) and **nadie que** (*no one who*).

Busco $\left\{\begin{array}{l}\textbf{quien}\\ \textbf{a alguien que}\end{array}\right\}$ **me ayude.**

I am looking for someone to help me.

No hay $\left\{\begin{array}{l}\textbf{quien}\\ \textbf{nadie que}\end{array}\right\}$ **lo comprenda.**

There is no one who understands it.

(ii) in place of **el que** to translate *he who*, *she who*, etc. used in a generalizing sense.

$\left.\begin{array}{l}\textbf{El que}\\ \textbf{Quien}\end{array}\right\}$ **trabaje más, ganará más.**

$\left.\begin{array}{l}\text{He who}\\ \text{Whoever}\end{array}\right\}$ works more will earn more.

NOTES: 1. With this section should be considered the examples quoted in § 151 (*c*) (4). **Yo soy quien lo hace** means, literally, *I am he who does it.*

2. In a similar generalizing sense **cuanto(s)** may replace **todo el que, todos los que**, etc.

Le quité $\left\{\begin{array}{l}\textbf{todo el dinero que}\\ \textbf{cuanto dinero}\end{array}\right\}$ **tenía.**

I took from him all the money he had.

Se engañan $\left\{\begin{array}{l}\textbf{todos los que}\\ \textbf{cuantos}\end{array}\right\}$ **piensan así.**

All who think like that are deceiving themselves.

153. OTHER RELATIVES

(a) cuyo (-a, -os, -as)   whose, of whom, of which

This is a relative adjective and agrees in number and gender with the thing possessed.

Vimos una casa cuyas ventanas estaban rotas.

We saw a house the windows of which were broken.

NOTE: When the principal function of the subordinate clause is to indicate the ownership (and not to say something further about the object owned) cuyo is avoided by the use of pertenecer a (*to belong to*).

Conozco a la chica a quien pertenece este libro.

I know the girl whose book this is.

(b) (en) donde   where, in which
adonde   where, to which
como   that, in which

Es el pueblo $\begin{Bmatrix} \text{a(l) que} \\ \text{adonde} \end{Bmatrix}$ **vamos ahora.**

It is the town we are going to now.

Ocurrió en la casa $\begin{Bmatrix} \text{en (la) que} \\ \text{(en) donde} \end{Bmatrix}$ **vivía.**

It happened in the house where he lived.

Lo que me desagrada es la manera como lo dice.

What displeases me is the way (in which) she says it.

NOTE: Cuando is best not used as a relative.

el día en que ocurra esto   the day when this happens
Fue el año en que murió su padre.   It was the year (when) his father died.

154. RELATIVE WITH INFINITIVE.

A relative may be followed by an infinitive in cases such as the following, where part of the verbs deber or poder is understood.

Tenía mucho que hacer.   I had a lot to do.

No tengo nada más que decir. — I have nothing more to say.

No tenía a quien visitar. — He had no one to visit.

No tenía amigos con quienes hablar. — He had no friends to talk to.

No encontraba ventana por la cual escaparme. — I couldn't find a window through which to escape.

Busqué un sitio desde el cual ver la procesión. — I looked for a place from which to see the procession.

155. INTERROGATIVES.   (*a*) Spanish interrogative adjectives, pronouns and adverbs are:

(a)**dónde**	where (to)	**cuánto -a -os -as**	how much; *pl.* how many
cómo	how	**qué**	what, which
cuál(es)	which, what	**quién(es)**	who, whom
cuándo	when	**de quién(es)**	whose

¿Adónde va usted?   Where are you going?

Me preguntó adónde iba.   He asked me where I was going.

¿Cómo lo van a hacer?   How are they going to do it?

No quiso decir cómo lo iban a hacer.   He wouldn't say how they were going to do it.

¿Cuánto han gastado?   How much have they spent?

No sabía cuántas pesetas habían gastado.   He didn't know how many pesetas they had spent.

¿De quién son estos libros?   Whose books are these?

¿Cuánto cuesta?
¿Qué precio tiene? } How much is it?   What is the price?
¿Cuál es el precio?

NOTES: 1. Interrogative words are used in direct and indirect questions.

2. Invariable **qué** (*what, which*) is both pronoun and adjective.

¿Qué hiciste?   What did you do?

¿Qué libros le prestó usted?   Which books did you lend him?

273

3. **Cuál(es)** (*which*) is a pronoun and indicates a more limited range of selection than the adjective **qué**.

¿Cuáles de estos libros le prestó usted?   Which of these books did you lend him?

¿Cuál de los hermanos no vino?   Which brother didn't come?

4. The English *which* and *what* before part of the verb *to be* is usually translated by **cuál(es)**. **Qué** is used only when a definition is asked for.

>   **¿Cuál es el mejor libro para empezar?**   Which is the best book to begin with?
>
>   **¿Cuáles son sus objeciones?**   What are his objections?
>
> *but*   **¿Qué es la filosofía?**   What is philosophy?
>
>   **¿Qué es esto?**   What is this?

5. **Cómo** means *how* (= *in what way*). Thus the English *how do you* (*did he*, etc.) *like* . . ., when it asks for an opinion rather than a choice, is not translated by **cómo + gustar**, but by **qué + parecer**.

¿Cómo le gusta el café?   How do you like your coffee? (*i.e.,* black or white, with or without sugar, etc.)

¿Qué le parece el café?   How do you like the coffee? (*i.e.,* what do you think of it?)

(*b*) An interrogative pronoun, adjective or adverb may be followed by an infinitive.

No sabíamos qué hacer.   We didn't know what to do.

No sabía por dónde empezar.   He didn't know where to begin.

No sabían qué libro escoger.   They didn't know which book to choose.

No sabían cuál escoger.   They didn't know which to choose.

¿Cómo explicarle lo que pasó?   How [are we] to explain to him what happened?

¿Por qué no hacerlo mañana?   Why not do it tomorrow?

156. EXCLAMATIVES. The most common of the Spanish exclamatives are:

cómo	what
cuánto -a -os -as	how much, what a lot
qué	what a, how
quién+*imperf. subj.*	would that I, if only I

¡Cómo! y ¡tú te atreves a decírmelo!   What, and you dare to tell me so!

¡Cuánto trabaja este hombre!   How hard (*or* What a lot) this man works!

¡Qué falta de inteligencia!   What a lack of intelligence!

¡Qué alegre está usted!   How cheerful you are!

¡Qué bien cantan!   How well they sing!

¡Quién fuera poeta!   If only I were a poet!

NOTE: **Qué** followed by a noun translates the English *what a!* A qualifying adjective may be placed before the noun or, more usually, placed after it and preceded by **más** or **tan**.

¡Qué buen chico eres!	What a good boy you are!
¡Qué señor más simpático!	What a(n exceedingly) nice gentleman!
¡Qué día más estupendo!	What a wonderful day!
¡Qué casa tan enorme!	What an enormous house!

Followed by an adjective or adverb alone, **qué** translates the English *how!* (See examples above.)

157. THE INFINITIVE. (*a*) The infinitive may be used in Spanish as a subject, complement, direct object or prepositional object. A masculine singular article is occasionally set before the infinitive to emphasize it as a noun.

Pintar
El pintar } **esto sería imposible.**

To paint this
The painting of this } would be impossible.

El no venir su padre le causó una gran desilusión.

The fact of his father's not coming caused him a great disappointment.

Morir es dormir.

To die is to sleep.

La casa fue difícil de encontrar.

The house was difficult to find.

Se mareaba con el ir y venir de tanta gente.

She was feeling faint with the coming and going of so many people.

Hubo un continuo moverse de gente.

There was a constant movement of people.

NOTES: 1. In the last two examples the infinitive has become a noun to such a point that **de** is necessary to introduce the subject. (Contrast the second example and notice the English translations.)

2. In general the article should be used: (i) when an infinitive used as a subject, complement or direct object has its own subject expressed (*cf.* second example), and (ii) when an infinitive used as a prepositional object has a subject expressed and introduced by **de** (*cf.* last two examples, but **con venir su hermano,** *with his brother's coming*). In certain other cases, and particularly when the infinitive has an object (*cf.* first example), the article may be used but is often literary or archaic.

(b) *Preposition + Infinitive*

So far the only cases given of a preposition with an infinitive have been as in English, with the subject of the infinitive the same as that of the main verb (**Lo hice antes de salir,** *I did it before going out*, i.e., before *I* went out). In Spanish, however, a prepositional infinitive may have a different subject from the main verb; this subject is then placed *after* the infinitive.

Lo hizo antes de venir yo.

He did it before I came.

Al no decir nada el padre, supusimos que ya no venía su hijo.

Since the father didn't say anything, we assumed his son was not coming.

El problema es muy difícil para resolverlo un estudiante tan joven.

The problem is very difficult for such a young student to solve.

¿Cómo quiere usted que él lo entienda sin explicárselo yo primero?

How do you expect him to understand it without my explaining it to him first.

(c) Also in the following cases a Spanish *preposition + infinitive* has adverbial sense and corresponds to an English adverbial clause:

(i) **de** + infinitive: to express condition (English *if*).

De haberlo sabido, no le hubiera dicho nada.

If I had known it I should not have told him anything.

NOTE: A is used in the same way in **a no ser** (*if...not*).

A no ser por mí, se hubiera caído.

If it had not been for me he would have fallen.

(ii) **con** + infinitive: to express concession (English *although*) and means (English *by -ing*).

Juan, con ser el mayor, no por eso deja de parecerme el menos inteligente.

John, although he is the eldest, nevertheless appears to me to be the least intelligent.

No se pierde nada con hacerle una visita.

We lose nothing by paying him a visit.

(iii) **por** + *infinitive*: to express cause (English *because*).

Lo hice así por no saber dónde estaba.

I did it like that because I didn't know where he was.

(d) In certain cases an active Spanish infinitive may have passive sense:

(i) after verbs of causing and perception [§ 100 (1) (ii) and (iii)].

Lo mandé escribir.

I ordered it to be written.

La oí cantar en un pueblo de la Mancha.

I heard it sung in a village of La Mancha.

(ii) after **por** and **sin** in cases like the following:

Esta lección aún queda $\begin{cases} \textbf{por terminar.} \\ \textbf{sin terminar.} \end{cases}$

This lesson still remains $\begin{cases} \text{to be finished.} \\ \text{unfinished.} \end{cases}$

Estos libros están sin mirar.

These books haven't been looked at.

(iii) after **que** and **de** in cases like the following:

No hay nada más que decir.

There is nothing more to say (*or* to be said).

Esto es muy difícil de resolver.

This is very difficult to solve.

(*e*) The infinitive (alone or preceded by the preposition **a**) is frequently used with imperative or exhortative force.

¡Dirigirse al portero!   Apply to the porter.

¡Venga, hombre, a trabajar!   Come on now, down to work!

158. DIMINUTIVES AND AUGMENTATIVES. (*a*) These are characteristic of Spanish but can only be acquired by studying Spanish usage. Consequently, the indications that follow aim to enable the student to recognize them but not to use them.

(*b*) *Diminutives*

A diminutive is formed by adding to a given word (most frequently, though not always, a noun) certain endings which add a sense of smallness and often suggest an emotional reaction. The commonest of such endings is **-ito** (**-cito**, **-ecito**, **-ececito**) which usually suggests, besides smallness, the favourable disposition of the speaker.

Una limosnita, señorito, que Dios se lo pagará.   Alms, young sir; God will repay you.

Mira qué mujercita más lista tengo.   Look what a clever little wife I have.

Espere un momentito.   Wait just one moment (will you?)

Other important diminutive endings are **-illo (-cillo, -ecillo, -ececillo)**, which is usually less emotive than **-ito** and its related forms, and **-uelo (-zuelo, -ezuelo, -ecezuelo)** which may add a pejorative sense. The endings **-ico, -ín, -ino, -iño** are generally regional in use.

NOTE: For the use of the different forms quoted (*e.g.*, **-ito, -cito, -ecito, -ececito**) the following may be stated briefly:

(i) the last two forms (the longer ones) are used generally after words of one syllable: **piececito** (*little foot*), **florecita** (*little flower*).

(ii) **-cito** is used after words of more than one syllable ending in **n** or **r**: **mujercita** (*little woman*), **corazoncito** (*little heart*).

(iii) **-ito** is used in most other cases (with the fall of any final vowel): **animalito** (*little animal*), **cuartito** (*little room*).

(c) Augmentatives

The augmentative endings are less used than the diminutives. They add a sense of bigness and may suggest also clumsiness or ugliness. The most frequent augmentative ending is **-ón**. Others are **-azo, -ote** and **-acho**.

un hombrón	a hefty chap
un hombrote, un hombrazo	a big brute of a fellow

(d) Many diminutives and augmentatives have established themselves as words in their own right.

la silla (chair)	**el sillín** (saddle)	**el sillón** (armchair)
la abeja (bee)		**el abejón** (hornet)
la niebla (fog, mist)	**la neblina** (mist, haze)	
la cera (wax)	**la cerilla** (match)	
la señora (lady)	**la señorita** (miss, unmarried woman)	
bueno (good)	**bonito** (nice)	

VOCABULARY

aceptable	acceptable	**arreglar**	to arrange, to
admirar	to admire		put right,
el alma	soul, mind		to mend

asegurar	to assure	**perdonar**	to forgive
cada uno	each one	**pertenecer**	to belong
el consejo	advice; council	**el presi-**	president
es decir ⎫	that is (to say)	**dente**	
o sea ⎭		**proponer**	to propose
despreciar	to scorn	**resultar**	to turn out, to
destinar	to destine		prove (to be),
la esposa	wife		to appear
el esposo	husband	**reunir**	to gather
felicitar	to congratulate	**ridículo**	ridiculous
humano	human	**la salud**	health
influir	to influence	**el secretario**	secretary
interesar	to interest	**simpático**	nice
el jefe	chief, head, boss	**la solución**	solution
libre	free	**suficiente**	sufficient
nacer	to be born	**de verdad** ⎫	really, truly
nombrar	to name, to appoint	**de veras** ⎭	

¡**Vaya!**   Well! I say! Come now!

¡**Vaya por Dios!**   Well I never!

EXERCISES

I. (a) *Study and translate:* Ésta es la fábrica en la que trabajo. Hubo un momento en que nos perdimos. Hay quien me aconseja que no lo haga. Siempre hay alguien que no está de acuerdo. Era ella la que me animaba a seguir. El profesor a cuyo lado andaba. Después de lo cual me acosté. Es el amigo con el que vine ayer. No hay quien le entienda. No sabía a quién pedir ayuda. Entérate de cómo se hace. ¡Quién supiera bailar! ¡Qué chica más estúpida! ¡Venga, a callaros! De no ser así. Se la oyó cantar a una chica andaluza. De haberlo sabido. Sólo con verle. ¿Por qué no escribirle en seguida? Un jardincito. Mi abuelita. Oye, chiquillo. Juanito. ¡Qué grandote!

(b) *Translate:* The man we saw yesterday. The lady for whom I did it. The room in which he slept. The door behind which she was sitting. Those who work most. The gentleman we were talking about. Whose ideas are

these? What is the explanation? What do you think of
the scheme? Which brother do you prefer? What a
lovely view! What a lot of people! How difficult these
last lessons have been! I had no one to go with. After his
father left for Spain. It would be difficult to think otherwise
(= in another way). If he hadn't broken his leg. They
ordered it to be done. On reading the first chapter. Come
on, off to sleep! This is very good to eat.

II. (a) *Study and translate:* 1. ¡Pero qué ridículo estás! ¡Que no
te vean así! 2. Sois vosotros los que tenéis que pensar en
la dificultad del problema. 3. De seguir las cosas así, no sé
cómo las vamos a arreglar. 4. Fui a buscar quien me
ayudara a resolver algunas de estas dificultades. 5.— Fue
usted la que me llamó, ¿verdad? — Le aseguro que no.
6. Le felicitaron por haber sabido ganarse la confianza de
personas tan distintas. 7. Vaya, don José, no parece bien
que se burle usted así de un hombre con quien pienso
casarme dentro de muy poco. 8. — Buenos días, señorita.
¡Qué tempranito llega usted! — Puesto que tengo un jefe
tan simpático, y además sin casar...9. Al día siguiente llegó
la esposa del ministro, la cual había influido mucho por lo
visto al nombrarse el nuevo secretario del Consejo.
10. Ahora bien: ya en el año 1895, o sea, tres años antes de
empezar la guerra con los Estados Unidos, Unamuno había
publicado unos ensayos sobre lo que se iba a llamar «el problema de España.»

(b) *Translate:* 1. It appears they have something difficult to
explain to us. 2. Have you seen the girl whose book we were
talking about? 3. The more people we invite, the less each
one will have to eat. 4. He assures us that this is the only
reason for his brother's not having come too. 5. Had I
known it, I should have written straight away asking them for
help. 6. Why do you suppose we were talking about you?
Are there no other things to talk about in the world?
7. When the sun rose (*or* At sunrise) we continued our journey towards the capital. 8. Which are the most important

towns in Spain, where are they situated, and to what do they owe their importance? 9. Up till now it has always been they who have helped me; now it is I who can do something for them. 10. We are not going to have sufficient money, unless you would kindly lend us a few pounds.

III. (a) *Study and translate:* 1. Me desprecian por creer que he faltado a mi palabra. 2. Yo soy quien no comprende bien lo que piensa hacer. 3. ¿Cuáles son las razones por las que Madrid llegó a ser la capital de España? 4. ¡Qué alegría encontrarme por fin con alguien que me comprende de verdad! 5. Estoy cansado de oír hablar mal de personas a quienes yo admiro mucho. 6. Entramos ahora en una época de dificultades, de la cual no sé cómo vamos a salir. 7. Hay ciertas personas para las cuales las ilusiones son lo peor que cabe en el alma humana. 8. El decirlo él me hubiera extrañado mucho, a no ser por algo que me escribió el año pasado. 9. Se hallaban reunidas muchas personas de importancia, entre las cuales se destacaba el señor Fernández, presidente del Consejo. 10. Resulta que el señor Martínez, con ser tan rico y tan amigo del ministro, no había podido encontrar quien se interesara por su nuevo proyecto.

(b) *Translate:* 1. For the present there is nothing more to be said. 2. It is not we who must change [our] opinion. 3. Which is the boy you were talking about the other day? 4. This is one of the problems that is still to be studied. 5. They took us to an old house the windows of which were all broken. 6. There's no one understands him when he starts talking about politics. 7. When his father came in, the boy escaped rapidly through the window. 8. It is important we should know who he was with and why he missed the meeting. 9. I have just discovered a secret of the greatest importance, but I don't want anyone to know what it is. 10. We should be interested (= It would interest us) to know for what reason you refuse to accept the remedy that has been proposed.

REVIEW AND DEVELOPMENT
SECTION (V)

159. There are three classes or conjugations of verbs in Spanish, known from their infinitive endings as **-ar** (or first-conjugation), **-er** (or second-conjugation) and **-ir** (or third-conjugation) verbs. Second- and third-conjugation verbs have the same endings almost throughout.

I. -ar *e.g.*, comprar	II. -er *e.g.*, vender	III. -ir *e.g.*, vivir

INFINITIVES
PRESENT

comprar, *to buy*	vender, *to sell*	vivir, *to live*

PERFECT

haber comprado, *to have bought*	haber vendido, *to have sold*	haber vivido, *to have lived*

GERUNDS
PRESENT

comprando, *buying*	vendiendo, *selling*	viviendo, *living*

PERFECT

habiendo comprado, *having bought*	habiendo vendido, *having sold*	habiendo vivido, *having lived*

PAST PARTICIPLE

comprado, *bought*	vendido, *sold*	vivido, *lived*

INDICATIVE MOOD

PRESENT

I buy, do buy, am buying, etc.	*I sell, do sell, am selling*, etc.	*I live, do live, am living*, etc.
compro	vendo	vivo
compras	vendes	vives
compra	vende	vive
compramos	vendemos	vivimos
compráis	vendéis	vivís
compran	venden	viven

IMPERFECT

I bought, was buying, used to buy, etc.	*I sold, was selling, used to sell*, etc.	*I lived, was living, used to live*, etc.
compraba	vendía	vivía
comprabas	vendías	vivías
compraba	vendía	vivía
comprábamos	vendíamos	vivíamos
comprabais	vendíais	vivíais
compraban	vendían	vivían

PRETERITE

I bought, did buy, etc.	*I sold, did sell*, etc.	*I lived, did live*, etc.
compré	vendí	viví
compraste	vendiste	viviste
compró	vendió	vivió
compramos	vendimos	vivimos
comprasteis	vendisteis	vivisteis
compraron	vendieron	vivieron

FUTURE

I shall buy, etc.	*I shall sell*, etc.	*I shall live*, etc.
compraré	venderé	viviré
comprarás	venderás	vivirás
comprará	venderá	vivirá
compraremos	venderemos	viviremos
compraréis	venderéis	viviréis
comprarán	venderán	vivirán

CONDITIONAL

I should buy, etc.	*I should sell*, etc.	*I should live*, etc.
compraría	vendería	viviría
comprarías	venderías	vivirías
compraría	vendería	viviría
compraríamos	venderíamos	viviríamos
compraríais	venderíais	viviríais
comprarían	venderían	vivirían

PERFECT

I have bought, etc.	*I have sold*, etc.	*I have lived*, etc.
he comprado	he vendido	he vivido
has comprado	has vendido	has vivido
ha comprado	ha vendido	ha vivido
hemos comprado	hemos vendido	hemos vivido
habéis comprado	habéis vendido	habéis vivido
han comprado	han vendido	han vivido

PLUPERFECT

I had bought, etc.	*I had sold*, etc.	*I had lived*, etc.
había comprado	había vendido	había vivido
habías comprado	habías vendido	habías vivido
había comprado	había vendido	había vivido
habíamos comprado	habíamos vendido	habíamos vivido
habíais comprado	habíais vendido	habíais vivido
habían comprado	habían vendido	habían vivido

PAST ANTERIOR

I had bought, etc.	*I had sold*, etc.	*I had lived*, etc.
hube comprado	hube vendido	hube vivido
hubiste comprado	hubiste vendido	hubiste vivido
hubo comprado	hubo vendido	hubo vivido
hubimos comprado	hubimos vendido	hubimos vivido
hubisteis comprado	hubisteis vendido	hubisteis vivido
hubieron comprado	hubieron vendido	hubieron vivido

FUTURE PERFECT

I shall have bought, etc.	*I shall have sold,* etc.	*I shall have lived,* etc.
habré comprado	habré vendido	habré vivido
habrás comprado	habrás vendido	habrás vivido
habrá comprado	habrá vendido	habrá vivido
habremos comprado	habremos vendido	habremos vivido
habréis comprado	habréis vendido	habréis vivido
habrán comprado	habrán vendido	habrán vivido

CONDITIONAL PERFECT

I should have bought, etc.	*I should have sold,* etc.	*I should have lived,* etc.
habría comprado	habría vendido	habría vivido
habrías comprado	habrías vendido	habrías vivido
habría comprado	habría vendido	habría vivido
habríamos comprado	habríamos vendido	habríamos vivido
habríais comprado	habríais vendido	habríais vivido
habrían comprado	habrían vendido	habrían vivido

IMPERATIVE MOOD

buy	*sell*	*live*
compra	vende	vive
comprad	vended	vivid

SUBJUNCTIVE MOOD

PRESENT

(that) I (may, should) buy, etc.	*(that) I (may, should) sell,* etc.	*(that) I (may, should) live,* etc.
compre	venda	viva
compres	vendas	vivas
compre	venda	viva
compremos	vendamos	vivamos
compréis	vendáis	viváis
compren	vendan	vivan

IMPERFECT (*Two Forms*)

(*that*) I bought, might (*should*) buy, etc.	(*that*) I sold, might (*should*) sell, etc.	(*that*) I lived, might (*should*) live, etc.
1. comprara	vendiera	viviera
compraras	vendieras	vivieras
comprara	vendiera	viviera
compráramos	vendiéramos	viviéramos
comprarais	vendierais	vivierais
compraran	vendieran	vivieran
2. comprase	vendiese	viviese
comprases	vendieses	vivieses
comprase	vendiese	viviese
comprásemos	vendiésemos	viviésemos
compraseis	vendieseis	vivieseis
comprasen	vendiesen	viviesen

PERFECT

(*that*) I (*may, should*) have bought, etc.	(*that*) I (*may, should*) have sold, etc.	(*that*) I (*may, should*) have lived, etc.
haya comprado	haya vendido	haya vivido
hayas comprado	hayas vendido	hayas vivido
haya comprado	haya vendido	haya vivido
hayamos comprado	hayamos vendido	hayamos vivido
hayáis comprado	hayáis vendido	hayáis vivido
hayan comprado	hayan vendido	hayan vivido

PLUPERFECT (*Two Forms*)

(*that*) I had bought, might (*should*) have bought, etc.	(*that*) I had sold, might (*should*) have sold, etc.	(*that*) I had lived, might (*should*) have lived, etc.
1. hubiera comprado	hubiera vendido	hubiera vivido
hubieras comprado	hubieras vendido	hubieras vivido
hubiera comprado	hubiera vendido	hubiera vivido

hubiéramos comprado	hubiéramos vendido	hubiéramos vivido
hubierais comprado	hubierais vendido	hubierais vivido
hubieran comprado	hubieran vendido	hubieran vivido
2. hubiese comprado	hubiese vendido	hubiese vivido
hubieses comprado	hubieses vendido	hubieses vivido
hubiese comprado	hubiese vendido	hubiese vivido
hubiésemos comprado	hubiésemos vendido	hubiésemos vivido
hubieseis comprado	hubieseis vendido	hubieseis vivido
hubiesen comprado	hubiesen vendido	hubiesen vivido

VOCABULARY

Revise Vocabularies XXI–XXV.

EXERCISES

I. (*a*) *Study and translate:* En cuanto lo termine. Se olvidará de nosotros. Se empeñó en acompañarnos. ¿Por qué no le escribís? Se había casado con una francesa. Antes de que lo hubiera publicado. Pronuncian muy mal. Mire usted lo que he comprado. Acababa de llegar cuando yo entré. Se marchó sin que nadie le viera. Le aconsejo que se quede aquí. Hemos pasado toda la mañana tomando el sol. ¿Qué hacemos si no llega a tiempo? Escríbale usted en seguida. Se reunieron todos en el salón. Le hemos invitado a cenar con nosotros. Márchate antes de que te vea. ¿Cómo lo hubiera explicado usted? Estaba preparando algo para el día siguiente.

(*b*) *Translate:* Before he accepted it. He was working in the garden. On condition that he finishes it. I used to accompany them. He swims very well. What would you have

288

replied? Don't fail to write to us. I am sorry they behaved like that. Who shall I hand it to? Did you speak to them? They have deceived you. Drink this milk up. We shall have finished. I shall try to do it. How much have you spent? He ordered her to explain what had happened. We visited him every day. Even if he had been appointed. I was very interested in such an idea. It will turn out cheaper than we expected.

II. (a) *Study and translate:* 1. ¿Cuál es el edificio más interesante que se encuentra por aquí? 2. Un caballero que acaba de llegar de Madrid pregunta por usted. 3. Yo estaba completamente de acuerdo con lo que había decidido el director. 4. Nos condujo al jardín donde su hijo estaba sentado sin hacer nada. 5. Existe también la posibilidad de que él se marche antes de haberlo terminado. 6. Por eso precisamente quiero saber quién es el médico de usted y qué ha hecho para devolverle la salud. 7. Resulta que cuanto más le hablamos de ella más la desprecia y anhela volver a su primer amor. 8. Aún no sabe con quién pasar el fin de semana cuando su hermano mayor se marche a Londres. 9. Le acusó de haber utilizado para sus propios fines dinero destinado al nuevo hospital. 10. En aquel momento comprendí que ya no sería posible volver a la vida de antes, que nos pertenecíamos ya definitivamente el uno al otro.

(b) *Translate:* 1. We must prepare it today and hand it in tomorrow. 2. My father forbade me to go into his room whilst he was working. 3. I'm looking for someone to teach me to drive this car I've just bought. 4. If this had happened a few days ago I should have known what to do. 5. What do you want me to do in order that she may forgive me? 6. We walked a lot that day, besides going up the highest mountain around there. 7. On another occasion he talked to us of what they had done on meeting one another after the war. 8. Even if what he says is true, I shall not let him leave here before nine o'clock. 9. He says he would rather spend the evening by himself than have to attend the meeting a second time. 10. He did wrong to renounce once and for all the scheme that had been proposed for the new hospital.

III. (a) *Study and translate:* 1. ¿A mí qué me importa que sigan diciendo tales cosas? 2. Han resultado dificilísimas todas las explicaciones que nos ha dado. 3. No somos nosotros los que debemos hablar con ellos, sino usted y su hermano. 4. Desde que marchaste no he vuelto a tener otro amigo que me comprenda como tú. 5. No creo que sea posible tenerlo todo hecho para mañana, pero haremos lo que se pueda. 6. No encontraban manera de llegar a una solución que fuera aceptable para todos. 7. A no ser por usted, no hubiera conocido mi propio corazón y me hubiera casado con otro. 8. Este chico no conoce tantos idiomas como su hermano, pero no por eso deja de parecerme más inteligente. 9. Le escribieron en seguida pidiéndole que no dejara de interesarse por un asunto de tanta importancia. 10. Conviene que busquemos la razón por la cual no han querido reconocer unos principios tan importantes para nosotros.

(b) *Translate:* 1. Although he appears rich he is much poorer than you think. 2. Don't believe John. He will tell you many things which are not true. 3. There have been many difficulties but we have always found some solution. 4. Velázquez was born in Seville on the sixth of June, fifteen hundred and ninety-nine. 5. If I had seen him before you [did], I should have told him not to come. 6. He did wrong not to remember what his father had told him before he left home. 7. I have just bought myself a new car, although it cost me quite a lot more than I expected. 8. If he has not written to you I assure you it is through no fault of mine. 9. I am pleased Peter has been to visit Mr Sánchez. I intend to write to him as soon as I have a free moment. 10. It is curious to think of the many times we have talked to him without realizing the importance of his ideas.

IV. *Re-translate the keys given for Lessons XXI–XXV [pp. 362–365] and compare your versions with the originals.*

REVIEW AND DEVELOPMENT
SECTION (VI)

160. WORD ORDER: VERB AND WEAK OBJECT PRONOUN. Against what has been stated in §§ 62 and 126, one should be prepared to find (though perhaps not to imitate) the occasional placing of a weak object pronoun after a finite verb part. Except in certain regional uses this indicates a literary or archaic style and is confined to cases where the verb is not bound up intimately with the immediately preceding element. It is found, then, most frequently, at the beginning of a main clause.

Dijérase que los odiaba a todos. One would think (*lit.*, say) he hated them all.

Vino y sentóse a mirar. He came and sat down to watch.

NOTES: 1. The use of the imperfect subjunctive **dijera,** in the first example, instead of the more usual conditional **diría,** is another indication of literary style.

2. For the accent on **sentóse** see § 4 (*d*) (i).

161. WORD ORDER: NOUN AND ADJECTIVE. Adjectives, except those which indicate or limit rather than describe, usually follow the noun in Spanish [§ 22 and § 38, Note 3]. However, describing adjectives, too, are placed before the noun when they are used in a less literal or more emotive sense, and when they do not therefore serve primarily to characterize or select.

la casa blanca	the white house (*the adjective helps to identify the house*)
but **la blanca nieve**	the white snow (*the adjective is logically unnecessary*)

    un caballo negro   a black horse (*literal sense of* black)
but **un negro pensamiento**   a black thought (*figurative sense of* black)

Similarly, common descriptive adjectives such as **pequeño** and **hermoso,** which are used frequently before the noun, nevertheless follow when they have full selective force. Thus, to the question *who did this*? one might reply **el nuevo colega**; to the question *which colleague did this?*, on the other hand, the reply **el colega nuevo** would be more appropriate.

An adjective modified by an adverb tends to become more selective, more analytical, and therefore follows the noun [§ 22 (4)].

Es un amigo muy bueno.   He is a very good (type of) friend.
el hermano más alto, the tallest brother

In a few cases, however, this analytical function is not present and the *adverb + adjective* precede.

Es muy buen amigo.   He's a very good friend.
la más profunda oscuridad, darkest night (*lit.*, the deepest darkness)

In the earlier cases the friend and the brother are individualized by the adjectives; in the latter ones the group *adverb + adjective + noun* is presented synthetically, as almost the equivalent of an absolute superlative [§ 132 (c)].

NOTES: 1. **Alguno,** *some,* placed after the noun, may have the negative sense of **ninguno: sin duda alguna,** *without any doubt*; **no hizo daño alguno,** *it didn't do any damage.*

2. A following **mismo** may intensify not only a noun [§ 22 (3)] but also a pronoun or adverb: **el padre mismo,** *the father himself*; **ellos mismos,** *they themselves*; **aquí mismo,** *on this very spot*; **ayer mismo,** *only yesterday*; **ahora mismo,** *this very instant, just now.*   Compare also the position of **no** in similar cases: **hoy no,** *not today*; **aquí no,** *not here*; etc.

162. WORD ORDER: MAIN ELEMENTS OF THE SENTENCE. The order of the main elements of the sentence in Spanish is far less rigid than in English and is largely a matter of style.   However, the following indications should prove useful:

(a) The Verb

The verb can be considered as the nucleus of the sentence.   If we disregard conjunctions, negative adverbs and weak pronoun objects, we can say that it almost always occupies the first or second position after a pause (i.e., usually, though not always, the first or second position in its own clause).   Here, then, lies the first important difference between English and Spanish: the verb in Spanish, in all types of sentence, appears frequently in initial position.   This is often because the subject is unexpressed apart from the verb ending, but also because the subject in Spanish may be used after the verb, particularly when it is composed of several words or when it is in a subordinate clause, or for reasons of emphasis.   The order *verb-subject* is compulsory when the verb is used parenthetically (i.e., after words quoted) and virtually compulsory when the verb is an infinitive or past participle.

Además, don Pablo no quiere ir.   Besides, Don Pablo doesn't want to go.

Durmieron toda la noche.   They slept all night.

Iremos en cuanto llegue mi hermano.   We shall go as soon as my brother arrives.

Mi padre trabaja mucho. }
Trabaja mucho mi padre. } My father works hard.

Viene un señor que usted no conoce.   There is a gentleman coming whom you don't know.

Y así llegamos todos.   And so we all arrived.

— Ven mañana — contestó el hermano.   "Come tomorrow," the brother replied.

Se marchó al llegar el dueño.   He went away when the owner arrived.

Terminada la lección, nos fuimos todos.   When the lesson was over we all left.

NOTES: 1. To say that the verb occupies the first or second position does not mean that it is the first or second word, but rather the first or second grammatical unit.   In **Y así llegamos todos** there is an example of inversion to prevent the verb's moving beyond the second position. The tendency to such inversion is not nearly so marked as in German, but it is none the less quite strong.

2. With the inverted order in the third example compare the popular English *He works hard, my father*. The stress is then alike in the two languages, though inversion in Spanish is by no means confined to popular usage. In English the addition of *there* before the verb may help to preserve the Spanish stress and order of words (*cf* example 5, above).

Luego se presentó otra dificultad. Then there appeared another difficulty.

(b) The Pre-Verbal Element

One main element may precede the verb. Usually, as in English, this element is the subject or an adverb or adverbial phrase; but often, too, it is the direct or indirect object, placed before the verb for emphasis, and especially in more literary style it may be a noun or adjective complement.

Su hijo llegó anoche. His son got here last night.

Luego se marchó a casa. Then he went off home.

A Juan le conozco muy bien. I know *John* very well.

Al verbo le acompaña la preposición *de*. The verb is accompanied by the preposition *de*.

Pero eso no lo encuentra usted aquí. But you don't find *that* here.

A mí no me han dicho nada. They haven't said anything to *me*.

Dueño eres de disponer de lo tuyo como mejor te parezca. You are the master of disposing of what is yours as best you think fit.

Muy difícil sería contarlo todo. It would be very difficult to relate it all.

NOTE: The order *object-verb*, so frequent in Spanish, is made possible: (i) by the existence of verb endings which often help to identify the subject irrespective of its position, and (ii) by the use of the personal *a* (even with inanimate objects if necessary, see example 4, above), which prevents confusion between a subject and direct object. Remember that the force of the Spanish inverted order may often be rendered into English by means of the passive voice [§ 145 (a)].

(c) Post-Verbal Elements

The normal order of elements used after the verb is the following: (1) adverb (or short adverbial phrase), (2) noun or adjectival complement, (3) subject, (4) direct object, (5) indirect object, (6) adverbial or prepositional phrase.

Se fía demasiado (1) **de su hermano** (6).   He trusts his brother too much.

Había venido alguna vez (1) **su padre** (3).   His father had come on the odd occasion.

Pues no es mala (2) **la solución** (3).   Well, the solution isn't bad.

¿Es muy grande (2) **vuestra casa** (3)?   Is your house very big?

Le había llamado ladrón (2) **a su hijo** (4).   He had called his son a thief.

Me pareció al principio (1) **muy buena** (2) **esta idea** (3).   This idea seemed very good to me at first.

No acusó nunca (1) **mi padre** (3) **a mi madre** (4) **de esto** (6).   My father never accused my mother of this.

Envié una felicitación (4) **a mi novia** (5) **desde Madrid** (6).   I sent my girl friend a greeting from Madrid.

This order, however, is far from absolute.   Much depends on the length of the different elements, for there is a strong tendency for short elements to be placed near the verb and for longer ones to be separated from it.

> **No lo ha hecho nunca** (1) **mi padre** (3).   My father has never done it.

but **No lo he hecho yo** (3) **nunca** (1).   I have never done it.

> **¿Es española** (2) **su madre** (3)?   Is your mother Spanish?

but **¿Es usted** (3) **española** (2)?   Are you Spanish?

> **No llegaba tarde** (1) **ninguno** (3).   None of them used to arrive late.

but **No llegaba ninguno** (3) **tan tarde como él** (6).   None of
    them used to arrive as late as he did.

This same tendency, as well as the desire for elements belonging
together to be placed together, frequently causes the attraction of
a noun by a following adjectival clause [see above, Section (*a*),
Example 5].

 Envié una felicitación (4) **a mi novia** (5).   I sent my girl
  friend a greeting.

but **Envié a mi novia** (5) **una felicitación** (4) **que no**
  esperaba.   I sent my girl friend a greeting that she wasn't
  expecting.

Finally, exceptional word order is often a reflection of emphatic
expression.

Trajo este libro para usted.   He brought this book for you.
Trajo para usted este libro.   He brought *this book* for you;
 or He brought this book *for you*.

But here one enters the realm of style.

NOTE: Distinguish carefully between the adjectival complement
used before the noun to which it refers and an ordinary adjective
used after the noun.   With parts of the body the latter is usual.

Tiene los ojos grandes y saltones.   He has big bulging eyes.
Tenía el pelo negro.   She had black hair.

163. THE PERSONAL **a.**   Besides the cases mentioned in § 47, the
personal **a** is used before personified things, and may be used
before collective nouns referring to individuals, and in other cases
to prevent ambiguity.

Teme la muerte.   He fears death.
Teme a la Muerte.   He fears Death.
Quiere mucho a su perro.   He is very fond of his dog.
¿Conoce usted a esa familia?   Do you know that family?
Al verbo sigue el pronombre.   The verb is followed by the
 pronoun.

164. Temer(se) AND **esperar.**   (*a*) **Temer** is a verb of emotion
and as such is followed by the subjunctive [§ 114 (6)].   However,

temerse meaning *to fear* in the sense of *to believe* is followed by the indicative unless there is definite doubt in the speaker's mind.

Me temo que no voy a poder ir.   I fear I'm not going to be able to go.

(*b*) **Esperar que** is often found instead of **esperar a que** with the meaning *to wait until* and is then followed by the subjunctive. With the meaning *to hope* and *to expect* it is found with both the indicative and the subjunctive according to the degree of doubt present in the speaker's mind.

Esperaré (a) que llegue.   I shall wait till he arrives.

Espero que sabrás explicármelo.   I hope (*or* trust) you will be able to explain it to me.

Esperemos que sea verdad.   Let us hope it is true.

165. Mucho.   Since **muy** cannot stand alone, **mucho** must be used in cases like the following:

— **¿Estás contento?**   — **Sí, mucho.**   "Are you happy?" "Yes, very."

Es alto, pero no mucho.   He's tall but not very.

Me gusta mucho (*or* muchísimo).   I like it very much.

166. FEMININE AND PLURAL ENDINGS

(*a*) *Formation of the Feminine*

Adjectives which in the masculine singular end in **-án, -ón** or **-or** (except the comparatives **mejor, peor, mayor, menor, superior, inferior**) take **-a** in the feminine, like adjectives of nationality [§ 20 (2)].

la idea abrumadora de la muerte   the overwhelming idea of death

una voz chillona y desagradable   a screeching, unpleasant voice

NOTE: Adjectives in **-or** and **-ón** frequently translate the English present participle used as an adjective. Remember that the Spanish gerund cannot be used in such cases [§ 45].

(b) *Formation of the Plural*

Against what was stated in §§ 9 and 20 the following two cases are to be noted:

(1) Nouns which in the singular end in *unstressed vowel* + s have the same form in the plural.

el paraguas, los paraguas	the umbrella(s)
el lunes, los lunes	on Monday(s)
but **el mes, los meses**	the month(s)
el revés, los reveses	the set-back(s)

(2) The few nouns and adjectives which end in a stressed vowel take **-es** in the plural.

el rubí, los rubíes	the ruby, the rubies
baladí, baladíes	worthless

EXCEPTIONS: Nouns in **-é** (**el café, los cafés**) and a few others: **el papá, los papás** (*dad, mum and dad*), **el sofá, los sofás** (*sofa[s]*)

167. PRONUNCIATION, ETC. Study the Introduction [§§ 1–7].

VOCABULARY

aparecer	to appear	**el objeto**	object
el cabo	cape, end	**no obstante**	nevertheless
al cabo	at last	**la patria**	homeland, (native) country
al cabo de	after, at the end of		
encantador	charming	**la paz**	peace
la estancia	stay, residence	**la prensa**	press
la fuente	fountain, source	**presentar**	to present, to introduce
incapaz	incapable		
indicar	to indicate, to point out	**presentarse**	to appear
		pronunciar	to pronounce
en medio de	amidst, in the midst of	**el respeto**	respect
		el sitio	place; siege
la memoria	memory; memoir	**la tierra**	earth, land
		trabajador	hard-working
nacional	national		

los dos, las dos both

NOTES: 1. Besides translating *earth* and *land,* **tierra** frequently expresses on a regional scale what **patria** expresses nationally: i.e., *homeland, native country.*

Vuelven a su tierra. They return home (*or* to their native villages).

2. When *to appear* can be replaced in English by *to seem,* **parecer** is used in Spanish; otherwise **aparecer** or, at times, **presentarse.**

3. In this and the remaining vocabularies new words are listed only if they appear in the English–Spanish exercises. The sentences in Spanish are taken from Spanish writers of the twentieth century and are covered by the general vocabulary at the end of the book. Between them, these sentences represent almost every aspect of Spanish grammar and should be studied closely as a means of general revision.

EXERCISES

I. (*a*) *Study and translate:* Estuve unas semanas en Nueva York. Sólo tenemos libres sábado y domingo. Sin explicárselo yo primero. Sin explicárselo primero su padre. A esta señora se le murió un hijo. Conozco a Pedro mejor que Juan. Conozco a Pedro mejor que a Juan. ¡Qué habladoras son las mujeres! A Felipe no se le escapa nada. Se le estaba durmiendo una pierna. A la guerra sigue la paz. ¿Por qué no espera usted a que termine esto? Espero que el próximo año te veremos casado. A mí no me importa nada que digan esas cosas. Al cabo de muchos años.

(*b*) *Translate:* She is a charming girl. Do you like wine? I like it very much. Through my not knowing anything. Then his brother appeared. The son took a present for his parents. Are they all Americans? On Saturdays the two sisters usually arrive together. As soon as they all finish. I hope you will both go. Shall we wait until he arrives? He is afraid to go with us. I fear he may not come. I am afraid it is true. But, in heaven's name, what does it matter to *you?* Amidst so many difficulties.

II. (*a*) *Study and translate:* 1. A mí me han reprochado el tener mal carácter; pero no creo que lo tenga tanto (P. Baroja). 2. La verdadera enseñanza de la vida no la dan los padres a los hijos, sino los hijos a los padres (J. Bergamín). 3. — ¿Entonces usted me aconseja oír la música como quien oye llover? — Exactamente: con la más profunda atención (J. Bergamín). 4. Se me ocurre un asunto bonito, cojo la pluma e inmediatamente me digo: — ¿Le gustará este tema al señor de Guadalajara? (J. Camba). 5. En medio de sus ridículos fracasos, había un grande y puro deseo de conocer la verdad; mas algo, que no acertaba a comprender, hacía estériles sus sacrificios (R. Léon). 6. Me acuerdo de que una de las veces que China cambió de régimen, tuvimos en un Consejo de Ministros una discusión acerca de las costumbres de aquel país (W. Fernández Flórez). 7. Yo, siendo niño, oía contar muchas veces que un vecino o un amigo estaba enfermo; luego, inmediatamente, la persona que contaba o la que oía se quedaba un momento pensativa (Azorín). 8. — ¡Si ella supiera quién soy! — Y cuando lo sepa, ya no serás el que fuiste: serás su esposo, su enamorado esposo, todo lo enamorado y lo fiel y lo noble que tú quieras y ella pueda desear (J. Benavente). 9. Llega a la torre y le dicen que el señor anda malucho; aunque suele madrugar, todavía no se ha levantado. — Esperaré que despierte — responde, y pregunta: — ¿Desde cuándo está enfermo . . .?, porque anteayer le vi (C. Espina). 10. Voy a escribir esta especie de Memorias con la ilusión de que pueden ser interesantes. Yo espero que a alguno le entretendrán. Quizá me engañe. No pienso inventar nada, sino contar lo que recuerde, más o menos transformado por la memoria (P. Baroja).

(*b*) *Translate:* 1. "Are her parents very wealthy?" "Not very, but they are extremely nice people." 2. I fear that most of those who were going to help us have been taken ill. 3. Whoever is not prepared to do the same has the door open, and it is best he should leave straight away. 4. I had thought of going with him to Brazil, but now I have resolved to give up such an idea for good. 5. Even if what you tell me is true

I shall none the less have complete confidence in any idea that that gentleman proposes to me. 6. Nevertheless, I trust I shall still be able to accompany my parents for a few days during their stay at Saragossa. 7. It seems very unlikely to us that such a solution will be accepted, so we have decided to talk no more about the matter. 8. "Your mother would be (= become) very pleased, wouldn't she, at seeing you the object of so much admiration in the national press?" "Yes, very." 9. Under this king Spain enjoyed an age of peace and work in which the name of the country came to be pronounced with respect and admiration throughout (= in all) the world. 10. He is a very hard-working boy and he has a very good memory for the things that interest him. The point is (= What happens is) that he is not at all interested in politics.

III. (a) *Study and translate:* 1. Venga usted conmigo. Me lo seguirá usted contando fuera. Me interesa tanto lo que usted dice, que me da fiebre (J. Grau). 2. Siempre he creído que, con un poco de buena voluntad, ambos señores concluirían por reconocer recíprocamente su error (W. Fernández Flórez). 3. Los sitios en que se deslizaron nuestros primeros años no se deben volver a ver; así conservamos engrandecidos los recuerdos de cosas que en la realidad son insignificantes (Azorín). 4. No, no ha sido en libros, no ha sido en literatos donde he aprendido a querer a mi patria: ha sido recorriéndola, ha sido visitando devotamente sus rincones (M. de Unamuno). 5. ¿Cómo es la España soñada por los escritores del 98?[1] No esperemos que sean idénticos los ensueños de todos ellos; conformémonos con que sean parecidos (P. Laín Entralgo). 6. — ¡Abrázame, querido! —exclamó con grande afecto, atrayendo sobre su

[1] *98 Generation* is the name commonly given to a group of Spanish writers whose work began to appear around the crisis year of 1898, the year in which Spain lost her last important colonies after a fiasco of a war with the United States. They were preoccupied largely with Spain and her historical destiny.

pecho a Jesús— ¡Qué deseos tenía de verte, ingrato! ¡Bendito sea Dios, que nos da al cabo esta alegría! (R. León). 7. Diríase que no entiende las preguntas que le hacen ni las contestaciones que da; tiene el aire de olvidar en un segundo las palabras que oye y las que pronuncia (C. Espina). 8. Ver un paisaje admirable, ver y escuchar a una mujer encantadora, oír algo de lo que más me gusta de Mozart o de Beethoven no me da ganas de dedicarme a la retórica, sino más bien de callarme (P. Baroja). 9. Cuando comenzaron las operaciones en Marruecos, no sabíamos apenas nada de los moros. Debíamos haber sabido mucho. En primer término, porque me parece imposible que lleguemos a conocernos a nosotros mismos en tanto que desconozcamos a los moros (R. de Maeztu). 10. Si yo fuera el hombre de libros que me creen los que no me conocen; si yo no anduviera de un sitio a otro, hablando con todo el mundo; si el sol no me hubiese mudado muchas veces la piel de la cara, ¿creéis que podría conservar este caudal de pasión? (M. de Unamuno).

(*b*) *Translate:* 1. They said it was possible I shouldn't sleep unless I closed the window. 2. I'll undertake to finish this work quickly provided that I am left completely alone. 3. They ordered him to get dressed and leave the hospital before the doctor arrived. 4. I was writing a letter when Philip came into the room and asked me for my brother's address. 5. We are both agreed that he should spend the first part of his stay working in some place that is near here. 6. I pointed out to them that this town was a lot bigger than those I had seen in South Africa. 7. There were many who believed that on the following morning they would be taking leave of their country for ever. 8. After three years he returned home (**a su tierra**) and married a girl he had once been introduced to at his grandfather's. 9. "I shall go with you," said the boy at last, "but on condition that you do not try to discover the secret of the fountain." 10. I assure you that my memory does not deceive me so much that I am incapable of remembering which is my own brother.

REVIEW AND DEVELOPMENT
SECTION (VII)

168. Radical-changing verbs are those which, in certain of their parts, undergo a change in the radical or stem vowel.

169. VERBS OF THE FIRST AND SECOND CONJUGATIONS. These undergo a change of stem vowel only when the main word stress falls upon that vowel: in the first, second and third persons singular and the third person plural of the present indicative and the present subjunctive, and in the imperative singular. In such cases a stem **e** becomes **ie** (**pensar—pienso, perder—pierdo**) and a stem **o** becomes **ue** (**contar—cuento, volver—vuelvo**).

I. **pensar,** *to think*

pres. ind.: pienso, piensas, piensa, pensamos, pensáis, piensan
pres. subj.: piense, pienses, piense, pensemos, penséis, piensen
imperative: piensa   pensad

Like **pensar** are:

acertar	to hit the mark	**desterrar**	to exile
apretar	to press, to squeeze	**empezar**	to begin, to commence
atravesar	to cross	**encerrar**	to enclose, to shut up
calentar	to warm		
cegar	to blind	**enterrar**	to bury
cerrar	to close, to shut	**errar**	to err, to wander
comenzar	to commence, to begin	**fregar**	to rub, to scour, to scrub
confesar	to confess	**gobernar**	to govern
despertar	to waken	**helar**	to freeze

303

manifestar	to make known, to reveal, to show	**reventar**	to burst
merendar	to have tea (a snack)	**segar**	to reap, to harvest
negar	to deny	**sembrar**	to sow (seeds), to scatter
nevar	to snow	**sentar**	to set down
plegar	to fold	**sosegar**	to quieten, to calm down
quebrar	to break, to shatter	**temblar**	to tremble
recomendar	to recommend	**tentar**	to touch; to incite, to tempt
regar	to water	**tropezar**	to stumble

NOTE: In **errar** the **i** of the diphthong **ie** becomes **y** to avoid an inadmissible initial **ie** (**yerro, yerras, yerra, erramos**, etc.).

I. contar, *to count, relate, tell*

pres. ind.: cuento, cuentas, cuenta, contamos, contáis, cuentan
pres. subj.: cuente, cuentes, cuente, contemos, contéis, cuenten
imperative: cuenta   contad

Like **contar** are:

acordar	to agree; to remind	**descolgar**	to unhook, to take down
acostar	to put to bed	**descontar**	to discount
almorzar	to (have) lunch	**encontrar**	to find, to meet
apostar	to bet	**esforzar**	to encourage
aprobar	to approve; to pass (in exam.)	**forzar**	to force
		mostrar	to show
		poblar	to colonize, to people
avergonzar	to shame, to make shy	**probar**	to try, to test, to prove
colgar	to hang up		
comprobar	to verify, to check	**recordar**	to remind
		reforzar	to reinforce
consolar	to console	**renovar**	to renew
costar	to cost	**resonar**	to resound, to echo
demostrar	to demonstrate, to prove, to show	**rodar**	to turn, to roll
		rogar	to request, to beg

soltar	to loosen, to release	trocar	to exchange
sonar	to sound	tronar	to thunder
soñar	to dream	volar	to fly
tostar	to toast, to tan	volcar	to overturn, to capsize

NOTE: Also to this group belongs **jugar** (*to play*), the only verb in which a stem **u** becomes **ue**.

II. **perder,** *to lose*

pres. ind.:   pierdo, pierdes, pierde, perdemos, perdéis, pierden
pres. subj.:   pierda, pierdas, pierda, perdamos, perdáis, pierdan
imperative: pierde   perded

Like **perder** are:

ascender	to ascend, to promote, to be promoted	encender	to light
atender	to attend to, to look after	entender	to understand
		extender	to spread, to extend
defender	to defend, to uphold	hender	to split
descender	to descend	tender	to hang out, to spread out
		verter	to pour, to spill

II. **mover,** *to move*

pres. ind.:   muevo, mueves, mueve, movemos, movéis, mueven
pres. subj.:   mueva, muevas, mueva, movamos, mováis, muevan
imperative: mueve   moved

Like **mover** are:

absolver	to absolve, to acquit	envolver	to enfold, to wrap up
conmover	to move (emotionally)	llover	to rain
		morder	to bite
desenvolver	to unroll, to unfold	oler	to smell
devolver	to return, to give back	remorder	to gnaw, to nag (*figuratively*)
disolver	to dissolve	remover	to remove, to stir
doler	to hurt, to pain, to ache	resolver	to determine, to solve

retorcer	to twist, to contort	**torcer**	to twist, to bend, to turn
revolver	to turn upside down	**volver**	to return, to go (come) back
soler	to be in the habit of, to be wont to		

NOTE: The letter **h** is placed before the diphthong of the strong parts of **oler** to avoid an inadmissible initial **ue: huele,** etc.

170. VERBS OF THE THIRD CONJUGATION. (a) As with verbs of the first and second conjugations so also with third-conjugation verbs there is a change of stem vowel when the stress falls on it, an **e** becoming **ie** in some verbs (**mentir—miento**) and **i** in others (**pedir—pido**), and an **o** becoming **ue** (**dormir—duermo**). There are therefore three groups where first- and second-conjugation verbs each had only two.

(b) But third-conjugation verbs also undergo a change of stem vowel in certain parts where the stress falls not on the stem but on the ending: namely, when that ending is in **-ió, -ie-** or **-a-**. In such cases a stem **e** becomes **i** and a stem **o** becomes **u**. This change affects the third persons singular and plural of the preterite, the first and second persons plural of the present subjunctive, the whole of the imperfect subjunctive, and the gerund.

mentir, *to lie*

pres. ind.:	miento, mientes, miente, mentimos, mentís, mienten
preterite:	mentí, mentiste, mintió, mentimos, mentisteis, mintieron
pres. subj.:	mienta, mientas, mienta, mintamos, mintáis, mientan
imp. subj.:	mintiera (mintiese), mintieras (mintieses), mintiera (mintiese), mintiéramos (mintiésemos), mintierais (mintieseis), mintieran (mintiesen)
imperative:	miente mentid
gerund:	mintiendo

Like **mentir** are:

adherirse	to adhere	**herir**	to wound
advertir	to notice, to warn	**hervir**	to boil, to seethe
arrepentirse	to repent	**inferir**	to infer, to imply
conferir	to grant, to concede, to confer	**pervertir**	to pervert
		preferir	to prefer
consentir	to consent	**presentir**	to have a presentiment of
convertir	to convert		
desmentir	to belie	**referir**	to refer
diferir	to defer; to differ	**sentir**	to feel
		sugerir	to suggest
divertir	to turn aside; to amuse	**transferir**	to transfer

NOTES: 1. With these verbs can be considered also **adquirir** (*to acquire*) and **inquirir** (*to inquire*). They retain their stem **i** whenever the stress does not fall upon the radical (*i.e.*, **adquiero, adquiera**, but **adquirimos, adquiría**).

2. **Erguir** (*to erect, raise*) may be included here (**yergo, yergues, yergue, erguimos**, etc.—For the **y** see § 169, Note) or below, under **pedir** (**irgo, irgues, irgue, erguimos**, etc.).

pedir, *to ask for*

pres. ind.:   pido, pides, pide, pedimos, pedís, piden

preterite: pedí, pediste, pidió, pedimos, pedisteis, pidieron

pres. subj.:   pida, pidas, pida, pidamos, pidáis, pidan

imp. subj.:   pidiera (pidiese), pidieras (pidieses), pidiera (pidiese), pidiéramos (pidiésemos), pidierais (pidieseis), pidieran (pidiesen)

imperative: pide   pedid

gerund: pidiendo

Like **pedir** are:

competir	to compete	**derretir**	to melt
concebir	to conceive	**despedir**	to say good-bye to
conseguir	to obtain, to achieve	**elegir**	to elect, to select
corregir	to correct	**embestir**	to rush upon, to assault

expedir	to dispatch	**reexpedir**	to forward, to send on
gemir	to moan, to groan	**regir**	to rule, to be in force
impedir	to hinder, to prevent	**rendir**	to overcome, to yield, to give up
medir	to measure		
perseguir	to pursue, to persecute	**repetir**	to repeat
proseguir	to proceed with, to continue	**seguir**	tò follow
		servir	to serve
reelegir	to re-elect	**vestir**	to clothe, to dress

NOTE: Also like **pedir** are verbs in **-eír** and **-eñir**, except that they lose the i of endings **-ió** and **-ie-**. In certain of their parts, verbs in **-eír** take a written accent in accordance with § 3 (c) (iv).

reír, *to laugh*

pres. ind.:   río, ríes, ríe, reímos, reís, ríen
preterite: reí, reíste, rió, reímos, reísteis, rieron
pres. subj.: ría, rías, ría, riamos, riais, rían
imp. subj.:   riera (riese), rieras (rieses), riera (riese), riéramos (riésemos), rierais (rieseis), rieran (riesen)
imperative: ríe   reíd
gerund: riendo

Other common verbs of this type are: **ceñir** (*to gird, girdle*), **freír** (*to fry*), **reñir** (*to quarrel*), **sonreír** (*to smile*) and **teñir** (*to dye*).

dormir, *to sleep*

pres. ind.:   duermo, duermes, duerme, dormimos, dormís, duermen

preterite: dormí, dormiste, durmió, dormimos, dormisteis, durmieron

pres. subj.: duerma, duermas, duerma, durmamos, durmáis, duerman

imp. subj.   durmiera (durmiese), durmieras (durmieses), dur-
          miera (durmiese), durmiéramos (durmiésemos),
          durmierais (durmieseis), durmieran (durmiesen)

imperative: duerme   dormid

gerund: durmiendo

Like **dormir** is **morir** (*to die*).

VOCABULARY

actuar	to act, to oper- ate	**gracias a**	thanks to
la conse- **cuencia**	consequence	**inferior**	inferior
		el interés	interest
contrario	opposite, con- trary	**la noticia**	(piece of) news, information; *pl.* news
al contrario	on the contrary	**el pensa-** **miento**	thought
duro	hard		
el duro	duro (= five pesetas)	**el poeta**	poet
		puro	pure
la edición	edition	**quitar(se)**	to take off, to take away
equivocado	mistaken		
equivocarse	to be mistaken	**realizar**	to bring about, to carry out
la esperanza	hope		
al extranjero	abroad (*move-* *ment*)	**el sombrero**	hat
		suelto	loose(d), un- leashed
en el **extranjero**	abroad (*position*)		

Study also the verbs listed within the lesson.

EXERCISES

I. (*a*) *Study and translate:* El agua estaba hirviendo. Le per-
siguieron. Nos lo han devuelto. Antes de que lo repitieran.
Sosiéguense, señores. Pruebe usted este café. Se esfuerza
por llegar. ¿A qué se refiere? No mientas. Me lo im-
pidieron. Se me está durmiendo una pierna. Con tal que
apruebe en francés. Me dicen que no viene. Se convirtió en
otra cosa. Le dijo que no compitiera. Le dijo que no

competiría. A no ser que le recomienden para otro puesto. ¿No recuerdas la idea que nos sugirió? A éstos no hay quien los conmueva. Se arrepintió de lo que había dicho. Sigamos durmiendo. Corríjale usted lo que ha escrito.

(b) *Translate:* They have repeated it. She is getting dressed. Close the door. They lied. I am beginning. He went to bed. They came back yesterday. It has rained. He was asking for a book. They would prefer. He is sleeping. They elected him president. How much does it cost? Before he acquired it. So that he might follow them. She laughed at this. When they conceived the idea. He lost the key. He asked me for permission. Even if it rains. Dissolve it in water. I don't understand you. Ask him to play with us. On the contrary, I find it extremely difficult. He prefers to live abroad.

II. (a) *Study and translate:* 1. Tome, tome su limosna y busque quien le favorezca en tomársela (M. de Unamuno). 2. ¡No me diga más! Hay que salvar la mentira cueste lo que cueste (A. Casona). 3. Desde que estoy en el pueblo, numerosas personas se me han acercado para que les diga sus nombres (J. Camba). 4. — ¿Se siente usted mal, señora? Está usted un poco pálida. — No, nada, muchas gracias. ¡Ideas que se le ocurren a una! (C. J. Cela). 5. Yo pienso que sin dinero no hay cosa que valga ni se estime en el mundo; que es el precio de todo (J. Benavente). 6. Hay quien salió jovencito de su pueblecillo sin conocer otra cosa, y os habla luego de España — por lo que lee en los periódicos (M. de Unamuno). 7. No son los grandes hombres quienes hacen a los escultores, sino los escultores quienes hacen a los grandes hombres (J. Camba). 8. Veinte años de su vida comenzaban a borrarse de la memoria; todo le parecía ahora hermoso y nuevo, como si lo mirara con ojos de niño (R. León). 9. Estoy persuadido de que para corregir nuestros defectos tenemos que conocerlos y objetivarlos, y que el camino para ello consiste en estudiar a los moros (R. de Maeztu). 10. Para la gente, era el tipo del escritor de las

calles de Madrid, el hombre a quien se escuchaba en un café,
y quizá hacía esto que le perdonaran como a un tipo pintoresco (P. Baroja).

(b) *Translate:* 1. Why doesn't he like reading poetry since he
himself is a poet?. 2. On entering the cathedral he had forgotten to take his hat off. 3. I am capable of finding what I
am asked for with my eyes closed. 4. Which is the most important city in the north-east of Spain and how many inhabitants has it [got]? 5. A few years later, in fourteen eighty-
seven, Bartholomew Diaz[1] got as far as the Cape of Good
Hope. 6. In such a situation there also operates the desire
of each one not to show himself inferior to the rest. 7. Finally, thanks to a friend of his, I was able to devote myself
completely for a year to the study of his work. 8. If I
manage to carry out my plan, you are certainly invited to
spend a few weeks with us in the country. 9. I don't like
my work but I console myself because I still haven't found
anyone who is satisfied with what he does. 10. People often
say the opposite of what they think, as if they believed that
thoughts should not be allowed to wander loose around the
world.

III. (a) *Study and translate:* 1. Me he de portar como un caballero, aunque me cueste el mayor sacrificio (C. Espina).
2. Don Pablo sonrió como quien, de repente, encuentra que
tiene toda la razón (C. J. Cela). 3. En general no concibo
que puedan interesar más los hombres que las ideas, las
personas que las cosas (J. Ortega y Gasset). 4. Tiene unos
ojos que le brillan mucho y debe ser un hombre que averigua
los secretos de los demás (P. Baroja). 5. ¡Caso triste, en
verdad, es el de un señor que no sabe quién es y que no
encuentra quien se lo diga! (J. Camba). 6. No digas nada,
no levantes la voz, no te muevas. . . .Tenemos que hablar;
siéntate. No dejes el sombrero, no fumes (J. Benavente).
7. Pero después de lo que acabo de oír veo que tenía razón;

[1] Bartolomé Díaz

si hay alguien capaz de salvarme, ese alguien es usted (A. Casona). 8. Reconcentró al cabo sus meditaciones en Hornedo, que continuaba inmóvil, muy pálido, sin atreverse a hablar (C. Espina). 9. Decir que se prefiere la creación a la destrucción no es nada. Casi todos los niños opinan lo contrario, sin que tampoco nos convenzan (R. de Maeztu). 10. ¿Cómo podría vivir una vida que merezca vivirse, cómo podría sentir el ritmo vital de mi pensamiento si no me escapara, así que puedo, de la ciudad, a correr por campos y lugares, a comer de lo que comen los pastores? (M. de Unamuno).

(b) *Translate:* 1. Show it to them when you see them and ask them what they think about it. 2. He seized his stick, put on his hat, and went out without saying a word to anyone. 3. I say, will you hand him this letter as soon as he arrives? I can't wait any longer. 4. He was afraid he wouldn't be able to go with them unless they paid his fare (= the journey) for him. 5. We were very sorry that he couldn't come, but perhaps we shall be able to see him after his trip to Canada. 6. I am very sorry to receive such information and I prefer not to think of the possible consequences of so mistaken a policy. 7. I merely wish to point out that if this had been a purely national problem, it would not have awakened so much interest abroad. 8. Look. What do you think of this book I have just bought? It's the first edition of Machado's poems and it only cost me two duros. 9. He is gradually overcoming the difficulties of the language and hopes to be able to speak it fairly well when he goes to Spain this summer. 10. No sooner had he got back home than he wrote them a letter denying that he had anything to do with the latest changes that had been proposed.

REVIEW AND DEVELOPMENT
SECTION (VIII)

171. A is used in Spanish in the following cases:

(1) to introduce a direct object referring to any specific person(s) (except weak pronoun objects).

Vimos a Juan y al señor Pérez.   We saw John and Mr Pérez.
Pero ellos no nos vieron a nosotros.   But *they* didn't see *us*.

NOTES: 1. The personal **a** is not used after **hay, había,** etc.; after **tener** it is used only in a few cases where **tener** does not indicate true possession.

Aquí tienes a mi hermana.   This is (*lit.,* Here you have) my sister.

2. **A** is used with direct-object indefinite pronouns even when they do not refer to *specific* persons [§ 47].
No hemos visto a nadie.   We have seen no one.

(2) to translate the English *to* before a noun, strong pronoun, or adjective with noun understood.
Se lo entregué a su señora.   I handed it to his wife.
Iremos a Francia e Italia.   We shall go to France and Italy.
Permaneció fiel a sus principios.   He remained faithful to his principles.
Es un problema ajeno a la filosofía.   It is a problem foreign to philosophy.
Al mayor le regaló un reloj y al otro una estilográfica.   He gave a watch to the elder one and a fountain pen to the other.
Se hicieron a la mar.   They put to sea.

(3) to indicate a person who is neither the subject nor the direct object of the verb yet who is directly interested in or related with the action of that verb [§ 149 (*b*)].

Póngale más azúcar a este chico. Put this boy more sugar in.
No perdona nada a nadie. He forgives no one anything.

In this section can be considered also the Spanish use of the dative with parts of the body and clothing, and to indicate the person *from* whom something is concealed, requested or acquired.

Les lavó la cara a los niños. She washed the children's faces.
Se lo han robado a mi padre. They have stolen it from my father.

(4) to translate English *in*, *into*, *on*, *on to*, when there is motion but little suggestion in the verb of complete enclosure.

    Se tiró al agua. He threw himself into the water.
    Échese al agua. Throw yourself into the water.
    Se arrojaron al mar. They flung themselves into the sea.
    Lo tiré todo al suelo. I tipped it all on the ground.
    Salió a la calle. He went out into the street.
    Subimos a la terraza. We went up on to the terrace.
but **Se metió en el agua.** He got into the water.
    Entré en el cuarto. I went into the room.
    Los metimos todos en una maleta. We put them all into a suitcase.

NOTE: *Into* indicating change or division is rendered by **en**:
Se convirtió en casa de huéspedes. It was turned into a guest house.
Lo partió en dos. He divided it into two.

(5) with a following infinitive to translate the English *to* + verb (also *and* + verb) after an indication of motion, beginning, exhortation, tendency and a few others [§§ 100 (2) (iv) and 101 (*c*) (1)].

¿Por qué no vienes a cenar? Why don't you come and have dinner?
Entré a buscarla. I went in to look for her.
Se puso a reír como un loco. He began to laugh like a madman.
Nos invitó a acompañarlos. He invited us to go with them.

¿Quieres que te ayude a escribirla? Do you want me to help you to write it?

Tiene propensión a dudar de todo. He has a tendency to doubt everything.

(6) to indicate a point of time (English *at* and others).

a la una, a las cuatro	at one o'clock, at four
a los tres días	after (by the end of) three days
a la mañana siguiente	on the following morning
a ratos	at times, at odd moments
a principios (mediados, finales) del siglo XIX	at the beginning (middle, end) of the nineteenth century
al + *infinitive*	on -ing, when he (I, you, etc.)—

A la media hora estaba ya cansada. By the end of half an hour she was tired.

Le vi a mediados del mes pasado. I saw him about the middle of last month.

Llegué a la hora en punto. I got there right on time.

No lo podrá terminar a tiempo. He won't be able to finish it in time.

Se asustó mucho al ver a su padre. He was very startled at seeing his father.

Al llegar la fecha del examen, se lo sabía todo. When the date of the examination arrived he knew it all.

NOTE: Time within which is indicated by **en: el día en que llegue mi hermano,** *the day my brother arrives.* **No le vi en todo el año,** *I didn't see him all year.* Notice, too, **en aquella (cierta, otra) ocasión,** *on that (a certain, another) occasion;* **en este (aquel, otro) momento,** *at this (that, another) moment.*

(7) to indicate position *where* in certain limited cases (English *at, on,* etc.).

a la izquierda, a mano izquierda	on the left
a la derecha, a mano derecha	on the right
al borde de	on the edge of

a orillas de	on the banks of
al sur (norte, este, oeste) de	to the south (north, east, west) of
a occidente, a poniente	to the west, to the east
al lado de	beside, at the side of
al pie de	at the foot of

Llame usted a la puerta. Knock at the door.

Todos estaban sentados a la mesa. They were all sitting at the table.

Toledo está a unos setenta kilómetros de Madrid. Toledo is about seventy kilometres from Madrid.

Estaban a cuatro millas de la ciudad. They were four miles from the town.

Vive a dos pasos de aquí. He lives only a few yards away (*lit.*, at two steps from here).

NOTE: In most cases English *at* indicating position is translated into Spanish by means of **en**. In certain of the above cases **en** would give a different meaning: *e.g.*, **Gibraltar está al sur de España** (*to the south of*) but **Andalucía está en el sur de España** (*in the south of*).

(8) to indicate price and rate (English *at*, *a*).

¿A cómo se venden las patatas? How much are your potatoes?

A dos pesetas el kilo. Two pesetas a kilogramme.

Lo he invertido al seis por ciento. I've invested it at six per cent.

Gana medio millón de pesetas al año. He earns half a million pesetas a year.

NOTE: **Por** also may indicate rate [§ 80 (8) Note].

(9) after words indicating love, hate, fear, and related emotions (English *of* and others).

el amor (odio) a la ciencia, the love (hatred) of knowledge
el miedo (temor) a la pobreza, the fear of poverty
una auténtica repugnancia a creerlo, a real reluctance to believe it

Tenían un respeto excesivo a la Dirección.   They had an
excessive respect for the management.
Es muy aficionado a la lectura.   He is very fond of reading.
Tiene mucha afición a los libros.   He is very keen on (has a
great liking for) books.

NOTE: After many such words **de** also may be used, but it is less
frequent than **a** in modern Spanish, probably because it may give
rise to a form of ambiguity which **a** avoids: **el amor del pueblo**
(*the people's love, love of the people*), **el amor al pueblo** (*love of the
people*).

(10) with a following infinitive to express condition [§ 157 (c)].

(11) as the final element of a few prepositional phrases.

en cuanto a	as for	**junto a**	beside
frente a	facing, opposite		

(12) in certain other expressions (principally of manner).

a caballo	on horseback	**un olor a**	a smell of
a pie	on foot	**saber a**	to taste of
a mano	by hand	**un sabor a**	a taste of
a máquina	by machine	**a mi parecer** ⎫	in my opinion,
a ciegas	blindly	**a mi juicio** ⎭	to my mind
a tientas	gropingly	**a lo largo de**	along
a oscuras	in the dark	**a causa de**	because of
a chorros	in sheets, abundantly	**a fuerza de**	by dint of
		a pesar de	in spite of,
a sabiendas	knowing(ly)		despite
a solas	alone, in private	**a través de**	across, through
poco a poco	gradually	**a condición**	on condition
a todo correr	at full speed	**(de) que**	that
oler a	to smell of		

a la española   in the Spanish manner

172. De is used in the following cases:

(1) to translate the English *of* (also *'s*) and *from*.

¿Está Vd. seguro de lo que dice?   Are you sure of what you
say?

Estoy harto de estar siempre repitiendo lo mismo. I am tired of always repeating the same thing.

Le desterraron del país. They banished him from the country.

NOTE: **A** also may at times translate *from* [§171 (3)] and *of* [§171 (9)].

(2) to translate *about* after certain verbs of communication and opinion.

Les hablé de mi viaje al Perú. I talked to them about my trip to Peru.

Se quejó del servicio. He complained about the service.

¿Qué opinas de esto? What do you think about this?

NOTE: **Sobre** and **acerca de** suggest a more detailed treatment than **de** [§ 94 (c)], *cf.* English *on* (*the subject of*).

(3) to indicate the cause of a given action or reaction (English *with*, *at*, *for*, etc.).

Me alegro mucho de su éxito. I'm very pleased at your success.

Se puso a saltar de alegría. He started to jump for joy.

Estaban temblando de frío. They were shivering with cold.

NOTE: **Por** expresses a stronger causal relationship than **de** [§ 146]; **ante** translates *at* with the meaning *when confronted with* [§ 94 (c)].

(4) to translate *with*, *in* and *by*, when they introduce the means or instrument of a given action.

Se le colmó de honores. He was loaded with honours.

Este campo está sembrado de trigo. This field is sown with wheat.

Se vistió de negro. She dressed in black.

Pintaron las puertas de verde. They painted the doors (in) green.

La cogí de la mano. I seized her by the hand.

La ciudad está rodeada de murallas. The city is surrounded by walls.

NOTE: In the last case the function of **de** comes close to that of **por** when it introduces an agent [§ 144]. **De** may in fact introduce the agent after the passive of a verb of feeling, but **por** is more usual in modern Spanish.

Era aborrecido por (*also* **de**) **todos.**   He was detested by all.

(5) to indicate in what capacity or with what status someone does something (English *as*+indefinite article).

Trabajó de enfermera en un hospital.   She worked as a nurse in a hospital.
Se alistó de soldado raso.   He joined up as a private.
Nos sirve de guía.   He acts as our guide.
¿Quién cantó de tenor?   Who sang (as) tenor?

NOTE: **Como** may often be used instead of **de**:
Trabajó como enfermera.   She worked as a nurse.

(6) to translate *in* in the sense of *as to, with respect to, as far as — is (are) concerned.*

Me encuentro mucho mejor de salud.   I feel much better in health.
Era muy pequeño de cuerpo.   He was very small in body.

NOTE: This Spanish construction frequently corresponds to an English compound adjective: **corto de vista**, *short-sighted*; **ancho de espaldas**, *broad-shouldered*; **un sombrero ancho de alas**, *a broad-brimmed hat*; **ágil de pies**, *nimble-footed*; **tierno de corazón**, *tender-hearted*; **pronto (corto) de genio**, *quick- (slow-) witted*, etc.

(7) to give adjectival function to a verb, noun, adverb or adverbial phrase.

la máquina de escribir	the typewriter
papel de fumar	cigarette paper
el campo de batalla	the battlefield
una mesa de roble	an oak table
la princesa de los ojos azules	the princess with the blue eyes
las excusas de siempre	the same old excuses
los vecinos de al lado	the next-door neighbours
los soldados de a pie y los de a caballo	the foot soldiers and those on horseback

NOTE: **Para** is similarly used to indicate function in cases where **de** might suggest content or composition.

> **un vaso para vino**   a wine glass
> **un cepillo para el pelo**   a hair-brush

But **un cepillo de dientes** (*a tooth-brush*), because no confusion is likely.

(8) to introduce an element in apposition (English *of*, or simply unexpressed).

Le aprobaron con calificación de sobresaliente. They passed him with distinction (grade).

¡Ay de mí! ¿Qué hago ahora? Woe is me! What shall I do now?

(9) in most cases to act as a link between a noun or adjective and a following infinitive, provided always that the infinitive cannot be interpreted as the real subject of the sentence (English *to*; § 101).

> **Esto es muy fácil de hacer.** This is very easy to do.
> *but* **Es muy fácil hacer esto.** It is very easy to do this.

> **No es mía la obligación de hacerlo.** The obligation to do it is not mine.
> *but* **No es mi obligación hacerlo.** It is not my obligation to do it.

REMEMBER: If **de** is required in a given case before an infinitive, it is used also before a corresponding noun clause.

Abrigo la esperanza de acompañarte.	I cherish the hope of going with you.
Abrigo la esperanza de que nos acompañes.	I cherish the hope that you will go with us.

(10) with a following infinitive to express condition [§ 157 (*c*)].

(11) as the final element of many prepositional phrases. To those listed in § 94 (*b*) can now be added the following:

acerca de	about, on (the subject of)	**a lo largo de**	along, in the course of
a causa de	because of	**en lugar de**	instead of
a fuerza de	by dint of	**en vez de**	
a pesar de	in spite of		

en medio de	amidst, in the midst of	**por medio de**	by means of

(12) in certain other expressions.

de antemano	previously, beforehand	**de buen humor**	in a good temper
de costumbre	usual(ly)	**de mal humor**	in a bad temper
de improviso	unexpectedly	**de espaldas**	on one's back; with one's back turned
de nuevo	again		
de paso	in passing		
de prisa	quickly	**de pie**	on foot
de una vez	once and for all	**de puntillas**	on tiptoe
de pronto		**de luto**	in mourning
de repente	suddenly	**de guardia**	on duty, on guard
de golpe			
de verdad	really	**de viaje**	travelling, on a trip
de veras			
de acuerdo	agreed	**de día**	by day, in the daytime
de memoria	by heart		
de buena gana	willingly	**de noche**	by night, at night
de mala gana	unwillingly		

de (tal) modo	
de (tal) manera	in (such a) way
de todos modos	
de todas maneras	at any rate, anyway
de ningún modo	
de ninguna manera	under no circumstances, by no means
estar de vuelta	to be back

173. Revise **por** and **para** [§§ 94 and 146].

VOCABULARY

el aficionado	lover, amateur	**la nieve**	snow
el autobús	(motor-)bus	**nombrar**	to appoint
avisar	to inform, to warn, to let know	**ordenar**	to put in order; to command
		el paso	step, pace
la casa	firm	**perfecto**	perfect
enorme	enormous, huge	**práctica-**	practically,
la invitación	invitation	**mente**	virtually
la milla	mile	**salvar**	to save

dar un paso to take a step

Study also the idioms listed in § 171 (11) and (12) and § 172 (11) and (12).

EXERCISES

I. (a) *Study and translate:* A orillas del Duero. Está de viaje. En otra ocasión. Él no había hecho tanto por mí. No tenían nada para él. Allí estuve muchos años de profesor. Tiene horror a las reuniones. Trabaja poco para su edad. Trabaja poco por su edad. Este asunto aún queda sin arreglar. España está por conocer para los españoles. Estaban vestidos de negro por la muerte de su padre. A veces las escribo a mano y a veces a máquina. Estaba cansada del silencio y de estar a solas consigo misma.

(b) *Translate:* At another hotel. Instead of doing it by himself. They are in mourning. At the foot of the mountains. We are all agreed. He lives three miles from here. He is very afraid of his father. He was in Germany as a soldier. He learnt it all by memory. This chapter has still to be read. A thousand pesetas a month. I shall come back tomorrow for the reply. If the weather is good I prefer to go on foot. Switzerland is to the north of Italy. It passed us at about a hundred kilometres an hour.

II. (a) *Study and translate:* 1. Y os aseguro que pocos países habrá en Europa en que se pueda gozar de una mayor variedad de paisajes que en España (M. de Unamuno). 2. Entramos en él [= el lugar]; son las cinco de la tarde; mañana hemos de ir a la venta famosa donde Don Quijote fué armado caballero (Azorín). 3. —Mira—decide—, no le hables de ello, que tal vez no le guste; sino que a solas, sin que nadie lo vea, le das este telegrama (C. Espina). 4. No es valor decidirse a aceptar la muerte, como no lo es decidirse a aceptar la vida. Tener valor es decidirse a saber por qué se aceptan (J. Bergamín). 5. Fué un engaño, un engaño más para traerte aquí. Pero no temas; pronto vendrá tu padre, pronto saldrás con él sin que nada tengas que reprocharme (J. Benavente). 6. Si el ideal de los hombres no consistiese sino en ser más ricos, acabarían por hacerse mejores, porque lo mejor, para hacerse más ricos, es ayudarse mutuamente (R. de Maeztu). 7. Aquí estamos para ayudarnos unos a otros; lo que pasa es que no se puede porque no queremos. Ésa es la vida (C. J. Cela). 8. Como sé que te vas a quedar, yo me encargo de que recibas aquí noticias nuestras, para que te reúnas con nosotros, cuando puedas huir, sin el menor riesgo (J. Grau). 9. Muchos años hace que se viene hablando en España de « europeización »: no hay palabra que considere más respetable y fecunda que ésta, ni la hay, en mi opinión, más acertada para formular el problema español (J. Ortega y Gasset). 10. ¿Cómo vais a razonar vuestra tristeza? No lo sabemos; pero presentimos vagamente, como si bordeáramos un mundo desconocido, que esta mujer tiene algo que no acertamos a explicar, y que al marcharse se ha llevado algo que nos pertenece y que no volveremos a encontrar jamás (Azorín).

(b) *Translate:* 1. As soon as you have got dressed I want you to go into town with me. 2. I live always in (= with) the hope of finishing it completely one of these days. 3. There are still many aspects of the problem for which no solution has been found. 4. There is an enormous difference between working through illusion and working out of necessity. 5. Then it became known that he had saved his brother's life during the last months of the war. 6. Mr Martínez told me to ask my brother for the books we had lent him the previous week. 7. "Why are you all so sad today?" "But, Don Joaquín, I assure you we are not the least bit (= in any way) sad." 8. He wants someone to explain to him what one must do in order to go as a guide with foreign tourists. 9. He warned them that by not accepting the solution proposed to them by the manager, they were making every kind of agreement virtually impossible. 10. I for my part am really grateful to you for having accepted the invitation I gave (= made) you. I am sure we shall both thoroughly enjoy ourselves.

III. (a) *Study and translate:* 1. Si hubiéramos sabido que le gustaban a Pomponina las flores, hubiéramos alfombrado de ellas el escenario (J. Grau). 2. De casi todos los sitios en que se entra fácilmente por la puerta, se suele salir por la ventana (J. Bergamín). 3. Cuando el marido no está en casa le fríe un huevo o le calienta un poco de café con leche al hermano (C. J. Cela). 4. Él no sabe por qué se esconde ni cuál es el motivo de su tristeza; siente un descontento profundo que le amarga la juventud, y al mismo tiempo una infinita piedad por todo cuanto vive y sufre (C. Espina). 5. Claro que el día en que los españoles razonemos con unos cerebros artificiales perderemos toda nuestra variedad, tan pintoresca. Pero acaso sea precisamente esto lo que nos está haciendo falta (J. Camba). 6. He aquí una mujer rubia, vestida de negro, en quien vosotros no habéis reparado al sentaros. Examinadla bien: los minutos van pasando; las olas van y vienen mansamente; el tren cruza los campos (Azorín). 7. Las calles no se han hecho para que la gente muera en ellas. La gente debe morir en una cama. Se exceptúa de esta costumbre tan sólo a los personajes de los dramas, que suelen morir en un sillón (W. Fernández Flórez). 8. La timidez del hombre hace ser más atrevidas a las mujeres. Y si lo dudas, aquí tienes a la inocente Silvia, que llega con el mayor sigilo y sólo espera para acercarse a ti que yo me retire o me esconda (J. Benavente). 9. Soy un hombre que ama verdaderamente el pasado. Los tradicionalistas, en cambio, no le aman: quieren que no sea pasado sino presente. Amar el pasado es congratularse de que efectivamente haya pasado (J. Ortega y Gasset). 10. El ansia de renombre y fama, la sed de gloria que movía a nuestro Don Quijote, ¿no era acaso en el fondo el miedo a oscurecerse, a desaparecer, a dejar de ser? La vanagloria es, en el fondo, el terror a la nada, mil veces más terrible que el infierno mismo (M. de Unamuno).

(*b*) *Translate:* 1. I am very grateful to him for the interest he shows in everything I do. 2. He told me to let him know as soon as the rest of the guests (= the remaining guests) arrived. 3. If you had asked your parents to accompany us, I am sure they would have agreed. 4. I am told that at the last meeting a very important step was taken towards a solution of the problem. 5. It appears he has now been appointed by the manager to attend the next meeting as the sole representative of the firm. 6. Most Spaniards have breakfast at about eight o'clock, lunch between two and three, and dinner after ten at night. 7. On the following morning the weather was perfect and the mountains, still covered with snow, stood out enormous against the blue sky. 8. We were wanting to catch the 12.45 bus, but at the hotel they don't serve lunch until one o'clock, so we shall have to set off a bit later. 9. Towards the end of the nineteenth century there appeared one day, in one of the least important papers of the capital, a notice of great interest to (= for) lovers of literature. 10. She was certainly paler than she had been on the previous evening, but the light was behind her and she approached him from the direction of the window.

REVISION

For general revision re-translate the keys given for all the Review and Development Sections (pp. 349, 353, 357, 361, 366–370), compare your versions with the originals, and re-study those points of grammar on which mistakes are still being made.

VERB TABLES

174. The verbs contained in the succeeding tables are the following:

andar, 28	**dar**, 32	leer, 26	reír, 10
apaciguar, 19	**decir**, 33	limpiar, 23	**saber**, 42
argüir, 20	delinquir, 13	llegar, 17	**salir**, 43
buscar, 12	distinguir, 18	mentir, 8	**ser**, 44
caber, 29	dormir, 11	mover, 7	situar, 24
caer, 30	enviar, 22	oír, 38	**tener**, 45
cazar, 14	**estar**, 34	pedir, 9	**traer**, 46
coger, 21	evacuar, 25	pensar, 4	**valer**, 47
comprar, 1	**haber**, 35	perder, 6	vencer, 15
conducir, 31	**hacer**, 36	**poder**, 39	vender, 2
conocer, 16	huir, 27	poner, 40	**venir**, 48
contar, 5	**ir**, 37	**querer**, 41	ver, 49
			vivir, 3

NOTES: 1. The numbers refer to the position of each verb in the tables below.

2. Bold type indicates the particular reason for the inclusion of each verb: regular verbs for their endings, radical-changing verbs for their stem vowel, orthography-changing verbs for the last letter of their stem, and irregular verbs for irregularities in whole verb parts. Similarly, in the tables that follow bold type indicates points of particular note: class changes when only certain letters are so printed (pienso, busqué) and individual irregularities when the whole word is in bold type (valgo, ven, tuve).

3. The conditional and the compound tenses have been excluded from the tables. The formation of the conditional should present no difficulty once the future is known [§§ 104 and 107]; and the use

of **haber** to form compound tenses has been set forth at length in § 159, so that here only the past participle of the different verbs need be given.

REGULAR

Infinitive	Gerund Past Part.	Imperative	Pres. Ind.	Imp. Ind.
(1) I comprar to buy	comprando comprado	compra compad	compro compras compra compramos compráis compran	compraba comprabas compraba comprábamos comprabais compraban
(2) II vender to sell	vendiendo vendido	vende vended	vendo vendes vende vendemos vendéis venden	vendía vendías vendía vendíamos vendíais vendían
(3) III vivir to live	viviendo vivido	vive vivid	vivo vives vive vivimos vivís viven	vivía vivías vivía vivíamos vivíais vivían

RADICAL-CHANGING

(4) I pensar to think	pensando pensado	piensa pensad	pienso piensas piensa pensamos pensáis piensan	pensaba pensabas pensaba pensábamos pensabais pensaban
(5) I contar to count	contando contado	cuenta contad	cuento cuentas cuenta contamos contáis cuentan	contaba contabas contaba contábamos contabais contaban

328

VERBS

Preterite	Future	Pres. Subj.	Imperfect Subjunctive	
compré	compraré	compre	comprara	comprase
compraste	comprarás	compres	compraras	comprases
compró	comprará	compre	comprara	comprase
compramos	compraremos	compremos	compráramos	comprásemos
comprasteis	compraréis	compréis	comprarais	comprasels
compraron	comprarán	compren	compraran	comprasen
vendí	venderé	venda	vendiera	vendiese
vendiste	venderás	vendas	vendieras	vendieses
vendió	venderá	venda	vendiera	vendiese
vendimos	venderemos	vendamos	vendiéramos	vendiésemos
vendisteis	venderéis	vendáis	vendierais	vendieseis
vendieron	venderán	vendan	vendieran	vendiesen
viví	viviré	viva	viviera	viviese
viviste	vivirás	vivas	vivieras	vivieses
vivió	vivirá	viva	viviera	viviese
vivimos	viviremos	vivamos	viviéramos	viviésemos
vivisteis	viviréis	viváis	vivierais	vivieseis
vivieron	vivirán	vivan	vivieran	viviesen

VERBS [§§ 84–87, 168–170]

pensé	pensaré	piense	pensara	pensase
pensaste	pensarás	pienses	pensaras	pensases
pensó	pensará	piense	pensara	pensase
pensamos	pensaremos	pensemos	pensáramos	pensásemos
pensasteis	pensaréis	penséis	pensarais	pensaseis
pensaron	pensarán	piensen	pensaran	pensasen
conté	contaré	cuente	contara	contase
contaste	contarás	cuentes	contaras	contases
contó	contará	cuente	contara	contase
contamos	contaremos	contemos	contáramos	contásemos
contasteis	contaréis	contéis	contarais	contaseis
contaron	contarán	cuenten	contaran	contasen

329

RADICAL-CHANGING VERBS—*cont.*

Infinitive	Gerund Past Part.	Imperative	Pres. Ind.	Imp. Ind.
(6) II perder *to lose*	perdiendo perdido	pierde perded	pierdo pierdes pierde perdemos perdéis pierden	perdía perdías perdía perdíamos perdíais perdían
(7) II mover *to move*	moviendo movido	mueve moved	muevo mueves mueve movemos movéis mueven	movía movías movía movíamos movíais movían
(8) III mentir *to lie*	mintiendo mentido	miente mentid	miento mientes miente mentimos mentís mienten	mentía mentías mentía mentíamos mentíais mentían
(9) III pedir *to ask for*	pidiendo pedido	pide pedid	pido pides pide pedimos pedís piden	pedía pedías pedía pedíamos pedíais pedían
(10) III reír *to laugh*	riendo reído	ríe reíd	río ríes ríe reímos reís ríen	reía reías reía reíamos reíais reían
(11) III dormir *to sleep*	durmiendo dormido	duerme dormid	duermo duermes duerme dormimos dormís duermen	dormía dormías dormía dormíamos dormíais dormían

330

Preterite	Future	Pres. Subj.	Imperfect Subjunctive	
perdí	perderé	pierda	perdiera	perdiese
perdiste	perderás	pierdas	perdieras	perdieses
perdió	perderá	pierda	perdiera	perdiese
perdimos	perderemos	perdamos	perdiéramos	perdiésemos
perdisteis	perderéis	perdáis	perdierais	perdieseis
perdieron	perderán	pierdan	perdieran	perdiesen
moví	moveré	mueva	moviera	moviese
moviste	moverás	muevas	movieras	movieses
movió	moverá	mueva	moviera	moviese
movimos	moveremos	movamos	moviéramos	moviésemos
movisteis	moveréis	mováis	movierais	movieseis
movieron	moverán	muevan	movieran	moviesen
mentí	mentiré	mienta	mintiera	mintiese
mentiste	mentirás	mientas	mintieras	mintieses
mintió	mentirá	mienta	mintiera	mintiese
mentimos	mentiremos	mintamos	mintiéramos	mintiésemos
mentisteis	mentiréis	mintáis	mintierais	mintieseis
mintieron	mentirán	mientan	mintieran	mintiesen
pedí	pediré	pida	pidiera	pidiese
pediste	pedirás	pidas	pidieras	pidieses
pidió	pedirá	pida	pidiera	pidiese
pedimos	pediremos	pidamos	pidiéramos	pidiésemos
pedisteis	pediréis	pidáis	pidierais	pidieseis
pidieron	pedirán	pidan	pidieran	pidiesen
reí	reiré	ría	riera	riese
reíste	reirás	rías	rieras	rieses
rió	reirá	ría	riera	riese
reímos	reiremos	riamos	riéramos	riésemos
reísteis	reiréis	riais	rierais	rieseis
rieron	reirán	rían	rieran	riesen
dormí	dormiré	duerma	durmiera	durmiese
dormiste	dormirás	duermas	durmieras	durmieses
durmió	dormirá	duerma	durmiera	durmiese
dormimos	dormiremos	durmamos	durmiéramos	durmiésemos
dormisteis	dormiréis	durmáis	durmierais	durmieseis
durmieron	dormirán	duerman	durmieran	durmiesen

ORTHOGRAPHY-CHANGING AN|

Infinitive	Gerund Past Part.	Imperative	Pres. Ind.	Imp. Ind.
(12)			busco	buscaba
		busca	buscas	buscabas
buscar	buscando		busca	buscaba
to look for			buscamos	buscábamos
	buscado	buscad	buscáis	buscabais
			buscan	buscaban
(13)			delinco	delinquía
		delinque	delinques	delinquías
delinquir	delinquiendo		delinque	delinquía
to trans-			delinquimos	delinquíamos
gress	delinquido	delinquid	delinquís	delinquíais
			delinquen	delinquían
(14)			cazo	cazaba
		caza	cazas	cazabas
cazar	cazando		caza	cazaba
to hunt			cazamos	cazábamos
	cazado	cazad	cazáis	cazabais
			cazan	cazaban
(15)			venzo	vencía
		vence	vences	vencías
vencer	venciendo		vence	vencía
to conquer			vencemos	vencíamos
	vencido	venced	vencéis	vencíais
			vencen	vencían
(16)			conozco	conocía
		conoce	conoces	conocías
conocer	conociendo		conoce	conocía
to know			conocemos	conocíamos
	conocido	conoced	conocéis	conocíais
			conocen	conocían
(17)			llego	llegaba
		llega	llegas	llegabas
llegar	llegando		llega	llegaba
to arrive			llegamos	llegábamos
	llegado	llegad	llegáis	llegabais
			llegan	llegaban

RELATED VERBS [§§ 135–143]

Preterite	Future	Pres. Subj.	Imperfect Subjunctive	
busqué	buscaré	busque	buscara	buscase
buscaste	buscarás	busques	buscaras	buscases
buscó	buscará	busque	buscara	buscase
buscamos	buscaremos	busquemos	buscáramos	buscásemos
buscasteis	buscaréis	busquéis	buscarais	buscaseis
buscaron	buscarán	busquen	buscaran	buscasen
delinquí	delinquiré	delinca	delinquiera	delinquiese
delinquiste	delinquirás	delincas	delinquieras	delinquieses
delinquió	delinquirá	delinca	delinquiera	delinquiese
delinquimos	delinquiremos	delincamos	delinquiéramos	delinquiésemos
delinquisteis	delinquiréis	delincáis	delinquierais	delinquieseis
delinquieron	delinquirán	delincan	delinquieran	delinquiesen
cacé	cazaré	cace	cazara	cazase
cazaste	cazarás	caces	cazaras	cazases
cazó	cazará	cace	cazara	cazase
cazamos	cazaremos	cacemos	cazáramos	cazásemos
cazasteis	cazaréis	cacéis	cazarais	cazaseis
cazaron	cazarán	cacen	cazaran	cazasen
vencí	venceré	venza	venciera	venciese
venciste	vencerás	venzas	vencieras	vencieses
venció	vencerá	venza	venciera	venciese
vencimos	venceremos	venzamos	venciéramos	venciésemos
vencisteis	venceréis	venzáis	vencierais	vencieseis
vencieron	vencerán	venzan	vencieran	venciesen
conocí	conoceré	conozca	conociera	conociese
conociste	conocerás	conozcas	conocieras	conocieses
conoció	conocerá	conozca	conociera	conociese
conocimos	conoceremos	conozcamos	conociéramos	conociésemos
conocisteis	conoceréis	conozcáis	conocierais	conocieseis
conocieron	conocerán	conozcan	conocieran	conociesen
llegué	llegaré	llegue	llegara	llegase
llegaste	llegarás	llegues	llegaras	llegases
llegó	llegará	llegue	llegara	llegase
llegamos	llegaremos	lleguemos	llegáramos	llegásemos
llegasteis	llegaréis	lleguéis	llegarais	llegaseis
llegaron	llegarán	lleguen	llegaran	llegasen

ORTHOGRAPHY-CHANGING AND RELATED VERBS—*cont.*

Infinitive	Gerund Past Part.	Imperative	Pres. Ind.	Imp. Ind.
(18)			distingo	distinguía
	distinguiendo	distingue	distingues	distinguías
distinguir		distingue	distingue	distinguía
to dis-	distinguido		distinguimos	distinguíamo
tinguish		distinguid	distinguís	distinguíais
			distinguen	distinguían
(19)			apaciguo	apaciguaba
	apaciguando	apacigua	apaciguas	apaciguabas
apaciguar		apacigua	apacigua	apaciguaba
to pacify	apaciguado		apaciguamos	apaciguábam
		apaciguad	apaciguáis	apaciguabais
			apaciguan	apaciguaban
(20)			arguyo	argüía
	arguyendo	arguye	arguyes	argüías
argüir		arguye	arguye	argüía
to argue	argüido		argüimos	argüíamos
		argüid	argüís	argüíais
			arguyen	argüían
(21)			cojo	cogía
	cogiendo	coge	coges	cogías
coger		coge	coge	cogía
to seize	cogido		cogemos	cogíamos
		coged	cogéis	cogíais
			cogen	cogían
(22)			envío	enviaba
	enviando	envía	envías	enviabas
enviar		envía	envía	enviaba
to send	enviado		enviamos	enviábamos
		enviad	enviáis	enviabais
			envían	enviaban
(23)			limpio	limpiaba
	limpiando	limpia	limpias	limpiabas
limpiar		limpia	limpia	limpiaba
to clean	limpiado		limpiamos	limpiábamos
		limpiad	limpiáis	limpiabais
			limpian	limpiaban

Preterite	Future	Pres. Subj.	Imperfect Subjunctive	
distinguí	distinguiré	distinga	distinguiera	distinguiese
distinguiste	distinguirás	distingas	distinguieras	distinguieses
distinguió	distinguirá	distinga	distinguiera	distinguiese
distinguimos	distinguiremos	distingamos	distinguiéramos	distinguiésemos
distinguisteis	distinguiréis	distingáis	distinguierais	distinguieseis
distinguieron	distinguirán	distingan	distinguieran	distinguiesen
apacigüé	apaciguaré	apacigüe	apaciguara	apaciguase
apaciguaste	apaciguarás	apacigües	apaciguaras	apaciguases
apaciguó	apaciguará	apacigüe	apaciguara	apaciguase
apaciguamos	apaciguaremos	apacigüemos	apaciguáramos	apaciguásemos
apaciguasteis	apaciguaréis	apacigüéis	apaciguarais	apaciguaseis
apaciguaron	apaciguarán	apacigüen	apaciguaran	apaciguasen
argüí	argüiré	arguya	arguyera	arguyese
argüiste	argüirás	arguyas	arguyeras	arguyeses
arguyó	argüirá	arguya	arguyera	arguyese
argüimos	argüiremos	arguyamos	arguyéramos	arguyésemos
argüisteis	argüiréis	arguyáis	arguyerais	arguyeseis
arguyeron	argüirán	arguyan	arguyeran	arguyesen
cogí	cogeré	coja	cogiera	cogiese
cogiste	cogerás	cojas	cogieras	cogieses
cogió	cogerá	coja	cogiera	cogiese
cogimos	cogeremos	cojamos	cogiéramos	cogiésemos
cogisteis	cogeréis	cojáis	cogierais	cogieseis
cogieron	cogerán	cojan	cogieran	cogiesen
envié	enviaré	envíe	enviara	enviase
enviaste	enviarás	envíes	enviaras	enviases
envió	enviará	envíe	enviara	enviase
enviamos	enviaremos	enviemos	enviáramos	enviásemos
enviasteis	enviaréis	enviéis	enviarais	enviaseis
enviaron	enviarán	envíen	enviaran	enviasen
limpié	limpiaré	limpie	limpiara	limpiase
limpiaste	limpiarás	limpies	limpiaras	limpiases
limpió	limpiará	limpie	limpiara	limpiase
limpiamos	limpiaremos	limpiemos	limpiáramos	limpiásemos
limpiasteis	limpiaréis	limpiéis	limpiarais	limpiaseis
limpiaron	limpiarán	limpien	limpiaran	limpiasen

ORTHOGRAPHY-CHANGING AND RELATED VERBS—*cont.*

Infinitive	Gerund Past Part.	Imperative	Pres. Ind.	Imp. Ind.
(24)			sitúo	situaba
		sitúa	sitúas	situabas
situar	situando		sitúa	situaba
to situate			situamos	situábamos
	situado	situad	situáis	situabais
			sitúan	situaban
(25)			evacuo	evacuaba
		evacua	evacuas	evacuabas
evacuar	evacuando		evacua	evacuaba
to			evacuamos	evacuábamos
evacuate	evacuado	evacuad	evacuáis	evacuabais
			evacuan	evacuaban
(26)			leo	leía
		lee	lees	leías
leer	leyendo		lee	leía
to read			leemos	leíamos
	leído	leed	leéis	leíais
			leen	leían
(27)			huyo	huía
		huye	huyes	huías
huir	huyendo		huye	huía
to flee			huimos	huíamos
	huido	huid	huís	huíais
			huyen	huían
				IRREGULAR
(28)			ando	andaba
		anda	andas	andabas
andar	andando		anda	andaba
to walk			andamos	andábamos
	andado	andad	andáis	andabais
			andan	andaban
(29)			**quepo**	cabía
		cabe	cabes	cabías
caber	cabiendo		cabe	cabía
to fit in			cabemos	cabíamos
	cabido	cabed	cabéis	cabíais
			caben	cabían

336

Preterite	Future	Pres. Subj.	Imperfect Subjunctive	
situé	situaré	sitúe	situara	situase
situaste	situarás	sitúes	situaras	situases
situó	situará	sitúe	situara	situase
situamos	situaremos	situemos	situáramos	situásemos
situasteis	situaréis	situéis	situarais	situaseis
situaron	situarán	sitúen	situaran	situasen
evacué	evacuaré	evacue	evacuara	evacuase
evacuaste	evacuarás	evacues	evacuaras	evacuases
evacuó	evacuará	evacue	evacuara	evacuase
evacuamos	evacuaremos	evacuemos	evacuáramos	evacuásemos
evacuasteis	evacuaréis	evacuéis	evacuarais	evacuaseis
evacuaron	evacuarán	evacuen	evacuaran	evacuasen
leí	leeré	lea	leyera	leyese
leíste	leerás	leas	leyeras	leyeses
leyó	leerá	lea	leyera	leyese
leímos	leeremos	leamos	leyéramos	leyésemos
leísteis	leeréis	leáis	leyerais	leyeseis
leyeron	leerán	lean	leyeran	leyesen
huí	huiré	huya	huyera	huyese
huiste	huirás	huyas	huyeras	huyeses
huyó	huirá	huya	huyera	huyese
huimos	huiremos	huyamos	huyéramos	huyésemos
huisteis	huiréis	huyáis	huyerais	huyeseis
huyeron	huirán	huyan	huyeran	huyesen

VERBS

anduve	andaré	ande	anduviera	anduviese
anduviste	andarás	andes	anduvieras	anduvieses
anduvo	andará	ande	anduviera	anduviese
anduvimos	andaremos	andemos	anduviéramos	anduviésemos
anduvisteis	andaréis	andéis	anduvierais	anduvieseis
anduvieron	andarán	anden	anduvieran	anduviesen
cupe	cabré	quepa	cupiera	cupiese
cupiste	cabrás	quepas	cupieras	cupieses
cupo	cabrá	quepa	cupiera	cupiese
cupimos	cabremos	quepamos	cupiéramos	cupiésemos
cupisteis	cabréis	quepáis	cupierais	cupieseis
cupieron	cabrán	quepan	cupieran	cupiesen

IRREGULAR VERBS—*contd.*

Infinitive	Gerund Past Part.	Imperative	Pres. Ind.	Imp. Ind.
(30)			**caigo**	caía
		cae	caes	caías
caer	cayendo		cae	caía
to fall			caemos	caíamos
	caído	caed	caéis	caíais
			caen	caían
(31)			**conduzco**	conducía
		conduce	conduces	conducías
conducir	conduciendo		conduce	conducía
to drive			conducimos	conducíamos
	conducido	conducid	conducís	conducíais
			conducen	conducían
(32)			**doy**	daba
		da	das	dabas
dar	dando		da	daba
to give			damos	dábamos
	dado	dad	dais	dabais
			dan	daban
(33)			**digo**	decía
		di	dices	decías
decir	diciendo		dice	decía
to say			decimos	decíamos
	dicho	decid	decís	decíais
			dicen	decían
(34)			**estoy**	estaba
		está	**estás**	estabas
estar	estando		**está**	estaba
to be			estamos	estábamos
	estado	estad	estáis	estabais
			están	estaban
(35)			**he**	había
		——	**has**	habías
haber	habiendo		**ha**	había
to have			**hemos**	habíamos
	habido	——	habéis	habíais
			han	habían

Preterite	Future	Pres. Subj.	Imperfect Subjunctive	
caí	caeré	**caiga**	cayera	cayese
caíste	caerás	**caigas**	cayeras	cayeses
cayó	caerá	**caiga**	cayera	cayese
caímos	caeremos	**caigamos**	cayéramos	cayésemos
caísteis	caeréis	**caigáis**	cayerais	cayeseis
cayeron	caerán	**caigan**	cayeran	cayesen
conduje	conduciré	conduzca	**condujera**	**condujese**
condujiste	conducirás	conduzcas	**condujeras**	**condujeses**
condujo	conducirá	conduzca	**condujera**	**condujese**
condujimos	conduciremos	conduzcamos	**condujéramos**	**condujésemos**
condujisteis	conduciréis	conduzcáis	**condujerais**	**condujeseis**
condujeron	conducirán	conduzcan	**condujeran**	**condujesen**
di	daré	dé	diera	diese
diste	darás	des	dieras	dieses
dio	dará	**dé**	diera	diese
dimos	daremos	demos	**diéramos**	**diésemos**
disteis	daréis	deis	dierais	dieseis
dieron	darán	den	dieran	diesen
dije	**diré**	diga	dijera	dijese
dijiste	**dirás**	digas	dijeras	dijeses
dijo	**dirá**	diga	dijera	dijese
dijimos	**diremos**	**digamos**	**dijéramos**	**dijésemos**
dijisteis	**diréis**	**digáis**	dijerais	**dijeseis**
dijeron	**dirán**	**digan**	dijeran	dijesen
estuve	estaré	**esté**	estuviera	estuviese
estuviste	estarás	**estés**	estuvieras	estuvieses
estuvo	estará	**esté**	estuviera	estuviese
estuvimos	estaremos	estemos	**estuviéramos**	**estuviésemos**
estuvisteis	estaréis	estéis	estuvierais	estuvieseis
estuvieron	estarán	**estén**	estuvieran	estuviesen
hube	**habré**	**haya**	hubiera	hubiese
hubiste	**habrás**	**hayas**	hubieras	hubieses
hubo	**habrá**	**haya**	hubiera	hubiese
hubimos	**habremos**	**hayamos**	**hubiéramos**	**hubiésemos**
hubisteis	**habréis**	**hayáis**	hubierais	hubieseis
hubieron	**habrán**	**hayan**	hubieran	hubiesen

IRREGULAR VERBS—*contd.*

Infinitive	Gerund Past Part.	Imperative	Pres. Ind.	Imp. Ind.
(36)			**hago**	hacía
		haz	haces	hacías
hacer	haciendo		hace	hacía
to do,			hacemos	hacíamos
make	**hecho**	haced	hacéis	hacíais
			hacen	hacían
(37)			**voy**	iba
		ve	vas	ibas
ir	yendo		va	iba
to go			vamos	íbamos
	ido	id	vais	ibais
			van	iban
(38)			**oigo**	oía
		oye	oyes	oías
oír	oyendo		oye	oía
to hear			oímos	oíamos
	oído	oíd	oís	oíais
			oyen	oían
(39)			**puedo**	podía
		puede	puedes	podías
poder	**pudiendo**		puede	podía
to be able			podemos	podíamos
	podido	poded	podéis	podíais
			pueden	podían
(40)			**pongo**	ponía
		pon	pones	ponías
poner	poniendo		pone	ponía
to put			ponemos	poníamos
	puesto	poned	ponéis	poníais
			ponen	ponían
(41)			**quiero**	quería
		quiere	quieres	querías
querer	queriendo		quiere	quería
to want			queremos	queríamos
	querido	quered	queréis	queríais
			quieren	querían

Preterite	Future	Pres. Subj.	Imperfect Subjunctive	
hice	haré	haga	hiciera	hiciese
hiciste	harás	hagas	hicieras	hicieses
hizo	hará	haga	hiciera	hiciese
hicimos	haremos	hagamos	hiciéramos	hiciésemos
hicisteis	haréis	hagáis	hicierais	hicieseis
hicieron	harán	hagan	hicieran	hiciesen
fui	iré	vaya	fuera	fuese
fuiste	irás	vayas	fueras	fueses
fue	irá	vaya	fuera	fuese
fuimos	iremos	vayamos	fuéramos	fuésemos
fuisteis	iréis	vayáis	fuerais	fueseis
fueron	irán	vayan	fueran	fuesen
oí	oiré	oiga	oyera	oyese
oíste	oirás	oigas	oyeras	oyeses
oyó	oirá	oiga	oyera	oyese
oímos	oiremos	oigamos	oyéramos	oyésemos
oísteis	oiréis	oigáis	oyerais	oyeseis
oyeron	oirán	oigan	oyeran	oyesen
pude	podré	pueda	pudiera	pudiese
pudiste	podrás	puedas	pudieras	pudieses
pudo	podrá	pueda	pudiera	pudiese
pudimos	podremos	podamos	pudiéramos	pudiésemos
pudisteis	podréis	podáis	pudierais	pudieseis
pudieron	podrán	puedan	pudieran	pudiesen
puse	pondré	ponga	pusiera	pusiese
pusiste	pondrás	pongas	pusieras	pusieses
puso	pondrá	ponga	pusiera	pusiese
pusimos	pondremos	pongamos	pusiéramos	pusiésemos
pusisteis	pondréis	pongáis	pusierais	pusieseis
pusieron	pondrán	pongan	pusieran	pusiesen
quise	querré	quiera	quisiera	quisiese
quisiste	querrás	quieras	quisieras	quisieses
quiso	querrá	quiera	quisiera	quisiese
quisimos	querremos	queramos	quisiéramos	quisiésemos
quisisteis	querréis	queráis	quisierais	quisieseis
quisieron	querrán	quieran	quisieran	quisiesen

IRREGULAR VERBS—*contd.*

Infinitive	Gerund Past Part.	Imperative	Pres. Ind.	Imp. Ind.
(42)			**sé**	sabía
	sabiendo	sabe	sabes	sabías
saber			sabe	sabía
to know	sabido		sabemos	sabíamos
		sabed	sabéis	sabíais
			saben	sabían
(43)			**salgo**	salía
		sal	sales	salías
salir	saliendo		sale	salía
to go out	salido		salimos	salíamos
		salid	salís	salíais
			salen	salían
(44)			**soy**	**era**
	siendo	**sé**	**eres**	**eras**
ser			**es**	**era**
to be	sido		**somos**	**éramos**
		sed	**sois**	**erais**
			son	**eran**
(45)			**tengo**	tenía
	teniendo	**ten**	tienes	tenías
tener			tiene	tenía
to have	tenido		tenemos	teníamos
		tened	tenéis	teníais
			tienen	tenían
(46)			**traigo**	traía
	trayendo	trae	traes	traías
traer			trae	traía
to bring	traído		traemos	traíamos
		traed	traéis	traíais
			traen	traían
(47)			**valgo**	valía
	valiendo	**val**	vales	valías
valer			vale	valía
to be	valido		valemos	valíamos
worth		valed	valéis	valíais
			valen	valían

Preterite	Future	Pres. Subj.	Imperfect Subjunctive	
upe	sabré	sepa	supiera	supiese
upiste	sabrás	sepas	supieras	supieses
upo	sabrá	sepa	supiera	supiese
upimos	sabremos	sepamos	supiéramos	supiésemos
upisteis	sabréis	sepáis	supierais	supieseis
upieron	sabrán	sepan	supieran	supiesen
alí	saldré	salga	saliera	saliese
aliste	saldrás	salgas	salieras	salieses
alió	saldrá	salga	saliera	saliese
alimos	saldremos	salgamos	saliéramos	saliésemos
alisteis	saldréis	salgáis	salierais	salieseis
alieron	saldrán	salgan	salieran	saliesen
ui	seré	sea	fuera	fuese
uiste	serás	seas	fueras	fueses
ue	será	sea	fuera	fuese
uimos	seremos	seamos	fuéramos	fuésemos
uisteis	seréis	seáis	fuerais	fueseis
ueron	serán	sean	fueran	fuesen
uve	tendré	tenga	tuviera	tuviese
uviste	tendrás	tengas	tuvieras	tuvieses
uvo	tendrá	tenga	tuviera	tuviese
uvimos	tendremos	tengamos	tuviéramos	tuviésemos
uvisteis	tendréis	tengáis	tuvierais	tuvieseis
uvieron	tendrán	tengan	tuvieran	tuviesen
raje	traeré	traiga	trajera	trajese
rajiste	traerás	traigas	trajeras	trajeses
rajo	traerá	traiga	trajera	trajese
rajimos	traeremos	traigamos	trajéramos	trajésemos
rajisteis	traeréis	traigáis	trajerais	trajeseis
rajeron	traerán	traigan	trajeran	trajesen
alí	valdré	valga	valiera	valiese
aliste	valdrás	valgas	valieras	valieses
alió	valdrá	valga	valiera	valiese
alimos	valdremos	valgamos	valiéramos	valiésemos
alisteis	valdréis	valgáis	valierais	valieseis
alieron	valdrán	valgan	valieran	valiesen

343

IRREGULAR VERBS—*contd.*

Infinitive	Gerund Past Part.	Imperative	Pres. Ind.	Imp. Ind.
(48)			**vengo**	venía
	viniendo	**ven**	**vienes**	venías
venir			**viene**	venía
to come			venimos	veníamos
	venido	venid	venís	veníais
			vienen	venían
(49)			**veo**	veía
	viendo	ve	ves	**veías**
ver			ve	veía
to see	**visto**		vemos	**veíamos**
		ved	veis	**veíais**
			ven	veían

344

Preterite	Future	Pres. Subj.	Imperfect Subjunctive	
vine	vendré	venga	viniera	viniese
viniste	vendrás	vengas	vinieras	vinieses
vino	vendrá	venga	viniera	viniese
vinimos	vendremos	vengamos	viniéramos	viniésemos
vinisteis	vendréis	vengáis	vinierais	vinieseis
vinieron	vendrán	vengan	vinieran	viniesen
vi	veré	vea	viera	viese
viste	verás	veas	vieras	vieses
vio	verá	vea	viera	viese
vimos	veremos	veamos	viéramos	viésemos
visteis	veréis	veáis	vierais	vieseis
vieron	verán	vean	vieran	viesen

KEY TO EXERCISES

LESSON I

II. (*a*) 1. You buy books and (news)papers. 2. We have a meal at the factory. 3. You sell pears. 4. I receive a letter from my friend. 5. We live in a house in Madrid. 6. My friend works in the hospital. 7. You send books to the girls. 8. The boy sells a newspaper to my wife. 9. The women work at a factory. 10. The boys eat pears in the hospital.

(*b*) 1. Los muchachos escriben a mi amigo. 2. Usted vende el libro a una muchacha. 3. Las muchachas reciben las cartas de mi amigo. 4. El muchacho manda un libro a mi mujer. 5. Escribimos a los hospitales. 6. Mi amigo trabaja en una fábrica en (*or* de) Madrid. 7. Viven en mi casa. 8. La mujer lee un libro. 9. Los muchachos mandan una carta a la muchacha. 10. Comemos en una tienda.

LESSON II

II. (*a*) 1. I write a letter to the boy's father. 2. Where are you going with John's father? 3. As I haven't any pears I eat apples. 4. The boys' mother lives in the town. 5. What do you read when you are not working?[1] 6. Which newspaper are you writing the letter to? 7. When are you going to buy the shop where I work? 8. There is a man who sells pencils. 9. I give my brother the pen I am writing the letter with. 10. What lessons is the boy talking about?

(*b*) 1. ¿Qué venden las mujeres? 2. ¿A quién escribe la carta? 3. Da mi pluma al muchacho. 4. ¿No recibe usted cartas de mi hermana? 5. ¿Adónde van ustedes? 6. Mi hermano no lee los libros que compra. 7. Hay una mujer que vende plumas a los muchachos. 8. ¿Por qué no leéis los periódicos? 9. ¿Con qué lápices escriben ustedes? 10. ¿Cómo escribe usted las cartas que manda a mi hermano?

[1] Notice that **usted** is not repeated.

347

Lesson III

II. (a) 1. There are many beautiful shops in Madrid. 2. Not many English gentlemen live in Andalusian houses. 3. Who are you going to give so many flowers to? 4. The Spanish girl sells many English newspapers. 5. Which books are the cheapest? 6. John studies the first lesson and my brother the third. 7. The blue flowers are very beautiful. 8. We are going to go with John's mother to the new English hospital. 9. How many letters does the Spanish girl write? 10. The woman sells the red flowers to my sister and the yellow ones to my mother.

(b) 1. Compro un lápiz verde y una pluma amarilla. 2. ¿Qué venden las muchachas españolas? 3. Bebéis mucho vino español. 4. ¿A quién vamos a vender las flores amarillas? 5. Mis amigos españoles venden plumas y lápices muy bonitos. 6. ¿Dónde compra usted tantas cosas baratas? 7. Estudian dos lecciones difíciles y una más fácil. 8. Las casas de Madrid son más grandes, pero las andaluzas son más bonitas. 9. ¿Con quién estudia usted la tercera lección? 10. Vendemos tantas cosas que mi padre va a comprar una nueva tienda.

Lesson IV

II. (a) 1. It is very easy to do that. 2. My mother is Spanish and my father English. 3. This gentleman has no friends in Madrid. 4. We all have the same ideas about this. 5. "Which factory do you work in?" "In this one." 6. We speak Spanish when we go to Spain. 7. Those Andalusian boys have to work hard. 8. "What is that?" "It is a good Spanish book that I am going to read some day." 9. The first chapter is very difficult but not as difficult as the third. 10. "How many tumblers have they got?" "Peter has two but John hasn't any."

(b) 1. Mi pobre hermano trabaja demasiado. 2. Aquellos señores no hablan inglés. 3. Ésta es una idea muy interesante. 4. ¿Por qué no compráis una casa más pequeña? 5. ¿Quién recibe todas estas cartas? 6. Esta casa es muy bonita y tiene muchos cuartos. 7. Pedro tiene muchos amigos, pero mi hermano no tiene ninguno. 8. Este hospital es demasiado grande para una ciudad tan pequeña. 9. Estas flores son muy hermosas, sobre todo las amarillas. 10. Esta tercera lección es mucho más difícil que la primera, pero no es tan difícil como la segunda.

Lesson V

II. (a) 1. His mother doesn't go to the town because she is very tired. 2. These Andalusian boys are quite clever. 3. "Where are you?" "I am here in my brother's room." 4. All my pencils are yellow. 5. This pen is broken. 6. "Whose are those extremely nice houses?" (*lit.*, those so nice houses). "They belong to (*lit.*, they are of) a gentleman from Seville." 7. What flowers have you in your garden? 8. The doors are all open. 9. It is not very difficult to do this. 10. That Andalusian girl is taller than many English women.

(b) 1. Esta ciudad tiene muchos hermosos jardines. 2. Vamos a leer el primer capítulo del libro. 3. Están tristes porque no van en el coche de su padre. 4. Los lápices son más baratos que las plumas. 5 — ¿ De quién es esta idea ? — Es de Pedro. 6. Bebemos mucho vino dulce, pero no estamos enfermos. 7. Seis y siete son trece. 8. Es un muchacho muy inteligente. 9. Aquí no es posible comprar vino barato. 10. Estoy muy contento porque todas las manzanas están maduras.

Review and Development Section (I)

II. (a) 1. We do the same thing twice. 2. These Andalusian wines are very good. 3. Those gentlemen receive many letters from their English friends. 4. How many times are you going to have to go to the same hospital? 5. Spain hasn't many big towns. 6. Where are you from and what are you doing in my house? (*Note Spanish punctuation.*) 7. This book isn't bad but I have a much more interesting one. 8. "Whose are these books?" "They belong to some friend of my father's." 9. It is the first time we have studied (*lit.*, are studying) this lesson. 10. He is pleased because today he is not working and he is going to go to Madrid with his wife.

(b) 1. Van a la nueva tienda de tu padre. 2. ¿Por qué coméis tantas manzanas? 3. Un señor que vive en la ciudad manda una carta a mi padre. 4. ¿Tiene usted algún libro de mi hermano? 5. ¿Qué hacen estas dos muchachas españolas? 6. Tienen una casa y un jardín muy bonitos en Madrid. 7. Estas ideas de Juan son muy interesantes. 8. Algún día voy a comprar una casa grande en

España.   9. Los hombres con quienes trabaja su padre son todos muy inteligentes.[1]   10. ¿A qué muchacho vas a escribir?

LESSON VI

II. (a) 1. It was very cold because all the doors were open. 2. During the good weather we used to go almost every day into the country.   3. Often they would send Spanish books and papers to their English friends.   4. What did you use to do when you went to the hospital?   5. I couldn't (lit., didn't) see very well the building where we had to go.   6. She doesn't bear in mind how cold it is now in Madrid.   7. Sometimes, when it was very hot or when we were hungry, we used to go to my grandparents'.   8. Many years ago there lived in this country a very intelligent king.   9. If he is not very careful he is going to have to go to the hospital.   10. It was very difficult to study so many languages.

(b) 1. — ¿Dónde estabas?   — Estaba en casa de mis abuelos. 2. Las puertas de la casa eran todas amarillas.   3. Mi madre y mi hermana vivían en Zaragoza.   4. Hablaba mucho español con sus amigos andaluces.   5. Usted trabajaba mucho más que él.   6. ¿Por qué tenían todos tanto miedo?   7. ¿Quién tenía razón?, ¿tú o yo? 8. Tenemos que tener en cuenta que en España hace mucho más calor que aquí.   9. Ella tenía hambre y ellos tenían mucha sed. 10. Hace muchos años yo vivía en un país donde siempre hacía buen tiempo.

LESSON VII

II. (a) 1. We used to spend many hours talking of the countries we were going to visit.   2. He was going to write the letter before visiting his friends.   3. Neither he nor she was right; nor were we.   4. I don't know the girl my brother was with.   5. I don't know where he lives nor in what factory he works.   6. I never receive so many visits as when I'm ill.   7. We didn't know where the station was.   8. He used to send all his children to Spain to learn the language.   9. Many of our neighbours worked in a factory that was very close to where we lived.   10. We used to visit all the most important people (lit., gentlemen or ladies and gentlemen) in the town.

[1] In Spanish the subject is often placed after the verb, particularly in subordinate clauses where it is longer than the verb, or is emphasized. Take note of examples as they occur.

(b) 1. Nunca estoy tan contento como cuando estoy trabajando en mi jardín. 2. No compraba nada para su hermano, ni para su hermana tampoco 3. Llevábamos a nuestros amigos a la estación cuando hacía mal tiempo. 4. Más vale pasar la tarde descansando en casa que salir con el calor que hace ahora. 5. El edificio de que estaba hablando está muy cerca de la plaza principal. 6. Al leer esto (or Cuando leemos esto), tenemos que tener en cuenta que en España hace mucho más calor que aquí. 7. ¿Sabe usted dónde está mi hermano? 8. Mi hermana tenía muchos amigos, pero mi hermano no tenía ninguno. 9. Al terminar (or Cuando terminaban), salían a buscar más libros. 10. Pasábamos las tardes visitando a viejos amigos y hablando de cosas de poca importancia.

Lesson VIII

II. (a) 1. Now, in the twentieth century, it is not difficult to know several countries. 2. Five hundred and sixty-seven plus seven hundred and fifty-four are one thousand three hundred and twenty-one. 3. He used to work from eight in the morning until five in the afternoon. 4. "At what time does the Seville train arrive?" "At about half past six." 5. On Mondays we used to go to my aunt and uncle's and on Wednesdays to my grandparents'. 6. "What was the date?" "It was the fourteenth of January." 7. I don't study as many languages as you. 8. His father used to go to the factory on the seven thirty-five train. 9. We all had to study until five to four. 10. At nine o'clock you weren't at home.

(b) 1. Cervantes vivía aún en el año mil seiscientos catorce. 2. Cuatrocientos cincuenta y tres más setecientos ochenta y nueve son mil doscientos cuarenta y dos. 3. Voy a terminar esto para mañana por la mañana. 4. Trabajo todos los días de nueve a cinco, pero él sólo trabaja seis horas. 5. Llega a Valencia el veinte de enero y tiene que estar en Barcelona antes del primero de marzo. 6. España tiene una población de más de treinta y un millones de habitantes. 7. Este tren llega a Sevilla a las seis diecinueve. 8. Teníamos que estar en la estación antes de las ocho y diez. 9. Hay ciento veintiuna casas en esta calle. 10. Va a llegar el veintisiete de diciembre hacia las seis de la tarde.

Lesson IX

II. (a) 1. He left Madrid on the twentieth of April, spent a few days in Saragossa, and reached Barcelona on the morning of the twenty-sixth. 2. It was just half past eight when they set out for your house. 3. He gave his son a drink because he (*lit.*, the latter) was very thirsty. 4. At that moment a tourist came in to ask where the *Hotel España* was. 5. We reached Murcia on Friday night, and on the following morning we went to see the cathedral. 6. "Good afternoon. How are you?" "Very well, thank you. And you?" 7. In the house next door there lived a gentleman who worked in the same hotel. 8. For three days it was terribly cold and no one went out into the street. 9. After visiting the cathedral, we went to have a meal in[1] a restaurant that was very close by. 10. The Moors reached Spain in the year seven hundred and eleven and were there for nine centuries, until sixteen hundred and ten.

(*b*) 1. Pasé todo el día escribiendo cartas. 2. Vivieron dos años en Valencia y luego fueron a vivir a[1] Barcelona. 3. ¿Vio usted a mi hermano cuando (éste) pasó por aquí? 4. Éste es uno de los amigos con quienes estudié en Madrid. 5. Estaban muy contentos porque sus hijos llegaban a las cuatro de aquella tarde. 6. Ella vivía aquí antes de ir a vivir a[1] Burgos. 7. En Granada vimos unos jardines muy hermosos, pero hacía un calor terrible. 8. El tercer capítulo fue demasiado difícil para mi hermano, pero hizo muy bien el primero. 9. Al lado de la catedral hay un restorán muy bonito adonde íbamos a comer. 10. Usted aprendió muchas canciones durante su viaje a España, ¿verdad?

Lesson X

II. (*a*) 1. My brother was here yesterday. Did you see him? 2. "Do you know this song that I learnt in Spain?" "Yes, we know it very well." 3. You were a long time in the east of Spain, weren't you? 4. If you don't understand this poem, I am going to explain it to you. 5. He was looking for his daughters in order to take them to the restaurant. 6. What did they reply to you when you talked to them about that idea? 7. What did you do with the present I gave you for your mother? 8. I gave it to my sister and she sent it to Saragossa. 9. There are great differences between the north of Spain and the south; there are also (them) between the east and the west. 10. I was going to give it him on the following day when I went to pay my respects to his parents.

---

[1] Notice the use of **a** to indicate the motion implied (cf. English *went to a restaurant to have a meal*, *went to Barcelona to live*, etc.).

(*b*) 1. ¿Por qué no les dio usted los buenos días al verlos en el mercado? 2. ¿Qué le dio usted cuando él fue a su casa? 3. ¿Por qué no nos lo explicó todo cuando nos vio la semana pasada? 4. Fui a darle las gracias y a enseñarle mi nuevo libro de poesías. 5. Voy a explicarles a ustedes la lección que miramos ayer. 6. Compró esta botella de vino y me la dio antes de salir para el sur. 7. Fui a visitarlos pero era tarde y no estaban en casa. 8. Estuvimos dos horas sin verlos. 9. Los estábamos buscando al pasar por los jardines. 10. En el siglo dieciséis España tenía una población de menos de ocho millones de habitantes.

REVIEW AND DEVELOPMENT SECTION (II)

II. (*a*) 1. *He* was very cheerful because his grandparents were arriving that day. 2. Who were the French people who were talking to your father? 3. Our idea was bad because we didn't take into account what the weather was like in the capital. 4. He arrived at night and on the following morning he left very early for the north. 5. I asked the policeman where the cathedral was. 6. Is this the restaurant where they have that excellent (*lit.*, so good) wine? 7. This lady is English but she knows many French and Spanish songs. 8. Last Wednesday we were all day without doing anything. 9. I read these poems when I was very young. 10. We were going to visit the cathedral but we didn't do so (=it).

(*b*) 1. La casa de sus abuelos estaba cerca de la plaza del mercado. 2. Estos señores pasaron varios años en Italia estudiando el idioma. 3. Estaba terminando el tercer capítulo cuando nosotros llegamos. 4. No conocían a la muchacha, pero sabían dónde vivía. 5. No comí ni las manzanas ni las peras porque aún no estaban maduras. 6. La última vez que estuve en España una libra valía más o menos ciento diez pesetas. 7. — ¿Qué edad tiene el chico más alto? — Tiene ocho o nueve años. 8. Tengo muchas ganas de leer el libro que compró mi hermano cuando estuvo (*or* estaba) en España. 9. Tenía que terminar la tercera lección antes de las cinco. 10. Le está enseñando a la señora unas flores que compró en el mercado.

LESSON XI

II. (*a*) 1. He had spent all morning working in the garden. 2. No one had arrived in time to explain all the difficulties to them. 3. He has plenty of pounds but he is short of pesetas. 4. As soon as he had left home he went to the main station where he took the Madrid train. 5. This year we didn't go to France, but to Germany and afterwards to Switzerland. 6. The telegram that I sent him from Barcelona has still not arrived. 7. We must bear in mind that in January and February it is very cold in Madrid. 8. On reaching London we went to the house of a lady and gentleman (*or* of some gentlemen) we had known in Austria. 9. I have liked very much the books that you bought me in Spain. 10. With the death of Philip and Isabella he (now) had only two children left.

(*b*) 1. Ya habíamos terminado el primer capítulo cuando dieron las cuatro. 2. La he visto y le he explicado la idea. 3. Hoy había muchos andaluces en el mercado, ¿verdad? 4. Después de visitar (Después de haber visitado; Después que visitó; Después que hubo visitado) a sus tíos, fue a saludar a su abuelo. 5. Apenas leí (Apenas hube leído) la primera poesía cuando mi padre cogió el libro y me preguntó dónde lo había comprado. 6. Aún no habían abierto las puertas cuando nosotros llegamos (*or* llegamos nosotros). 7. Ha aprendido varios idiomas enseñándolos a otros. 8. Me preguntaron por qué no les había dejado mi dirección. 9. Para mis padres España ha sido siempre el país más hermoso y más interesante de Europa. 10. Acabo de contestar a la carta de que le hablé ayer.

Lesson XII

II. (*a*) 1. He likes Andalusian wines very much. 2. I don't know any lecture room as small as this one. 3. The important thing was to finish it all before tea time. 4. He had talked a lot during supper of his trip to India and Japan. 5. What an unhappy life to have to be always teaching the same thing! 6. In a certain village of southern Spain there lived, many years ago, a certain Mr Martínez. 7. As he was not a soldier we didn't know how to explain the difference to him. 8. She raised her eyes towards the window where she had seen him a few minutes before. He was no longer there. 9. These lessons are much more difficult than those we were studying last year. 10. Next week we are all leaving for South America.

(*b*) 1. No tengo clase hasta el miércoles que viene. 2. Lo importante es hacerlo ahora, antes de salir para España. 3. Su hermano es profesor de idiomas en el Instituto. 4. Estos libros son mucho más difíciles que los del año pasado. 5. Es un soldado muy bueno y le van a hacer oficial. 6. El español no es tan difícil como el álgebra que estudiábamos en el colegio. 7. Lo que no comprendo es por qué no nos escribió explicando lo que había pasado (or ocurrido). 8. No sé si los caballos son más útiles que los perros, pero sí son más inteligentes. 9. Los españoles no saben hacer una buena taza de té, ni los ingleses saben (or sabemos) hacer café. 10. Vamos a ir primero a Francia y Alemania, y después, si nos queda bastante dinero, a Suiza e Italia.

Lesson XIII

II. (a) 1. She asked him for a glass of water and gave it to her child. 2. When it rains Mr and Mrs Martínez usually come by car. 3. This reminds me of something that happened to me once in Málaga. 4. It seems they have gone to the station to see a friend of the family off. 5. I find [it] very difficult to understand the policy that those of the government defend. 6. Now I am beginning with the difficulties of algebra and I just can't (lit., I find no means to) understand them. 7. The things she buys in the market cost her much less than those she buys near home. 8. He prefers to continue living in the same house where his parents and grandparents[1] lived years ago. 9. Tomorrow begins the most important and difficult part,[1] and I tremble to think of it. 10. At half past eleven at night he goes up to his room, switches on the light and begins his day's lesson.

(b) 1. Quiero ver lo que ha hecho. 2. Pero ¿no se lo pidió a usted hace dos meses? 3. La leche cuesta más que el vino en muchas partes de Europa. 4. Mintió (or Mentía) al decir (or cuando dijo) que su hermano venía al día siguiente. 5. Quiere calentar la leche antes de acostar a sus hijos. 6. Me preguntaron qué hora era y les dije que eran las siete y media. 7. Siempre llueve cuando quiero ir a la ciudad a visitar a mi hermano. 8. Dicen que los españoles prefieren el café al té, pero no comprendo por qué. 9. Recuerdo que mi hermano decía más o menos la misma cosa cuando volvió del Brasil (or al volver del Brasil). 10. Siguieron al extranjero hasta el mercado, pero allí le perdieron y tuvieron que volver a casa.

[1] The absence of repetition of the possessive in 8 and of the article in 9 (contrary to § 21, Note and § 34, Note) emphasizes the oneness of the nouns thus brought together: the parents and grandparents (i.e., almost ancestors) in 8, and the importance and difficulty in 9.

355

Lesson XIV

II. (a) 1. They entered the room and sat down without saying anything to one another. 2. You never know what people think if you don't ask them. 3. They went away without saying anything to the police or to the proprietor of the hotel. 4. He brought his bottle of wine and sat down to eat beside my wife. 5. It appears that during this voyage things were discovered of great interest to (*lit.*, very interesting for) scientists. 6. He fell on his way back from school and broke the watch that his parents had bought him. 7. Nothing is heard save the water that loses itself in dreams amongst the trees. 8. They say that in China people dress in white when someone dies. 9. I heard this said one day by a lady who was coming out of the house of a minister of the last government. 10. When we wakened up in the morning we felt more cheerful and made plans for the days we intended to remain there.

(b) 1. Se levanta a las siete y se acuesta a las diez. 2. Se lo comieron todo sin guardar nada para sus amigos. 3. — Se puede pensar una cosa y decir otra. — Sí, pero no se debe. 4. Se vistieron y fueron a comer a casa de un amigo. 5. Suelo acostarme a las doce y me levanto hacia las siete y media. 6. Durmió durante una hora y, al despertarse, pidió un vaso de agua. 7. Los ingleses que piensan esto de sus vecinos se engañan sin saberlo. 8. Llevamos ya más de un año sin vernos, pero nos escribimos cada semana (*or* todas las semanas). 9. A estas horas de la tarde, cuando ya se han marchado todos los turistas, los jardines quedan en silencio. 10. Nunca se han visto tantos aviones ni tantos soldados como desde la visita del rey Pedro IV (Pedro cuarto).

Lesson XV

II. (a) 1. They were all behind the house, amusing themselves with the boys next door. 2. They did it all under the direction of a (gentle)man from Madrid. 3. I have read a very interesting book on the travels of an Englishman through Spain. 4. The others think the same as you but they don't want to go back to things as they were. 5. These boys can't swim but they can dance and they do it very well too. 6. He continues thinking the same as ever and I don't know how we are going to convince him of his error. 7. My parents live a little beyond the main square, not very far from where *you* live. 8. We could see the cathedral from outside the city, long before reaching the station.   9. After saying this he went out with me to visit some friends we had got to know at the meeting. 10. Like good tourists we had to look at the whole cathedral inside and out.

(b) 1. A mí no me importa lo que dicen, pero a él sí.   2. Fui con él a ver si le podía ayudar.   3. El gato saltó sobre la mesa con el perro detrás.   4. Encima de la puerta veía un letrero, pero no pudo leerlo.   5. Ha vendido todas las sillas y las mesas y ahora tienen que comer fuera.   6. Estaba sentada delante de la puerta preparando las patatas para la cena.   7. Además, él ha hablado contra el proyecto sólo porque vive dentro de la ciudad.   8. Había llevado a su mujer a comer a un pequeño restorán que conocía al lado del mercado. 9. Yo suelo llegar antes que mi hermano, pero él se marcha generalmente mucho después que yo.   10. Estaba buscando la salida cuando alguien le cogió por detrás.

Review and Development Section (III)

II. (a) 1. The important thing is not to tell anybody what they intend to do.   2. It's very nice here (lit., one is very well here), isn't it, with the weather we have been having since we arrived. 3. There has been a lot of fog and the windows are very dirty. 4. "Where is the station exit?"   "I am not sure, but I think it is over there."   5. He wrote to me three or four days ago but he didn't give me his new address.   6. The poor sparrow had a broken wing and *we* didn't know what to do.   7. We were talking to him for more than half an hour but he wouldn't believe what we were telling him.   8. I had to leave without having talked to the proprietor or studied the new scheme.   9. For many years now he has been repeating the same thing and asking favours of the different ministers.   10. We had already been waiting more than twenty minutes for a certain Andalusian friend when a German tourist approached us.

(b) 1. Los jueves vuelve del instituto a las seis.   2. Me pidió el libro de español que le di a usted.   3. Las paredes de mi cuarto son amarillas, pero ahora están muy sucias.   4. ¿No ha ido usted a ver lo que están haciendo con el nuevo hospital?   5. Hace mucho calor hoy, pero tenemos calor porque hemos bebido varias tazas de té. 6. Todos estábamos muy cansados después de haber trabajado tanto en la fábrica.   7. — Tenía mucha sed y quería un vaso de agua.

—¿Por qué no lo pidió? 8. La verdad es que a las siete, cuando sus padres llegaron, aún no había terminado la tercera lección. 9. Pero todos le hablaron en alemán y no pudo comprender lo que decían. 10. Todos los días a las tres, entra, cierra la puerta, y cuenta el dinero que han ganado en la tienda.

Lesson XVI

II. (a) 1. We must try to have it all done by next week. 2. I seemed to think I had seen him several times at the prime minister's house. 3. People are always needed [who are] prepared to work in the small towns. 4. She never ceases to tell us everything she has done with her children. 5. It was then that she began to feel ill and to insist on returning home. 6. I remembered that they had decided not to come back until the following week. 7. I believe that the need for earning one's living by working is gradually being accepted. 8. It has been said that he did right not to reply to the letter they had sent him. 9. We were tired of the visit and of talking all the time of such unimportant things. 10. I find it difficult to get used to the idea of living alone in such a big city as this.

(b) 1. Estoy seguro de que es capaz de hacerlo solo. 2. Prometieron no decir nada a nadie. 3. Me alegro de haber tenido (or Me alegra haber tenido) la oportunidad de conocerle. 4. Convinieron en esperar hasta el lunes siguiente. 5. Tenía la idea de que no quería venir a comer con nosotros. 6. ¿Está usted dispuesto a enseñarme a conducir este nuevo coche que acabo de comprar? 7. Hay que (or Tenemos que or Debemos) reconocer la necesidad de aceptar tal proyecto. 8. Se olvidó de decirle (or Se le olvidó decirle) que su hermano quería venir a verle. 9. Acababa de leer el primer capítulo cuando mi hijo subió a despedirse. 10. Hace un año tenía la idea de que usted no trabajaba bastante y ahora casi me da miedo verle trabajar tanto.

Lesson XVII

II. (a) 1. It will take quite a time to feed the little ones. 2. Shall I open the window or shall I leave it closed? 3. "The others won't have heard anything, will they?" "I hope not." 4. We shall have breakfast very early and at eight o'clock we shall (already) be at North Station. 5. The same thing will happen with the new neighbours and we shall only be able to go out on Thursday nights. 6. I suppose they will take grandfather's visit as a pretext to amuse themselves. 7. Will you take these suitcases up to room number a hundred and forty seven? It is on the fifth floor. 8. This guide (-book) will be very useful to us for the trip we intend to make through the south of Spain. 9. Do you think she will realize what we intend to do when we leave her with Mr and Mrs Cantón? 10. I shall keep these flowers always as my best souvenir of the (so) lovely days we have spent here.

(b) 1. ¿Qué hará usted si su hermano se niega a ayudarle? 2. Se encargó de (or Se comprometió a) hacerlo él mismo, pero no quiso decir para cuándo. 3. Tendremos que preparar toda la lección para el jueves que viene. 4. Usted debería tratar de encontrar otra manera (or otro modo) de resolver todas estas dificultades. 5. — Le invitaré a comer con nosotros mañana. — Eso sí que no (lo harás). 6. Sería mejor encontrar algún pretexto para ir a visitarle a su casa. 7. Será difícil persuadirle a marcharse sin ella. 8. No quiere permitirnos ir solos si no prometemos volver antes de las nueve. 9. No puedo reconocer la necesidad de tal proyecto, ni le ayudaré (a usted) a convencer a otros de su importancia. 10. Usted habrá oído decir lo que piensa hacer el nuevo ministro con los que tomaron parte en la revolución.

Lesson XVIII

II. (a) 1. However much he works he will never have as much money as his brother. 2. I advise you to think it over carefully (lit., that you think it well) before it is too late. 3. Does it also seem wrong to you that he should feel the death of a friend? 4. There certainly isn't room for any more people here (lit., It is without doubt that no more people will fit in here). 5. It is best he shouldn't know what we did with the other money that he let us [have]. 6. I am (lit., I have become) mad with joy because it no longer seems impossible that he loves me. 7. What does it matter that we don't have the same ideas on life if we live happily with one another? 8. It is better that nobody should know anybody's name. Then (lit., Thus) there is no danger of too much being discovered. 9. Is it not true that a few days before leaving here you spent more than two thousand pesetas buying things for your trip? 10. There is nothing that attracts more in love than the impossible, "the vain phantom of mist and light" that Bécquer talked of (lit., said).

(b) 1. Prefiero quedarme aquí hasta que vengan. 2. Es posible que lo haga mañana por la mañana. 3. Está buscando una mujer que sepa leer esto. 4. Me alegro de que hayan tenido tanta suerte. 5. ¿Quiere usted que le diga lo que haría yo? 6. Tenemos que impedir que se dé cuenta de lo que hemos hecho. 7. Dudo que llueva, aunque el cielo sí está bastante negro. 8. Usted tiene que prometerme que no volverá a salir sin que yo lo sepa. 9. No he de parar hasta que él quiera a esta chica tanto como quería a la de enfrente. 10. No ha devuelto aún el libro que le presté, pero dice que se lo dará a mi hermano cuando éste pase por Londres.

Lesson XIX

II. (a) 1. "What do you advise me to do?" "Do what you want." 2. Go and tell your brother to come and see me at once. 3. Don't go and believe all that these (gentle)men say. 4. Come on, man, help me to put my coat on. 5. Come in (*Notice this very common use of* pasar). It is a real joy that you have decided to come and see us. 6. Whilst we have a head on our shoulders let us use it as we should. 7. But (my) son, what have you done? How have you got so dirty? Go and wash yourself at once. 8. Present my respects to her (*or* Greet her in my name) and tell her that as soon as I finish here I shall be (very) pleased to attend to her. 9. When you see her tell her to think it over carefully, to look to what she is doing, for you don't find a husband like him every day. 10. "But we are all standing. Let us sit down." "If you will allow me *I* prefer to stand." "As you wish. Consider yourself at home (*lit.*, You are in your house). Let *us* sit down."

(b) 1. No vayas demasiado lejos, que te vas a perder. 2. Hace demasiado calor aquí. Vamos dentro. 3. No lleve usted esa carta a su padre. Démela a mí. 4. No les deje nunca pensar que nos hayan (*or* han *if I believe they really have convinced us*) convencido de su sinceridad. 5. Vamos a ver lo que dice si le acusamos de habernos mentido. 6. Dígale que venga a verme en seguida, y usted venga con él. 7. ¿Me haría el favor de darle estos libros míos cuando le vea? 8. Isabel, pon la mesa, ¿quieres?, que vamos a comer en seguida. 9. No le diga usted (nada) más. Tiene que aceptar nuestra explicación, por increíble que parezca. 10. Tenga la bondad de escribirles a todos invitándoles a venir (*or* a que vengan) a pasar la semana con nosotros en el campo.

Lesson XX

II. (*a*) 1. You heard him demand last night that you should stay until Friday. 2. If they had come yesterday we should have talked to them. 3. Heavens! And I who was so pleased that he was a soldier. 4. Nevertheless, it was natural that he should think only of his own family. 5. We didn't know how to prevent his coming (*or* managing) to speak to the minister. 6. But, in heaven's name, what do you expect (*lit.*, want) me to do? You know he hasn't left me so much as a peseta. 7. She would be adorable if she were more cheerful and if she didn't become so jealous. 8. *I* shouldn't have let myself be deceived like that, even if he had confessed his love to me a thousand times. 9. If God willed that this girl should fall in love with a man like you the poor mother would be the happiest of women. 10. Until he reached the age of eighteen, he had neither been out of his village nor did he know there existed, outside books, countries where any other language but Spanish was spoken.

(*b*) 1. Sin embargo, si esto fuera verdad, yo no estaría aquí ahora. 2. Es evidente que ha pensado mucho en usted. 3. Si él tiene razón, tendremos que aceptar el nuevo proyecto. 4. Quiero pedirle que vuelva a considerar la respuesta que dio a nuestro representante. 5. Le mandaron que repitiera lo que había dicho al oficial. 6. Si se hubiera acercado a la casa, se hubiera dado cuenta de lo que pasaba. 7. Aunque ya no pueden defender su política de antes, siguen convenciendo a la gente de su sinceridad. 8. En cuanto entraron en el cuarto, el padre de Juan abrió todas las ventanas. 9. Si se hubiera comprometido a hacerlo solo, le hubiera dado permiso para trabajar en la casa. 10. Nos esforzamos por guardar el secreto, pero no pudimos impedir que por fin se supiera la verdad.

(*Except in the second half of Nos.* 6 *and* 9 *the* -iese *form of the imperfect subjunctive may replace the* -iera *form used above.*)

Review and Development Section (IV)

II. (*a*) 1. It matters as much to me as it does to him that this difficulty should be solved as soon as possible. 2. I say, will you lend me your car? I'm in a great hurry to get to the station. 3. And what am I to do if he doesn't consent to receive us or if he refuses to accept this scheme? 4. I'm not going to finish it all unless I spend the whole night working on it. 5. When he reached London he had only two pounds left and about a hundred and fifty pesetas. 6. We did everything possible to convince him but he did not want to leave his mother alone. 7. If you had been at home you would have no need to ask it of anybody. 8. Since you don't like talking of politics let us talk of poetry. You write poems, don't you? 9. He hasn't much confidence in our ideas although I don't think that his are of any outstanding value. 10. But they are not the only ones to think like that. I have been saying the same thing for some (considerable—*Translates the notion expressed by the Spanish* ya) time.

(b) 1. Le hablé ayer, pero no pude persuadirle a aceptar el nuevo proyecto. 2. Lo difícil es resolver el problema sin pedir ayuda a nadie. 3. ¿Por qué no le escribimos una carta invitándole a tomar parte en la organización de la reunión? 4. — ¿Vamos a pie? — Si no le importa, preferiría (*or* me gustaría más) ir en coche. 5. No deje usted de visitarle cuando vaya a Madrid. Se pondrá muy contento al verle (*or* Se alegrará mucho de verle). 6. Aunque esto fuera verdad, no me gustaría comprometerme a seguir tal política. 7. No los acompañaré (*or* No iré con ellos) hasta que esté seguro de que lo desean. 8. Confiesa haber tomado el libro sin decir nada a nadie. 9. No cabe duda de que el ministro hizo bien en no aceptar la política que querían seguir los demás. 10. Le persuadí a que volviera a casa y que se quedara allí hasta que hubiera hablado (*or* hasta haber hablado) con su padre.

Lesson XXI

II. (a) 1. He spoke clearly, concisely and most elegantly. 2. Without doubt this is not the best time to know the south of Spain. 3. Autumn is (gradually) arriving and the trees are beginning to lose their leaves. 4. This gentleman has the most curious accent I have heard in my life. 5. Now there was nothing (*lit.*, no remedy) left for us but to accept the scheme as they had prepared it. 6. The most important rivers in Spain are the Tagus, the Duero, the Ebro, the Guadiana and the Guadalquivir (*Notice that in Spanish rivers are always masculine*). 7. The first chapters of this book are extremely difficult (*or* most difficult) but we are (gradually) coming to understand them. 8. Peter is older than his sister but not so old as his friend Philip. 9. No, no; I want her to satisfy her smallest whims. Is she not the most beautiful woman in all Madrid? Then let her also be the one who dresses most expensively (*lit.*, with most luxury). 10. From time to time something re-awakes within me

KEY TO EXERCISES

and I dream again and I begin once more to make plans and to deceive myself again a little more. But this is becoming less and less frequent, and it also lasts progressively less.

(b) 1. Tengo menos libras ahora que cuando salí de casa. 2. Ésta es la única manera de hacerlo rápidamente sin que nadie nos vea. 3. Este problema es más difícil de resolver de lo que parece a primera vista. 4. No conozco ninguna vista tan preciosa como la que tengo desde mi ventana. 5. Ésta es la montaña más alta de la Península Ibérica, pero no es la más alta de España. (*The highest mountain in Spain is the Pico de Teide (12,180 ft.) in the Canary Islands; the second highest, and the highest in the Iberian Peninsula, is the Mulhacén (11,420 ft.).*) 6. Inmediatamente después de cenar salimos a dar un paseo por la parte más antigua de la ciudad. 7. Los padres de Isabel han estado enfermos, pero ahora están mejor e Isabel quiere volver a la escuela. 8. Hágalo inmediatamente para que (yo) sepa si me hará falta una maleta más grande. 9. Este chico no tiene más que diez años, pero anda mucho más rápido que sus hermanos, que son todos mayores que él. 10. El río más largo de España es el Tajo, que tiene una longitud de más de mil kilómetros.

Lesson XXII

II. (a) 1. Carry on reading, for we are getting near the end. 2. We are all agreed that the change should be brought about in such a way. 3. She has been very nervous since I handed her that letter at the end of last week. 4. It is important that you should fix as soon as possible the date of your arrival in Paris. 5. Let us pick up these sheets, and let us go and show them to his father when he arrives home. 6. I simply can't understand (*lit.*, I don't manage to understand) how you have been able to spend a whole year without doing anything. 7. It is as well that all should know how this man goes against the will and the heart of his daughter. 8. The better I know Spain the more I like it and the more keen I am to go and settle there. 9. I approached the window where she was, and rapidly, without anybody's seeing me, I handed her the letter. 10. It is best you speak to the manager so that he himself may explain to you the position he has found himself in since Mr López left.

(b) 1. Al principio no quería que nadie leyera sus poesías. 2. Hacía frío y estaba lloviendo cuando llegué al hotel. 3. ¿Le

363

pedimos que busque a alguien que nos enseñe a conducir? 4. La señora de Sánchez me envía a hablar con el dueño de esta casa. 5. Me dijo que siguiera leyendo porque ya íbamos llegando al final. 6. Si esto es verdad, entonces ella misma debe hacerlo cuando llegue a casa. 7. Cuando usted llegó, estaba leyendo un ensayo interesantísimo sobre la vida en la Inglaterra del siglo xv (quince). 8. A pesar de esto sigo (*or* continúo) pensando que la mayor dificultad consistirá en convencerlos de nuestra buena voluntad. 9. Averigüe usted si el ministro los acompañará (*or* irá con ellos) cuando salgan para el Canadá. 10. Ésta será una buena oportunidad para persuadirle a que nos deje publicar sus obras completas.

Lesson XXIII

II. (*a*) 1. Everything that can be done for this poor lady is already done. 2. At the end of the month we are going off to Spain for a few weeks. 3. The Iberian Peninsula is situated in the extreme south-west of Europe. 4. They knew that neither by menaces nor by tears could anything be achieved. 5. The work was dedicated by him with all affection to his master Don Ramón Menéndez Pidal. 6. How do you expect (*lit.*, want) us to convince others if we are not convinced ourselves? 7. But the cathedral is a very long way off, so that they will take quite a time to get back however quickly they go. 8. The English word *now* is generally translated by **ahora,** though also at times by **ya,** and other times by **ahora bien.** 9. On the other hand I like very much the translation that Mr Ramírez published years ago. 10. I shall try to study the lesson tomorrow morning, though Philip says he intends to have it finished by tonight.

(*b*) 1. ¿Quiere usted hacerlo por mi hermano? 2. Todos los que la conocen la quieren. 3. Mire usted esta traducción. Está muy bien hecha, ¿verdad? 4. Me parece que he oído decir algo de Segovia a mi hermano (*or* Me parece que mi hermano me ha hablado algo de Segovia). 5. Le castigué por haber vendido todos sus libros por unas cuantas pesetas. 6. A la mañana siguiente, nos levantamos temprano e inmediatamente después del desayuno salimos para Toledo. 7. Voy a intentar traducir este capítulo al español, aunque me dicen que será bastante difícil. 8. Se llamó (*or* Llamaron) en seguida al médico, pero era demasiado tarde para que pudiera hacer algo. 9. Desde luego creo que le han engañado, pero ¿no le parece que el engaño fue justificado por su propia conducta? 10. Indudablemente estos problemas son difíciles, pero no lo son tanto que no los pueda resolver un buen estudiante.

Lesson XXIV

II. (a) 1. I am not expecting anyone nor am I available to anyone. 2. Your uncle, especially, did not cease for one moment to think of you. 3. He does not dare to confess what he has thought of me during these last days. 4. May I ask you a question? There's no need to answer it if you don't want. 5. Look closely at (lit., Note well) the colour of this tree. And look how pretty the leaves are. 6. I wanted to remember his name but it had quite slipped my memory. 7. It was a very pleasant evening, especially for those of us who were interested in political questions. 8. I know that he hasn't ceased a single day to ask you for forgiveness for the bad way he has behaved towards you. 9. Certainly this matter is very well known to me, but I'd rather be silent than make him doubt his own opinions. 10. I should be very grateful to you, gentlemen, if you would be so good as to say a few words to my son before leaving.

(b) 1. Me gustaría más hacerlo yo solo que dejar que me lo haga ella (or Preferiría hacerlo yo solo a dejar que me lo haga ella). 2. Quiero aprovechar esta visita para conocer sus propios sentimientos. 3. Por otra parte, no debemos contar demasiado con la posibilidad de tal revolución. 4. Se ha dicho que los jóvenes pasan el tiempo soñando con lo imposible. 5. Los viernes ella se lava el pelo, y los sábados se lo lava a sus hijos. 6. Le estoy esperando ahora, pero siempre llega tarde. Deben de ser ya las cinco. 7. Le pidió veinticinco pesetas, diciendo que se las devolvería a la mañana siguiente. 8. El otro día di con (or me encontré con) un antiguo amigo que estaba para casarse con una chica andaluza. 9. Durante la semana anterior había triunfado de sus enemigos al ser elegido ministro en el nuevo gobierno. 10. Siento no tener el libro aquí. Se lo presté la semana pasada al señor Fernández y no me lo ha devuelto todavía (or aún).

Lesson XXV

II. (a) 1. (But) how ridiculous you look! Don't let them see you like that. 2. It is you who have to think of the difficulty of the problem. 3. If things go on like this, I don't know how we are going to put them right. 4. I went to look for someone to help me to solve some of these difficulties. 5. "It was you who called me, wasn't it?" "I assure you it was not." 6. They congratulated him on having been able to win the confidence of such different people. 7. Come now, Don José, it doesn't seem right that you should make fun like that of a man I intend to marry very shortly. 8. "Good morning, Miss [López]. How nice and early you have arrived." (*Present tense in Spanish because she is just arriving; the diminutive* tempranito *here suggests a bantering tone*). "Seeing that (*lit.,* Since) I have such a nice boss, and what's more, unmarried (*or* and unmarried at that)." 9. On the next day arrived the minister's wife who had exerted great influence, it appeared, when the new secretary of the Council was appointed. 10. Now, already in the year 1895, that is, three years before the war with the United States began, Unamuno had published some essays on what was going to be called "the problem of Spain".

(*b*) 1. Parece que tienen algo difícil que explicarnos. 2. ¿Ha visto usted a la muchacha de cuyo libro hablábamos? 3. Cuantas más personas invitemos, menos tendrá que comer cada una. 4. Nos asegura que ésta es la única razón por la que no ha venido también su hermano. 5. De haberlo sabido (*or* Si lo hubiera sabido), les hubiera escrito en seguida pidiéndoles ayuda. 6. ¿Por qué supones que estábamos hablando de ti? ¿No hay otras cosas de que hablar en el mundo? 7. Al salir el sol, continuamos nuestro viaje hacia la capital. 8. ¿Cuáles son las ciudades más importantes de España, dónde se hallan situadas, y a qué deben su importancia? 9. Hasta ahora siempre han sido ellos los que me han ayudado a mí; ahora soy yo el que puede hacer algo por ellos. 10. No vamos a tener dinero suficiente (*or* bastante dinero), a no ser que usted nos quiera prestar unas cuantas libras.

REVIEW AND DEVELOPMENT SECTION (V)

II. (*a*) 1. Which is the most interesting building to be found around here? 2. A gentleman who has just arrived from Madrid is asking for you. 3. I was in complete agreement with what the manager had decided. 4. He led us to the garden where his son was sitting doing nothing. 5. There also exists the possibility that he may leave before having finished it. 6. That is precisely why I want to know who your doctor is and what he has done to give you back your health. 7. It turns out that the more we speak to him about her the more he scorns her and longs to return to his first love.   8. He still doesn't know who to spend the weekend with when his elder brother goes off to London.   9. He accused him of having utilized for his own ends money destined to the new hospital. 10. At that moment I realized that it would no longer be possible to return to life as it was (*lit.*, the life of formerly), that we now belonged to each other once and for all.

(*b*)   1. Tenemos que (*or* Hay que) prepararlo hoy y entregarlo mañana.   2. Mi padre me prohibió que entrara en su cuarto mientras estuviera trabajando.   3. Estoy buscando a alguien que me enseñe a conducir este coche que acabo de comprar.   4. Si esto hubiera ocurrido hace unos días, hubiera sabido qué hacer (*or* lo que tenía que hacer).   5. ¿Qué quiere usted que haga para que ella me perdone?   6. Anduvimos mucho aquel día, además de subir la montaña más alta de por allí.   7. En otra ocasión nos habló de lo que habían hecho al encontrarse después de la guerra.   8. Aunque sea verdad lo que dice, no le permitiré que salga de aquí (*or* no le dejaré salir de aquí) antes de las nueve.   9. Dice que preferiría pasar la tarde solo a tener que (*or* le gustaría más pasar la tarde solo que tener que) asistir a la reunión por segunda vez.   10. Hizo mal en no renunciar ya definitivamente al proyecto que se había propuesto para el nuevo hospital.

Review and Development Section (VI)

II. (*a*)   1. I have been reproached with having a bad character; but I don't think it's as bad as that (*lit.*, I don't think that I have it [bad character] so much).   2. The real education of life is not given by parents to children but by children to parents.   3. "Then you advise me to listen to music like someone listening to it raining?" "Exactly, with the greatest attention."   4. I think of a nice subject, take up my pen and immediately say to myself: "Will the gentleman of Guadalajara like this topic?"   5. Amidst his ridiculous failures there was a great and pure desire to know the truth.   But something that he could not quite (*lit.*, that he did not manage to) understand made his sacrifices sterile.   6. I remember that one of the times that China changed its régime, we had a discussion in the Council of Ministers about the customs of that country.   7. I, as a child, often heard it related that a neighbour or a friend was ill; then, immediately, the person who was relating or the one who was listening would remain pensive a moment.   8. "If she knew who I am!"   "And when she knows, you will not be the person you were: you will be her husband, her loving husband, as loving and as faithful and as noble as you wish and she can desire." 9. She reaches the tower and is told that the master is off colour; although he usually gets up early he is not yet out of bed. "I'll wait until he awakes," she replies, and asks, "How long has he been ill, because I saw him the day before yesterday?" 10. I am going to write this sort of Memoirs with the illusion that they may be interesting. I hope that they will entertain someone. Perhaps I am mistaken. I don't intend to invent anything, but to relate what I remember, more or less transformed by memory.

(b) 1. — ¿Son muy ricos sus padres? — No mucho (or Mucho no *which suggests greater wealth*), pero son gente simpatiquísima. 2. Me temo que se han puesto enfermos la mayor parte de los que nos iban a ayudar. 3. El que no esté dispuesto a hacer lo mismo tiene abierta la puerta, y es mejor que se marche en seguida. 4. Había pensado en acompañarle al Brasil, pero ahora he resuelto renunciar definitivamente a tal idea. 5. Aunque sea verdad lo que usted me dice, no por eso dejaré de tener confianza completa en cualquier idea que me proponga aquel señor. 6. No obstante (or Sin embargo), confío en que aún podré acompañar unos días a mis padres, en su estancia en Zaragoza. 7. Nos parece muy difícil (or muy poco probable) que se acepte tal solución, por lo cual (or de modo que) hemos decidido no hablar más del asunto. 8. — Se pondría muy contenta su madre, ¿verdad?, al verle objeto de tanta admiración en la prensa nacional. — Sí, mucho. 9. Bajo este rey, España disfrutó de una época de paz y trabajo en la que el nombre del país (or, *more emotively*, de la patria) llegó a pronunciarse con respeto y admiración en todo el mundo. 10. Es un chico muy trabajador (or que trabaja mucho) y tiene muy buena memoria para las cosas que le interesan. Lo que pasa es que no le interesa nada la política (or no se interesa nada por la política).

REVIEW AND DEVELOPMENT SECTION (VII)

II. (a) 1. Here, take your alms and look for someone who will do you the favour of taking it from you. 2. Tell me no more! We must save the lie whatever the cost (or cost what it may). 3. Since I have been in the town numerous people have approached me in order that I should tell them their names. 4. "Do you feel ill, madam (or Mrs . . .)? You are a little pale." "No, [it's] nothing, thank you very much. [Just] ideas that occur to one." 5. I think that without money there is nothing valued or esteemed in the world, for it is the price of everything. 6. You find the man (*lit.*, There is he) who [as a mere] stripling left his village without knowing anything else, and then he talks to you about Spain — from what he reads in the newspapers (*The Spanish* quien *of generalization may also be translated by the English plural: i.e.*, There are those who . . .) 7. It is not great men who make sculptors, but sculptors who make great men. 8. Twenty years of his life were beginning to be erased from his memory; everything now appeared to him lovely and new as if he looked at it with [the] eyes of [a] child. 9. I am persuaded that in order to correct our defects we must know them and view them objectively, and that the road for that lies in studying the Moors. 10. For the people he was the typical writer of the streets of Madrid, the man who was listened to in a café; and perhaps it was this that made them forgive him as a picturesque type.

(*b*) 1. ¿Por qué no le gusta leer poesías siendo él mismo poeta? 2. Al entrar en la catedral, se le había olvidado (*or* se había olvidado de) quitarse el sombrero. 3. Soy capaz de encontrar lo que se me pida con los ojos cerrados. 4. ¿Cuál es la ciudad más importante del noreste de España y cuántos habitantes tiene? 5. Unos años más tarde, en mil cuatrocientos ochenta y siete, Bartolomé Díaz llegó hasta el cabo de Buena Esperanza. 6. Actúa también en tal situación el deseo de cada uno de no mostrarse inferior a los demás. 7. Finalmente, gracias a un amigo suyo, pude dedicarme completamente durante un año al estudio de sus obras. 8. Si logro realizar mi proyecto, desde luego quedas (*or* estás) invitado a pasar unas cuantas semanas con nosotros en el campo. 9. Mi trabajo no me gusta, pero me consuelo porque todavía no he encontrado a nadie que esté contento con lo que hace. 10. Se dice muchas veces lo contrario de lo que se piensa, como si se creyera que no se debe permitir a los pensamientos andar sueltos por el mundo.

REVIEW AND DEVELOPMENT SECTION (VIII)

II. (*a*) 1. And I assure you that there will be few countries in Europe where one can enjoy a greater variety of scenery than in Spain. 2. We enter it [=the village]; it is five in the afternoon; tomorrow we are to go to the famous inn where Don Quixote was armed a knight. 3. "Look [here]," she decides, "don't talk to her about it, for perhaps she won't like it, but alone, without anyone's seeing, you give her this telegram." 4. It is not valour to decide to accept death, as it is not to decide to accept life. To have valour is to decide to know why they are accepted. 5. It was a deception, another deception to bring you here. But have no fear; soon your father will come, soon you will go out with him having nothing to reproach me with. 6. If men's ideal consisted only in being wealthier, they would end up by becoming better, because the best thing, in order to become wealthier, is to help one another. 7. We're here to help each other. The thing is (*lit.*, What happens is that) it can't be so because we don't want to. That's life. 8. As I know you are going to stay, I'll ensure that you receive news of us here so that, when you can make your escape, you can join us without the least risk. 9. For many years now there has been talk in Spain of "Europeanization." There is no word that I consider more respectable and fruitful than this one, nor is there any, in my opinion, more suited to epitomize the Spanish problem. 10. How are you going to reason out your sadness? We don't know, but we have a vague presentiment, as if we were touching on an unknown world, that this woman has something that we can't quite explain, and that with her departure she has taken away something that belongs to us and that we shall never find again.

(*b*) 1. En cuanto usted se haya vestido, quiero que me acompañe a la ciudad. 2. Vivo siempre con la esperanza de acabarlo ya definitivamente un día de éstos. 3. Quedan aún muchos aspectos del problema para los cuales no se ha encontrado ninguna solución. 4. Hay una diferencia enorme entre trabajar por ilusión y trabajar por necesidad. 5. Luego se supo que le había salvado la vida a su hermano durante los últimos meses de la guerra. 6. El señor Martínez me dijo que le pidiera a mi hermano los libros que le habíamos prestado la semana anterior. 7. — ¿Por qué estáis todos tan tristes hoy? — Pero, don Joaquín, le aseguro que no lo estamos de ninguna manera. 8. Quiere que alguien le explique cómo (*or* lo que) hay que hacer para acompañar de guía a los turistas extranjeros. 9. Les advirtió que al no aceptar la solución que les proponía el director, hacían prácticamente imposible toda clase de acuerdo. 10. Yo por mi parte te agradezco de verdad que hayas aceptado la invitación que te hice. Estoy seguro de que nos divertiremos muchísimo los dos.

VOCABULARY

The vocabulary aims to be complete for the purposes of this course. It does not, however, include articles [§§ 10-11, 77-78], possessives [§§ 34, 118], numerals [§§ 35, 50-51] or personal pronouns [§§ 124-127]. Nor does it include in the Spanish-English section proper nouns that are identical in the two languages. Adverbs in **-mente** are included only in special cases. Numbers refer to paragraphs; *via* indicates that a change of construction is necessary; N. = Note.

SPANISH-ENGLISH

a, to, at [171]
abierto, open
abrazar, to embrace
el **abrigo,** overcoat
abril (*m.*), April
abrir, to open
la **abuela,** grandmother
el **abuelo,** grandfather
los **abuelos,** grandparents
acabar, to finish; **acabar de,** to have just
acaso, perhaps; **por si acaso,** (just) in case
el **acento,** accent
aceptable, acceptable
aceptar, to accept
acerca de, about
acercarse (a), to approach, to draw near (to)

acertar (ie), to hit the mark, to succeed, to happen
acompañar, to accompany, to go with
aconsejar, to advise
acordar (ue), to agree; **acordarse,** to remember
acostar (ue), to put to bed; **acostarse,** to go to bed
acostumbrar, to accustom; **acostumbrarse a,** to get used to
actuar, to act, to operate
el **acuerdo,** agreement; **de acuerdo,** agreed, in agreement
acusar, to accuse
además (de), besides

371

admirable, admirable, remarkable

la **admiración,** admiration

admirar, to admire

adonde, (to) where, to which; **¿adónde?** where (to)?

adorable, adorable

adquirir (ie), to acquire

advertir (ie), to notice, to warn

el **afecto,** affection

aficionado, fond, amateur, lover

el **África** (*f.*), Africa

agosto (*m.*), August

agradable, pleasant

agradecer, to be grateful for

el **agua** (*f.*), water

aguantar, to stand, to put up with

ahora, now [133]; **ahora bien,** now [133]

el **aire,** air, appearance

el **ala** (*f.*), wing

alegrarse, to be glad

alegre, cheerful, gay

la **alegría,** joy, cheerfulness

alemán, German

Alemania (*f.*), Germany

alfombrar, to carpet

el **álgebra** (*f.*), algebra

algo, something

alguien, someone, somebody

alguno, some

el **alma** (*f.*), soul, mind

alrededor (de), around, about [94 (*c*)]

alto, high, tall

allá, there; **más allá (de),** beyond

allí, there; **por allí,** through there, over there, that way

amar, to love

amargar, to embitter

amarillo, yellow

ambos, both

la **amenaza,** menace

amenazar, to threaten

América (*f.*), America

americano, (Latin) American

el **amigo,** friend; **amigo de,** friendly with

la **amistad,** friendship

el **amor,** love

andaluz, Andalusian

andar, to walk; to go, to run; to be [134]

anhelar, to long (for)

animar, to encourage, to urge, to brighten, to liven, to cheer (up)

anoche, last night

el **ansia** (*f.*), longing

ante, before, at [94 (*c*)]

anteayer, the day before yesterday

anterior, previous

antes, before(hand); **antes de,** before [94 (*c*) and (*e*)]; **antes (de) que,** before; **cuanto antes, lo antes posible,** as soon as possible

antiguo, old, ancient

anunciar, to announce, to advertise

el **año,** year; **tener ... años,** to be ... (years old)

apaciguar, to appease, to pacify

aparecer, to appear, to come into view

apenas, scarcely, no sooner

apostar (ue), to bet

aprender, to learn

aprobar (ue), to approve (of); to pass (exam.)

aprovechar, to take advantage of

aquel, -ella, -ellos, -ellas, that, the former

aquí, here

el árbol, tree

la Argentina, Argentine

argentino, Argentinian

argüir, to argue, to object

armar, to arm

arreglar, to arrange, to put right, to mend

arrepentirse (ie), to repent

arrimarse a, to lean against

arrodillarse, to kneel

artificial, artificial

asegurar, to assure

así, thus, like this (that); **así que,** as soon as

asistir a, to attend, to be present at

el aspecto, aspect

el asunto, matter, subject

la atención, attention

atender (ie), to attend to

atento, attentive

atraer, to attract, to draw

atreverse, to dare

atrevido, bold, daring

el aula (f.), lecture room, classroom

aun, even

aún, still, yet

aunque, although, even though

Austria (f.), Austria

austriaco, Austrian

el autobús, (motor-)bus

autorizar, to authorize

avergonzarse (ue), to be ashamed

averiguar, to ascertain, to find out

el avión, aeroplane

avisar, to inform, to warn, to let know

ayer, yesterday

la ayuda, help

ayudar, to help

azul, blue

bailar, to dance

bajar, to go (come, take, bring) down, to lower

bajo, under [94 (c)]

barato, cheap

bastante, rather, fairly, quite, enough

el bastón, stick

beber, to drink

bendito, blessed, praised

bien, well; **más bien,** rather

blanco, white

la bondad, goodness; **tener la bondad de,** to be so good as to

bonito, nice, pretty

bordear, to touch on

borrar, to erase

la botella, bottle

el Brasil, Brazil

brillar, to shine, to sparkle

bueno, good
burlarse de, to mock, to ridicule, to make fun of
buscar, to look for, to seek

el caballero, gentleman, knight
el caballo, horse
caber, to fit in [111]; **no cabe duda,** there is no doubt
la cabeza, head
el cabo, cape, end; **al cabo,** at last; **al cabo de,** after, at the end of
cada, each; **cada uno,** each one
caer(se), to fall; to suit [93]
el café, coffee, café; **café con leche,** white coffee
calentar (ie), to warm
caliente, warm, hot
el calor, warmth, heat; **tener calor,** to be warm, hot (*persons*); **hacer calor,** to be warm, hot (*weather*)
callar(se), to be silent
la calle, road, street
la cama, bed
cambiar, to change
el cambio, change; **en cambio,** on the other hand
el camino, road, way
el campo, country(side), field
el Canadá, Canada
la canción, song
cansado, tired; tiresome
cantar, to sing
capaz, able, capable
a capital, capital

el capítulo, chapter
el capricho, whim
la cara, face
el carácter, character
caro, dear
la carta, letter
la casa, house; firm; **a casa,** (to) home; **en casa,** at home
casarse (con), to marry, to get married
casi, almost, nearly
el caso, case
castigar, to punish
la catedral, cathedral
el caudal, store, wealth
celoso, jealous
la cena, evening meal (dinner, supper)
cenar, to have one's evening meal, to dine
el censo, census
cerca, close, near by; **cerca de,** close to, near
el cerebro, brain
cerrar (ie), to close, to shut
cesar, to cease
el cielo, sky
el científico, scientist
ciento, (a) hundred
cierto, (a) certain
la ciudad, town, city
claro, clear; clearly, of course
la clase, lecture, class, kind
el coche, car
coger, to seize, to catch, to take (up)
el colegio, (private) school
colgar (ue), to hang (up)
el color, colour

comenzar (ie), to commence, to begin

comer, to eat, to have a meal, to have lunch; **comerse,** to eat up

la comida, food, meal, midday meal (lunch, dinner)

como, as, like; **¿cómo?,** how?

competir (i), to compete

complacerse (en), to take pleasure (in)

completo, complete, full (*bus,* etc.)

la compra, purchase; **ir de compras,** to go shopping

comprar, to buy

comprender, to understand

comprometerse, to undertake

con, with

conceder, to grant

conciso, concise

concluir, to conclude, to finish

la conclusión, conclusion

a condición (de) que, on condition (that)

conducir, to lead, to drive

la conducta, conduct

confesar (ie), to confess

la confianza, confidence

confiar (en), to confide, to trust, to hope

conformarse, to agree; to be satisfied

confundir, to confuse

congratular, to congratulate

conmover (ue), to move (emotionally)

conocer, to know [49]

conque, then, so [133]

la consecuencia, consequence

conseguir (i), to manage, to obtain, to achieve

el consejo, advice, council

consentir (ie), to consent

conservar, to preserve

considerar, to consider

consistir, to consist

consolar (ue), to console

constituir, to constitute

construir, to construct, to build

contar (ue), to count, to relate, to tell

contentarse, to content oneself

contento, pleased, contented, happy

la contestación, reply

contestar, to answer, to reply

continuar, to continue

contra, against

contrariar, to go against

contrario, opposite

al contrario, on the contrary

contribuir, to contribute

convencer, to convince

convenir, to agree, to be fitting, to be appropriate

convertir (ie), to convert

el corazón, heart

corregir (i), to correct

correr, to run

la **cosa,** thing; **otra cosa,**
   something else, anything
   else

costar (ue), to cost

la **costumbre,** custom, habit

la **creación,** creation

creer, to believe, to think

cruzar, to cross, to pass
   through

cuál(es), which [155]; **el
(la) cual, los (las)
cuales** [151]

cualquiera, any(one),
   whichever

cuando, when; **¿cuando?**
   when?

cuanto, all that; **en cuánto,**
   as soon as; **cuanto antes,**
   as soon as possible;
   unos cuantos, a few;
   ¿cuánto?, how much?
   pl. how many?

el **cuarto,** room; quarter,
   fourth

cubrir, to cover

el **cuchillo,** knife

la **cuenta,** account, bill;
   darse cuenta, to realize;
   tener en cuenta, to bear
   in mind, to take into
   account, to consider

la **cuestión,** question

el **cuidado,** care; **tener
cuidado,** to be careful

cumplir, to fulfil, to accom-
   plish

curioso, strange, curious

la **chica,** girl

el **chico,** boy

dar, to give [57]

de, of, from, about [172]

debajo (de), under(neath)
   [94 (*c*)]

deber, to have to, must

decidir(se), to decide

decir, to say, to tell; **es
decir,** that is (to say)

declarar, to declare

dedicar, to dedicate, to devote

el **defecto,** defect

defender (ie), to defend

definitivo, final, definitive

dejar, to leave, to let, to
   allow; to put down, to
   leave go of; **dejar de,** to
   leave off, to stop; **no
dejar de,** not to fail to,
   to be sure to

delante (de), in front (of)
   [94 (*c*)]

delinquir, to transgress

lo(s) **demás,** the rest, the
   others

demasiado, too, too much,
   too many

dentro (de), inside, within

la **derrota,** defeat

desaparecer, to disappear

desayunar, to have breakfast

el **desayuno,** breakfast

descansar, to rest

desconocer, not to know

el **descontento,** discontent

descubrir, to discover

desde, since, from [94 (*c*)];
   desde luego, certainly;
   desde que, since

desear, to desire, to wish

el deseo, desire

desilusionado, disappointed

deslizarse, to slip away

despacio, slowly

la despedida, farewell

despedir (i), to dismiss, to see off, to say good-bye to; **despedirse de,** to take leave of, to say goodbye to

despertar (ie), to wake (up); **despertarse,** to awake, to wake up

despreciar, to scorn

después, after(wards); **después de,** after [94 (c) and (e)]; **después (de) que,** after

destacarse, to stand out

destinar, to destine

la destrucción, destruction

detenerse, to stop

detrás (de), behind

devolver (ue), to give back, to return

devoto, devout, fond

el día, day; **buenos días,** good morning

diario, daily, a (=per) day

diciembre (m.), December

la diferencia, difference

difícil, difficult, hard, unlikely

la dificultad, difficulty

el dinero, money

Dios (m.), God; **¡por Dios!,** for heaven's sake! in heaven's name! **¡Dios mío!,** good heavens! dear me!

la dirección, address, direction

el director, manager

la discusión, discussion

disfrutar (de), to enjoy

disponer, to dispose, to arrange, **disponerse,** to prepare, to get ready

dispuesto, prepared, willing

distinguir, to distinguish

distinto, different

disuadir, to dissuade

divertir (ie), to amuse

el doctor, doctor

domingo (m.), Sunday

don, master, Mr [80 (5) N. 4]

donde, where; **¿dónde?,** where?

dormir (ue), to sleep; **dormirse,** to go to sleep

dos, two; **los dos, las dos,** both, the two

el drama, drama

dudar, to hesitate, to doubt, to question

el dueño, proprietor, master

dulce, sweet

durante, during, for

durar, to last

duro, hard

el duro, duro (=five pesetas)

e, and [75]

echar, to throw; **echar(se) a,** to begin to

la edad, age

la edición, edition

el edificio, building

efectivamente, in fact, actually

efectuar, to bring about

el **ejemplar,** copy (of book)

la **elegancia,** elegance

elegante, elegant, smart

elegir (i), to elect, to choose

sin **embargo,** nevertheless

empeñarse, to insist

empezar (ie), to begin

el **empleado,** employee, clerk

en, in, at, on [94 (c)]

enamorado, in love, loving

enamorarse de, to fall in love with

encantador, charming

encargar, to entrust, to give to do; **encargarse,** to undertake, to take charge of, to ensure

encender (ie), to light, to switch on

encima (de), on top (of), over

encontrar (ue), to find, to meet; **encontrarse,** to find oneself, to be [99, N. 2]; **encontrarse con,** to meet, to find (out)

el **enemigo,** enemy

enero (m.), January

enfermo, ill; invalid, sick person

enfrente (de), in front (of), opposite

engañar, to deceive; **engañarse,** to be mistaken

el **engaño,** deception

engrandecer, to enlarge, to augment

enorme, huge, enormous

el **ensayo,** essay

la **enseñanza,** education

enseñar, to teach, to show

el **ensueño,** (day)dream, illusion

entender (ie), to understand

enterarse de, to discover, to find out

entonces, then [133]

entrar, to go (come) in, to enter

entre, between, among(st)

entregar, to hand over, to hand in

entretener, to entertain

enviar, to send

la **época,** period, time, age

equivocarse, to be mistaken

el **error,** mistake

es que, the fact is that

escapar(se), to escape

el **escenario,** stage

escoger, to choose

esconder, to hide

escribir, to write

el **escritor,** writer

escuchar, to listen to

la **escuela,** (primary) school

el **escultor,** sculptor

ese, -a, -os, -as, that

esforzarse (ue), to strive, to try hard

el **esfuerzo,** effort

a **eso de,** at about

España (f.), Spain

español, Spanish, Spaniard

la **especie,** sort, kind

la **esperanza,** hope

esperar, to wait (for), to hope, to expect [164]

la **esposa,** wife

el **esposo,** husband

establecer, to establish

la **estación,** station

los **Estados Unidos,** U.S.A.

la **estancia,** stay, residence

estar, to be [30–33, 57, 97, 99, 144]

este, -a, -os, -as, this, the latter

el **este,** east

estéril, sterile, unfruitful

estimar, to esteem

el **estudiante,** student

estudiar, to study

el **estudio,** study

estúpido, stupid

Europa (*f.*), Europe

la **europeización,** Europeanization

evidente, obvious

evitar, to avoid

exacto, exact

examinar, to examine

exceptuar, to except

exclamar, to exclaim

exclusivo, exclusive

exigir, to demand

existir, to exist

la **explicación,** explanation

explicar, to explain

exponerse, to expose oneself

extranjero, foreign

el **extranjero,** foreigner; foreign parts, abroad

extrañar, to surprise, to seem strange to

extraordinario, extraordinary

extremo, extreme; el **extremo,** extreme, end

la **fábrica,** factory

fácil, easy

falso, false

la **falta,** lack; **hacer falta,** to be necessary, to be needed; *via* to need [76]

faltar, to be missing; *via* to be short of, to lack [76]; **faltar a,** to break (word, promise, etc.)

la **fama,** fame

la **familia,** family

familiar, familiar, family

famoso, famous

el **fantasma,** phantom

el **favor,** favour; **hacer el favor de,** *via* please, kindly [109 (*f*)]

favorecer, to favour

febrero (*m.*), February

fecundo, fertile, fruitful

la **fecha,** date

felicitar, to congratulate

Felipe, Philip

feliz, happy

fiarse de, to trust

la **fiebre,** fever; **dar fiebre,** to put into a fever

fiel, faithful

fijar, to fix; **fijarse en,** to notice, to take note of

el **fin,** end, aim; **por fin,** finally, at last

el **final,** end

finalmente, finally

la **flor,** flower

el **fondo**, bottom
formular, to formulate, to express, to epitomize
forzar (ue), to force
el **fracaso**, failure
francés, French
Francia (*f.*), France
frecuente, frequent
freír (i), to fry
frío, cold
el **frío**, cold; **tener frío**, to be cold (*persons*); **hacer frío**, to be cold (*weather*)
la **fuente**, fountain, source
fuera (de), outside
la **fuerza**, force; *pl.* strength
fumar, to smoke

la **gana**, desire; **tener ganas de**, to want to, to be keen to, to feel like; **dar ganas de**, to make (someone) want to
ganar, to earn, to win
gastar, to spend
el **gato**, cat
general, general
generalmente, generally
la **gente**, people
la **gloria**, glory
el **gobierno**, government
el **gorrión**, sparrow
gozar, to enjoy
gracias, thanks, thank you; **dar las gracias a**, to thank, to say thank you to
grande, big, great
Guadalajara, *Spanish town*
guardar, to keep, to save; **guardarse de**, to take care not to

el **guardia**, policeman
la **guerra**, war
el **guía**, guide
la **guía**, guide(-book)
gustar, to please; *via* to like [76]
el **gusto**, pleasure

haber, to have [66, 74]
haber de, to be to [74, 109 (*b*)]
el **habitante**, inhabitant
hablador, talkative, gossiping
hablar, to talk, to speak
hacer, to do, to make [44]; **hacerse**, to become
hacia, towards, (at) about [94 (*c*)]
hallar, to find; **hallarse**, to be [99 N. 2]
el **hambre** (*f.*), hunger; **tener hambre**, to be hungry
hartarse, to grow tired
hasta, until, as far as, (up)-to; **hasta que**, until
hay, there is, there are; **hay que**, one (we, you, etc.) must
la **hermana**, sister
el **hermano**, brother
hermoso, beautiful, lovely
hervir (ie), to boil
la **hija**, daughter
el **hijo**, son
los **hijos**, children, sons, son(s) and daughter(s)
la **historia**, history, story
la **hoja**, leaf, sheet
el **hombre**, man
el **hombro**, shoulder

la **hora,** hour
el **horror,** horror
el **hospital,** hospital
el **hotel,** hotel
hoy, today
el **huevo,** egg
huir, to flee
humano, human

ibérico, Iberian
la **idea,** idea
el **ideal,** ideal
idéntico, identical
el **idioma,** language
la **ilusión,** illusion
impedir (i), to prevent
la **importancia,** importance
importante, important;
    poco importante, unim-
    portant
importar, to matter
imposible, impossible
incapaz, incapable
inclinado, inclined
el **inconveniente,** inconveni-
    ence, disadvantage, ob-
    stacle
increíble, incredible
la **India,** India
indicar, to indicate, to
    point out
indudable, without doubt,
    indubitable
inferior, inferior
el **infierno,** hell
infinito, infinite
influir, to influence
Inglaterra (*f.*), Britain,
    England
inglés, English

ingrato, ungrateful, thank-
    less
inmediato, immediate
inmóvil, motionless
inocente, innocent
insignificante,   insignifi-
    cant
insistir, to insist
el **instante,** instant
el **instituto** (state grammar)
    school
insustituible, irreplaceable
inteligente, intelligent
intentar, to try
el **interés,** interest
interesante, interesting
interesar, to interest; **in-**
    teresarse (por), to be
    interested (in), to take an
    interest (in)
inventar, to invent
la **invitación,** invitation
el **invitado,** guest
invitar, to invite
ir, to go [18, 57]; **irse,** to go
    away, to go off; **ir bien a,**
    to suit
Isabel, Elizabeth, Isabella
Italia (*f.*), Italy
italiano, Italian

jactarse, to boast
jamás, not . . . ever, never
el **Japón,** Japan
el **jardín,** garden
el **jefe,** chief, head, boss
Jesús, Jesus (*a common*
    christian name in Spain)
joven, young
jovencito, *dimin. of* **joven**
Juan, John

jueves (*m.*), Thursday
julio (*m.*), July
junio (*m.*), June
junto, together; **junto a,**
  close to
justificar, to justify
la juventud, youth

el kilo, kilogramme
el kilómetro, kilometre

el lado, side; **al lado,** at the
  side, next door; **al lado
  de,** beside, by the side of
la lágrima, tear
el lápiz, pencil
largo, long
lavar, to wash
la lección, lesson
la leche, milk
leer, to read
lejos, far, distant; **lejos de,**
  far from
la lengua, language, tongue
el letrero, sign, notice
levantar, to raise, to lift up;
  levantarse, to get up
la ley, law
la libertad, freedom
la libra, pound
libre, free
el libro, book
la limosna, alms
listo, clever; ready
el literato, writer, man of
  letters
la literatura, literature
loco, mad
lograr, to succeed
Londres (*m.*), London
la longitud, length

luchar, to fight
luego, then, next [133];
  desde luego, certainly
el lugar, place, spot, village
el lujo, luxury
lunes (*m.*), Monday
la luz, light

llamar, to call
la llave, key
la llegada, arrival
llegar, to arrive; **llegar a,**
  to reach, to arrive at, to
  come to
llevar, to take, to carry; to
  wear; to be, to spend
  (time) [73]; **llevarse,** to
  take away
llover (ue), to rain

la madre, mother
la madrugada, (early) morning
madrugar, to get up early
maduro, ripe, mature
(el) maestro, master
mal, badly; **hacer mal,** to
  do wrong
la maleta, suitcase; **hacer
  una maleta,** to pack a
  suitcase
malo, bad, ill
malucho, off colour
mandar, to send; to order,
  to command
la manera, manner, means,
  way; **de esta (tal, otra)
  manera,** in this (such a,
  another) way
la mano, hand; **a mano,** by
  hand

manso, soft, gentle
la manzana, apple
la mañana, morning
mañana, tomorrow
la máquina, machine; a máquina, by machine; escribir a máquina, to type(write)
maravillarse, to wonder, to marvel
marchar(se), to go away, to go off
el marido, husband
Marruecos (m.), Morocco
martes (m.), Tuesday
marzo (m.), March
mas, but
más, more, most, plus; más allá de, beyond; más bien, rather; no ... más que, only
mayo (m.), May
mayor, older, greater; oldest, greatest
la medianoche, midnight
el médico, doctor
medio, half (a); en medio de, amidst, in the midst of
el mediodía, midday
la meditación, meditation
Méjico (m.), Mexico
mejor, better, best
la memoria, memory, memoir
menos, less, minus; a menos que, unless; no poder menos de, not to be able to help but
mentir (ie), to (tell a) lie
la mentira, lie
el mercado, market

merecer, to deserve
meridional, southern
el mes, month
la mesa, table
meter, to put (in); meterse en, to meddle in
mi, my
el miedo, fear, fright; dar miedo, to frighten; tener miedo, to be afraid
mientras, while, whilst
miércoles (m.), Wednesday
mil, (a) thousand
el ministro, minister
el minuto, minute
mirar, to look at, to watch
mismo, same, very; self [161 N. 2]
el modo, way, means; de este (tal, otro) modo, in this (such a, another) way
el momento, moment
la montaña, mountain
el monumento, monument
morir(se) (ue), to die
el moro, Moor
mostrar (ue), to show
el motivo, motive, reason
mover(se) (ue), to move
la muchacha, girl
el muchacho, boy
mucho, much, a lot of; pl. many, a lot of; (of time) long; very [165]
mudar, to change
la muerte, death
la mujer, woman, wife
el mundo, world; todo el mundo, everybody, everyone

la **muralla,** wall (of town)
la **música,** music
mutuamente, mutually, one another
muy, very

nacer, to be born
nacional, national
nada, nothing, not at all
la **nada,** nothingness
nadar, to swim
nadie, no one, nobody
natural, natural
necesario, necessary
la **necesidad,** need, necessity
negar (ie), to deny; **negarse,** to refuse
negro, black
nervioso, nervous
ni, neither, nor; **ni (siquiera),** not even
la **niebla,** fog, mist
la **nieve,** snow
ninguno, none, (not) any, no
el **niño,** child
no, no, not; **no ... más que,** only
noble, noble
la **noche,** night
nombrar, to name, to appoint
el **nombre,** name
el **noreste,** north-east
el **norte,** north
norteamericano, American
notar, to note
la **noticia,** (piece of) news, information; *pl.* news
la **novela,** novel

noviembre(*m.*), November
Nueva York, New York
nuevo, new; **de nuevo,** again
el **número,** number
numeroso, numerous
nunca, never

o, or
objetivar, to view objectively
el **objeto,** object
obligar, to oblige, to compel
la **obra,** work
no obstante, nevertheless
la **ocasión,** occasion, opportunity
Oceanía (*f.*), Australasia
octubre (*m.*), October
ocuparse, to busy oneself
ocurrir, to happen, to occur
el **oeste,** west
el **oficial,** officer
ofrecer, to offer
oír, to hear, to listen to; **oye, oiga,** I say
ojalá, would that, I wish
el **ojo,** eye
la **ola,** wave
olvidar(se), to forget
la **operación,** operation
opinar, to think
la **opinión,** opinion
oponerse a, to oppose
la **oportunidad,** opportunity
oportuno, suitable, opportune
ordenar, to put in order; to command
la **organización,** organization

a orillas de, on the banks of
oscurecerse, to grow dim,
to fade away
el otoño, autumn
otro, (an)other

el padre, father
los padres, parents
pagar, to pay (for)
la página, page
el país, country
el paisaje, scenery, landscape
la palabra, word
pálido, pale
el papel, paper
para, for, by, (in order) to
[94, 146]; para que, in
order that
parar, to cease
parecer, to seem, to appear;
via to think (of) [76]
parecido, similar
la pared, wall (of house)
la parte, part; por mi parte,
for my part, on my side;
por otra parte, on the
other hand; en (or por)
todas partes, everywhere
el pasado, past
pasado, past; el año pa-
sado, last year
pasar, to pass, to go (come)
in; to spend (time); to
happen
el paseo, walk; dar un paseo,
to go for a walk
la pasión, passion
el paso, step, pace; dar un
paso, to take a step
el pastor, shepherd
la patata, potato

la patria, homeland, (native)
country
la paz, peace
el pecho, breast, bosom, chest
pedir (i), to ask (for)
Pedro, Peter
el peligro, danger
peligroso, dangerous
el pelo, hair
la pena, grief, pain, trouble;
valer la pena, to be
worth while
la península, peninsula
el pensamiento, thought
pensar (ie), to think, to intend
pensativo, pensive
pequeño, small, little
la pera, pear
perder (ie), to lose
el perdón, forgiveness; ¡perdón!, forgive me, I beg
your pardon
perdonar, to forgive
perfecto, perfect
el periódico, (news)paper
el permiso, permission
permitir, to permit, to allow
pero, but
el perro, dog
perseguir (i), to pursue, to
persecute
la persona, person; pl. people
el personaje, personage, character (in play)
persuadir, to persuade
pertenecer, to belong
el Perú, Peru
a pesar de, in spite of
la peseta, peseta (Spanish
money, approx. ½p.)

el pie, foot; **ir a pie,** to go on foot, to walk; **estar de pie,** to be standing

la piedad, piety, pity, compassion

la piel, skin

la pierna, leg

pintoresco, picturesque

el piso, floor, flat

el plato, plate

la plaza, square

la pluma, pen

la población, population

pobre, poor

poco, little, not much; *pl.* few, not many; **poco a poco,** gradually, little by little

poder to be able (can)

la poesía, poem, poetry

el poeta, poet

la policía, police

la política, politics, policy

político, political

poner, to put, to place [111]; **ponerse,** to become, to go, to get; **ponerse a,** to set about, to burst out; **poner la mesa,** to lay the table

por, through, by, for [80 (8) N., 94, 144, 146]; **por allí,** over there, that way; **por . . . que,** however; **¿por qué?,** why?; **por entonces,** about that time

porque, because

portarse, to behave

portugués, Portuguese

la posibilidad, possibility

posible, possible

la postal, postcard

práctico, practical

el precio, price

precioso, delightful, lovely

preciso, necessary, precise

preferir (ie), to prefer

la pregunta, question; **hacer una pregunta,** to ask a question

preguntar, to ask

la prensa, press

preocuparse, to be worried

preparar, to prepare

prescindir, to leave aside, to omit, to do without

presentar, to present, to introduce; **presentarse,** to appear

presente, present

presentir (ie), to have a presentiment

el presidente, president

prestar, to lend

el pretexto, pretext

primero, first

principal, main, principal

el principio, beginning, principle

la prisa, haste; **tener prisa,** to be in a hurry; **de prisa,** quickly

probable, probable

probar (ue), to try, to test, to prove

el problema, problem

procurar, to try

el profesor, teacher, lecturer

profundo, profound, deep, sound

prohibir, to forbid

prometer, to promise
pronto, soon; **de pronto,**
  suddenly
pronunciar, to pronounce
propio, own
proponer, to propose
próximo, near, next
el **proyecto,** plan, scheme
publicar, to publish
el **pueblecillo,** *dimin. of*
  pueblo
el **pueblo,** town, village
la **puerta,** door
pues, then [133]
el **puesto,** position, post
puesto que, since
en **punto,** exactly (*of time*)
puro, pure

que, who, whom, which,
  that; than, as; for; **¿qué?**
  what? which?; **¡qué!,**
  how! what (a)!
quedar, to remain, *via* to
  have (left) [76]; **que-**
  darse, to remain, to stay
querer, to want, to like, to
  love
querido, dear, beloved
quien(es), who, whom;
  ¿quién(es)?, who?
  whom?; **¿de quién(es)?,**
  whose?
Don Quijote, Don Quixote
quitar(se), to take off, to
  take away
quizá(s), perhaps

la **radio,** wireless
rápido, quick

la **razón,** reason; **sin razón,**
  wrongfully; **tener razón,**
  to be right
razonar, to reason (out)
reaccionar, to react
la **realidad,** reality
realizar, to bring about, to
  carry out
recibir, to receive
recíproco, reciprocal,
  mutual
recoger, to collect, to
  gather
recomendar (ie), to recommend
reconcentrar, to concen-
  trate
reconocer, to recognize, to
  acknowledge
recordar (ue), to remind,
  to recall, to remember
recorrer, to travel over, to
  wander about
el **recuerdo,** recollection,
  souvenir, memory
referirse (ie), to refer
regalar, to give (as a present), to present with
el **regalo,** present, gift
el **régimen,** régime
reír(se) (i), to laugh
el **reloj,** watch, clock
el **remedio,** remedy
el **renombre,** renown
renunciar (a), to renounce
reñir (i), to scold; to quarrel
reparar (en), to notice
de **repente,** suddenly
repetir (i), to repeat
el **representante,** representative

reprochar, to reproach (with)

resignarse, to resign oneself

resolver (ue), to solve, to resolve

respetable, respectable

el **respeto,** respect

responder (de), to answer (for), to reply

la **respuesta,** reply

el **restorán,** restaurant

resuelto, resolved, solved

resultar, to turn out, to prove (to be), to appear

retirar(se), to withdraw

la **retórica,** rhetoric

la **reunión,** meeting

reunir, to gather; **reunirse,** to join, to gather

la **revolución,** revolution

el **rey,** king

rezar, to pray

rico, rich, wealthy

ridículo, ridiculous

el **riesgo,** risk

el **rincón,** corner, out-of-the-way place

el **río,** river

el **ritmo,** rhythm

robar, to steal, to rob

rojo, red

romper, to break, to tear

roto, broken

rubio, fair, blond

ruso, Russian

sábado (*m.*), Saturday

saber, to know, to be able (can) [49]

el **sacrificio,** sacrifice

la **salida,** exit, way out, departure

salir, to go (come) out, to leave, to depart; to rise (*sun*) [49]

el **salón,** sitting-room

saltar, to jump

la **salud,** health

saludar, to greet, to pay one's respects to

salvar, to save

santo, holy, saint(ly)

satisfacer, to satisfy

o **sea,** that is (to say)

el **secretario,** secretary

el **secreto,** secret

la **sed,** thirst; **tener sed,** to be thirsty

en **seguida,** at once, immediately, straight away

seguir (i), to follow, to continue

según, according to

el **segundo,** second

seguro, sure, certain

la **semana,** week

semejante, such (a)

sentar (ie), to set down; **sentarse,** to sit down

el **sentimiento,** feeling

sentir (ie), to feel, to be sorry (about); **sentirse,** to feel

el **señor,** gentleman, master, Mr; **(los) señores,** Mr and Mrs, lady and gentleman, ladies and gentlemen

la **señora,** lady, wife; **la señora de . . .,** Mrs . . .

se(p)tiembre (*m.*), September

ser, to be [30–33, 57, 97–98, 144]; **a no ser que,** unless

serio, serious

servir (i), to serve

Sevilla (*f.*), Seville

si, if

sí, yes

siempre, always, ever

el sigilo, secrecy, reserve

el siglo, century

siguiente, following; **al día siguiente,** on the following day

el silencio, silence

la silla, chair

el sillón, armchair

simpático, nice

sin, without; **sin que,** without

la sinceridad, sincerity

sino, but [75]; **no ... sino,** only

el sitio, place, siege

la situación, situation, position

situar, to situate

sobrar, to be more than enough, *via* to have more than enough [76]

sobre, on, upon, about [94 (*c*)]; **sobre todo,** especially

sobrevivir (a), to survive

el sol, sun

solamente, only

a solas, alone

el soldado, soldier

soler (ue), to be wont to, *via* usually

solo, alone

sólo, tan sólo, only

la solución, solution

el sombrero, hat

sonreír (i), to smile

soñar (ue) (con), to dream (of)

sorprender, to surprise

sosegar(se) (ie), to quieten, to calm down

subir, to go (come) up, to take (bring) up

sucio, dirty

suelto, loose(d), unleashed

el sueño, sleep, dream; **tener sueño,** to be sleepy

la suerte, luck, fortune; **tener suerte,** to be lucky

suficiente, sufficient

sufrir, to suffer

sugerir (ie), to suggest

Suiza (*f.*), Switzerland

suizo, Swiss

suponer, to suppose, to presuppose

el sur, south

sustituir, to substitute, to replace

el Tajo, Tagus

tal, such (a); **un tal,** a certain; **con tal que,** provided that; **tal vez,** perhaps

también, also, as well, too

tampoco, neither

tan, so, such

tanto, so much; *pl.* so many; **en tanto que,** insomuch as, so long as

la tapia, (garden) wall

tardar, to take (a long time)

tarde, late
la tarde, afternoon, evening
la taza, cup
el té, tea
el telegrama, telegram
el tema, theme, subject, topic
temblar (ie), to tremble
temer, to fear [164]
temprano, early
tener, to have [28, 44]; tener (tal hora), to make it (such a time)
tercero, third
terminar, to finish
el término, limit, end, boundary; en primer término, in the first place
terrible, terrible
el terror, terror
la tía, aunt
el tiempo, weather; time; a tiempo, in time
la tienda, shop
la tierra, earth, land; homeland
la timidez, timidity
tímido, timid
el tío, uncle; los tíos, uncles, aunt and uncle
el tipo, type, sort
todavía, still, yet
todo, all, every [110]; todo el mundo, everybody, everyone
tomar, to take; tomar el sol, to sunbathe
la torre, tower
trabajador, hard-working
trabajar, to work
el trabajo, work; costar trabajo a, to be difficult for

el tradicionalista, traditionalist
la traducción, translation
traducir, to translate
traer, to bring, to fetch
transformar, to transform
el tranvía, tram
tras, after [94 (c)]
tratar, to try; tratarse de, to be a question of, to be about
a través de, through, across [94 (c)]
el tren, train
triste, sad, unhappy
la tristeza, sadness
triunfar, to triumph
tropezar (ie), to stumble; tropezar con, to run into, to run up against
el turista, tourist

u, or [75]
último, last, latest
único, only, sole
la universidad, university
usar, to use
útil, useful
utilizar, to utilize, to use

vago, vague
valer, to be worth, to have power [49]
el valor, value, worth, valour
la vanagloria, vainglory
vano, vain
la variedad, variety
varios, several
el vaso, tumbler, glass

¡vaya!, well! I say! come now!; ¡vaya por Dios!, well I never!

el vecino, neighbour

vencer, to conquer, to overcome

vender, to sell

venir, to come; venga, come on; que viene, next

la venta, inn

la ventana, window

ver, to see; tener que ver con, to have to do with

el verano, summer

de veras, really, truly

la verdad, truth; de verdad, really, truly; ser verdad, to be true; ¿(no es) verdad?, isn't it?, didn't he?, aren't they?, etc.

verdadero, real

verde, green

vestir (i), to dress; vestirse, to get dressed

la vez, time; otra vez, again; de vez en cuando, from time to time; muchas veces, often; cada vez más, more and more; cada vez menos, less and less; tal vez, perhaps

viajar, to travel

el viaje, journey, trip, voyage; de viaje, travelling, on a trip

la vida, life; ganarse la vida, to earn one's living

viejo, old

viernes (m.), Friday

el vino, wine

la Virgen, (Blessed) Virgin

la visita, visit

visitar, to visit

la vista, sight, view

vital, vital

vivir, to live

la voluntad, will

volver (ue), to return, to go (come) back; volver a ..., to ... again; volverse, to become, to turn, to go

la voz, voice

la vuelta, walk (run) round, spin; dar una vuelta, to go for a walk round (a spin); to turn, to twist

y, and

ya, already [133]; ya no, now ... not, no longer

Zaragoza, Saragossa

ENGLISH–SPANISH

able, capaz; **to be able,** poder

about, de, sobre, acerca de; unos, hacia, alrededor de [94 (c)]; **at about,** hacia; **to be about to,** estar para

abroad, extranjero (m.)

accent, acento (m.)

to **accept,** aceptar

to **accompany,** acompañar

according to, según

account, cuenta (f.); **to take into account,** tener en cuenta

to **accuse,** acusar

to **achieve,** conseguir (i)

to **acknowledge,** reconocer

to **acquire,** adquirir (ie)

across, a(l) través de; **to come across (meet),** dar con

address, dirección (f.)

admiration, admiración (f.)

adorable, adorable

advantage, ventaja (f.); **to take advantage of,** aprovechar

to **advise,** aconsejar

aeroplane, avión (m.)

affection, afecto (m.)

afraid: to be afraid, tener miedo, temer(se) [164]

Africa, África (f.)

after, después; después de, tras [94 (c) and (e)]; al cabo de; después (de) que

afternoon, tarde (f.); **good afternoon,** buenas tardes

afterwards, después

again, otra vez, de nuevo; *via* volver (ue) a

against, contra

age, edad (f.); (*period*) época (f.)

ago, hace [44 (c)]

to **agree,** acordar (ue), convenir, quedar, estar de acuerdo

agreed, de acuerdo

agreement, acuerdo (m.)

algebra, álgebra (f.)

alive: to be alive, vivir

all, todo; **not at all,** nada

to **allow,** permitir, dejar

almost, casi

alms, limosna (f.)

alone, solo, a solas

already, ya

also, también

although, aunque

always, siempre

a.m., de la madrugada (mañana) [52 (b)]

America, América (f.)

American, norteamericano

393

amidst, entre, en medio de
among(st), entre
to **amuse,** divertir (ie); **to be amused,** divertirse
and, y, e [75]
Andalusian, andaluz
to **announce,** anunciar
another, otro; **one another,** se (... el uno al otro, etc.) [91]
answer, respuesta (*f.*)
to **answer,** contestar
  any, alguno, cualquiera; *after neg.* ninguno; **anyone, anybody,** alguien; *after neg.* nadie; **anything,** algo, cualquier cosa; *after neg.* nada
  apparently, por lo visto
to **appear,** parecer; aparecer, presentarse
  apple, manzana (*f.*)
to **appoint,** nombrar
to **approach,** acercarse (a)
  April, abril (*m.*)
to **arm,** armar
  around, alrededor de, por; (*about*) hacia, alrededor de, unos
  arrival, llegada (*f.*)
to **arrive,** llegar
  as, como, tal como; cuando, al; **(such) as,** tal como; **as ... as,** tan ... como; **as far as,** (*up to*) hasta; **as much, as many,** tanto(s); **as soon as,** en cuanto; **as well,** (*also*) también
to **ascertain,** averiguar
  aside: to leave aside, prescindir de

to **ask,** (*enquire*) preguntar; (*request*) pedir (i); **ask for,** pedir (i); **ask a question,** hacer una pregunta
  aspect, aspecto (*m.*)
to **assure,** asegurar
  at, en, a, ante [94 (*c*)]
to **attend,** asistir a; **attend to,** atender (ie) a
  attention, atención (*f.*)
to **attract,** atraer
  August, agosto (*m.*)
  aunt, tía; **aunt and uncle,** tíos (*m. pl.*)
  Austria, Austria (*f.*)
  autumn, otoño (*m.*)
to **awake(n),** despertar(se) (ie)
  away: to go away, irse, marcharse

  bad, malo
to **be,** ser, estar [30–33, 57, 97–99, 144]; tener, hacer [44, 99 N. 1]; haber [74]; quedar, encontrarse (ue), hallarse [99 N. 2]; **be (destined, intending) to,** haber de
to **bear in mind,** tener en cuenta
  beautiful, hermoso
  because, porque
to **become,** volverse (ue), hacerse, ponerse
  bed, cama (*f.*); **to get out of bed,** levantar(se); **to go to bed,** acostarse (ue); **to put to bed,** acostar (ue)
  before, hacía [44 (*c*)]; antes (de), delante (de), ante [94 (*c*), (*e*)]; antes (de) que

to **begin,** empezar (ie), comenzar (ie)

to **behave,** portarse

behind, detrás (de)

to **believe,** creer

to **belong,** pertenecer

beside, al lado de, junto a

besides, además (de)

best, mejor; **to be best,** (*fitting*) ser mejor, convenir

better, mejor; **to be better,** ser (estar) mejor; valer más

between, entre

beyond, más allá de

big, grande

bill, cuenta (*f.*)

bit, poco

black, negro

blue, azul

to **boil,** hervir (ie)

book, libro (*m.*)

born: to be born, nacer

boss, jefe (*m.*)

both, los dos, las dos

bottle, botella (*f.*)

boy, muchacho (*m.*), chico (*m.*)

Brazil, Brasil (*m.*)

to **break,** romper

breakfast, desayuno (*m.*); **to (have) breakfast,** desayunar

to **bring,** traer; **bring about,** efectuar; **bring up(stairs),** subir

broken, roto

brother, hermano (*m.*)

to **build,** construir

building, edificio (*m.*)

bus, autobús (*m.*)

but, pero, mas; sino [75]

to **buy,** comprar

by, por; (*time*) para

café, café (*m.*)

to **call,** llamar

can (to be able), poder, saber [88]

Canada, Canadá (*m.*)

capable, capaz

cape, cabo (*m.*)

capital, capital (*f.*)

car, coche (*m.*)

careful: to be careful, tener cuidado

to **carry,** llevar; **carry on,** seguir (i); **carry out,** realizar

cat, gato (*m.*)

to **catch,** coger

cathedral, catedral (*f.*)

to **cease,** cesar, parar

century, siglo (*m.*)

certain, cierto; (*sure*), seguro, cierto; **a certain,** cierto; un tal; **certainly,** desde luego

chair, silla (*f.*)

change, cambio (*m.*)

to **change,** cambiar

chapter, capítulo (*m.*)

character, carácter (*m.*)

charming, encantador

cheap, barato

cheerful, alegre

child, niño (*m.*), niña (*f.*); (*offspring*) hijo (*m.*), hija (*f.*)

China, China (*f.*)

to **choose,** escoger, elegir (i)

city, ciudad (*f.*)

class, clase (*f.*)
clear, claro
clever, listo
clock, reloj (*m.*); **o'clock**
[52]
close, cerca (de)
to **close,** cerrar (ie)
coat, abrigo (*m.*)
coffee, café (*m.*)
cold, frío; frío (*m.*); **to be
cold,** (*persons*) tener frío,
(*weather*) hacer frío; **to
catch cold,** resfriarse
colour, color (*m.*); **off
colour,** malucho
to **come,** venir; **come now!,**
vaya; **come on!,** venga;
come to, llegar a; **come
across,** (*meet*) dar con,
encontrarse (ue) con;
come back, volver (ue);
come down, bajar; **come
in(to),** entrar (en); **come
out,** salir; **come up,** subir
to **commit oneself,** comprometerse
complete, completo; **completely,** completamente,
por completo; (*finally*) definitivamente
to **conceive,** concebir (i)
concise, conciso
conclusion, conclusión (*f.*)
condition, condición (*f.*);
on condition that, a condición (de) que
conduct, conducta (*f.*)
to **confess,** confesar (ie)
confidence, confianza (*f.*)
congratulate, felicitar
consent, consentir (ie)

consequence, consecuencia
(*f.*)
consequently, por lo tanto
to **consider,** considerar; (*bear
in mind*) tener en cuenta
to **consist,** consistir
to **console,** consolar (ue)
to **constitute,** constituir
content(ed), contento
to **continue,** seguir (i), continuar
to **contribute,** contribuir
to **convince,** convencer
copy, ejemplar (*m.*)
to **correct,** corregir (i)
to **cost,** costar (ue)
council, consejo (*m.*)
to **count,** contar (ue)
country, (*rural*) campo (*m.*);
(*state*) país (*m.*); (*native*)
patria (*f.*); (*region*) tierra
(*f.*)
to **cover** cubrir
covered, cubierto
cup, taza (*f.*)
curious, curioso
custom, costumbre (*f.*)

to **dance,** bailar
danger, peligro (*m.*)
to **dare,** atreverse
date, fecha (*f.*)
daughter, hija (*f.*)
day, día (*m.*); **good day,**
buenos días
dear, caro; (*beloved*) querido
death, muerte (*f.*)
to **deceive,** engañar
December, diciembre (*m.*)
deception, engaño (*m.*)
to **decide,** decidir(se)

to **declare,** declarar
to **dedicate,** dedicar
deep, profundo
defeat, derrota (*f.*)
to **defeat,** vencer
defect, defecto (*m.*)
to **defend,** defender (ie)
delightful, precioso
to **demand,** exigir
to **deny,** negar (ie)
departure, salida (*f.*); *via* marcharse
to **depend (on),** depender (de)
to **deserve,** merecer
desire, deseo (*m.*)
to **desire,** desear
to **devote,** dedicar
to **die,** morir(se) (ue)
difference, diferencia (*f.*)
different, distinto
difficult, difícil; **to find it difficult,** encontrar (ue) difícil, *via* costar (ue) trabajo
difficulty, dificultad (*f.*)
dinner, (*midday*) comida (*f.*); (*evening*) cena (*f.*); **to have dinner,** comer; cenar
direction, dirección (*f.*)
dirty, sucio
disappointed, desilusionado
to **discover,** descubrir
discussion, discusión (*f.*)
to **dismiss,** despedir (i)
disposed, dispuesto
to **dissolve,** disolver (ue)
distant, lejos
to **do,** hacer; **to have to do with,** tener que ver con

doctor, médico (*m.*)
dog, perro (*m.*)
door, puerta (*f.*)
doubt, duda (*f.*); **without doubt,** indudable(mente), sin duda
to **doubt (whether),** dudar (que)
doubtful, dudoso; **to be doubtful,** caber duda
doubtless, indudable(mente), sin duda
dozen, docena (*f.*)
to **draw near,** acercarse
dream, sueño (*m.*)
to **dream (of),** soñar (ue) (con)
to **dress,** vestir(se) (i)
to **drink,** beber
to **drive,** conducir
a **drop of,** (*a little*) un poco de
during, durante

each, cada; cada uno; **each other,** se (... el uno al otro, etc.) [91]
early, temprano
to **earn,** ganar
east, este (*m.*)
easy, fácil
to **eat,** comer; **eat up,** comerse
edition, edición (*f.*)
education, enseñanza (*f.*)
either, o; *after neg.* tampoco
elder, eldest, mayor
to **elect,** elegir (i)
elegant, elegante
Elizabeth, Isabel
else, más
end, fin (*m.*), final (*m.*), cabo (*m.*); extremo (*m.*)

to **end up,** acabar
enemy, enemigo (*m.*)
England, Inglaterra (*f.*)
English, inglés
to **enjoy,** gozar (de), disfrutar (de), *via* gustar [76]; **enjoy oneself,** divertirse (ie)
enormous, enorme
enough, bastante
to **ensure,** encargarse
to **enter,** entrar
to **entertain,** entretener
to **entrust,** encargar
to **epitomize,** formular
to **erase,** borrar
escape: to make one's escape, huir
to **escape,** escapar(se)
especially, especialmente, sobre todo
essay, ensayo (*m.*)
to **establish,** establecer
to **esteem,** estimar
Europe, Europa (*f.*)
Europeanization, europeización (*f.*)
even, aun; **even if, even though,** aunque; **not even,** ni (siquiera)
evening, tarde (*f.*); **good evening,** buenas tardes
ever, siempre; alguna vez; *after neg.* nunca, jamás
every, todo, cada; **everybody,** todo el mundo (*m.*); **everything,** todo; **everywhere,** en todas partes, por todas partes
evident, evidente
exactly, exactamente; (*of time*) en punto

to **examine,** examinar
to **exceed,** pasar de
exclusively, exclusivamente
to **exert influence,** influir
to **exist,** existir
exit, salida (*f.*)
to **expect,** esperar, confiar en [164]
to **explain,** explicar
explanation, explicación (*f.*)
extraordinary, extraordinario
extreme, extremo (*m.*); **extremely,** -ísimo [132 (*c*)]
eye, ojo (*m.*)

factory, fábrica (*f.*)
to **fail: not to fail to,** no dejar de
failure, fracaso (*m.*)
fairly, bastante
faithful, fiel
to **fall,** caer
false, falso
family, familia (*f.*)
famous, famoso
far (from), lejos (de); **as far as,** (*up to*) hasta
father, padre (*m.*)
favour, favor (*m.*); **to do the favour of,** hacer el favor de; favorecer en
to **favour,** favorecer
fear, miedo (*m.*)
to **fear,** temer(se) [164]
February, febrero (*m.*)
to **feed,** dar de comer
to **feel,** sentir(se) (ie)
feeling, sentimiento (*m.*)
few, pocos; **a few,** algunos, unos (cuantos)

field, campo (*m.*)
finally, finalmente, por fin, por último
to **find,** encontrar (ue), hallar
fine, bueno
to **finish,** terminar, acabar
firm, casa (*f.*)
first, primero; **at first,** al principio
to **fit in,** caber
to **fix,** fijar
flat, piso (*m.*)
floor, suelo (*m.*); (*storey*) piso (*m.*)
flower, flor (*f.*)
fog, niebla (*f.*)
to **follow,** seguir (i)
following, siguiente
fond, aficionado; **to be fond of,** querer; *via* gustar [76]; ser aficionado a
foot, pie (*m.*); **on foot,** a pie
for, para, por, durante [146 (*b*)]; que, puesto que
to **forbid,** prohibir
force, fuerza (*f.*)
to **force,** forzar (ue), obligar
foreign(er), extranjero
to **forget,** olvidar(se)
to **forgive,** perdonar; **forgive me,** perdón
forgiveness, perdón (*m.*)
former, anterior, de antes
fortune, suerte (*f.*)
fountain, fuente (*f.*)
France, Francia (*f.*)
French, francés
frequent, frecuente
Friday, viernes (*m.*)
friend, amigo (*m.*)
friendship, amistad (*f.*)

to **frighten,** dar miedo
from, de, desde [94 (*c*)]
front: in front (of), delante (de)
fruitful, fecundo
to **fry,** freír (i)
fun: to make fun of, burlarse de

garden, jardín (*m.*)
gay, alegre
generally, generalmente
gentleman, señor (*m.*), caballero (*m.*)
German, alemán
Germany, Alemania (*f.*)
to **get,** conseguir (i); persuadir; (*become*) ponerse; (*to a place*) llegar; **get to,** llegar a; **get to know,** (llegar a) conocer; **get back,** volver (ue); **get down,** bajar; **get dressed,** vestirse (i); **get in,** entrar; **get lost,** perderse (ie); **get out,** salir; **get up,** levantarse; **get up early,** madrugar
girl, muchacha (*f.*), chica (*f.*)
to **give,** dar; **give back,** devolver (ue); **give up,** renunciar a
glad, contento; **to be glad,** alegrarse, estar contento
glass, vaso (*m.*)
to **go,** ir; (*mech.*) andar; (*become*) volverse (ue); **go against,** contrariar; **go away, go off,** irse, marcharse; **go back,** volver (ue); **go down,** bajar; **go**

in, entrar; **go on,** seguir (i); **go out,** salir; **go to bed,** acostarse (ue); **go to sleep,** dormirse (ue); **go up,** subir; **go with,** acompañar, ir con

God, Dios

good, bueno; **to be so good as to,** tener la bondad de; **for good,** definitivamente

good-bye, adiós; **to say good-bye,** despedir(se) (i)

government, gobierno (*m.*)

gradually, poco a poco [57 (*c*)]

grammar school, instituto (*m.*)

grandfather, abuelo (*m.*)

grandmother, abuela (*f.*)

grandparents, abuelos (*m.*)

grateful: to be grateful, agradecer

great, grande

green, verde

to **greet,** saludar

to **grow tired,** cansarse, hartarse

guest, invitado (*m.*)

guide, guía (*m.*); (*book*) guía (*f.*)

hair, pelo (*m.*)

half, medio (*adj.*); mitad (*f.*)

hand, mano (*f.*); **on the other hand,** por otra parte

to **hand** (**over, in**), entregar

to **happen,** pasar, ocurrir

happy, feliz, contento

hard, duro; (*difficult*) difícil; **hard-working,** trabajador

hat, sombrero (*m.*)

to **have,** tener [28]; haber [66, 73]; **have to,** tener que, deber; **have just,** acabar de [73 (*b*)]

head, cabeza (*f.*)

to **hear,** oír; **hear (said),** oír decir; **hear about,** oír hablar de, oír decir

heart, corazón (*m.*)

heat, calor (*m.*)

heaven, cielo (*m.*); (**good**) **heavens,** Dios mío; **for heaven's sake, in heaven's name,** por Dios

help, ayuda (*f.*)

to **help,** ayudar

here, aquí

hereabouts, por aquí

high, alto

history, historia (*f.*)

to **hold,** *via* caber [111]

home, casa (*f.*); (**to**) **home,** a casa; **at home,** en casa

hope, esperanza (*f.*)

to **hope,** esperar

horse, caballo (*m.*)

hospital, hospital (*m.*)

hot, caliente; **to be hot,** tener calor

hotel, hotel (*m.*)

hour, hora (*f.*)

house, casa (*f.*)

how, cómo; **how!** ¡qué! **how much, how many,** cuánto(s)

however, sin embargo; por . . . que

hundred, ciento

hunger, hambre (*f.*)

hungry: to be hungry, tener hambre
hurry, prisa (*f.*); **to be in a hurry,** tener prisa
husband, marido (*m.*)

Iberian, ibérico
idea, idea (*f.*)
ideal, ideal (*m.*)
if, si; **even if,** aunque
ill, enfermo, malo
illusion, ilusión (*f.*)
immediate, inmediato
importance, importancia(*f.*)
important, importante
impossible, imposible
in, en; **in(to),** a, en [171 (4)]
incapable, incapaz
incredible, increíble
India, India (*f.*)
inferior, inferior
information, noticia (*f.*)
inhabitant, habitante (*m.*)
inn, venta (*f.*)
inside, dentro (de)
to insist, empeñarse, insistir
instead of, en vez de
intelligent, inteligente
to intend, pensar (ie)
interest, interés (*m.*)
to interest, interesar; **to be interested in,** interesarse por
interesting, interesante
into, a, en [171 (4)]
to introduce, presentar
invalid, enfermo
to invent, inventar
invitation, invitación (*f.*)

to invite, invitar
Italian, italiano
Italy, Italia (*f.*)

January, enero (*m.*)
Japan, Japón (*m.*)
jealous, celoso
John, Juan
to join, reunirse
journey, viaje (*m.*)
joy, alegría (*f.*)
July, julio (*m.*)
to jump, saltar
June, junio (*m.*)
just, (*time*) en punto; **to have just,** acabar de [74 (*b*)]
to justify, justificar

keen, aficionado; **to be keen on,** ser aficionado a; **to be keen to,** tener ganas de
to keep, guardar; (*continue*) seguir (i)
key, llave (*f.*)
kilogramme, kilo (*m.*)
kilometre, kilómetro (*m.*)
kind, clase (*f.*)
kindly, *via* querer *or* hacer el favor
king, rey (*m.*)
knight, caballero (*m.*)
to know, conocer, saber [49]; **know how to,** saber (cómo); **get to know,** (llegar a) conocer; **let know,** avisar

lack, falta (*f.*)
to lack, carecer de; *via* faltar [76]
lady, señora (*f.*)

language, lengua (*f.*), idioma (*m.*)

last, último; **last night,** anoche; **last year,** el año pasado; **at last,** por fin, al fin, al cabo

late, tarde

latest, último

latter, éste

to laugh, reír(se)

law, ley (*f.*)

to lay the table, poner la mesa

to lead, conducir

leaf, hoja (*f.*)

leaning, apoyado

to learn, aprender

least, menos

leave: to take one's leave, despedirse (i)

to leave, salir, irse, marcharse; dejar, salir de [49]

lecture, clase (*f.*); **lecture-room,** aula (*f.*)

lecturer, profesor (*m.*)

left: to have left, *via* quedar [76]

leg, pierna (*f.*)

to lend, prestar

length, longitud (*f.*)

less, menos; menor; **less and less,** cada vez menos; **none the less,** no por eso dejar de

lesson, lección (*f.*)

to let, dejar, permitir; **let know,** avisar

letter, carta (*f.*)

lie, mentira (*f.*); **to tell a lie,** mentir (ie)

to lie, mentir (ie); (*consist*) consistir

life, vida (*f.*)

to lift (up), levantar

light, luz (*f.*)

to light, encender (ie)

like, como; **like this, like that,** así; **to be (look) like,** parecerse a

to like, querer, *via* gustar [76]

to listen (to), escuchar, oír

literature, literatura (*f.*)

little, (*amount*) poco; (*size*) pequeño

to live, vivir

living: to earn one's living, ganarse la vida

London, Londres (*m.*)

long, largo; (*time*) mucho; **how long,** cuánto tiempo; desde cuándo; **a long way off,** lejos

longer, más largo; más; **no longer,** ya no

to look, parecer; **look at,** mirar; **look for,** buscar; **look like,** parecerse a; **look (out) on to,** dar a

loose, suelto

to lose, perder (ie)

lost: to get lost, perderse (ie)

lot: a lot of, mucho(s); **what a lot of,** cuánto(s)

love, amor (*m.*); **to fall in love with,** enamorarse de

to love, querer, amar

lovely, hermoso, precioso

lover, aficionado (*m.*)

loving, enamorado

to lower, bajar

luck, suerte (*f.*)

lucky: to be lucky, tener suerte

lunch, comida (*f.*); **to have lunch,** comer
to lunch, comer
luxury, lujo (*m.*)

mad, loco
Madrid, Madrid (*m.*)
main, principal
to make, hacer; **make it,** (*time*) tener
man, hombre (*m.*), señor (*m.*)
to manage, conseguir (i), lograr, llegar, acertar (ie)
manager, director (*m.*)
manner, manera (*f.*)
many, muchos; **how many,** cuántos; **not many,** pocos; **so many, as many,** tantos; **too many,** demasiados
March, marzo (*m.*)
market, mercado (*m.*)
to marry, casar(se)
married: to get married, casarse
master, (*teacher*) maestro (*m.*), (*owner*) dueño (*m.*), (*of servants*) señor (*m.*)
matter, asunto (*m.*)
to matter, importar
may, poder
May, mayo (*m.*)
meal, comida (*f.*); **to have a meal,** comer
means, manera (*f.*)
to meet, encontrar(se con) (ue); **meet with,** dar con, encontrarse con
meeting, reunión (*f.*)
memoir, memoria (*f.*)

memory, memoria (*f.*); **from memory,** de memoria
menace, amenaza (*f.*)
merely, no . . . más que, sólo
midday, mediodía (*m.*)
midnight, medianoche (*f.*)
mile, milla (*f.*)
milk, leche (*f.*)
million, millón (*m.*)
mind: to bear in mind, tener en cuenta
minister, ministro (*m.*)
minus, menos
minute, minuto (*m.*)
to miss, faltar a
Miss, señorita (*f.*)
mist, niebla (*f.*), neblina (*f.*)
mistake, error (*m.*)
mistaken, equivocado; **to be mistaken,** engañarse, equivocarse
moment, momento (*m.*)
Monday, lunes (*m.*)
money, dinero (*m.*)
month, mes (*m.*)
monument, monumento (*m.*)
Moor, moro (*m.*)
more, más; **more and more,** cada vez más
morning, mañana (*f.*); (*early*) madrugada (*f.*); **good morning,** buenos días
most, más; -ísimo [132 (*c*)]; la mayor parte (de)
mother, madre (*f.*)
mountain, montaña (*f.*)
mourning, luto (*m.*); **in mourning,** de luto

403

to move, mover (ue)
Mr, señor (*m.*)
Mrs, señora (de) (*f.*)
much, mucho; how much, cuánto; not much, poco; so much, as much, tanto; too much, demasiado
music, música (*f.*)
must, deber, tener que, *via* hay que [74]
my, mi

name, nombre (*m.*)
national, nacional
natural, natural
near, cerca (de)
nearly, casi
necessary, preciso, necesario
necessity, necesidad (*f.*)
need, necesidad (*f.*)
to need, necesitar, *via* hacer falta [76]
negation, negación (*f.*)
neighbour, vecino (*m.*)
neither, tampoco; ni uno ni otro; neither . . . nor, ni . . . ni
nervous, nervioso
never, nunca, jamás
nevertheless, sin embargo, no obstante
new, nuevo
news, noticia(s) (*f.*)
newspaper, periódico (*m.*)
next, que viene, próximo, siguiente; luego; next to, junto a; next door, (de) al lado
nice, bonito; (*likeable*) simpático

night, noche (*f.*); good night, buenas noches; last night, anoche
no, no; ninguno; no one, nadie
noble, noble
nobody, nadie
none, ninguno; none the less, no por eso dejar de
nor, ni
north, norte (*m.*); northeast, noreste (*m.*)
not, no; not at all, nada
to note, fijarse en
nothing, nada
notice, letrero (*m.*); (*news*) noticia (*f.*)
to notice, fijarse en
novel, novela (*f.*)
November, noviembre (*m.*)
now, ahora, ya, ahora bien [133]; now and then, de vez en cuando
number, número (*m.*)
numerous, numeroso

object, objeto (*m.*)
to object, oponerse
objectively: to view objectively, objetivar
to oblige, obligar
occasion, ocasión (*f.*)
o'clock [52]
October, octubre (*m.*)
of, de
officer, oficial (*m.*)
often, a menudo, muchas veces
old, viejo; (*ancient, former*) antiguo; to be . . . years old, tener . . . años [44]

on, en, sobre, encima de [94
(c)]; **on foot,** a pie

once, una vez; **at once,** en
seguida

one, uno *or not translated*
[25 (a) N. 6]; **one an-
other,** se (. . . el uno al
otro, etc.) [91]

only, único; sólo, solamente,
no . . . más que

open, abierto

to **open,** abrir

to **operate,** actuar

opinion, opinión (f.)

opportunity, oportunidad
(f.), ocasión (f.)

opposite, contrario; enfrente (de)

or o, u [75]; *after neg.* ni

to **order,** mandar

in **order to,** para; **in order
that,** para que

organization, organización
(f.)

other, otro; **others,** otros,
los demás; **each other,**
se (. . . el uno al otro, etc.)
[91]

otherwise, de otro modo, de
otra manera

ought, deber [123 (6)]

out, fuera; **out of,** (*because
of*) por

outside, fuera (de)

over, (por) encima de, (*more
than*) más de; **over there,**
por allí

overcoat, abrigo (m.)

to **overcome,** vencer

to **owe,** deber

own, propio

to **pack a suitcase,** hacer una
maleta

page, página (f.)

pale, pálido

paper, papel (m.); **(news)-
paper,** periódico (m.)

parents, padres (m. pl.)

Paris, París (m.)

part, parte (f.)

to **pass,** pasar

to **pay (for),** pagar; **pay respects,** saludar

peace, paz (f.)

pear, pera (f.)

pen, pluma (f.)

pencil, lápiz (m.)

peninsula, península (f.)

pensive, pensativo

people, personas (f. pl.),
gente (f.); *via the reflexive*

perfect, perfecto

perhaps, tal vez, quizá(s),
acaso

period, época (f.)

permission, permiso (m.)

person, persona (f.)

to **persuade,** persuadir

Peru, Perú (m.)

peseta, peseta (f.)

Peter, Pedro

phantom, fantasma (m.)

Philip, Felipe

to **pick up,** recoger

picturesque, pintoresco

place, sitio (m.), lugar (m.)

plan, proyecto (m.)

to **play,** jugar (ue)

pleasant, agradable

to **please,** gustar; *via* hacer el
favor de

pleased, contento; **to be pleased,** alegrarse, estar contento, *via* alegrar; tener mucho gusto

pleasure, gusto (*m.*)

plenty: to have plenty, *via* sobrar [76]

plus, más

p.m., de la tarde (noche) [52 (*b*)]

poem, poesía (*f.*)

poet, poeta (*m.*)

poetry, poesía(s) (*f.*)

to point out, indicar

police, policía (*f.*); **policeman,** guardia (*m.*)

policy, política (*f.*)

political, político

politics, política (*f.*)

poor, pobre

population, población (*f.*)

Portugal, Portugal (*m.*)

Portuguese, portugués

position, situación (*f.*); (*job*) puesto (*m.*)

possibility, posibilidad (*f.*)

possible, posible

postcard, postal (*f.*)

potato, patata (*f.*)

pound, libra (*f.*)

to prefer, preferir (ie)

to prepare, preparar; **prepared** (*willing*), dispuesto

present, (*gift*) regalo (*m.*); **for the present,** por ahora

to present, presentar; (*gift*) regalar

presentiment: to have a presentiment, presentir (ie)

press, prensa (*f.*)

pretext, pretexto (*m.*)

pretty, bonito

to prevent, impedir (i)

previous, anterior

price, precio (*m.*)

prime minister, primer ministro (*m.*)

probable, probable

probably, probablemente; *via future or conditional* [108]

problem, problema (*m.*)

progressively, cada vez

to promise, prometer

to pronounce, pronunciar

to propose, proponer

proprietor, dueño (*m.*)

provided that, con tal que

to publish, publicar

to punish, castigar

pure, puro

to put, poner; **put on,** ponerse; **put to bed,** acostar (ue); **put right,** arreglar

quarter, cuarto (*m.*)

question, pregunta (*f.*); (*problem*) cuestión (*f.*)

quick, rápido

quickly, rápidamente, de prisa

quite, bastante; completamente

Quixote: Don Quixote, Don Quijote

to rain, llover (ue)

to raise, levantar

rapid, rápido

rather, bastante, (*preferably*) más bien; *via* preferir (ie), gustar más

to **reach,** llegar a; **reach the age of . . .,** cumplir los . . . años
to **react,** reaccionar
to **read,** leer
ready, listo
real, verdadero; **really,** verdaderamente, de verdad, de veras
to **realize,** darse cuenta de
reason, razón (*f.*)
to **reason** (**out**), razonar
to **reawake,** volver a despertarse
to **recall,** recordar (ue)
to **receive,** recibir
to **recognize,** reconocer
to **recommend,** recomendar (ie)
to **reconsider,** volver (ue) a considerar
red, rojo
to **refuse,** negarse (ie)
régime, régimen (*m.*)
to **regret,** sentir (ie)
reign, reinado (*m.*)
to **relate,** contar (ue)
to **remain,** quedar(se)
remaining, (*other*) demás
remedy, remedio (*m.*)
to **remember,** acordarse (ue) de, recordar (ue)
to **remind,** recordar (ue)
to **repeat,** repetir (i)
to **repent,** arrepentirse (ie)
reply, contestación (*f.*), respuesta (*f.*)
to **reply,** contestar, responder
representative, representante (*m.*)
to **reproach,** reprochar

to **resolve,** resolver(se) (ue), decidir(se)
respect, respeto (*m.*); **to pay respects,** saludar
respectable, respetable
rest, descanso (*m.*); (*other[s]*) lo(s) demás
to **rest,** descansar
restaurant, restorán (*m.*)
to **return,** volver (ue); (*give back*) devolver (ue)
revolution, revolución (*f.*)
ridiculous, ridículo
right: to be right, tener razón; **to put right,** arreglar
ripe, maduro
to **rise,** (*sun*) salir
risk, riesgo (*m.*)
river, río (*m.*)
road, camino (*m.*), calle (*f.*)
room, cuarto (*m.*); **to be room** *via* caber [111]
round, alrededor de; (*through*) por; **to walk round** (**something**), dar la vuelta (a algo)

sacrifice, sacrificio (*m.*)
sad, triste
sadness, tristeza (*f.*)
same, mismo
Saragossa, Zaragoza (*f.*)
satisfied, contento, satisfecho
to **satisfy,** satisfacer
Saturday, sábado (*m.*)
save, excepto; **nothing . . . save,** no . . . más que
to **save,** salvar; (*keep*) guardar

to **say**, decir; **I say**, (*listen!*) oye, oiga; **say good-bye to**, despedir(se de) (i); **say good morning**, dar los buenos días; **say thank you**, dar las gracias

scarcely apenas

scheme, proyecto (*m.*)

school, escuela (*f.*), colegio (*m.*), instituto (*m.*)

scientist, científico (*m.*)

sculptor, escultor (*m.*)

second, segundo

secret, secreto (*m.*)

secretary, secretario (*m.*)

to **see**, ver; **see off**, despedir (i)

to **seem**, parecer; **seem to think**, *via* parecer

to **seize**, coger

self, mismo

to **sell**, vender

to **send (on)**, mandar, enviar

September, se(p)tiembre (*m.*)

to **serve**, servir (i)

to **set: set out, set off**, salir; **set down**, sentar (ie)

to **settle**, establecerse

several, varios

Seville, Sevilla (*f.*)

shall [103, 105, 107–109]

sheet, hoja (*m.*)

shop, tienda (*f.*)

shopping, compras (*f. pl.*); **to go shopping**, ir de compras

short: to be short of, *via* faltar [76]

shortly, dentro de poco

should [104, 106–109]

shoulder, hombro (*m.*)

to **show**, enseñar, mostrar (ue), demostrar (ue)

to **shut**, cerrar (ie)

sick, enfermo, malo; **sick person**, enfermo (*m.*)

side, lado (*m.*); **at the side (of)**, al lado (de)

sight, vista (*f.*)

silence, silencio (*m.*)

silent: to be silent, callar(se)

since, desde; (*time*) desde que, (*because*) puesto que

sincerity, sinceridad (*f.*)

to **sing**, cantar

sister, hermana (*f.*)

to **sit (down)**, sentarse (ie)

sitting, sentado

to **situate**, situar

situation, situación (*f.*)

sky, cielo (*m.*)

sleep: to go (off) to sleep, dormirse (ue)

to **sleep**, dormir (ue)

sleepy: to be sleepy, tener sueño

to **slip the memory**, escaparse de la memoria

slowly, despacio

small, pequeño

to **smell**, oler (ue)

snow, nieve (*f.*)

so, tan; lo; que sí; conque; **so much, so many**, tanto(s); **so (that)**, de modo que, de manera que; para que

soldier, soldado (*m.*)

sole, único

solution, solución (*f.*)

to **solve**, resolver (ue)

some, alguno; **somebody**, alguien; **someone**, alguien, alguno; **something**,

algo; **sometimes,** a veces, algunas veces; **somewhere,** en alguna parte
son, hijo (*m.*)
song, canción (*f.*)
soon, pronto; **as soon as,** en cuanto; **as soon as possible,** cuanto antes, lo antes posible; **no sooner,** apenas
sorry: to be sorry (about), sentir (ie)
sort, especie (*f.*); tipo (*m.*)
sound, profundo
south, sur (*m.*)
southern, meridional
souvenir, recuerdo (*m.*)
Spain, España (*f.*)
Spaniard, español (*m.*)
Spanish, español
sparrow, gorrión (*m.*)
to **speak,** hablar
to **spend,** gastar; (*time*) pasar
spite: in spite of, a pesar de
square, plaza (*f.*)
to **stand,** estar de pie; **stand out,** destacarse
standing, de pie
to **start,** empezar (ie), ponerse
station, estación (*f.*)
stay, estancia (*f.*)
to **stay,** quedar(se)
to **steal,** robar
step, paso (*m.*); **to take a step,** dar un paso
sterile, estéril
stick, bastón (*m.*)
still, aún, todavía
story, historia (*f.*)
straight away, en seguida
strange, extraño, curioso

street, calle (*f.*)
strength, fuerzas (*f. pl.*)
to **strike (the hour),** dar la hora
stripling, jovencito
to **strive,** esforzarse (ue)
to **study,** estudiar
study, estudio (*m.*)
stupid, estúpido
subject, asunto (*m.*)
to **succeed,** lograr, conseguir (i)
such, tan; tal, semejante
suddenly, de pronto, de ·repente
to **suit,** ir bien [57 (*c*)], caer bien [93 N. 3]
suitcase, maleta (*f.*)
suited, acertado
summer, verano (*m.*)
sun, sol (*m.*)
Sunday, domingo (*m.*)
to **suppose,** suponer
sure, seguro
to **surprise,** sorprender
sweet, dulce
to **swim,** nadar
to **switch on,** encender (ie)
Switzerland, Suiza (*f.*)

table, mesa (*f.*)
Tagus, Tajo (*m.*)
to **take,** tomar, coger; (*along*) llevar; **take away,** quitar; llevarse; **take care of,** cuidar de; **take down,** bajar; **take off,** quitarse; **take up,** subir; coger; **take time, take long,** tardar; **to be taken ill,** ponerse enfermo

talk: to have a talk, hablar
to talk, hablar
tall, alto
tea, té (*m.*)
to teach, enseñar
teacher, profesor (*m.*)
tear, lágrima (*f.*)
to tear, romper
telegram, telegrama (*m.*)
to tell, decir; (*relate*) contar
(ue); tell a lie, mentir (ie)
terrible, terrible
than, que, de [130]
to thank, dar las gracias, agradecer; thanks, thank you,
gracias; thanks to, gracias
a
that, ese, aquel; que; that is
(to say), o sea, es decir
then, entonces; luego; pues
[133]
there, allí, allá, ahí; over
there, por allí; there is,
there were, etc., hay,
había, etc. [74]
thereabouts, por allí, por
allá, por ahí
thing, cosa (*f.*)
to think, pensar (ie), *via*
ocurrir; (*believe*) creer;
(*opinion*) pensar (ie), *via*
parecer [76]; think over
carefully, pensar bien
third, tercero
thirst, sed (*f.*)
thirsty: to be thirsty, tener
sed
thoroughly, muchísimo
though, even though, aun-
que
thought, pensamiento (*m.*)

to threaten, amenazar
through, por, a(l) través de
[94 (*c*)]
Thursday, jueves (*m.*)
thus, así
time, tiempo (*m.*); (*occasion*)
vez (*f.*); (*age*) época (*f*);
at times, a veces; in time,
a tiempo; what time, qué
hora; from time to time,
de vez en cuando
tired, cansado; to grow
tired, cansarse, hartarse
tiresome, cansado
to, a, (*up to*) hasta; (*in order
to*) para [100–101]
today, hoy
together, juntos
tomorrow, mañana
tonight, esta noche
top: on top (of), encima (de)
too, demasiado; (*also*) también; too much, too
many, demasiado(s); to
have too much, too
many, *via* sobrar [76]
topic, tema (*m.*)
to touch, tocar; touch on,
bordear
tourist, turista (*m.*)
towards, hacia
tower, torre (*f.*)
town, ciudad (*f.*), pueblo
(*m.*)
train, tren (*m.*)
tram, tranvía (*m.*)
to transform, transformar
to translate, traducir
translation, traducción (*f.*)
to travel, viajar
travels, viajes (*m. pl.*)

tree, árbol (*m.*)
to tremble, temblar (ie)
trip, viaje (*m.*)
to triumph, triunfar
true, verdadero; to be true, ser verdad
to trust, fiarse de; (*hope*) confiar
truth, verdad (*f.*)
to try, procurar, intentar, tratar
Tuesday, martes (*m.*)
tumbler, vaso (*m.*)
to turn out, salir
twice, dos veces
type, tipo (*m.*)

uncle, tío (*m.*)
under, bajo, debajo de [94 (*c*)]
underneath, debajo (de)
to understand, comprender, entender (ie)
to undertake, encargarse, comprometerse
unimportant, poco importante
United States, Estados Unidos (*m. pl.*)
university, universidad (*f.*)
unknown, desconocido
unless, a menos que, a no ser que
unlikely, poco probable, difícil
until, hasta (que)
up: to eat up, comer(se); to get up, levantarse; to wake up, despertar(se) (ie); up to, hasta
upon, sobre

to use, emplear, usar, utilizar; *via the imperfect* [41]; to get used to, acostumbrarse a
useful, útil
usually, *via* soler (ue) [41]
to utilize, utilizar

vague, vago
vain, vano
valour, valor (*m.*)
value, valor (*m.*); to be of value, to be valued, valer
variety, variedad (*f.*)
very, muy; mucho [165]; very much, muchísimo
view, vista (*f.*)
village, pueblo (*m.*), pueblecillo (*m.*), lugar (*m.*)
virtually, prácticamente
virtue, virtud (*f.*)
visit, visita (*f.*)
to visit, visitar
voice, voz (*f.*)
voyage, viaje (*m.*)

to wait (for), esperar [164]
to wake (up), despertar(se) (ie)
walk, paseo (*m.*); to go for a walk, dar un paseo; to go for a walk round, dar una vuelta
to walk, andar, ir a pie; walk round (something), dar la vuelta a (algo)
wall, (*house*) pared (*f.*); (*garden*) tapia (*f.*); (*city*) muralla (*f.*)
to wander, andar
to want, querer

war, guerra (*f.*)

warm, caliente; **to be warm,** tener calor [44 (*b*)], hacer calor [44 (*c*)]

to warm, calentar (ie)

warmth, calor (*m.*)

to warn, advertir (ie)

to wash, lavar

watch, reloj (*m.*)

to watch, mirar

water, agua (*f.*)

way, camino (*m.*); (*manner*) manera (*f.*), modo (*m.*); **that way,** (*manner*) de ese modo; (*direction*) por allí; **way in,** entrada (*f.*); **way out,** salida (*f.*)

wealth, riqueza (*f.*)

wealthy, rico

to wear, llevar

weather, tiempo (*m.*); **to be fine (bad) weather,** hacer buen (mal) tiempo [44 (*c*)]

Wednesday, miércoles (*m.*)

week, semana (*f.*); **weekend,** fin de semana (*m.*)

well, bien; **as well,** (*too*) también; **to be as well,** (*fitting*) convenir; **wellknown,** familiar

west, oeste (*m.*)

what, qué, cuál [155]; lo que [79]; ¡**what (a)!,** ¡qué!; **what's more,** además

whatever, todo lo que, cuanto

when, cuando; cuándo [17]

where, donde; dónde [17]; **where . . . (to),** adonde; adónde [17]

whether, si

which, que, el que, el cual [151–154]; qué, cuál [155]

while, whilst, mientras

whim, capricho (*m.*)

white, blanco

who(m), que, quien, el que, el cual [151–154]; quién [17, 155]

whoever, el que

whole, todo

whose, cuyo [153]; de quién(es) [155]

why, por qué

wife, mujer (*f.*), señora (*f.*), esposa (*f.*)

will, voluntad (*f.*)

will, (*verb*) querer [103, 105, 107–109]

to win, ganar

window, ventana (*f.*)

wine, vino (*m.*)

wing, ala (*f.*)

wish, deseo (*m.*)

to wish, desear, querer

with, con

within, dentro (de)

without, sin (que)

woman, mujer (*f.*)

wont: to be wont to, soler (ue)

word, palabra (*f.*)

work, trabajo (*m.*), (*of art, science, etc.*) obra (*f.*)

to work, trabajar

world, mundo (*m.*)

worse, worst, peor

worth: to be worth, valer; **to be worth while,** valer la pena

would [104, 106–109]; **would that,** ojalá

to **write,** escribir
  writer, escritor (*m.*)
  wrong, (*a bad thing*) mal

year, año (*m.*); **to be . .**
  years old, tener . . . años
yellow, amarillo
yes, sí

yesterday, ayer; **the day**
  before yesterday, anteayer
yet, todavía, aún; ya [133
  (*a*)]
young, joven
younger, menor
youth, juventud (*f.*)

INDEX

*The references are to paragraphs and their sub-sections
(N. = Note). The treatment of peculiarities pertaining to
individual words is referred to in the preceding Vocabularies.*

414